Mental Toughness

The Mindset Behind Sporting Achievement

Second edition

Michael Sheard

Routledge
Taylor & Francis Group

LONDON AND NEW YORK

First published 2010
by Routledge

This edition published 2013
by Routledge
27 Church Road, Hove, East Sussex BN3 2FA

Simultaneously published in the USA and Canada
by Routledge
711 Third Avenue, New York NY 10017

Routledge is an imprint of the Taylor & Francis Group, an informa business

British Library Cataloguing in Publication Data
A catalogue record for this book is available
from the British Library

Library of Congress Cataloging-in-Publication Data
Sheard, Michael, 1968
   Mental toughness : the mindset behind sporting achievement/
Michael Sheard.—2nd ed.
     p.cm
   Includes bibliographical references and index.
   ISBN 978-0-415-57895-0 (hardback)—ISBN 978-0-415-
57896-7 (paperback) 1. Sports—Psychological
aspects. 2. Athletes—Psychology. 3. Mental
discipline. 4. Achievement motivation. I. Title.
   GV705.4.S45 2012
   796.01–dc23

                                            2012002352

ISBN: 978-0-415-57895-0 (hbk)
ISBN: 978-0-415-57896-7 (pbk)
ISBN: 978-0-203-10354-8 (ebk)

Typeset in Times
by RefineCatch Limited, Bungay, Suffolk
Cover design by Andrew Ward

Printed and bound in Great Britain by the MPG Books Group

Mental Toughness

Mental toughness is one of the most common terms used in sport – by athletes, coaches, spectators and the media. However, it is also one of the least understood terms. This book examines the characteristics and development of mentally tough sport performers, and presents the cutting-edge research in this area. In these chapters, the author proposes that mental toughness is a personality style and mindset, and presents a compelling case for its inclusion within the positive psychological paradigm.

This second edition has been updated to include new material on the characterisation, conceptualisation, measurement, and development of mental toughness. As in the first edition, the book includes a historical overview of empirical research, and also describes the conceptual arguments behind this research.

Now packed with even more rigorous scientific evidence and bang up-to-date anecdotes from the world of sport, the book presents a fascinating explanation of why some athletes are successful, and how and why they stay on top. *Mental Toughness: The Mindset Behind Sporting Achievement* will be essential reading for all sport psychology, sport science, sport studies, and coaching students.

Michael Sheard has enjoyed a distinguished teaching, research and consultancy career. Specialising in teaching Research Methods, and Sport and Exercise Psychology, Michael has presented his investigative work at conferences worldwide. He is currently working on his first novel. Michael lives in the northeast of England, and can be contacted on drsheard@ hotmail.com.

"This book authoritatively updates what was already an excellent and highly readable exposition on mental toughness in sports. All major theoretical and research bases are touched and supported with up-to-date citations. Additionally, scientific concepts are fleshed out with vivid anecdotal citations that make the book come alive. Michael Sheard has established himself as a leading authority on mental toughness." – **Arnold LeUnes, Professor of Psychology, Texas A and M University, USA**

"Michael Sheard has managed to successfully draw together a wide range of academic and applied material to dissect the phenomenon of mental toughness. The underlying academic credentials are extremely sound and are coupled with an engaging presentation style which I find very appealing. The book updates the previous edition very well, and the new material is excellent." – **John Kremer, Honorary Research Fellow, Queen's University, Belfast, UK**

"Solidly anchored in scientific research, the second edition of Mental Toughness goes even further in the analysis of what mental toughness is, how to assess it, and its determinants. Written in a lively style, the book contains both research and anecdotes that make it accessible to both scholars and students alike." – **Robert J. Vallerand, Lab Recherche sur le Comport Social, Department of Psychology, University of Québec, Canada**

"This book is an ideal companion for coaches, athletes and sports studies students who are interested in sport psychology. The references and quotes from key academics and sporting greats allow the reader to understand the concept of mental toughness, its relationship to sporting success and the ways in which it can be nurtured through practice and training." – **John F. Mathers, Director of Learning and Teaching, School of Sport, University of Stirling, UK**

"The scholarly review of existing mental toughness research presented in this book is informative, and in particular, the critical analysis of previous attempts to create measures of mental toughness provides an insightful summary for scholars and students alike. Dr. Sheard's discussion of the factors which contribute to the development of mental toughness – cultural influences in particular – is also illuminating." – **Robert Harmison, Kibler Professor of Sport Psychology, James Madison University, USA**

For Julie

Tempores mutant et nos mutamus in illis,
sed amantium nostrum est fidelis.

Nothing on earth can stop the man with the right mental attitude; nothing on earth can help the man with the wrong mental attitude.

Thomas Jefferson

Opportunities multiply as they are seized.

Sun Tzu

What we call results are beginnings.

Ralph Waldo Emerson

No one can make you feel inferior without your consent.

Eleanor Roosevelt

Whatever you can do, or dream you can, begin it. Boldness has genius, power, and magic in it.

Johann Wolfgang von Goethe

To travel hopefully is a better thing than to arrive.

Robert Louis Stevenson

Character and self-control.

Marcus Aurelius

Possunt quia posse videntur.

Virgil

Contents

Figures

Tables

The Mental Toughness Code

With clarity of mind and firmness of purpose, mentally tough performers aspire to be great. Settling for being good is never enough. They know how to win, and have the courage to stand tall in the face of adversity. It is not denial of the problem, but the efficiency of the response. Champions do the ordinary things better than anyone else. They make fewer mistakes and possess a work ethic, winning mentality, and self-confidence. Mentally tough performers refuse to be intimidated; instead, they intimidate the opposition with their presence. It is about holding yourself together, dealing with the inevitable nerves that are fluttering around, however much you wish they weren't. Winning is not all that matters. Character also matters. Compete with talent, enthusiasm, guts, dignity, and integrity. Mentally tough athletes do not dwell on defeat, but, rather, accept losing as an inevitable consequence of meeting someone better on a particular day. In defeat, they remain gracious. They remain positive about the future. They believe in themselves and in all they can achieve. This is to take the first step on the path to achievement. Success does not come with time; it comes with toil. Ultimately, we are responsible for our success. And we measure success by the experiences we live. Mental toughness is the stuff of champions.

Preface and acknowledgements

Mental toughness enjoys the status of being one of the most ubiquitous terms used in sport; it is used by performers, managers, coaches, spectators, owners, and administrators. The sporting print and broadcast media, in particular, continue to be preoccupied with 'mental toughness'. The term is used frequently in interviews, newspaper reports, and during match commentaries. However, it also remains one of the least understood terms. It is the aim of this second edition of *Mental Toughness: The Mindset Behind Sporting Achievement* to continue to help clarify what this construct is and, just as important, what it is not.

Personality is a meaningful concept and the measurement of it a useful tool. However, there is a growing tendency to put everything that is desirable in terms of personality attributes under the umbrella term 'mental toughness'. This is misguided and is also a failure to recognise that there are perfectly adequate existing psychological constructs that represent many attributes. It has also added weight to claims that mental toughness is too broad a construct even to consider defining. This is nonsense. The problem is, as it always has been, that it is a phrase that everyone takes for granted: 'Mental toughness . . . you know what I mean . . . you know . . . resilient . . . you know . . . digs deep . . . you know . . .' Well, actually, I didn't know – until the first edition of this book.

The book is targeted primarily towards psychology, sport psychology, sport science, and sport studies students, but its audience domain is likely to include related fields such as coaching, health psychology, occupational psychology, and social psychology. The first edition of this text, *Mental Toughness: The Mindset Behind Sporting Achievement*, was published in 2009 with the global purpose of summarising the state of knowledge with regard to research in mental toughness. Like its predecessor, this edition of the text has also been written to provide a comprehensive and up-to-date review of the issues germane to this most intriguing of psychological concepts. Again, the text has been written in such a way that, if desired, it may be read from cover to cover. However, it is more likely that specific chapters will be dipped into. With this in mind, I have written each chapter so that it may stand alone. It is hoped that, having read the entire book, the reader will have developed a greater appreciation of mental toughness in sport, and will have been made aware of the important advances in its origins, characterisation, conceptualisation, measurement, development and maintenance, and possible hereditary traits.

Specific chapter content has changed significantly, in response to changes that have occurred in the field. The book's introductory chapter looks at the anecdotal evidence that suggests mental toughness is a contributory (some would say even a decisive) factor in successful sport performance. The end of the chapter begins to consider situational evidence of displays of mental toughness and suggests that it is a personality style and mindset. This is rigorously extended in Chapter 2, where a theoretical exposition of the characteristics constitutive of mental toughness is given. This is considered further in Chapter 3, which deals with a number of antecedents in the history of its conceptual clarification that have informed its development. It is also in this chapter that the case for mental toughness to be considered within the positive psychological paradigm is presented.

As valid and reliable instruments are essential to the study of any defined construct, Chapter 4 explores the validation of various measures of mental toughness. Dealing as it does with psychometrics, this chapter may appear somewhat esoteric and separated from the rest of the book. It is written and presented in a deliberately more academic style, reflecting the topic's intricacies. I respectfully ask for your, the reader's, indulgence, because the chapter has been written with a researcher-based audience in mind. Chapter 5 investigates how mental toughness can be acquired and, crucially, maintained. This chapter also examines the research evidence of cultural and nationality differences in mental toughness in sport performers, and considers mental toughness in that all too common band of sport brothers and sisters – the injured athlete. Finally, Chapter 6 offers a concluding commentary and possible directions for future mental toughness research. This includes giving consideration to the genetic inheritance × environmental mediation interaction debate, presently at the forefront of personality theory. Specifically, it is proffered that perhaps, as well as being learned, an element of mental toughness is innate. Perspectives on explaining the attainment of superior sport performance vary, considering dedicated practice over many years and hereditary contributors. The premise that genetic determinants are as powerful as experiences and environments in life is not new. The evidence is clear from adoption studies and identical twin studies that genetic transmission is, at best, 50 per cent, though more likely in the order of 16–25 per cent. However, considering the potential contribution of genetic factors to mental toughness is a novel departure. I must emphasise at this point that the suggestion is not one of a predetermined inherited mental toughness capacity. That would ignore the effect of environmental influences. Rather, it is advocated that research should be conducted to pursue this potentially fruitful orchard of possibility. It is also stressed that it is not the aim of this book to demonstrate an interaction between genetic and environmental factors. Compelling research evidence exists already to this effect. Rather, the model depicted ultimately in Chapter 6 shows the interaction between genetic and environmental factors, their contribution to a combination of physical, physiological, perceptual-cognitive, and sociological factors, and their contribution to superior sport performance. Whether this interaction is related to mental toughness, or indeed any other key correlate positive psychological constructs, is yet to be determined. More research must be conducted if the null hypothesis is to be rejected.

Sport reveals character. Sport examines and exposes the robustness and the frailties of human nature – often, brutally. I am sure we can all think of examples of talented sportspeople who get so far (indeed, beyond most), but who do not fulfil that potential by becoming 'a great'. For many, this is due to personality deficiencies, be they mental frailties or more serious disorders that are contributors to maladaptive behaviours. I would argue that all greats obviously have talent, but that the manifestation of consistently optimal performance is given expression due to a package of mental attributes that I call an 'achievement mindset'. Certainly, talent and this achievement mindset (I call it 'mental toughness') are inextricably linked. Indeed, in this book, I state clearly that the two enjoy a symbiotic relationship. No sporting contest is decided exclusively by any one variable.

Two particular sporting events prompted my decision to write a second edition of this text. First, FC Barcelona's victory over Manchester United FC in the 2009 Uefa Champions League final, when Barcelona played better football on that particular Wednesday evening. (They repeated the feat over the same opponents in 2011.) However, I would proffer that their doing so was, to a great extent, afforded by their opponent's tactical play that was, in turn, influenced by the defensive mindset that evening of the Manchester United manager and players. Second, I suspect that Everton FC couldn't believe their good fortune in the first minute of the FA Cup final three days later. But Chelsea FC's self-belief (a core component of mental toughness) was more evident and eventually won through. Witness the frequency with which Everton surrendered possession of the ball. As you will discover later in the book, there is a whole lot more to mental toughness than mere defensive, rearguard action or reaction. Each of these exemplars showed that, even in defeat, there remains an alternative and more desirable way to lose – demonstrable mental toughness.

My point is that mental toughness is one (albeit a crucial one) variable that distinguishes between performers. Yet, it's a case of different strokes for different folks. Athletes demonstrate equivalent expressions of mentally tough behaviour in all manner of situations across a variety of sports. And that is the point: the mentally tough mindset is a composite of core attributes. Others of a more peripheral nature may be more sport-specific. Some attributes are more apposite in certain situations than others. But, surely, what is beyond doubt is that, whether singly or in combination, these constituents of the mental toughness mindset make a substantial contribution to separating the great from the merely very good, the winners from the vanquished, the achievers from the also-rans.

My earliest recollection of watching a sporting contest is the 1974 Fifa World Cup final. As a 5-year-old, I knew nothing of mental toughness. But, whenever I read about or see footage of that match in Munich's Olympiastadion, it is clear which side was the mentally tougher. For all their talent (and showboating), Holland's arrogance (like triumphalism, not a component of the mentally tough mindset) lost out to West Germany's discipline, fortitude, and seizing of the opportunity given them. Yes, admittedly, a dubious equalising penalty; but resulting ultimately from Dutch contemptuousness. Holland ought to have had the new World Cup boxed up and wrapped in orange after only 20 minutes. That they didn't was due to a lack of the equivalent mental toughness demonstrated by the West German team. For an engaging narrative of Holland's 'Lost Final', I recommend David Winner's *Brilliant Orange*. (See References for details.)

Many reading this book will know what is constitutive of talent. There is precious little variation in what separates performers operating at the highest competitive standards in sport. The evidence, both anecdotal and empirical, is that mentality is the clincher.

It is believed that the reader will find this edition of *Mental Toughness: The Mindset Behind Sporting Achievement* to be even more interesting than its predecessor. The text contains additions, changes, and expansions, which reflect the proliferation of published research in the field. In offering such a comprehensive overview of the literature, it is hoped that the reader will appreciate the balance that has been struck in this latest effort between breadth – giving the audience a sense of the scope of the field – and depth – stimulating thought and reflection. Its publication coincides with the 2012 Olympics, and I hope to witness many feats of mental toughness deserving of the sporting legacy the London Games will bequeath.

I have always believed that the true definition of a champion or great athlete is someone who wins a title or championship and then goes out and defends it successfully, at least once, and/or someone who repeatedly demonstrates behaviour that overcomes seemingly intolerable adversity.

Raising the achievable standard is the function of the champion. Suffice to say, most readers will recognise the mental toughness mindset presented in this book in the likes of champions and greats such as: Maggie Alphonsi, Lance Armstrong, Mike Atherton, Sir Roger Bannister, David Beckham, Allan Border, Sir Ian Botham, Geoffrey Boycott, Sir Donald Bradman, Mark Cavendish, Sir Bobby Charlton, Kim Clijsters, Dónal Óg Cusack, Laurie Daley, Novak Djokovic, Charlotte Edwards, John Elway, Jessica Ennis, Sir Nick Faldo, Andy Farrell, Roger Federer, Sir Alex Ferguson, Sir Ranulph Fiennes, Andrew Flintoff, Clare Francis, Jack Gibson, Steffi Graf, Dougal Haston, Sally Haynes, Stephen Hendry, Dame Kelly Holmes, Sir Chris Hoy, Tomaž Humar, Phil Jackson, Magic Johnson, Martin Johnson, Vivien Jones, Michael Jordan, Jens Lehmann, Jeremy Lin, Darren Lockyer, Dame Ellen MacArthur, Richie McCaw, Tony McCoy, Phil Mickelson, Joe Montana, José Mourinho, Ambrose Murtagh, Rafael Nadal, Martina Navratilova, Jack Nicklaus, Brian O'Driscoll, Manny Pacquiao, Victoria Pendleton, Michael Phelps, Oscar Pistorius, Ricky Ponting, Paula Radcliffe, Sir Steve Redgrave, Sir Vivian Richards, Joannie Rochette, Pete Sampras, Michael Schumacher, Doug Scott, Kevin Sinfield, Mark Spitz, Martin Strel, Mike Stroud, Claire Taylor, Phil Taylor, Tim Tebow, Sachin Tendulkar, Bert Trautmann, Beth Tweddle, Grete Waitz, Shane Warne, Steve Waugh, Erik Weihenmayer, Kepler Wessels, Jonny Wilkinson, Betty Wilson, Tiger Woods, Louis Zamperini, to name but a few. Each of these performers did the best they could with the talent they had, because they had mental toughness.

I am compelled to add three more names. First is Eddie Izzard – the British actor, comedian, and (he would be the first to admit it) non-athlete. I was privileged, and humbled, to watch a BBC television programme of his completion of 43 marathons in 51 days. In the summer of 2009, Izzard ran the length and breadth of the United Kingdom to raise money for the charity Sport Relief. He covered 1,160 miles, and this supreme effort is awe-inspiring. If ever I have witnessed a demonstrable example of the mental toughness mindset, then this astonishing achievement is it. What makes this achievement all the more incredible is his ability to remain cheerful though he is in agony. He even had enough energy to perform an impromptu gig. 'I'm a little exhausted,' he told the audience in the Lake District, 'because I ran here from London.' Second is former Royal Marine and SAS member Chris Foot, who spent more than 70 days pulling a sledge 1,400 miles on his own across Antarctica in order to raise funds for Combat Stress, the mental health charity that helps ex-soldiers suffering from psychological injuries. And third is Major Phil Packer, whose completion of the 2009 London Marathon is astonishing. Packer, who was told he would never walk again after suffering a severe spinal injury while serving in Iraq, raised over £1 million for charity by walking for two weeks to cover the 26 miles and

385 yards. Each of these deeds, their every painful step, is a testament to Izzard, Foot, and Packer's courage, determination, and mental toughness; each an utterly remarkable achievement.

I thank David Fallais and his colleagues at Middlesbrough Central Library for their invaluable help in retrieving archived news reports. I thank Psychology Press for its immediate interest in publishing a second edition of my book. At Routledge, I thank Sharla Plant, Michael Fenton, Mary O'Hara, and Natalie Meylan. I am also deeply indebted to Project Manager, Kirsty Holmes, and my diligent copy editor, Kevin Eaton. I thank Andrew Ward for designing such an eye-catching cover. But, above all, thank you, to Julie and to my mother Kathleen. Your encouragement kept me going; your own mental toughness is inspirational.

1   Introducing mental toughness

A leader is a dealer in hope.

Napoleon Bonaparte

Introduction

It has been suggested that: 'A sporting contest is defined by the pursuit of a victor. Other benefits of a more altruistic and social nature may accrue from sport, but, in essence, the challenge is set down: to find a winner' (G. Davies, 2007: 19). This is a sentiment echoed by Olympic champion Sir Matthew Pinsent: 'Sport is all about rising to the challenge, whether it is laid down by your own limitations, the prowess of your opposition or the magnitude of the event; to win you have to have the ability to overcome' (Pinsent, 2009: 62). Indeed, our enduring fascination with sport may very well be attributed to 'its sole objective criterion – winning' (B. Moore, 2009b: S17). Nowhere is this struggle for quantifiable supremacy more intense than at the very highest competitive levels, where sport is no longer a pastime, run and organised by amateurs. Sport's essence is 'competition, if not conflict; more so when it is the livelihood of the participants' (B. Moore, 2009c: S15), and it exists in a culture where, as Manchester United FC's manager Sir Alex Ferguson said: 'The pressure never eases . . . where if you're not winning every game then swoosh, kick in the teeth' (as cited in Winter, 2009d: S5) and 'you are in to win and you can't lose too many or you lose your job . . . we are all subject to winning' (as cited in Rich, 2010: 5). Wales rugby union head coach Warren Gatland summed up such a culture after a narrow loss: 'At the end of the day it's about winning and we lost' (as cited in S. James, 2010c: S19).

Competitive sport has developed into a well-established global industry, operating in an increasingly competitive world (Stead, 2003); and, to some extent, functions to make money (see Hannon, 2010; Hirshey & Bennett, 2010; Pearson, 2011), too often with deplorable consequences and sapping much of the joy. Nowadays, there is a far greater commercial importance attached to how individuals and teams achieve success. Sport is a multi-billion pound business that competes for scarce resources and uses, among other things, commercial and professional management techniques (Robinson, 1999, 2003). These developments have moved sport organisations towards a more professional and bureaucratic structure (Byers, 2004; Old, 2004; Slack & Hinnings, 1992). In this push towards efficiency, effectiveness, and value for money, it has become of even greater interest to players, coaches, administrators, spectators, and owners (and, increasingly, shareholders and sponsors) to identify qualities associated with superior sport performance as a first stage in facilitating their development. When it comes down to it, there are two qualities that are necessary for victory in any sport: ability and mental toughness.

I am concerned primarily with the latter although, naturally, each affects the other. The two enjoy a symbiotic relationship. Mental toughness is just as important as natural talent. At the top level of any sport, all the challengers have the requisite technical skills, but it necessitates mental toughness to use that talent consistently to become a champion athlete. As Dutch international footballer Robin Van Persie stated: 'I think it's the combination you have to have – the mental toughness and the talent. You have to put in the quality but as well as have the mental strength to do it over and over again' (as cited in Hytner, 2010b). Such a viewpoint corroborates the observation of experienced football manager Sam Allardyce: 'You can only play in the Premier League if you have that mental toughness . . . The ability comes after that' (as cited in Szczepanik, 2009: 8). Similarly, Steve Bruce's eulogy of his former Manchester United FC teammate Ryan Giggs: 'His natural ability has made him the player he is but so has his mentality' (as cited in L. Taylor, 2009: 5) – reflects that it is about matching sporting capability with an evoking mentality. Manchester United and Scotland midfielder Darren Fletcher reflected: 'In the big games especially, I'm of the opinion that sometimes it's more psychological than about actual ability. I'm a great believer in that. A big percentage of the game is played in your head' (as cited in Ducker, 2010a: 9). In the aftermath of back-to-back title-damaging defeats, France international footballer, and then of Arsenal FC, Samir Nasri spoke of the team being galvanised: 'We wanted to prove we have the strength and the mentality to be winners . . . Last year we made some mistakes . . . We are stronger in our heads. Now it is 90 per cent in the mind. If you don't have the mentality you can't use your technique' (as cited in Lawrence, 2010: 4). England cricketer Ian Bell recognised the need to work on his mental toughness in addition to his technical skills (Hoult, 2009d). It has been suggested that the travails of Australian cricket captain Ricky Ponting in the 2010–11 Ashes series were born of mental turmoil: 'If you accept that batting is 25 per cent technical and 75 per cent mental, and that his technique, while not flawless, has held him in pretty good stead all these years, it must have been a mental aberration . . . his mind is scrambled' (S. Hughes, 2010e: S6). While the longest tennis match in history elicited this summary: 'It is very rare that a single sports match takes players to the edge of their capacity in so many different areas: physical fitness, mental toughness, competitive fire' (E. Smith, 2010).

To place emphasis on the identification of ability and a personality style is to subscribe to the view that 'sport is neither a moral nor a philosophical undertaking but an athletic and a psychological one' (Syed, 2007: 71), and that the person is a psychophysical unity – something that has both physical and mental attributes (McGinn, 2008). Personality is known as a source of moderator variables, and is more likely to manifest in interaction effects, such as influencing the likelihood of actualising one's ability into achievement (Aidman & Schofield, 2004). The field of sport psychology, in particular, has striven to understand and predict performance excellence primarily on the basis of personality (P. S. Miller & Kerr, 2002). Considerable evidence exists within the extant sport psychology literature that desirable psychological attributes contribute significantly to superior sport performance. (See Note 1.) Moreover, it has been suggested that as sport performers move up towards elite levels, only those with adaptive personality characteristics advance (Deaner & Silva, 2002). This is exemplified by former Great Britain No. 1 tennis player Annabel Croft's admission to lacking the emotional toughness necessary to cope with the defeats she suffered in trying to move upward in her sport (Preston, 2008).

At this level, the differences between competitors in technical, tactical, and physical ability are minimal (Moran, 2004). Improvements in diet, hygiene, and medical science have led to the healthiest, most physically robust sportspeople ever known, with, at the highest competitive level, a generation of near equals 'stronger, hardier and more resistant than at any time in history' (Goodbody, 2002: 32). Athletes are carefully prepared, both physically and technically. Physical and technical abilities are more evenly matched at higher levels especially, so personality becomes increasingly significant, thus demonstrating that 'sport is about the revealing of character and inner spirit as much as it is about technical brilliance' (Cleary, 2005b: S6). This is evidenced in the words of three-time Tour de France champion Alberto Contador, who spoke of his 2010 contest with Andy Schleck, after a particularly gruelling stage, as 'a psychological war, we're both at more or less the same level physically and this was a test of minds' (as cited in Fotheringham, 2010: 15). Team Sky and Great Britain's cycling general manager Dave Brailsford recognised the importance of rider psychology:

'To keep going for three weeks on a bike is such a monumental physical effort, to carry on must largely be in the mind. That is where there is an opportunity. Psychology will be everything' (as cited in White, 2010c: S10).

As long ago as the 1960s and, in particular, in readiness for their magnificent 1970 Fifa World Cup triumph, the Brazil soccer team recognised that psychological preparation was as important as technical and tactical arrangements. Four decades later, in preparation for the 2010 tournament, England head coach Fabio Capello employed a sport psychologist, Christian Lattanzio, who doubled as a translator (Burt, 2010). World champion boxer Alex Arthur insists that: 'It's important your mind is as strong as your body. Boxing makes demands of you that no other sport does. The real battlefield is in the mind, not in the gym or on the road' (as cited in Halliday, 2010: 11). Formula One's 2008 and 2009 world champions, respectively, sum it up – Lewis Hamilton: 'The biggest challenge is defeating your opponents mentally' (as cited in Ross, 2007), and Jenson Button: 'Mentally it's so, so draining . . . It's more tough mentally than physically' (as cited in Weaver, 2011: 11).

To this end, athletes' ability to focus attention, to control performance imagery, and a total commitment to the pursuit of excellence have been identified as critical psychological attributes (Orlick & Partington, 1988). Undoubtedly, the advice of one of the most successful Test cricket captains, the West Indies' Clive Lloyd, holds true: 'If you want to improve at your sport, you have to be dedicated, do little else, train hard' (Lloyd, 2007: 90). But, ultimately, those athletes with the appropriate psychological attributes make the transition upward because their personalities facilitate the adjustment. Success in any sport starts in the mind. The New Zealand rugby union team, 2011 world champions and the consistently world-ranked No. 1 All Blacks, has an idiom that sums it up perfectly: 'It's all about the top two inches' (Loe, 2007). The failing is in the head. Indeed, it has been written of the All Blacks that: 'They have a mindset that is unique. It is what sets them apart' (Greenwood, 2010b: S2).

From findings of the current literature, it is apparent that several specific personality characteristics have been indicated that ameliorate sport performance. After reviewing this research, sport psychologists Jean Williams and Vikki Krane concluded: 'Regardless of the source of data or the nature of the sport, a certain psychological profile appears to be linked with successful performance' (J. M. Williams & Krane, 2001: 174–175). This general profile cited self-regulation of arousal, high self-confidence, heightened concentration, coping skills for dealing with distractions and unexpected events, feeling in control, a positive preoccupation with sport, and determination and commitment (the very attributes which we will see later are constitutive of mental toughness) as key psychological characteristics distinguishing successful from less successful athletes.

In two separate studies, Dan Gould and his associates reported that 73 per cent and 82 per cent, respectively, of their sample pools (i.e., sport performers, coaches, parents, siblings, significant others) identified 'mental toughness' as a vital characteristic associated with successful performance (D. Gould, Dieffenbach, & Moffett, 2002; D. Gould, Hodge, Peterson, & Petlichkoff, 1987). Indeed, in the D. Gould *et al.* (2002: 186) study, the largest higher-order theme from their interviews was 'mental toughness', comprised of raw data responses such as 'mentally tough, perseverance, resilient, and persistent'. In a similarly explorative study of the mental skills of National Hockey League players, one interviewee stated that: 'Mental toughness is probably the biggest thing [needed for success] in hockey' (Barbour & Orlick, 1999: 29). In addition, high-performance kick-boxers were in agreement that psychological hardiness and mental toughness were necessary in order to become a successful tournament fighter (Devonport, 2006). More recent research has also recognised mental toughness as important for success (Bullock, Gulbin, Martin, Ross, Holland, & Marino, 2009). Thus, this personality style appears to be central to overall performance excellence.

However, mental toughness is probably one of the most used but least understood terms in sport psychology. Stemming in part from Jim Loehr's research, it is widely alluded to by athletes and coaches, as well as in the popular media and in applied sport psychology, as a crucial prerequisite of success in sport (Loehr, 1986). Indeed, researchers have felt the need to re-label sport psychology as 'mental toughness' in order to sell it to English soccer academy directors and national coaches (Pain & Harwood, 2004). Why do some athletes and teams perform a little better in pressure situations? How do some performers cope with being 'iced' (e.g., dealing with a time-out called just before taking a field-goal or free-throw, or facing a goal-keeper who continually mucks about ahead of a penalty)? What separates those who thrive on elite competition from those who collapse under pressure? Why do some athletes and teams succeed in the face of adversity while others fail? Why do some performers bounce back from personal failure whereas others are beleaguered by it? Why have some athletes consistently underachieved? Many suggest that the answer lies in mental toughness.

According to Jason Robinson, a Rugby World Cup winner in 2003 and an all-time great in both rugby codes: 'Mental toughness is as important as physical toughness' (as cited in Lynch, 2008). While former Republic of Ireland international footballer Tony Cascarino placed even greater emphasis on its influence, suggesting that: 'Mental toughness can make the difference between success and failure' (Cascarino, 2009: 14). Again from soccer, it has been suggested that: 'On the pitch, mental toughness is a most important attribute' (The Secret Footballer, 2012, p.1). Accepting the enormous challenge of tackling southern hemisphere supremacy in rugby league, England head coach Steve McNamara acknowledged: 'Mental toughness is an area that we need to look at' (as cited in Bott, 2010). Indeed, it has been suggested that at the highest competitive levels 'the essential extra element is mental toughness' and that 'this mental toughness needs training just as much as the ability to hit a ball straight and far' (G. Faulkner, 2006: 27). In the second of her Olympic triumphs in Athens in 2004 (the 1,500 metres), Kelly Holmes' 'mental toughness was truly awesome as she dominated the race' (Redgrave, 2011). And, in the midst of the fallout from his infidelity scandal, Tiger Woods has been described as 'still the mentally toughest athlete on the planet' (Gregory, 2010). It would appear that to progress from strong performer to champion, the breakthrough ingredient is mental toughness. It is this attribute that allows sport performers to act in an instinctive and automatic way at the most important moments and the turning points of a competition or other high-stakes situations. But what exactly is 'mental toughness'?

Popular mental toughness

Across a multitude of sports, athletes often attribute achievement and success to 'mental toughness'. Upon reaching the considerable milestone of a century of centuries in first-class cricket, and becoming only the 25th player in the history of the game ever to do so, Surrey and England batsman Mark Ramprakash said: 'I had so many knocks, so many low scores, so many setbacks, and have shown a lot of mental toughness to keep going – despite the blows' (as cited in Kimmage, 2008: 19). Also from cricket, of Alastair Cook's second innings century for England against Sri Lanka in Galle, it was written that: 'Amid the disappointments, it was great to see such mental toughness from someone so young, right at the end of the tour' (Hoggard, 2007: 62). Interviewed on his recall to the England One-Day International side, wicketkeeper Matt Prior reflected: 'When you are left out, people give you stick and say that is the end and he will never be back. To come back and perform for Sussex the way I have I am quite proud of. It shows mental toughness' (as cited in Hoult, 2008: S20). And, on the eve of what turned out to be a hugely successful tour of Australia, England batsman Kevin Pietersen said: 'We've got to be mentally tougher' (as cited in Booth, 2010: 23).

Claire Taylor, captain of the all-conquering England women's cricket team said: 'It took a while but my mental toughness was built on an understanding that I wasn't the best player technically' (as cited in McRae, 2010d: 6–7). Former Australian spin bowler Shane Warne described India's talisman Sachin Tendulkar as 'very tough mentally' (Warne, 2009: 15). Upon acceptance of the captaincy of the Australian Test cricket team, the immensely successful Steve Waugh reflected in his autobiography that: 'All that was required was the mental toughness to carry out my plan' (Waugh, 2006: 52). And, in addition to the requisite physical fitness for long spells of bowling, also needed 'is the mental toughness to be able to bowl your 24th over of the day as hard and as optimistically as your first' (S. Hughes, 2010c: S15).

Reflecting upon his Olympic gold medal-winning performance in Beijing, British yachtsman Ben Ainslie spoke reverentially of other high-achieving athletes: 'The mental toughness of those guys, especially [Michael] Schumacher, was amazing' (as cited in Snow, 2008: 32). Admitting the need for urgent psychological repair following a disastrous semi-final perform-ance in the winter Olympics in Vancouver, British speed-skating coach Nicky Gooch said: 'It takes a lot of mental toughness to come back and that's what we're going to work on now' (as cited in Hart, 2010a: S17). Of getting through to the third round of the Wimbledon tennis championships for the first time in seven attempts, Australian player Samantha Stosur reflected: 'I think my mental toughness wavered in and out, it certainly wasn't there all the time, but I got it back' (as cited in P. Wilson, 2009). And ahead of the 2011 US Masters, British golfer Graeme McDowell said: 'I have been blessed with a certain mental toughness which has stood me in good stead during my career' (as cited in Donegan, 2011a: 7).

From rugby league, ahead of a Super League grand final victory, Leeds Rhinos forward Jamie Jones Buchanan attributed his team's resurgence to 'mental toughness and work ethic' (as cited in Irvine, 2007b: 79). In praise of their opponent's challenge after his side's third consecutive Rugby League Challenge Cup triumph, St Helens full-back Paul Wellens said: 'They gave us as tough a game as any we've had all season. The heat and intensity really took its toll in the second half. In the end our mental toughness got us through' (as cited in Malin, 2008: 14). Even rugby league's world No. 1 referee, Ashley Klein, attributed a large part of his success to mental tough-ness: 'It is about being mentally tough. It is about being able to make a deci-sion and forget about it and not letting external factors cloud your judgement' (personal communication, June 24, 2008). And from golf, 2009 World Match Play champion Ross Fisher's assessment: 'In all, I think it was mental toughness that pulled me through' (as cited in Dixon, 2009b: 79).

From rugby union: 'mental toughness and unyielding self-belief in the tightest of corners are two of Jonny Wilkinson's great attributes' (Fitzgerald, 2011, p. 94). Speaking prior to his side's surprise semi-final victory over hosts France in the 2007 Rugby World Cup, England captain Phil Vickery acknowledged: 'We know it will be tough, but I feel we have the players not just with the skills but with the mental toughness' (as cited in Slot, 2007a: 120), adding that: 'This is a once-in-a-lifetime opportunity. It's mental toughness we need now, not game plans galore. It's about physicality, about bravery, about guts' (as cited in Cleary, 2011e: S6). Subsequently, teammate Lawrence Dallaglio wrote of England's win: 'In the end, it came down to mental toughness' (Dallaglio, 2007: 427). Of the rejuvenation of his international career under a new head coach, Wales star Gavin Henson said: 'It is all about concentration and it has given us a mental toughness' (as cited in Rees, 2008: 11). Ahead of a showdown with the world champion South African rugby union team, of his own teammates, British and Irish Lion Nathan Hines spoke of the 'mental toughness throughout the group. Many of the players have reached the highest level and sustained that standard' (as cited in Pearce, 2009). Attributing a personally successful debut season in the English Premiership, South African Schalk Brits said: 'You have to be so tough mentally' (as cited in Cleary, 2010c: S20). Mental toughness was strongly referred to by Wales international rugby player Shane Williams (since retired) during his team's impressive World Cup showing: '[This is] mentally the toughest squad I've ever been involved in . . . We've been pretty switched on. The most important thing is that we realise it's all about working hard if we want to be successful. That's where this mental toughness comes from' (as cited in Cleary, 2011g: S7), and: 'We are far more mentally strong as a team these days' (as cited in Slot, 2011c: 72).

And, from American football, New England Patriots kicker Stephen Gostkowski explained:

> You have to be able to focus for that one time you get a chance in a game. Your margin for error is really thin and you only get so many opportunities and if you don't take advantage of them you won't have a job . . . Not everybody has the mental toughness to be put in situations like that or bounce back when you don't succeed.
>
> (as cited in Dart, 2009b)

In order to become a championship-calibre team, Washington Redskins linebacker and defensive co-captain London Fletcher said: 'In pro sports, you have to be mentally tough. That mental toughness part . . . you have to be extremely mentally tough' (as cited in J. Reid, 2010).

Retired performers have also written of the positive contribution of mental toughness to sporting achievement. Of 2008 Junior Wimbledon tennis champion Laura Robson, Annabel Croft wrote of her 'impression that she is very tough, mentally' (as cited in A. Baker, 2008: S5). Writing of the positive impact a new national coach has made on Welsh rugby union fortunes, former Wales and Great Britain international rugby union and league star Jonathan Davies observed: 'Most rugby nations nowadays are on a par in terms of fitness and technique, but the major difference Warren Gatland has made is mental toughness. It's all in the head' (J. Davies, 2008: 86). While in response to the question of where yet another defeat to the New Zealand All Blacks leaves Wales, former Welsh international legend Gerald Davies commented: 'In need of the mental toughness and relentless will to win as expressed by New Zealand on Saturday' (G. Davies, 2009: 72). England cricket legend Geoffrey Boycott wrote of another hugely talented international batsman: 'Jonathan Trott is mentally strong . . . Other batsmen have been better stroke-players but did not have the mental toughness to succeed' (Boycott, 2011c: S10). And, former world No. 1 and winner of five grand slam titles Martina Hingis has suggested that: 'Maria Sharapova's greatest strength has always been her mental toughness – she gives opponents nothing . . . Sharapova is so strong in the mind' (Hingis, 2011: F6).

Similarly, coaches have spoken of mental toughness in terms of its contribution to performance and results. Ahead of Amir Khan's Olympic boxing lightweight semi-final in Athens, Great Britain team manager Terry Edwards considered that: 'An important factor for the rest of this tournament will be mental toughness. This is something that we have been developing' (as cited in Goodbody, 2004b: 50). Seeking to rectify a dip in his Australian rugby league team's form, Newcastle Knights coach Brian Smith commented: 'We need mental toughness to grind out the win for the whole game' (as cited in McDonald, 2008). Craig Bellamy, coach of Melbourne Storm spoke of his side's mindset: 'One of the things that, during the pre-season, we wanted to make sure we had is a mentally tough team . . . we certainly trained for them to be a team capable of being a mentally tough team with plenty of resolve . . . I'd like to think they're a pretty mentally tough footy team' (as cited in R. Gould, 2011). Of the St George-Illawarra team, Brisbane Bronco's Darren Lockyer said: 'The Dragons are by far the best team in the competition . . . They're all mentally tough players' (as cited in McDonald, 2011). And ahead of the 2011 State of Origin series, Queensland's coach Mal Meninga pinpointed the influence of his opposite number, New South Wales' Wayne Bennett: 'One of Wayne's great attributes is his man-management skills, being able to talk to the players and make them mentally tough' (as cited in McDonald, 2011).

Reacting to criticism, former Leicester Tigers (English rugby union) coach Marcelo Loffreda countered: 'I have felt high-pressure situations with the [Argentina] national side but that wasn't about professionalism, this is. I'll tackle it with a lot of hard work, commitment and mental toughness' (as cited in Hands, 2008a: 68). Also from rugby union, Glasgow coach Sean Lineen spoke of injured Scotland flanker Donnie Macfadyen's efforts during rehabilitation: 'I've been very impressed, he has shown a real mental toughness' (as cited in L. Stuart, 2008: 85). While across Scotland, appointed to shore up the defence of Edinburgh, coach Billy McGinty said:

'My outlook is that it's going to be a game where you hurt afterwards. Hopefully, I can instil a kind of mental toughness' (as cited in A. Reid, 2011). Of the England team's change in fortune during the 2007 Rugby World Cup, former rugby league icon and present Wales rugby union defensive coach Shaun Edwards wrote: 'Ashton's men had the character, the mental toughness, to turn things round in France last autumn' (Edwards, 2008: 9). While ahead of the British and Irish Lions 2009 tour of South Africa, and working as the assistant Lions coach, he asserted: 'We've certainly tried to select players who have that mental toughness' (as cited in Ackford, 2009).

Reflecting on his side's heroic defensive effort, London Irish director of rugby Toby Booth said: 'Mental toughness and resilience are often words that are bandied around and if you look at the sequence of defence in our own 22 . . . it indicates that people care about what they are doing' (as cited in Mairs, 2010c: S20). On retirement from playing Australian Rules football, Collingwood coach Mick Malthouse reminisced: 'When a new season starts you tend to forget the agony that you went through, how hard it becomes to get up and running, the cold, the injuries, the effort and mental toughness' (Malthouse, 2008).

Ahead of trips to Northwestern and Michigan State, coach of the undefeated Michigan Wolverines, Brady Hoke, said: 'I'm interested to see how we react and what we're made of, our mentality, our mental toughness' (as cited in Lage, 2011). Of selection controversies, the University of Southern California athletic director, Pat Haden mused: 'Every quarterback goes through this. It's why the position requires such mental toughness' (as cited in Foster, 2011). And from soccer, Glasgow Rangers FC coach Ally McCoist stated: 'It is about mental toughness, a little bit of luck, a certain attitude as well, and a desire as much as anything' (as cited in Spiers, 2008b: 108). Reflecting on a come-from-behind victory, Brendan Rodgers, manager of Swansea City FC, said: 'We talked about the definition of mental toughness and how it's about coming back from disappointment and setbacks and not dwelling on the negatives . . . our mental toughness was put into question and we came up with all the answers' (as cited in Lucas, 2011: 49). While Sir Alex Ferguson spoke of his championship-winning team: 'There is a mental toughness about the team these days and that will stand us in good stead as the pressure builds' (as cited in Ogden, 2009).

Similarly, athletes' below-par performances and failures have often been attributed to a lack of mental toughness. Of her defeat in the final of the 2009 French Open, Russian tennis star Dinara Safina suggested: 'I put pressure on myself because I wanted to win so much. I didn't handle it. I didn't stay tough mentally' (as cited in Pitt, 2009: 11). When another former world No. 1, Jelena Jankovic, suffered a shock first round exit at the China Open, she admitted that she had been lacking 'mental toughness' (as cited in P. Simpson, 2011). Of the Wales international rugby union team's decline in fortunes since its 2005 Six Nations grand slam triumph: 'No one doubts that talent but it's been legitimate over the last two seasons to question their resolve and their mental toughness' (Ackford, 2007). When Scotland failed for the first time to qualify from the group stage of a Rugby World Cup, hooker Ross Ford said: 'It is a mental thing' (as cited in L. Stuart, 2011: 67), adding that Scotland had to start finding the mental toughness to convert game opportunities into victories.

When his Denver Broncos side were pounded by the Baltimore Ravens in the National Football League (NFL), coach Josh McDaniels said: 'For the first time I thought our mental toughness was questioned' (as cited in Hensley, 2010). Of Dallas Cowboys quarterback Tony Romo, NFL Hall of Famer Deion Sanders (2011) said: 'He proved that he has heart, he has mental toughness.' While Baltimore Orioles manager Buck Showalter said of Zach Britton, the team's pitcher: 'You don't do the things he has done over a long period and not have some mental toughness. The mental toughness part of it is never a question with him' (as cited in Connolly, 2011). And, Everton footballer Tim Cahill attempted to explain a dreadful run in the team's form: 'It's the overall attitude and mental toughness . . . nothing's going to fix it except our mental attitude' (as cited in Hunter, 2009a).

Other examples include: 'His [Dimitar Berbatov] encouraging response removed the doubts about his appetite and mental toughness in adversity' (Hayward, 2010b); 'They're [Celtic and Rangers] supposed to have the nurturing skills and coaching sophistication required when presented with a young player with abundant ability but perhaps lacking mental toughness' (A. Smith, 2010: 13); 'Now is the time for a new wave of northern hemisphere player to emerge with the mental toughness to put behind them last weekend's failure' (Best, 2005); 'Shane Williams has hit back at critics who question the character and mental toughness of the British and Irish Lions' (as cited in D. Lewis, 2009); 'The statistics back up Behrami's point about a side lacking mental toughness' (D. Kent, 2010); 'Scotland midfielder Rhona Simpson criticised her team's lack of mental toughness after their hopes of a top-six finish at the European Nations Cup fell by the wayside against Ukraine' (C. Middleton, 2003). Indeed, the player herself stated: 'At this level you need attention to detail because every touch matters. There's no point huffing and hiding; if you have that attitude you should get off the pitch. You have to grind out the phases that count – it's about mental toughness' (as cited in ibid.). Launching a stinging attack on his players, Sam Allardyce reiterated comments mentioned earlier in this chapter: 'In the Premiership, the mental side is even more important than the ability side. You can only play in this league if you have that mental toughness and resilience. Ability comes after that. But, at the moment, the mental resilience is not there' (as cited in Fifield, 2009b: 8). While counterpart Alex McLeish said of one player that he has 'certainly shown the mental toughness to handle it' (as cited in McLoughlin, 2011: 105). And, enduring their third game in eight days in pursuit of a play-off place, Gloucester RUFC players were reminded by their coach Bryan Redpath: 'The key thing is that everyone going to Saracens gets there with a mindset that they've got to be mentally strong' (as cited in P. Morgan, 2011).

Occasionally, individuals somehow avoid using the term 'mental toughness', even when we pretty much know that is what is being referred to; for example, '[Manchester] United possess resilience in their DNA' (Winter, 2012e). Here, Hibernian manager John Hughes vents spleen and laments his team's apparent lack of mental toughness after a particularly dismal showing: 'We are turned over, we do not have that resolve, that character, that toughness to see games out, to win ugly, that mental attitude' (as cited in Hardie, 2010). Similarly, the England football team's 'psychological fragility' (Kay, 2011f: 96) has been apparent; indeed, the players' mental toughness, when faced with a penalty shoot-out situation, is being questioned in this example: 'It is hoped that Capello's decisiveness will strengthen the players' often brittle psychological resolve' (Winter, 2010i: S4).

Arsenal FC manager, Arsène Wenger, sought to explain a surprise reversal in terms of his team's being 'not completely there on the mental side' (as cited in Rich, 2008: S2). In addition, it has been noted that: 'Wenger is less worried about his players' physical attributes than their mental strength ... psychological weaknesses have undermined Arsenal' (M. Hughes, 2010b: 4); while Champions League and FA Cup exits coupled with four Premier League draws meant that 'the mental toughness of Wenger's squad has been questioned' (Hytner, 2011a: 4). Approaching the end of Arsenal's 2010–11 season, it was written: 'Here ... was a demonstration of how profoundly a lack of mental fortitude has damaged a campaign that once contained such promise' (R. Williams, 2011d: 10). Further, 'mental fragility' has been attributed to indifferent runs of form for not only Arsenal (Hytner, 2010a: 7; Kay, 2011c: 84), but also Chelsea FC (M. Hughes, 2010c: 3). Tim Henman's failings were suggested as evidence of 'mental frailty under pressure' (Bierley, 2001). And a 'fragile mental state' was blamed for tennis player Tommy Haas' squandering a two-set lead to Roger Federer in the 2009 French Open (Hodgkinson, 2009: S20).

The phrase 'mental toughness' appears to be used somewhat liberally in the popular media. For example, an examination of the print media, and their respective websites, yields a plethora of reports where the term has been used to explain preparation, performances, and results in a variety of sports, ranging from American football through to tennis. (See Note 2 for a comprehensive list.) The following are examples of the term's appeal in the sporting media: 'Lennon's view is simple: that his players all too often lack mental toughness' (Murray, 2011c: 7); 'England's ... mental toughness took them to a famous victory' (Walsh, 2008a: 2); 'Wasps, the champions, are the benchmark for any aspiring team, for their mental toughness, and their sheer cussedness' (Cleary, 2008: S12); 'Wenger praised the grit and determination of his young side, pinpointing their mental toughness' (Dall, 2007); 'Gordon Strachan insisted yesterday that Scotland's players possess the mental toughness required to finish their Euro 2008 qualifying job' (P. Gordon, 2007: 96); 'Now bubbling Boro are a mentally tougher team' (Vickers, 2011b: 38); '. . . a common trait in all the champions . . . including Prost, Senna, Michael Schumacher and Mika Hakkinen, has been an immense mental toughness. They all had the willpower to burn . . . the difference between winning and losing' (Garside, 2008: 15); 'It's a three-way battle for the title and mental toughness will be a major factor' (Perry, 2008); 'India claim to be the best in the world. To pull off a remarkable victory here to go with their recent defeat of Australia, will prove they have the requisite self-belief and mental toughness to go with their undoubted skill' (S. Hughes, 2008b); '. . . a tactical triumph and a glorious vindication of Leeds' mental toughness to recover from their mauling by Saints in the qualifying semi-final two weeks earlier' (Irvine, 2008b); 'Kidney cannot be criticised for checking Sexton's mental toughness' (O'Reilly, 2011: 2); 'Leicester . . . Theirs is a game based on mental toughness' (Souster, 2011a: 62); 'Ryder Cup captain Colin Montgomerie has hailed Graeme McDowell's mental toughness' (US Open 2010); 'Danny Lennon insists his St Mirren players need to develop a mental toughness to deal with flak from the fans' (Baillie, 2011); 'No one can doubt the South Africans' mental toughness' (B. Moore, 2009d: S9); 'The match starting at the Oval today is not about ability – there is nothing between the teams – it's about character, commitment and mental toughness' (Boycott, 2009c: S4); 'Certainly, McIlroy seems mentally tougher than 18 months ago' (Donegan, 2011b: 12); 'We should hope McIlroy can find the mental toughness to return and win' (B. Moore, 2011: S11); in the obituary of tennis great Jack Kramer: 'As an outstanding Wimbledon and US champion of the 1940s, he developed a powerful, ruthless serve and volley game, with one of the best second serves in history and immense mental toughness' (Gray, 2009); of England cricketer Paul Collingwood's batting: 'He never reflects on what has gone before. He shuts out a play and miss or an lbw appeal, retaining a calm composure. Mentally, he must be one of the toughest men ever to play for England' (S. Hughes, 2010a: S4), and of goalkeeper Robert Green's potential selection ahead of the 2010 Fifa World Cup: 'Does he have the sheer belief and mental toughness to do football's loneliest job, at a World Cup, for England?' (Northcroft,

2010: 8). Even Her Majesty, Queen Elizabeth II, in her capacity as a race-horse owner and, therefore, with experience of receiving bad news from trainers, can empathise that 'dealing with fragile racehorses on a regular basis develops a certain mental toughness' (J. A. McGrath, 2011: S18).

However, what constitutes mental toughness as reported in the popular media comes in various guises. Several other terms and phrases are used interchangeably to describe those characteristics that are constitutive of popular mental toughness. The annals of sporting history are chronicled with examples of memorable encounters, where the determinant of success has been attributed anecdotally to performers' 'mental strength' (see Note 3) or performance failure blamed on its absence (see Note 4). For example, Marc Lièvremont, former coach of the French international rugby union team, spoke of the psychological requirement to overhaul England ahead of their Rugby World Cup quarter-final: 'We know it's going to be hard and we will need a lot of mental strength' (as cited in Rees, 2011d: 11). And from the same tournament, after their own quarter-final defeat of Ireland, Wales' Shane Williams said: 'We have the mental strength now to win tight matches' (as cited in Rees, 2011f: 4). Former Formula One world champion Damon Hill suggested of the 2008 champion, and the then youngest ever winner of the drivers' championship, Lewis Hamilton: 'What Hamilton has proved this year more than anything else is that he has huge mental strength' (Hill, 2008: 3). While Arsène Wenger said of his team's response to adversity: 'Going out of the Champions League hurt and it was a massive disappointment and you go through a period of grief, and of denial, and then you have to start showing you have the mental strength to respond and the team has done that remarkably well' (as cited in Scott & Hunter, 2011: 1). Cricket coach Kepler Wessels, speaking up in defence of the often-criticised spin bowler Monty Panesar, said: 'People underestimate Monty's mental strength' (as cited in Hopps, 2006). Responding to suggestions of his gaining a psychological edge over Olympic champion Usain Bolt, American sprinter Tyson Gay said: 'I honestly believe that he [Bolt] is mentally strong' (as cited in Hart, 2011a: S13). Trying to explain Serena Williams's astonishing comeback from serious injury, it was written: 'The biggest thing in Williams's favour is her mental strength' (Cambers, 2011). And, of British diver Tom Daley's return to competition in the wake of his father's death, it was written: 'Daley's extraordinary mental strength. You do not get to be a world champion at the age of 15 without it' (Hart, 2011b: S13).

Former England cricket coach Duncan Fletcher wrote of the 'mentality', 'mindset', and 'mentally tough' requisites for a successful tour of India (Fletcher, 2008: 9). Zimbabwean cricketer Dale Benkenstein reflected on a relatively disappointing season with Durham CCC: 'When you move up the order you have to be a bit sharper, and I wasn't fit enough mentally' (as cited in Rae, 2011: 12). Shane Warne wrote of a change in 'England's mindset' as a contributor to their winning the 2010 ICC Twenty20 World Cup (Warne, 2010: S2). Often, the media use words such as 'grit', 'determination', and 'belief' to describe behaviours constitutive of mental toughness; for example: 'Having been given little or no chance against an apparently peerless St Helens, Leeds achieved back-to-back league championships ... with a performance in last night's Super League Grand Final that examined their reservoirs of self-belief and gritty determination and found them overflowing' (Patrick, 2008).

Similarly, sporting achievement has been credited with coaches who built up a psychology of winning by concentrating on their team's strengths, while failure is due, in part, to adoption of the mentality of defeat (Anthony, 2007). Thus, when the England national soccer team lost at home in its final qualification match and, as a consequence, failed to reach the 2008 European Championships, the pens (and laptops) were ready: 'The quality Croatia possess in particular abundance is self-belief ... England players may need to find greater mettle on their travels' (Winter, 2007: S2); while 'players' state of mind' (as cited in J. Wilson, 2007: S2–S3) and 'some sort of mental block' (as cited in Jenson, 2007: 2) were suggested by Fabio Capello. Of the flaws that have blighted a succession of Arsenal FC campaigns, lacking 'the mental fortitude to deal with the tests of character that are presented over the course of a season. Or to put it in more crude terms – bottle' has been proposed (Kay, 2011c: 85). In response to setbacks for the Ireland national rugby union team, former coach Eddie O'Sullivan recognised: 'We've got to become mentally tougher' (as cited in Kitson, 2004). And, in the aftermath of golfer Rory McIlroy's meltdown on the final round of the 2011 US Masters, it was suggested that 'it is the mind that most needs strengthening' (Dixon, 2011: 56).

Each of the aforementioned anecdotal explanations is related by a synonymous theme: 'mental toughness' (or lack of), and its assumed constitutive characteristics, were a contributory variable partly responsible for performers' success or loss. (For additional examples of phrases used synonymously to infer mental toughness, see Note 5.) Seven-times Formula One world champion Michael Schumacher was renowned for his 'mind games' and, for many observers and commentators of sport, is the epitome of mental toughness (see Cashmore, 2002; Goodbody, 2002). Yet, occasionally, it was known for the tables to be turned, in particular when he came up against Jacques Villeneuve. Of his battles with the French-Canadian driver, it was noted that: 'The disconcerting thing for him [Schumacher] about Villeneuve was that he was a tough character, mentally very strong' (J. Allen, 2007: 189). To highlight further the observation of terms used synonymously with mental toughness, I draw on the print media's coverage of seven high-profile sporting events: The 2003 Rugby World Cup, the 2005 Ashes cricket series, the 2007 Rugby World Cup, the 2008–09 soccer season, the 2009 British and Irish Lions rugby union tour of South Africa, the 2009 Wimbledon tennis championships, and the 2009 Ashes cricket series.

The 2003 Rugby World Cup

Of England's 2003 Rugby World Cup triumph, reflections included: 'The task of beating Australia in a World Cup final in Australia needed a colossal mental shift. The England rugby union side has certainly made one: and it was enough . . . Now they are world champions and that represents a serious shift of attitude' (Barnes, 2003: 38); 'Observers . . . were forced to admit that their own Wallabies had been beaten in a thrilling contest by a more skilful and resolute side' (R. Williams, 2003: 2); 'Woodward never talked of England doing their best or of them trying to get to the final. He spoke of winning the damn thing from the start . . . His achievements with England have come about because Woodward understands winning. He has a clear purpose and, perhaps most important of all, vigorous self-belief. His absolute determination that he is on the right path, and doing the right thing, gave him the courage to push for what he believed England needed in order to be the best' (Kervin, 2003: 36). Paying tribute to the victors, Australia captain George Gregan said: 'They [England] are very professional, do what they have to do to get victories . . . That's why they are world champions . . . They delivered under pressure and delivered when it counted' (as cited in Souster, 2003: 35).

The 2005 Ashes cricket series

This memorable sporting encounter provided many observations: 'Their [the cricketers'] play is . . . psychologically gruesome in its exposure of character' (Nicholas, 2005: VI); 'Australian cricketers are like cockroaches. You can damage their legs, cuff them on the head and poison their knees, but you can't crush them. Their spirit is unbreakable' (S. Hughes, 2005a: VI); 'Character. That's what got England over the line. Muscle, at such tense moments, turns to jelly. Only inner self-belief can hold the body together' (S. Hughes, 2005b: VII); 'Pietersen, mentally strong enough to absorb the immensity of the occasion without being cowed' (C. Ellis, 2005: V); 'He [Pietersen] is a belligerent individual. He is cocky and confident; there is a touch of arrogance about him. All the great players have had self-confidence and self-belief' (Boycott, 2005: S6). Kevin Pietersen himself stated: 'In the over against Brett Lee it was either me or him and I backed myself to succeed' (as cited in Hoult, 2005: S5). While team-mate Marcus Trescothick reflected: 'Fighting back from adversity is what we have done so well recently' (as cited in Pringle, 2005: II).

The 2007 Rugby World Cup

And, from coverage of the 2007 Rugby World Cup tournament: 'On the field they [South Africa] had the backbone to win under pressure. Off it, their shirt buttons were done up, their ties on straight, shoes polished. They looked like a team who were proud of what they had achieved. In short, they looked like world champions' (Greenwood, 2007: S14); 'They [England] made the quarter-finals . . . sustained by courage, coolness and sheer bloody-mindedness' (Rees, 2007: 4); 'A triumph against the odds, a stunning turn of events, one that speaks of many things: of inner strength, of fortitude, of togetherness, of bloody-mindedness and of duty' (Cleary, 2007: S2); 'This team [England] has got where it has through commitment, hard work, courage and a desire to prove people wrong' (Souster, 2007: 72); 'It's what you do when it matters most . . . You have no duty to enter-tain, if people cannot find inspiration or compulsion from your courage, fortitude and honesty, it's their problem, not yours' (B. Moore, 2007: S3).

The 2008–09 soccer season

Reporting on good times: 'The mental fortitude which West Bromwich have shown is worth a mention' (Macaskill, 2009: S8); 'In thumping Arsenal, Chelsea rubbed in the importance of power and resolve, bouncing back from their Champions League distress against Barcelona with real character' (Winter, 2009b: S6); Uefa Champions League winning coach Pep Guardiola of FC Barcelona: 'I concern myself only with what we can control' (as cited in Garside, 2009a: S7); 'It is when the machine has misfired that United have produced their most memorable moments of the campaign, drawing on their reserves of character, as well as their famed cavalier spirit, to turn defeat into victory against Aston Villa and Tottenham Hotspur in April' (Kay, 2009b: 4); Sir Alex Ferguson speaking of Wayne Rooney: 'The most important attribute is his fantastic hunger and desire . . . he's got resilience' (as cited in Winter, 2009d: S5); speaking prior to the final of his desire to win the European Under-21 soccer championship, England coach Stuart Pearce: 'We have come to win it and we have one team standing in our way. It is now down to who has the guts to win it' (as cited in Lansley, 2009b: 15); and, of qualifying for the final, England goal-keeper Joe Hart: 'We didn't make it easy but, down to ten men, we showed a lot of character and won the game' (as cited in ibid.: 15).

. . . And on those not so good times, of Sunderland FC's woes: 'Their collapse after taking the lead away to Portsmouth on Monday was not that of a team blessed with mental fortitude' (Kay, 2009c: 75); of Newcastle United FC's collapse: '. . . shortage of determination' (Winter, 2009e: S2); 'When it came to the club's day of reckoning, the players were as guilty as anyone for failing to show any desire to embrace the opportunity that was there to be taken' (Kay, 2009d: 2); of Middlesbrough FC's relegation: 'No leader, no spine, no confidence' (Jacob, 2009a: 8); lamenting Arsenal FC's deficiencies: 'For all their undoubted talent and potential, this Arsenal team have never appeared to have the necessary mental fortitude to flourish at the very highest level' (Kay, 2009a: 2); and, regretting his team's semi-final penalty shoot-out defeat to England, Swedish coach Jörgen Lennartsson reflected of taking penalties: 'It is 90 per cent mental and 10 per cent technical' (as cited in Lansley, 2009a: 14).

The 2009 British and Irish Lions rugby union tour of South Africa

The requisite tone was set ahead of the tour with acknowledgement of an 'emphasis on spirit and character' (Ackford, 2009). The particularly intense contest itself between hosts and world champions South Africa and the touring British and Irish Lions provided many comments. For example, Lions wing Shane Williams stated: 'You can't go into your shell, dwell on past mistakes, sometimes things don't go your way . . . I'll be a better player if I can cope with that' (as cited in Hands, 2009a: 81); 'Character as much as skill will make the difference in the Tests. Guts and gumption take you a long way. With the scores level with four minutes to go, the Lions' unbeaten record endured because of their grit, their togetherness, their all-important sense of themselves . . . They are winning. Self-belief is no longer an abstract concept' (Cleary, 2009f: S12); of his disappointment after the first Test, the Lions' Ugo Monye reflected: 'Sport can take you to the greatest peaks and drag you to the deepest troughs. It was quite a tough pill to swallow but you can't go feeling sorry for yourself. You've got to pick yourself up and dust yourself down' (as cited in Cleary, 2009h: S15); of South African half-back Ruan Pienaar:

> As he lined up another crack at goal . . . the referee tried to hurry him because he was getting near the end of his allotted minute. 'Come on 10,' he said, but he might as well have been speaking to himself. Pienaar never heard him, and he did not hear the crowd all day. He is a player who goes into 'The Zone', does what he has to do, never allows anyone to distract him from his chosen path, and gets the job done . . . Frighteningly efficient.
>
> (Greenwood, 2009b: S4)

Of the second Test in Pretoria, it was written that: 'It was a game of noble stature, one that revealed and, in some cases, exposed character' (Cleary, 2009g: S8). And following the Lions' emphatic victory in the third and final Test, and in the process refuting suggestions that Lions tours may be consigned to history: 'Saturday's landmark victory, testimony to the nerve, the character and the unquenchable spirit of the tourists, has seen to that' (Cleary, 2009j: S16).

The 2009 Wimbledon tennis championships

Despite the absence from this tournament of the injured defending champion Rafael Nadal, there was still much alluding to popular mental toughness: 'She has a rare ability to handle everything that has been thrown at her so far' (Harman, 2009b: 63); 'It all began with that lapse of concentration, that mental packing of the bags' (Barnes, 2009c: 10); 'The sheer irresistible force of Hewitt's will to win' (J. Henderson, 2009: 5); British No. 1 Andy Murray was the object of many observations: 'Murray yesterday played with complete and rather frightening self-certainty, mixed with a little playfulness, a sense of delight in the whole business. Yesterday, he looked like a champion' (Barnes, 2009b: 84); 'It was Murray's will, competitiveness, and desire that were swaying the course of a tight and compelling contest' (Bierley, 2009b: 1); 'Murray has that champion's ability of being unembarrassed by his own difficulties, of always concentrating on the fight. A champion must be happy to get down and dirty in a fight if he has to and Murray did exactly that' (Barnes, 2009d: 64); 'The real test of a competitor is how they respond to adversity' (White, 2009b: 3). And of the final, where Roger Federer, arguably the greatest tennis player of all time, won his record-breaking 15th grand slam title: 'Here was Federer in crisis, growing not shrinking' (Chadband, 2009d: S4); 'He had the experience and character to stand there as Roddick came forward and attacked, and even though he was not having his best day, Federer knew he would make it hard for Roddick to win. That is the quality that he has' (Becker, 2009: S3); 'Poor Roddick. The American tried his heart out, only to come up short again on this hallowed ground. "I had two options out there, I either lay down or I keep going. The second option sounded better to me," he said' (Harman, 2009f: 68). And from the champion himself: 'I feel like I've got the game, the mental approach and experience to win at Wimbledon many more times' (as cited in Chadband, 2009c: S10).

The 2009 Ashes cricket series

Of former England cricket captain Michael Vaughan, it was written: 'He took on the leadership of his team and made it believe it was destined to win' (O Captain, our Captain, 2009: 2); then Vaughan himself: 'The team who win the Ashes this summer will be the one that capitalises on pressure situations and nails them' (Vaughan, 2009: S10); of Australian opening batsman Simon Katich: '... ready to assert himself with renewed self-belief' (Atherton, 2009b: 10); of England matchwinner Andrew Flintoff: 'His courage in adversity should set an inspiring example to the whole England team' (Briggs, 2009f: S3). Again of Flintoff, former Australian opening batsman Justin Langer, with whom he enjoyed many contests, stated admiringly: 'The main thing for me, though, is his spirit. He can lift an entire team with his character and attitude as well as his talent, just like Shane Warne did for us' (as cited in Johnson, 2009: 16). Other examples included: '... a bloody minded refusal to get out or give up' (Roebuck, 2009a: 59); 'bloody-minded' and 'unyielding Aussie attrition' (Lawton, 2009b: 60); 'implacable will' and 'resilient character' (Briggs, 2009d: S4); '... deeply committed Australia team' (Atherton, 2009e: 3); 'character and skill' and '... a mind coldly determined to fulfil every last drop of talent he possessed' (Barnes, 2009i: 92); 'It is now about bottle as much as talent' (Garside, 2009e: S11); 'Self-belief and confidence are keys to quickly turning around poor results' (Lawson, 2009: S14); 'They could appreciate what bloody-minded commitment was needed to stay with the Australians' (S. Hughes, 2009b: S8); 'Yet in the death throes of an already lost Test, there was enough chutzpah, bloody-mindedness and defiance in pursuit of a forlorn cause' (Chadband, 2009j: S4); '... this was a failure of nerve and character ... questionable mental fortitude' (Pringle, 2009c: S2).

What emerges is a constellation of desirable personality attributes, each a reflection of mental toughness. The key characteristics identified from these quotes are summarised in Table 1.1.

Clearly, these encounters provided fertile ground for journalists' and performers' comments. Writing after the Australian cricket team's dramatic second Test victory against England in Adelaide, one newspaper journalist stated: 'They turned an apparently lost cause into a triumph' (Roebuck, 2006: 57). Of one performer's individual impact on the match, the same correspondent, the late Peter Roebuck, added:

> Shane Warne's contribution counts among the mightiest of his career. Pounded by the batsmen and berated by the critics after a lacklustre showing in the first innings, he produced a stirring performance ... But it is not only about skill. Greatness is a state of mind ... A lesser man might have wilted. Not Warne. Instead, he wanted to make amends and convinced himself it could be done.
>
> (ibid.: 57)

Table 1.1 Characteristics identified anecdotally from the print media as contributory to sporting achievement

2003 Rugby World Cup	2005 Ashes cricket series	2007 Rugby World Cup	2008–09 soccer season	2009 British and Irish Lions	2009 Wimbledon	2009 Ashes cricket series
Colossal mental shift	Exposure of character	Backbone to win under pressure	Mental fortitude	Spirit	Handle things thrown at you	Belief
Serious shift of attitude	Unbreakable spirit	Proud	Power and resolve	Character	Concentration	Capitalise on pressure situations
Resolute	Character	Look like World Champions	Control what you can	Don't dwell on mistakes	Force of will	Self-belief
Understand winning	Inner self-belief	Courage	Reserves of character	Guts	Self-certainty	Courage in adversity
Clear purpose	Mentally strong	Coolness	Spirit	Grit	Look like a champion	Character
Vigorous self-belief	Belligerent	Bloody-mindedness	Hunger and desire	Togetherness	Competitiveness	Attitude
Absolute determination	Touch of arrogance	Inner strength	Resilience	Sense of oneself	Desire	Bloody minded
Courage	Self-confidence	Fortitude	Guts	Self-belief	Concentrating on the fight	Unyielding attrition
Professional	Self-belief	Togetherness	Character	Pick oneself up	Happy to get down and dirty	Implacable will
Do what you have to	Backing oneself to succeed	Duty	Determination	No distractions	Respond to adversity	Resilient character
Deliver under pressure	Fighting back	Commitment	Desire	Efficient	Growing in crisis	Deeply committed
Deliver when it counts	from adversity	Hard work	Leadership	Nerve	Character	Determined mind
		Desire to prove people wrong	Spine	Unquenchable spirit	Make it hard for opponent to win	Bottle
		What you do when it matters most	Confidence		Keep going	Confidence
		Honesty	Mental		Mental approach	Bloody-minded commitment
						Nerve
						Mental fortitude

The manner of Australia's victory was profound. I stayed up through the early hours of the morning at home in England to watch the final day's play. I just had a feeling that the game was not going to end in a draw, as most pundits were predicting. The circumstances on the morning of the fifth day were intriguingly poised: one side was playing for the draw (England); the other (Australia) could win. As it transpired, the latter prevailed. Why? Mindset. On that day, in that particular situation, England did not have it. Australia turned up to the ground with the right mindset. I attributed the manner of the triumph to: 'You have a plan, stick to it (self-belief), execute it (determination), and impose your will on the opposition to secure your desired outcome (unyielding attitude). Two words – mental toughness' (Sheard, 2006: 18).

Such desirable psychological attributes have been offered as explicative reasons for high profile sporting triumphs and failures. Interestingly, growing public awareness and acknowledgement of the potential influence of psychological factors on sport performance have prompted sufficiently motivated readers to write to newspapers' editors. Reasons for success include: '. . . a determination to imbue his team-mates to believe in their ability to win' (Barlow, 2006: S17); and 'Toughness of the mental, not physical kind gave Australia a scare and England hope. The ability of the Aussies in the first half was sensational. But in the second England played without inhibition or respect for reputation' (Sheard, 2009c: 10). Among those suggested for failure: 'They [England] do not have the mental capabilities to win consistently around the world in all conditions . . . get a lesson on mental toughness' (M. Ryan, 2005: S10); and 'At the highest level, victory and defeat are often attributed to an athlete's mental toughness . . . Rusedski exploded and Andy Roddick capitalised' (Sheard, 2003: 25). Evidently, people are thinking increasingly about sporting success and failure in terms of the possession or absence of mental toughness as a contributory factor.

Winning and losing

So it would appear, anecdotally at this stage, that there exists an awareness of the psychological attributes considered contributory to sporting success. But does such success equate only with winning? Rudyard Kipling may have exhorted individuals to meet with the twin impostors of triumph and disaster just the same. Yet, it is probably unrealistic to expect athletes to deal with winning and losing in an equivalent manner. As mentioned in the opening of this chapter, a sporting event is a struggle for supremacy in which every athlete and coach seeks to emerge victorious. Thus, it would be naïve to assert that winning is not an important part of sport. Indeed, as was

put to me by a professional rugby league footballer: 'Why keep a scoreboard if the score does not matter?' (Alker, personal communication,
November 28, 2007). In a similar vein, Gerald Davies wrote: 'Competition
is a selfish taskmaster and winning is the exclusive and unshareable gift'
(G. Davies, 2003: 36). While it is abundantly clear that victory over London
Irish in rugby union's Premiership final is all that mattered to Leicester's
fly-half Sam Vesty: 'No-one remembers how you became champions in
2009. All that matters is we are champions' (as cited in Lowe, 2009: 11).
Andy Murray's answer to being asked what aspects of tennis he enjoys was
pointedly straightforward: 'Winning' (as cited in Harrell, 2010: 42). For
professional sportspeople, the scoreboard is their judge and jury. It is what
it is. Results will always be the final arbiter.

However, while it is agreed that winning is an inherent part of competition, and therefore an important aim, it has been argued that it is not the
only, or most important, objective (Martens, 2004; R. E. Smith & Smoll,
2002; J. Thompson, 2003). Rather, winning should be viewed as a consequence of performers' physical and psychological development and not as
the primary focus of athletic involvement (S. P. Cumming, Smoll, Smith, &
Grossbard, 2007). This is particularly emphasised in relation to youth sport.
Herein lies the separation of philosophies. It is likely that the importance of
winning and losing increases with age and/or the level of competition. A
developmental model of sport, with an emphasis on giving maximum effort,
working to develop one's skills, and enjoying the social and competitive
aspects of the sport experience, rather than the only objective being to beat
one's opponent, is advocated for youth sport (S. P. Cumming *et al.*, 2007;
Martens, 2004; Smoll & Smith, 2005). This environment should increase
the likelihood of athletes realising their potential for personal growth.

Moreover, the prevalence of fear of failure in achievement settings, and
its negative effects on psychological and physical well-being, represents an
important social concern (Conroy, 2001; Sagar, 2009; Sagar & Stoeber,
2009; Wankel & Mummery, 1990). Particularly alarming is the finding
from a cricket-sponsored study that more than a quarter of 1,000 polled
children aged 8 to 16 years admitted to emulating the cheating behaviours
demonstrated by their favourite players in order to win in competition
(Bingham, 2009). Overemphasising competition in the early phases of
training will always cause shortcomings in athletic abilities later in
performers' careers (Balyi & Hamilton, 2003). It will also remove all the
joy, and make youngsters less likely to think of sport as enjoyable. Sport
represents one of the most significant achievement domains for children,
and the emphasis ought to be on reducing fear of failure in young athletes
and helping them with both performance-related factors and their social
development (Conroy & Coatsworth, 2006; Côté & Fraser-Thomas, 2007;

Fraser-Thomas, Côté, & Deakin, 2005; Saferstein, 2005, 2006; Sedor, 2008).

However, the higher the competitive level, there must be a concomitant rise in an additional attribute. For performers to be successful in the win- and profit-oriented environment that characterises professional sport, they must develop and nurture a 'killer instinct' or 'winning mentality'. Posses- sion of this mentality is particularly crucial when 'even when less than his best, the champion is better than his opponent at winning' (Barnes, 2008e: 71) or when, as the previously mentioned Sam Vesty put it: 'An ugly win keeps us on our toes' (as cited in Cleary, 2009c: S16). Coaches are also aware of the importance of a 'winning mentality' (M. Hughes, 2012a; Hytner, 2009c). To be the best, you must think you are the best. To win, you have to believe you will win. I hasten to stress that this winning mentality is in conjunction with, and does not replace, the developmental model attributes mentioned previously. The late George Steinbrenner, former owner of the New York Yankees baseball franchise, famously said: 'Winning is the most important thing in my life, after breathing. Breathing first, winning next' (as cited in George Steinbrenner, 2010: 55). Forget such hyperbole: winning isn't everything. It is neither the only thing. And it never should be. But its proportionate emphasis increases with the level of competition.

Particularly noteworthy is the observation of the great Australian rugby union star Mark Ella, who recognised that the uplifting effect of winning is not only associated with a final score: 'It is always great to come off the field as victors, but knowing you and your team-mates absolutely and without any doubt won every facet of the battle as well as on the scoreboard is the sweetest moment in a sportsman's career' (Ella, 2009a). Indeed, winning has been found to result in 'a range of pleasant emotional outcomes and reductions in arousal and stress' (G. V. Wilson & Kerr, 1999: 85). On the other hand, the same study reported that losing produces unpleasant emotional reactions and reduced arousal. Another study found that athletes have reported significantly higher levels of anxiety, humiliation, and sullen- ness following losses compared with after victories (Kerr, Wilson, Bowling, & Sheahan, 2005). Winning feels good. As England cricket captain Andrew Strauss put it: 'Winning lifts the spirit of the team. It gives everyone confi- dence' (as cited in Weaver, 2009: 1). Victory serves to refresh the conquerors' endeavours and, many would say, justifies the means. Losing is painful. Defeated athletes often suffer an according collapse of will. However, an erroneous display of mental toughness is to project oneself as a bad loser. A bad loser is not the same as a mentally tough athlete. Mental toughness is being gracious and magnanimous in defeat, and retiring respectfully to the sidelines to give the victors their deserved limelight.

Although beaten, the mentally tough athlete may, for example, hold on to the 'proud memory of courage and unyielding commitment shown in the face of overwhelming force' (A. O'Connor, 2003: 39). A mentally tough losing athlete does not get expelled from the field of play, does not look like death has visited him, and certainly makes no excuses for defeat. A captain does not have an emotional breakdown. Such an athlete possesses the courage to endure the misery of defeat. Similarly, the victorious athlete is decorous and honourable so as not to bask in the despair of a downed opponent. Sir Alex Ferguson ordered his players to tone down their celebrations after defeating Arsenal FC in a European Champions League semi-final out of respect to the hosts (Stone, 2009). The way athletes react to winning is every bit as important as how they respond to losing (see Clayton, 2009). The victory should be enjoyed, but there ought to be no place for triumphalism in the heart of the mentally tough performer, for whom there is no laziness or easing off. Quite rightly, take delight in finding yourself a winner, but remember: the mentally tough athlete stays honest.

Ever-higher levels of excellence are not achieved with self-congratulation. Greatness has never recognised coasting. The pursuit of the next horizon is a characteristic of the mentally tough performer. As the most successful soccer manager in the history of the British game, the aforementioned Sir Alex Ferguson, said after a victory which put his Manchester United FC team ahead in the league championship and on course for their record-equalling 18th title: 'It's time to kick on' (as cited in Syed, 2009b: 71). Unerring focus. Manchester United, led by Ferguson, subsequently broke the record in 2011. This is the mentality of a serial winner. His players take responsibility, find strength at times of adversity, and, when challengers wilt, reveal the mental toughness that wins titles.

The philosopher A. C. Grayling sums it up perfectly: 'It is what we aspire to be that colours our characters – and it is our trying, not just our succeeding, which ennobles them' (Grayling, 2001: 25). For the athlete, there are lessons to be learnt from suffering defeat. Very often, the best ones are also the hardest; and defeat counts among these. As New Zealand All Black Dan Carter put it:

> You learn a lot more from your disappointments and defeats. When you get setbacks it builds up a lot of motivation and gives you more drive to succeed. Before we [New Zealand] lost in the 2007 World Cup [to France] I'd already been the IRB Player of the Year and won numerous Tri-Nations and Super 14s. So it had been pretty smooth sailing for me until that point. But it's how you bounce back from disappointment that gives a true reflection of your character.
>
> (as cited in McRae, 2009h: 10)

Correspondingly, Paul Collingwood reflected: 'Failure builds resistance . . . I've had my struggles but I now feel more confident and mentally strong' (as cited in S. Hughes, 2010b: S23). When mentally tough athletes lose, they toughen up, they learn their lessons, and move on all the wiser. They enjoy better performances that often emerge from the biggest defeats.

Defeat comes to the best, and it comes to the rest. It is part of the texture of sport. It is as Uncle Henry Skinner instructs the young Maximilian in the motion picture *A Good Year*: 'You'll come to see that a man learns nothing from winning. The act of losing, however, can elicit great wisdom. Not least of which is, uh . . . how much more enjoyable it is to win. It's inevitable to lose now and again. The trick is not to make a habit of it' (Lustig, Payne, Ellzey, & Scott, 2007). The mark of top athletes is how they react to and bounce back from defeat. Being a bad loser is just that – a bad loser. As Franz Beckenbauer, Germany's most revered footballer, said: 'Defeat belongs to life like victory' (as cited in Cameron, 1995: 112). Although remembered as a winner, Beckenbauer suffered losses during his playing and managing career. Indeed, he remains the only man to have played for (1966) and coached (1986) World Cup losing finalists. Disappointments are as common as triumphs, arguably, more so. Yet his comment reflects an inclination to the philosophical outlook of the mentally tough performer, accepting that 'defeat is part of the routine of a sportsman's life; it happens to them all, and it is the way players deal with defeat that separates the champions from the rest' (Barnes, 2009e: 4). Similarly, having won the final race of the season but, ultimately, missing out on the 2008 Formula One drivers' championship by a single point, Felipe Massa was gracious in defeat: 'I know how to win and I know how to lose. It is one more day of my life and we are going to learn a lot from this' (as cited in Gorman, 2008b: 76). The gratitude, humility, and sportsmanship demonstrated by American golfer Kenny Perry having just lost the 2009 US Masters play-off had the attending media spellbound by such benevolence we too seldom witness (Reason, 2009b); the Corinthian spirit in which sport should be played, yet rarely is. Sportsmanship commands respect (Chadband, 2009d; Epic of sportsmanship, 2009), and, appropriately, belongs with mental toughness.

Despite possessing an unyielding winning mentality, Ben Ainslie still acknowledges that: 'It is about being able to lose gracefully as well' (as cited in Winter, 2009g: S23). Following a series of media-perceived lacklustre performances, it was written of 2009 Formula One champion Jenson Button that: 'He possesses a remarkably balanced and controlled temperament that enables him to surf over great waves of disappointment without getting wet' (Gorman, 2009b: 77). While of his semi-final defeat to Andy Roddick at Wimbledon 2009, Andy Murray magnanimously reflected:

'It's a pathetic attitude to have if you lose one match and you go away and let it ruin your year' (as cited in Hart, 2009a: S1), and 'Sometimes you have to say, "That was too good and the other guy played better" ' (as cited in A. Baker, 2009: S7). To see this requires the courage that, along with the other personality attributes identified in this chapter, is constitutive of mental toughness.

A final word on winning and losing: the mentally tough performer is not dedicated to the philosophy of winning at all costs. Taken to its extreme, such a philosophy inevitably will entertain, perhaps even condone, acts of cheating. This is particularly concerning as financial stakes increase. The more money matters in sport, the more sport becomes a business. Top athletes and sport organisations do better financially when they perform well in the sports arena. But alongside the extra cash, comes a huge amount of pressure on coaches and performers to achieve and, on occasion, there has been coercion to cross the line into dishonesty. Cheating, in any guise (for a variety of methods, see Note 6) does not belong with mental toughness. Results are not the only currency in which sport trades. Winning at all costs is not winning at all. Mentally tough performers compete, and strive to win, with integrity. They are honourable. Anything worth having is not worth cheating for. No pride should be taken in a victory achieved in the absence of integrity. As Simon Barnes of *The Times* quite rightly observed at the time of a particularly nasty Test cricket series between Australia and India that dripped with mutual enmity: 'The way you win matters just as much' (Barnes, 2008d: 66). Sport is about a great deal more than winning.

A championship mindset

Finally in this chapter, I wish to begin the process of conceptualising mental toughness (Chapter 2 takes this much further). Several years ago I received a letter from Professor Allan Snyder of the Centre for the Mind at the University of Sydney. He was intrigued by a report he had read in the *New Scientist* (E. Young, 2001). In it, I stated that psychological superiority alone could explain why Australia had won six consecutive Rugby League World Cup tournaments between 1975 and 2000. Since previous research into rugby league football has not identified significant differences in physical and tactical preparation (Brewer & Davis, 1995), I argued it seems that, regardless of physical attributes, the tougher athlete often prevails, and the difference between success and failure is often more easily, and perhaps more appropriately, attributable to psychological factors. This struck a chord. In accordance with my own view, Snyder had stated in a publication at the time: 'Two athletes may enter a race with similar bodies, even similar training, but their mindset will be different' (A. W. Snyder, 1999: 71). He added: 'It is our mindset that ultimately limits our expectations of ourselves and which circumscribes our boundaries. It is our mindset which determines whether or not we have the courage to challenge others and to expand our horizons' (ibid.: 73). My view is that mental toughness should be conceptualised as a personality style and mindset, shaped by experiences, culture, society, training, and, quite possibly, genetics. Snyder believes that it is, and that 'the world is viewed in its totality through this mindset' (ibid.: 73). Moreover, he advocates that such a mindset 'is the transferable commodity, not the skill itself' (ibid.: 73).

Psychologist Carol Dweck has suggested that the mindset distinguishes great athletes (i.e., the champions) from others. Without denying the importance of an individual's talent, we ought to look more closely at the commitment, discipline, and perseverance that go into success. Of Jackie Joyner-Kersee, Mia Hamm, and Muhammad Ali, Dweck (2006) observed that, yes, they had talent; but they also had the right mindset. Perhaps one of the best definitions of mental toughness comes from the late Vince Lombardi, Green Bay Packers football coach and NFL Hall of Famer. In the early 1960s, Lombardi transformed the Packers from perennial losers to winners. He was known as a person who demanded excellence and never accepted mediocrity. He said: 'Mental toughness is many things and rather difficult to explain. Its qualities are sacrifice and self-denial. Also, most importantly, it is combined with a perfectly disciplined will that refuses to give in. It's a state of mind – you could call it character in action' (as cited in Curtis Management Group, 1998: 20). I agree with Lombardi, Dweck, and Snyder. A world of opportunities exists. The saddest words in the English language are 'could have . . . might have . . . should have . . . would have . . . didn't.' Mental toughness affords great minds to think big. If you believe you can do it, you probably can.

Conclusion

This introductory chapter has discussed the characteristics purportedly constitutive of mental toughness as reported by the popular media. Further, consideration was given to the moderating role of mental toughness in guiding athletes to consider appropriate reactions to win–lose outcomes. As a conclusion to this introduction to mental toughness, I would like to give the last words to two sporting greats. Swimming legend Michael Phelps (dual record holder of most gold medals, and most won at a single Olympic Games) stated of the 'mental' contribution to his success: 'Our mental outlook is one of the few things that we can truly control. Training we must view as a privilege, and act accordingly. We must first look inward to find solutions to challenges. The solution lies with us' (as cited in Lord,

2007: 70). Seven-times winner of the Tour de France, Lance Armstrong epitomises mental toughness. After suffering from cancer, most competitors would be thankful that they were alive. Instead, Armstrong, who had been told by doctors that he would not ride again (physicians gave him less than a 40 per cent chance of survival), got on his bike and returned to competitive cycling to accomplish the seemingly impossible: winning what is considered to be the most physically and mentally demanding event in all of sport. Interviewed after his fifth Tour triumph, he reflected: 'When you feel like giving up, you have to ask yourself which you would rather live with. What the Tour de France teaches you is that pain is temporary, quitting is forever' (as cited in Philip, 2004a: S5). These defining qualities truly reflect a mentally tough and championship mindset.

2 Characterising mental toughness

The reward of a thing well done is to have done it.

Ralph Waldo Emerson

Introduction

Mental toughness has often been associated with peak sport performance, particularly in popular sporting discourse (see Chapter 1) as a synonym for determination or resilience (Moran, 2004). As mentioned also in the previous chapter, top sportspeople have frequently cited mental toughness as the crucial prerequisite of sporting success (e.g., D. Gould *et al.*, 1987, 2002). Moreover, research findings have emphasised the importance of mental toughness in developing champion sport performers (e.g., Durand-Bush & Salmela, 2002; Norris, 1999).

The term has also been used as a euphemism for sport psychology in re-labelling efforts to sell the benefits of the latter to English soccer players and their coaches (Pain & Harwood, 2004). Virtually any positive and desirable psychological characteristic associated with success has been, at some time, labelled as mental toughness. However, perhaps due to its seemingly amorphous structure, the term 'mental toughness' is seldom found in academic psychology. Indeed, it is a new topic requiring exploration relative to the psychology of sporting excellence (D. Gould, 2002). Though the term is intuitively appealing and used equally generously by players, coaches and the sport media, an adequate definition has been elusive (Cashmore, 2002; Clough, Earle, & Sewell, 2002). Several definitions have been proffered to address this lack of conceptual clarity, including an ability to cope with stress and pressure (e.g., Goldberg, 1998), to rebound from failures (e.g., Woods, Hocton, & Desmond, 1995), and to show resilience (e.g., Tutko & Richards, 1976). However, research on stress, resilience, and vulnerability in sport has been characterised by definitional circularity. Mental toughness, in particular, has suffered from a general lack of conceptual clarity. Indeed, the construct has been criticised as being 'rather nebulous' (Moran, 2004: 10). Therefore, a theoretical model of the construct of mental toughness would provide terminological refinement on the vulnerability–resilience continuum and address this criticism.

While athletes and coaches often talk about mental toughness, seldom has it been precisely defined. This is in spite of the literature including numerous contributions dedicated to the notion of developing mentally tough sport performers. In this chapter, the attempts of the extant literature to gain a consensual definition of mental toughness, and its constitutive characteristics, are presented.

In search of mental toughness

Fons et origo

As part of his pioneering sport psychology work, Coleman Griffith (1926, 1928) examined the personality profiles of successful athletes. Through observations of, and interviews with, university and professional athletes, Griffith identified 11 characteristics attributable to their success (see Table 2.1). Many sport performers since have completed many more personality inventories. Interestingly, Griffith's inter-war characteristics and those elicited from the first sport-specific personality inventory, Tutko and co-workers' Athletic Motivation Inventory (AMI; Tutko, Lyon, & Ogilvie, 1969), more than 40 years later, reveal a striking commonality (Table 2.1). Particularly noteworthy is the AMI's ninth characteristic – mental toughness.

Table 2.1 Personality characteristics associated with superior athletes

Griffith (1926)	*Tutko* et al. *(1969)*
Ruggedness	Drive
Courage	Determination
Intelligence	Leadership
Exuberance	Aggressiveness
Buoyance	Guilt proneness
Emotional adjustment	Emotional control
Optimism	Self-confidence
Conscientiousness	Conscientiousness
Alertness	Mental toughness
Loyalty	Trust
Respect for authority	Coachability

The quest for a definition

Mental toughness is a bit like 'talent' or 'charisma': instinctively recognis-able, but endlessly tricky to pin down in a definition. The earliest attempts to define mental toughness proposed that it was a personality trait (Cattell, Blewett, & Beloff, 1955; Kroll, 1967; Werner & Gottheil, 1966). Consid-ered as 'tough-mindedness', and manifested in realistic, self-reliant, and cynical behaviour, this trait was one of 16 that described personality (Cattell, 1957). Interestingly, mental toughness has also been viewed as a state of mind (A. Gibson, 1998). Subsequent contributions have attempted to elucidate the term; however, the literature has struggled to arrive at a definitional consensus. (For examples of the varied definitions provided by research, see Note 7.)

Characteristics of mentally tough performers

Similarly, the proposed characteristics of mentally tough performers in the extant literature have been wide ranging, with varying examples given in Note 8.

Interestingly, American coach and educationalist Harvey Dorfman prefers to use the term *mental discipline* rather than *mental toughness*. Whatever the preferred term, he refers to the aspects of mental toughness as disciplines of one's mind; namely: courage, intensity, competitiveness, consistency of focus, a confrontational attitude, aggressiveness under control, relentlessness, responsibility to do what the situation requires, responsibility for one's own behaviour, honesty, self-sacrifice, self-trust, an ability to make necessary adjustments, an ability to compete with pain, a positive approach to task and circumstance, an ability to cope effectively with adversity, an indifference to an opponent's presence or posturing, and an ability to do always what needs to be done (Dorfman, 2003). Somewhat modestly, he admits that these aspects may not be all-inclusive of mental toughness. However, I would suggest that they go some way to characterising a particular state of mind; that is, a mentally tough mindset. Conceptual refinement of the aspects may be required; however, as Dorfman (ibid.: 167) states: 'An athlete who checks off all of the above as being representative of his own makeup qualifies as a mentally tough individual.'

Qualitative developments

Given the aforementioned diverse range of characteristics, it is perhaps unsurprising that efforts to provide a narrow definition have, arguably, contributed to mental toughness being one of the least understood terms in sport psychology. Rather than criticising the construct for its historical propensity to be defined in diverse ways, research should be directed towards categorising those characteristics required to be a mentally tough performer. Despite the apparent breadth of opinion, there appears to be broad agreement on the requisite attributes of mentally tough performers. However, qualitative research on the issue of mental toughness has still concerned itself with defining the construct and determining the essential attributes required to be a mentally tough performer.

For example, Sansonette Fourie and Justus Potgieter investigated the components of mental toughness as reported in written statements by 131 expert coaches and 160 elite-level sport performers recruited from 31 different sports (Fourie & Potgieter, 2001). Data responses from the coaches ($n = 534$) and from the athletes ($n = 488$) were content analyzed through a consensual procedure. Inductive content analysis resulted in 41 higher-order themes that were summarised into 12 mental toughness umbrella categories; namely: motivational level, coping skills, confidence mainte-nance, cognitive skill, discipline and goal-directedness, competitiveness, possession of prerequisite physical and mental requirements, team unity, preparation skills, psychological hardiness, religious convictions, and ethics.

In another qualitative investigation of mental toughness, Graham Jones and co-workers asked 10 international sportspeople to (a) define mental toughness, and (b) identify and describe their perception of the attributes of the ideal mentally tough performer (G. Jones, Hanton, & Connaughton, 2002). Subsequently, the interviewees were asked to place these attributes in rank order of importance. Twelve attributes were identified from the first question (see Table 2.2).

The athletes defined the construct of mental toughness as the cognitive and behavioural efforts of a performer to have superior self-regulatory skills (G. Jones *et al.*, 2002). Their perception of the mentally tough performer was someone who is able, generally, to cope better than opponents with the many competition, training, and lifestyle demands that sport places on him/her. Of equal interest, was the assessment of how a performer, specifically, is more consistent and better than opponents in remaining determined, focused, confident, and in control under pressure. Using similar investiga-tive techniques to their 2002 study, the same authors verified their earlier definition of mental toughness in a follow-up study (G. Jones, Hanton, & Connaughton, 2007). 'Super-elite' sport performers (i.e., Olympic or World champions), coaches, and sport psychologists categorised 30 attributes under 13 sub-components that were essential to being mentally tough. These attributes (see Table 2.3) were clustered under four separate

Table 2.2 Mental toughness attributes and importance ranking

Overall rank	Attribute
1	Having an unshakable self-belief in your ability to achieve your competition goals
2	Bouncing back from performance setbacks as a result of increased determination to succeed
3	Having an unshakable self-belief that you possess unique qualities and abilities that make you better than your opponents
=4	Having an insatiable desire and internalised motives to succeed
=4	Remaining fully focused on the task at hand in the face of competition-specific distractions
6	Regaining psychological control following unexpected, uncontrollable events (competition-specific)
7	Pushing back the boundaries of physical and emotional pain, while still maintaining technique and effort under distress (in training and competition)
8	Accepting that competition anxiety is inevitable and knowing that you can cope with it.
=9	Thriving on the pressure of competition
=9	Not being adversely affected by others' good and bad performances
11	Remaining fully focused in the face of personal life distractions
12	Switching a sport focus on and off as required

Source: Adapted from G. Jones *et al.* (2002).

dimensions (namely: attitude/mindset, training, competition, and post-competition) within an overall framework of mental toughness.

The attitude/mindset dimension was divided into two sub-components (belief and focus), which enabled mentally tough performers to remain on course in achieving their ultimate goal, irrespective of obstacles and circumstances. The training dimension reflected how mentally tough performers were able to keep motivation levels high, and used every aspect of the training environment and challenging situation to their advantage when dealing with years of patience, discipline, and work required to reach the highest standards. The third dimension, competition, explained how the ideal mentally tough performer behaved under the extreme pressure of high-level competitions. Post-competition, the final dimension, contained two sub-components that described the rationalisation of competition failures and successes (G. Jones *et al.*, 2007).

Focusing on professional soccer, Richard Thelwell and co-workers (Thelwell, Weston, & Greenlees, 2005) aimed to confirm the findings of the G. Jones *et al.* (2002) study. The main aim of their study was to examine further the definition and attributes of mental toughness within a specific

Table 2.3 G. Jones and co-workers' (2007) mental toughness framework

Dimension	Sub-category	Rank and description	
Attitude/ mindset	Belief	1	Having an unshakable self-belief as a result of total awareness of how you got to where you are now
		2	Having an inner arrogance that makes you believe that you can achieve anything you set your mind to
		3	Having the belief that you can punch through any obstacle people put in your way
		4	Believing that your desire or hunger will ultimately result in your fulfilling of your potential
	Focus	5	Refusing to be swayed by short-term gains (financial, performance) that will jeopardise the achievement of long-term goals
		6	Ensuring that achievement of your sport's goal is the number-one priority in your life
		7	Recognising the importance of knowing when to switch on and off from your sport
Training	Using long-term goals as the source of motivation	1	When training gets tough (physically and mentally) because things are not going your way, keeping yourself going by reminding yourself of your goals and aspirations and why you're putting yourself through it
		2	Having the patience, discipline, and self-control with the required training for each specific developmental stage to allow you to reach your full potential
	Controlling the environment	3	Remaining in control and not controlled
		=4	Using all aspects of a very difficult training environment to your advantage
	Pushing yourself to the limit	=4	Loving the bits of training that hurt
		6	Thriving on opportunities to beat other people in training
Competition	Handling pressure	1	Loving the pressure of competition
		3	Adapting to and coping with any change/distraction/threat under pressure
		5	Making the correct decisions and choosing the right options that secure optimal performance under conditions of extreme pressure and ambiguity
		8	Coping with and channelling anxiety in pressure situations
	Belief	2	Total commitment to your performance goal until every possible opportunity of success has passed

(Continued overleaf)

Table 2.3 Continued

Dimension	Sub-category	Rank	and description
		4	Not being fazed by making mistakes and then coming back from them
	Regulating performance	6	Having a killer instinct to capitalise on the moment when you know you can win
		7	Raising your performance 'up a gear' when it matters most
	Staying focused	9	Totally focusing on the job at hand in the face of distraction
		11	Remaining committed to a self-absorbed focus despite external distractions
		=12	In certain performances, remaining focused on processes and not solely outcomes
	Awareness and control of thoughts and feelings	10	Being acutely aware of any inappropriate thoughts and feelings and changing them to help perform optimally
	Controlling the environment	=12	Using all aspects of a very difficult competition environment to your advantage
Post-competition	Handling failure	1	Recognising and rationalising failure and picking out the learning points to take forward
		2	Using failure to drive yourself to further success
	Handling success	3	Knowing when to celebrate success and then stop and focus on the next challenge
		4	Knowing how to rationally handle success

Source: Adapted from G. Jones *et al.* (2007).

soccer population. The authors' approach was to counter the effect of inter-sport variations, which they suggested had arisen from research attempts to identify mental toughness characteristics from a general, rather than specific, sport perspective. These authors reported two studies, with interviews from the first suggesting a general consensus with the G. Jones *et al.* definition. The sole variation was the finding that mentally tough soccer players should always (as opposed to 'generally') cope better than their opponents with the demands of the sport. There were also slight variances with regard to the attributes deemed essential for mental toughness, which may be attributable to the specificity of the sport.

Despite ten qualities being identified, not all participants mentioned each of them. Key mental toughness characteristics were perceived as more important than others. Specifically, all six participants mentioned that having the total self-belief at all times that one will achieve, having the ability to react to situations positively, to hang on and be calm under pressure, and to ignore distractions and remain focused, were critical to the mentally tough performer. Five participants identified that wanting the ball at all times (when playing well and not so well), knowing what it takes to grind oneself out of trouble, and controlling emotions through performance, were vital qualities. Four participants commented on the importance of having a presence that affects opponents, and having everything in control outside of the game, while three commented on the need to enjoy the pressure associated with performance (Thelwell *et al.*, 2005).

Dealing with pressure and coping with stress appear to be important constituents of mental toughness. A key characteristic of the mentally tough athlete has been suggested as the ability to deal with pressure and maintain confidence, determination, game sense, leadership, regulation of performance state, and regulation of attentional focus (Holland, Woodcock, Cumming, & Duda, 2010). Similarly, mental toughness has been defined as the ability to stay focused, composed, and confident in stressful situations (DeWiggins, Hite, & Alston, 2010).

Other researchers (S. C. Middleton, Marsh, Martin, Richards, & Perry, 2004a), however, asserted that the G. Jones *et al.* (2002) study was inadequate as it only described the outcomes of being mentally tough and did not define mental toughness itself. Employing a qualitative grounded theory approach following semi-structured interviews, Cory Middleton and colleagues defined mental toughness as 'an unshakeable perseverance and conviction towards some goal despite pressure or adversity' (S. C. Middleton *et al.*). These authors also identified 12 key mental toughness characteristics; namely: *self-efficacy* in one's ability to achieve in a chosen sport, belief in one's own *potential* and capacity for growth and development, a strong and positive *mental self-concept* with regards to dealing with adversity, *task familiarity* and understanding adversity, *task value* in the quality and success of performance, intrinsic motivation to achieve *personal bests*, intellectual and emotional *goal commitment*, *perseverance* in the face of adversity, *task-specific attention* while being able to block out distracting or negative thoughts, *positivity* when faced with adversity, *stress minimisation* when under pressure or adversity, and *positive comparisons* with one's opponents in coping better with adversity.

Importantly, S. C. Middleton *et al.* (2004a) used existing theory that had parallels with the emergent mental toughness characteristics (i.e., self-concept theory, attentional styles, self-determination theory) in order to develop a preliminary conceptual model. This model was both multidimensional and hierarchical, attempting to capture the complexity of mental toughness with greater specificity, and separating mental toughness into orientation and strategy. The authors argued that their definition and model illustrate not only what mental toughness is, but also describe the actions of mental toughness (e.g., perseverance, task focus, emotion management), coupled with the personality characteristics that orientate people to be mentally tough (e.g., self-belief, motivation, commitment).

Similar actions and personality characteristics emerged from two qualitative single-sport investigations of mental toughness. Interviews with elite English cricketers yielded five mental toughness general dimensions; namely: developmental factors, personal responsibility, dedication and commitment, belief, and coping with pressure (S. J. Bull, Shambrook, James, & Brooks, 2005). Of particular interest, analysis of the focused interview transcripts identified the critical role of the players' environments in influencing tough character, tough attitudes, and tough thinking, and how these manifest in players' actions. A study of experienced Australian Rules football coaches identified and ranked 11 characteristics in the following descending order of importance: self-belief (that is, belief in mental and physical ability), work ethic (pushing one's physical and mental boundaries to their limits), personal values (valuing becoming a better person and footballer through one's experiences), self-motivated (desire success and competitive challenges to showcase one's abilities), tough attitude (discipline, commitment, positivity, professionalism, and sacrifices towards becoming the best that one can be), concentration and focus (ability to focus on goals and objectives when confronted with distractions), resilience (ability to overcome adversities, challenges, and pressures), handling pressure (ability to execute skills and procedures effectively under pressure), emotional intelligence (an awareness and understanding of one's emotions and ability to manage emotions to perform successfully), sport intelligence (understand training and competitive environments and accept one's role within the team), and physical toughness (not easily affected by minor injuries or physical fatigue, and enjoy 50-50 situations that involve physical risk) (Gucciardi, Gordon, & Dimmock, 2008). The study's authors proposed that mental toughness is 'a quality that brings together several human features and allows a footballer to consistently get the best out of his physical ability' (ibid.: 278). Their findings also identified those situations that demand mental toughness and the behaviours commonly displayed by mentally tough Australian Rules footballers. Specific to Australian Rules football, Gucciardi *et al.* determined that mental toughness:

> is a collection of values, attitudes, behaviours, and emotions that enable you to persevere and overcome any obstacle, adversity, or pressure experienced, but also to maintain concentration and motivation when things are going well to consistently achieve your goals. (ibid.: 278)

The same authors (Gucciardi, Gordon, & Dimmock, 2009a) subsequently presented a conceptual process model of mental toughness that is grounded in the theoretical framework of personal construct psychology (Kelly, 1955/1991). Within this 'constructive alternativism' conceptual framework, Gucciardi *et al.* propose that the key components of mental toughness influence the way in which an individual overtly and covertly approaches, appraises, and responds to events demanding varying degrees of adversity, challenge, and pressure. Self-referenced and others' feedback is then used to evaluate the processes an individual has undergone in dealing with an event in relation to his or her personal goals. Gucciardi *et al.* (ibid.: 69) ultimately proffered the definition of mental toughness:

> [It] is a collection of experientially developed and inherent sport-general and sport-specific values, attitudes, cognitions, and emotions that influence the way in which an individual approaches, responds to, and appraises both negatively and positively construed pressures, challenges, and adversities to consistently achieve his or her goals.

In a further development, as a consequence of the data yielded from their qualitative study to identify concepts of mental toughness (e.g., characteristics, situations, behaviours, cognitions) in soccer, Coulter, Mallett, and Gucciardi (2010) slightly revised Gucciardi *et al.*'s (2009a) definition, suggesting that:

> mental toughness is the *presence of some or the entire* collection of experientially developed and inherent values, attitudes, emotions, cognitions, *and behaviours* that influence the way in which an individual approaches, responds to, and appraises both negatively and positively construed pressures, challenges, and adversities to consistently achieve his or her goals.
>
> (Coulter *et al.*, 2010: 715)

It is particularly noteworthy that Coulter *et al.* removed Gucciardi *et al.*'s emphasis of sport-specific components of mental toughness.

An emerging consensus

A summarised overview of the aforementioned qualitative studies is presented in Table 2.4. A consistent picture has appeared from the spate of qualitative studies and a consensus has emerged of what is constitutive of mental toughness. My criticism levelled at much of the qualitative research presented in this chapter is that it has contributed little to furthering our

Table 2.4 Summary of key published studies investigating mental toughness

Study	Method	Data obtained	Participants	Sports represented	N	Findings	Limitations
Fourie and Potgieter (2001)	Written statements	Qualitative	Expert coaches (mean age = 42.7 years; range = 22–85) who had an average of 14.3 years coaching experience. Elite-level sport performers (mean age = 21 years; range = 14–35) competing at international, national, provincial, or 1st-team university level.	31 sport codes (unspecified by authors).	131 coaches (93 males, 38 females). 160 sport performers (87 males, 73 females).	The identification of 12 components of mental toughness. Coaches and sport performers differed in their opinion as to the most important characteristics.	The coaches and sport performers were quite varied in their description of the characteristics of mental toughness. Fails to relate findings to extant mental toughness research literature, especially Loehr's work.
Clough et al. (2002)	Questionnaires	Qualitative/ quantitative	Sport performers (no further demographic data available).	A range of sports (unspecified by authors).	>600 (males and females).	The design and development of an instrument to measure mental toughness (MT48). [See Chapter 4 for more information on the subsequent MTQ48]	Much additional validation evidence is required before the MT48 can be accepted as a worthwhile tool for the measurement of mental toughness.

Study	Method	Design	Participants	Sports	Sample	Findings	Limitations
G. Jones et al. (2002)	Individual interviews and focus groups	Qualitative	International sport performers (mean age = 31.2 years; SD = 5.3) who had achieved full international honours and represented their country in major events (e.g., Olympic/Commonwealth Games) and had an average of five years' international experience.	Swimming, sprinting, artistic and rhythmic gymnastics, trampoline, middle-distance running, triathlon, golf, rugby union, and netball.	10 (7 males, 3 females).	A definition of mental toughness and 12 attributes of the ideal mentally tough performer emerged. The resulting definition emphasised both general and specific dimensions.	Range and number of sports sampled. Small sample size. Using only one focus group with three individuals.
Middleton et al. (2004a)	Individual interviews	Qualitative	Elite sport performers (mean age = 37.7 years; SD = 13.4; range = 25–70).	Track and field, swimming, boxing, hockey, rowing, archery, basketball, mountain running, mountain climbing, marathon, rugby union, rugby league, Australian Rules football, baseball, cricket, cycling, water polo, squash, netball, triathlon, power lifting, and physically disabled track and field.	33 (21 males, 12 females) of whom 25 were sport performers, and 8 were non-athletes.	The identification of 12 mental toughness characteristics.	Conclusion that mental toughness exists only in relation to overcoming adversity. The relative contribution of each of the 12 characteristics has not yet been established.

(Continued overleaf)

Table 2.4 Continued

Study	Method	Data obtained	Participants	Sports represented	N	Findings	Limitations
Thelwell et al. (2005)	Individual interviews	Qualitative	Professional soccer players (mean age = 28.8 years; SD = 4.8), all with international playing experience.	Soccer.	6 (all males).	A definition of mental toughness and 10 qualities were identified (though not all participants mentioned each of them).	Very small sample size. Only one sport represented. Focus group rather than individual interviews may have been more appropriate.
Bull et al. (2005)	Individual interviews	Qualitative	Professional cricketers (nominated by coaches for their 'mental toughness') who had represented England in international Test and one-day competition.	Cricket.	12 (all males).	The identification of 5 general dimensions within 4 structural categories.	Only one sport represented.

Study	Method	Design	Sample	Sport	Participants	Findings	Limitations
G. Jones et al. (2007)	Focus groups and individual interviews	Qualitative	Olympic or world champion sport performers (age range = 25–48 years) who had an average of six years' experience at this 'super-elite' level and who had won at least one gold medal at an Olympic Games or world championship. Coaches (age range = 38–60 years) and sport psychologists (age range = 35–45 years) who had coached or consulted with Olympic or world champions on a long-term basis.	Boxing, swimming, athletics, judo, triathlon, rowing, pentathlon, squash, cricket, and rugby union.	8 sport performers (5 males, 3 females). 3 coaches (all males). 4 sport psychologists (all males).	The identification of 30 attributes clustered under 4 separate dimensions.	Omission of coaches and sport psychologists in the focus group.
Gucciardi et al. (2008)	Individual interviews	Qualitative	Coaches (mean age 42 years; SD = 9.6), all with considerable elite-level playing and coaching experience.	Australian Rules football.	11 coaches (all males).	The identification of 11 key characteristics within 3 independent categories.	Use of self-report data. Reliance on elite-level volunteers only.

(Continued overleaf)

Table 2.4 Continued

Study	Method	Data obtained	Participants	Sports represented	N	Findings	Limitations
Coulter et al. (2010)	Individual interviews	Qualitative	Coaches (mean age 44 years; SD = 3.4), all with extensive coaching experience, players (mean age 29 years; SD = 3.8), and parents (mean age 59 years; SD = 3.3).	Soccer.	4 coaches (all males). 6 players (all males). 5 parents (3 mothers, 2 fathers).	The identification of situations demanding mental toughness characteristics, cognitions, and behaviours.	Use of self-report data and retrospective recall methodology. Single interviews. Limited generalisability.

understanding of mental toughness. As we shall see, it can be argued that a comparison of these recent qualitative findings with what was already known yields substantial similarities. It is also apparent that the G. Jones *et al.* (2002) study is often cited by other researchers of mental toughness seeking confirmation of the validity of their own qualitative findings (e.g., Lane, Thelwell, & Gill, 2007; Thelwell *et al.*, 2005). Given the overlap between the rationales and methods of the G. Jones *et al.* (2002, 2007) studies, it is worth taking a closer look at participants' responses. The definitions elicited from volunteers in these studies highlight the multivariate nature of the mental toughness construct and assume the necessity of aggregating such psychological skills into meaningful mental toughness attributes. Moreover, when the participants were invited to elaborate on their answers, it is apparent that their perception of the attributes of the ideal mentally tough performer reflects those of athletes many years earlier (see Tables 2.5 and 2.6).

Table 2.5 The commonality of attributes identified by G. Jones and co-workers (2002) and Loehr's (1986) previously identified mental toughness subscales

G. Jones et al. mental toughness attributes	Examples of participant quotes from G. Jones et al. *(pp. 210–213)*	Loehr subscales
Having an unshakable self-belief in your ability to achieve your competition goals.	'Mental toughness is about your self-belief and not being shaken from your path . . . it is producing the goods and having the self-belief in your head to produce the goods.'	Self-confidence
Bouncing back from performance setbacks as a result of increased determination to succeed.	'Nobody's rise to the top is completely smooth, there are always little hiccups or turns in the road.'	Attitude control
Having an unshakeable self-belief that you possess unique qualities and abilities that make you better than your opponents.	'He had the self-belief in his ability to know he was making the right decisions.'	Self-confidence
Having an insatiable desire and internalised motives to succeed.	'You've really got to want it, but you've also got to want to do it for yourself. You've also got to really understand why you're in it.'	Motivation
Remaining fully focused on the task at hand in the face of competition-specific distractions.	'If you want to be the best, you have got to be totally focused on what you are doing. There are inevitable distractions and you just have to be able to focus on what you need to focus on.'	Attention control

(Continued overleaf)

Table 2.5 Continued

G. Jones et al. *mental toughness attributes*	*Examples of participant quotes from G. Jones et al. (pp. 210–213)*	*Loehr subscales*
Regaining psychological control following unexpected, uncontrollable events (competition-specific).	'It's definitely about not getting unsettled by things you didn't expect or can't control. You've got to be able to switch back into control mode.'	Negative energy control Attention control
Pushing back the boundaries of physical and emotional pain, while still maintaining technique and effort under distress (in training and competition).	'In my sport you have to deal with the physical pain from fatigue, dehydration, and tiredness . . . you are depleting your body of so many different things. It is a question of pushing yourself . . . it's mind over matter, just trying to hold your technique and perform while under this distress and go beyond your limits.'	Motivation Attitude control
Accepting that competition anxiety is inevitable and knowing that you can cope with it.	'I accept that I'm going to get nervous, particularly when the pressure's on, but keeping the lid on it and being in control is crucial.'	Negative energy control
Thriving on the pressure of competition.	'If you are going to achieve anything worthwhile, there is bound to be pressure. Mental toughness is being resilient to and using the competition pressure to get the best out of yourself.'	Positive energy
Not being adversely affected by others' good and bad performances.	'The mentally tough performer uses others' good performances as a spur.'	Motivation
Remaining fully focused in the face of personal life distractions.	'Once you're in the competition, you cannot let your mind wander to other things. It doesn't matter what has happened to you, you can't bring the problem into the performance arena.'	Attention control
Switching a sport focus on and off as required.	'The mentally tough performer succeeds by having control of the on/off switch.'	Attention control

Source: Adapted from G. Jones *et al.* (2002) and Loehr (1986).

Table 2.6 The commonality of descriptions identified by G. Jones and co-workers (2007) and Loehr's (1986) previously identified mental toughness subscales

G. Jones et al. mental toughness descriptions [sub-category]	Examples of participant quotes from G. Jones et al. (pp. 248–260)	Loehr subscales
Having an inner arrogance that makes you believe that you can achieve anything you set your mind to. [Belief]	'It's that inner arrogance, that bit of an attitude towards things that I set my mind to. It is never ever giving up and knowing that if I just persevere I know that I am going to be able to do it . . . I believe I will be able to do it.'	Self-confidence
Refusing to be swayed by short-term gains (financial, performance) that will jeopardise the achievement of long-term goals. [Focus]	'The mentally tough performer will not be swayed by short-term goals, such as money or minor successes, in their desire to achieve their ultimate goal. You can think of many athletes who turn down vast amounts of money that are offered by promoters or sponsors to run in marathons . . . or compete or play in competitions . . . or go on tours, so that they can focus on their long-term goal . . . you know . . . the Olympics or Worlds.'	Motivation
When training gets tough (physically and mentally) because things are not going your way, keeping yourself going by reminding yourself of your goals and aspirations and why you're putting yourself through it. [Using long-term goals as the source of motivation]	'Life gets difficult, training gets difficult, but the mentally tough athletes know exactly why they are doing it . . . They know what their goals and aspirations are and why they are putting themselves through the hard work.' 'I am doing this because I want to win gold . . . Mentally tough performers acknowledge that they are tired but realize and remind themselves that if they are to achieve their goal they have to get back in the gym and work.'	Motivation Attitude control

(Continued overleaf)

Table 2.6 Continued

G. Jones et al. mental toughness descriptions [sub-category]	Examples of participant quotes from G. Jones et al. (pp. 248–260)	Loehr subscales
Using all aspects of a very difficult training environment to your advantage. [Controlling the environment]	'At training camps you don't always get things your way . . . You've got to be able to train with other people in the training environment there. It may not be ideal for you but you've got to deal with that and use it to your advantage. The mentally tough performer can handle the environment he is put in and use it to his advantage.'	Negative energy control Attitude control
Thriving on opportunities to beat other people in training. [Pushing yourself to the limit]	'Their identity is caught up with . . . "I am very good, I am going to prove it, I am going to take you out of this and beat you." . . . They thrive on opportunities of beating other people and are not afraid to put themselves on the line.'	Self-confidence Attitude control
Making the correct decisions and choosing the right options that secure optimal performance under conditions of extreme pressure and ambiguity. [Handling pressure]	'Sometimes it is about curbing your initial instincts in a pressure situation, because the instinct says 'go for it now,' whereas, actually, the best option might be to wait 5 minutes before you go for it. Mentally tough performers are able to make the right decisions . . . and know when that is. . . . They will make the right decision when it is required.'	Attention control
Not being fazed by making mistakes and then coming back from them. [Belief]	'Mistakes would get some people down because they start worrying and thinking about failure. The ideal mentally tough performer can put a mistake to one side and carry on performing regardless. They have a resilience, a toughness, they are not fazed by mistakes. They stay mentally strong when things do go wrong, they are able to bounce back from mistakes or errors . . . and then produce it again.'	Negative energy control Positive energy Attitude control

Raising your performance 'up a gear' when it matters most. [Regulating performance]	'If somebody in a heat breaks the world record, you know you are going to have to do the same. In a final you might have to break the world record to win, you have to be prepared to break the world record to win, and the mentally tough performer can and, importantly, knows how to do that.'	Self-confidence Positive energy
Remaining committed to a self-absorbed focus despite external distractions. [Staying focused]	'They are in a cocoon almost, absorbed in themselves, committed to what they're doing, what they need to do, how they're going to react. Regardless of what happens, mentally tough performers remain committed to what they should be focused on, despite the efforts of other people and circumstances that try to draw them out of it.'	Attention control
Being acutely aware of any inappropriate thoughts and feelings and changing them to help perform optimally. [Awareness and control of thoughts and feelings]	'They have this recognition mechanism that kicks in, but the key difference between them and other athletes is that the mentally tough ones are able to change that thought or feeling so that they can perform at their best.'	Negative energy control Attitude control
Using all aspects of a very difficult competition environment to your advantage. [Controlling the environment]	'You need to be able to handle any situation that's thrown at you. At the Olympics you cannot isolate yourself . . . it involves team-mates, coaches, doctors, management. You may not get on with all of them but you've got to hold it together, you have to be consistent. You may have to compete in conditions that you didn't wish for . . . you have to be able to cope with that . . . Mentally tough performers are able to handle all the environments, all the personal and impersonal relationships, and use them to his advantage.'	Negative energy control Positive energy Attitude control

(Continued overleaf)

Table 2.6 Continued

G. Jones et al. mental toughness descriptions [sub-category]	Examples of participant quotes from G. Jones et al. (pp. 248–260)	Loehr subscales
Recognising and rationalising failure and picking out the learning points to take forward. [Handling failure]	'He is able to analyze his performance and learn to adapt to whatever caused the errors so that he can reach his ultimate goal. The mentally tough performer is able to move on from that failure and it's not an issue or a mental block for him. He uses this knowledge for future performances.'	Motivation Positive energy
Knowing when to celebrate success and then stop and focus on the next challenge. [Handling success]	'The mentally tough performer has an acute awareness of his own ability, his levels of fitness, his strength, limitations, and what needs to be done in order to achieve the level of performance required to win . . . He also knows when to stop celebrating and how long it will take to reach that top-level performance again.'	Motivation Positive energy

Source: Adapted from G. Jones *et al.* (2007) and Loehr (1986).

Loehr's mental toughness attributes

According to Jim Loehr (1986), mentally tough performers are disciplined thinkers who respond to pressure in ways which enable them to remain feeling relaxed, calm, and energised because they have the ability to increase their flow of positive energy in crisis and adversity. They also have the right attitudes regarding problems, pressure, mistakes, and competition. Under competitive pressure, mentally tough performers can continue to think productively, positively, and realistically, and do so with composed clarity (Loehr, 1995). Specifically, Loehr's (1986) seven attributes of mental toughness include: self-confidence (knowing that one can perform well and be successful), negative energy control (handling emotions such as fear, anger, anxiety, and frustration, and coping with externally-determined events), attention control (remaining fully focused on the task at hand), visualisation and imagery control (thinking positively in pictures rather than words, and being able to control the flow of mental pictures and images in positive and constructive directions), motivation (the ability to set meaningful goals and be willing to persevere with training schedules and to endure the pain, discomfort, and self-sacrifice associated with forward progress), positive energy (the ability to become energised from such sources as fun, joy, determination, positiveness, and team spirit), and attitude control (reflecting a performer's habits of thoughts, with particular emphasis on being unyielding and showing obstinate insistence on finishing rather than conceding defeat).

An enduring blueprint

While the previously examined qualitative research supports Loehr's (1986) propositions on mental toughness, this has not substantially added to the debate. There is considerable overlap between Loehr's original factors and attributes subsequently identified by other researchers that are based, to some extent, on his research (cf. G. Jones *et al.*, 2002; Thelwell *et al.*, 2005). For example, G. Jones *et al.* (2002: 209) suggested that mental toughness is 'having the natural or developed psychological edge that enables you to, generally, cope better than your opponents with the many demands (competition, training, lifestyle) that sport places on a performer and, specifically, be more consistent and better than your opponents in remaining determined, focused, confident, and in control under pressure'. Similarly, Cashmore (2002: 166–167) described mental toughness as a package of intellect qualities that includes 'an unusually high level of resolution, a refusal to be intimidated, an ability to stay focused in high-pressure situations, a capacity for retaining an optimum level of arousal throughout a competition, an unflagging eagerness to compete when injured, an unyielding attitude when being beaten, a propensity to take risks when rivals show caution and an inflexible, perhaps obstinate insistence on finishing a contest rather than conceding defeat'. Interestingly, Cashmore (ibid.: 138) shares Loehr's view that 'mentally tough athletes are not emotionless: they are just skilled in subordinating emotions to the greater requirement of winning competitions'. Consequently, Loehr's remains a useful and enduring blueprint for examining the construct of mental toughness. This shall be considered more closely in Chapter 3.

A mindset for all sports

As mentioned earlier in this chapter, it has been suggested that there may be inter-sport variance in mental toughness. For example, Thelwell *et al.* (2005) derived definitions of mental toughness that were applicable specifically to a football context (e.g., 'wanting the ball at all times'). Furthermore, G. Jones *et al.* (2002) proffered that a distinction should be made between emotional pain resulting from failure (arguably a sport-generic factor) and physical pain (more specific to, for example, rowing than snooker). Consequently, it has been suggested that mental toughness characteristics may be sport-specific. However, more likely is the suggestion that there exists a core set of attributes that characterise the mental toughness mindset, but that these personality characteristics can be exhibited in very different behaviours. For example, S. J. Bull *et al.* (2005) suggest that the maintenance of self-control at the critical moment in order to sink a short golf putt, taking calculated risks in high-speed, high-risk motor sport, the ability to handle the incredibly high volumes of training for endurance sports, and a willingness to enter into the high-intensity confrontation between batsman and bowler in cricket (and revel in it), are contrasting types of mental toughness. However, each of the scenarios above is only one behavioural response from an athlete with a mentally tough mindset. There are a multitude of other scenarios in golf (for example, the confidence to drive over the water from a tee-shot), motor sport (the ability to hold off pursuers and maintain a lead over 60 laps), endurance sports (the ability to visualise particular components of the sport), and cricket (the ability to stick around and grind it out as a batsman when one's team-mates are losing their wickets) where another, more appropriate mentally tough response is desirable.

Not only is it the nature of the sport that elicits the appropriate behavioural manifestation of mental toughness. More accurately, it is the nature of specific scenarios at any given time in different sports that elicit the apposite response from the mentally tough performer. Some mental toughness attributes are peripheral components to the requirements of specific sports. However, the core components of mental toughness are broad enough to encompass all sports. There are equivalent expressions of mental toughness in every sport. Ultimately, at the core of the mentally tough mindset are self-belief, honesty and integrity, resolve, and a well-developed sense of ethical principles. Armed with these attributes, sport performers are more likely to adapt positively and respond unerringly to situations. These apply regardless of the sport played.

Conclusion

Mental toughness is a notion that enjoys considerable popular appeal. As discussed in this chapter, several researchers have devoted empirical attention to addressing the nature of mental toughness and such psychological skills used by sport performers in order to manage the stressful demands encountered in training and competition. For example, Fourie and Potgieter (2001) suggested that mentally tough performers are those athletes who have developed the necessary psychological hardiness. Mental toughness has been described as the ability to maintain an optimal mindset (J. W. Jones, Neuman, Altmann, & Dreschler, 2001) and as a package of intellect qualities (Cashmore, 2002, 2005). For Clough *et al.* (2002), mentally tough performers have a high sense of self-belief, an unshakeable faith that they control their own destiny, and that such individuals remain relatively unaffected by adversity. D. Gould *et al.* (2002) described mental toughness in terms of resilience, perseverance, and the ability to deal successfully with adversity. G. Jones *et al.* (2002) suggested that mental toughness is having a natural or developed psychological edge that enables performers to cope with the plethora of demands made upon them. The same authors subsequently proposed that an essential quality of mentally tough athletes is their ability to harness the anxiety experienced in stressful competitive situations to enhance rather than debilitate performance (G. Jones *et al.*, 2007). Thelwell *et al.* (2005) described mental toughness in terms of having a presence that affects opponents, having the ability to react to situations positively, and to be calm under, and even to enjoy, pressure. While Loehr (1986) described mentally tough performers as disciplined thinkers who respond to pressure in ways which enable them to remain feeling relaxed, calm, and energised because they have the ability to increase their flow of positive energy in crisis and adversity. Such athletes also have the right attitudes regarding problems, pressure, mistakes, and competition. Mental toughness assumes effort. Mentally tough performers are effortful, tackling challenges that lie just beyond their competence.

This chapter has presented the characteristics historically associated with mental toughness within the extant literature. Acknowledging the widespread use of the phrase mental toughness by sport psychologists, researchers in sport psychology, coaches, and performers, the present chapter has examined the concept in terms of how it is defined and its constitutive attributes. The present chapter has shown that, within the literature, there is common agreement that accomplished sport performers are mentally tough. Despite the breadth of constitutive attributes, a consensus is emerging as to what is characteristic of mental toughness. For sure, there is a strong argument that this collection of characteristics represents a particular mindset. The debate over a definition of mental toughness can now be advanced to an examination of its conceptual clarification. Specifically, Chapter 3 will consider the multi-faceted role of mental toughness and question an emerging conceptualisation that its sole function is that as a moderator of the stress response.

3   Conceptualising mental toughness

Self-control and resistance to distractions. Optimism in adversity. A personality in balance.

Marcus Aurelius

Introduction

The potentially stressful nature of being involved in competitive sport is well documented. Athletes participating in training and competition frequently encounter stressors, whether in individual (e.g., Cohn, 1990; Giacobbi, Foore, & Weinberg, 2004; Giacobbi, Lynn, Wetherington, Jenkins, Bodendorf, & Langley, 2004; McKay, Niven, Lavallee, & White, 2008; Nicholls, Holt, & Polman, 2005) or team (e.g., Anshel, 2001; Holt & Hogg, 2002; Nicholls, Holt, Polman, & Bloomfield, 2006; Noblet & Gifford, 2002; Noblet, Rodwell, & McWilliams, 2003) sport environments. Sport performers, particularly those operating at the highest professional levels, must cope with the stressors they experience in order to sustain high levels of performance and maintain their status. Participating in competitive sport requires athletes not only to develop and maintain a high level of sport ability, but also to assemble a collection of skills to cope with stressful encounters in a challenging environment. Put simply, they are expected to deal with pressure. To this end, the lessons of success in sport are often linked with the ability to display mental toughness in stressful situations.

Mental toughness as a moderator of stress

As discussed in Chapter 2, for many researchers of mental toughness, a strong mindset exists in relation to overcoming adversity (e.g., Dorfman, 2003; Fourie & Potgieter, 2001; G. Jones *et al.*, 2002; S. C. Middleton *et al.*, 2004a; Thelwell *et al.*, 2005). In a study of the stressors facing cricketers, reported coping strategies included: 'see the pressure as a challenge', 'tell myself to fight', 'tell myself to focus', 'tell myself to be patient', 'tell myself to control the controllables', 'be ice cold to the opposition', 'stay level-headed', 'maintain composure', 'get myself calm before a game', and 'look for a confrontation' (Thelwell, Weston, & Greenlees, 2007). Each of these is constitutive of mental toughness. Others have pursued this direction. For example, Fletcher (2005: 1246) conceptualised mental toughness as 'an individual's propensity to manage the demands of environmental stressors, ranging from an absolute resilience to extreme vulnerability'. He argued that it represents a composite variable that is a conglomerate of the more manifest moderators of the stress process. Furthermore, Fletcher suggested that a complete understanding of mental toughness and human performance would only be obtained if it were studied within the context of a transactional conceptualisation of stress.

   Fletcher's (2005) facet model outlines the moderating role of mental toughness in the stress process and its theoretical relationship with performance (see Figure 3.1). According to the model, the relevance of the attributes that constitute mental toughness will depend on the combination of different personal, organisational, and competitive stressors encountered by performers in a particular situation. These attributes moderate the relationship between stressors and responses by influencing athletes' appraisal and coping. Mental toughness, therefore, plays a pivotal role in determining

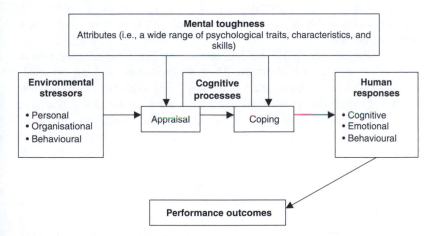

Figure 3.1 A facet model of mental toughness and human performance.

Source: Adapted from Fletcher (2005), reprinted by permission of Taylor & Francis Ltd, www. informaworld.com

how athletes cognitively, emotionally, and behaviourally respond to stressors, which will in turn affect their performance.

Developing the idea of mental toughness as a moderator of the stress response, Fletcher and Fletcher (2005) offered a supra-ordinate perspective of the stress–emotion–performance relationship. The authors proposed that stressors arise from the environment in which athletes operate, are mediated by the processes of perception, appraisal and coping, and, consequently, result in positive or negative responses, feeling states and outcomes. They added that this is an ongoing process, moderated by various personal and situational factors, including athletes' levels of mental toughness. With regard to causal sequence, it could be argued that the ability to withstand stress is an indication of a mentally tough performer, and that, consequently, being mentally tough is predictive of the ability to handle stress.

The aforementioned conceptualisation of mental toughness has much in common with the Cognitive-Affective Processing System (CAPS) model of personality advanced by Walter Mischel and Yuichi Shoda (Mischel & Shoda, 1995). This model accounts for personality coherence in terms of a stable system, whose functioning underlies both consistency and situationally-based variability in behaviour. It is a dynamic network of cognitive, affective, motivational, and behaviour-generation units that interacts with situational factors to produce both coherence and cross-situational variability in behaviour. Within the CAPS framework, mentally tough performers are likely to exhibit the following characteristics: they encode demanding situations as challenges and opportunities, rather than threats; they confidently view themselves as having the personal resources needed to cope successfully with pressure situations; and they feel in control of self and capable of producing a positive outcome.

According to the CAPS model, mentally tough athletes also have a distinctive motivational structure. Their goals include seeking out challenging situations with uncertain outcomes. They value personal improvement and skill mastery, are high in positive achievement motivation, and relatively low in fear of failure. Mentally tough athletes are also self-motivated and self-directed in their efforts to improve; and they do not require external pressure to work hard. Their commitment to their sport often sets them apart.

The affective responses of mentally tough athletes facilitate, rather than impair, performance by enhancing their ability to remain focused on the task at hand under even the most demanding and potentially distracting conditions. Their self-reinforcement standards involve giving maximum effort at all times, especially in the face of adversity. Self-standards are self-referenced, realistic, and oriented towards skill improvement. They have the self-regulation skills needed to persist in the face of adversity, and their ability to delay gratification contributes to the commitment they exhibit to skill development. Mentally tough athletes know how to develop action plans, how to learn, and how to improve. All of these characteristics facilitate their development and performance under pressure. Interestingly, within the CAPS framework, reference is made to personality 'hardiness': mentally tough performers are able to function in the face of difficulties that would interfere with the performance of less hardy individuals (Mischel & Shoda, 1995).

Developing this connection, particularly noteworthy is the conclusion of Fourie and Potgieter (2001: 71) that: 'Athletes should develop the necessary psychological hardiness.' Indeed, psychological hardiness was one of the 12 umbrella mental toughness categories identified in that study and was defined as the 'ability of the athlete to reveal a strong personality, emotional and psychological well-being, to take charge, and show autonomy' (ibid.: 68). Similarly, Clough *et al.* (2002: 38), writing of mentally tough performers, stated that: 'With a high sense of self-belief and an unshakeable faith that they control their own destiny, these individuals can remain relatively unaffected by competition or adversity.' This definition suggests operationalising mental toughness in terms of psychological resilience or stress-resistance; in effect, individuals' positive responses to situations of stress and adversity (Braddock, Royster, Winfield, & Hawkins, 1991; L. Miller, 2008; Rutter, 1987; Tugade & Fredrickson, 2004). Although the aforementioned descriptions of hardiness are in stark contrast to that originally put forward by Suzanne Kobasa (1979), such resilient responses have often been described in terms of demonstrations of the hardy personality. Moreover, some researchers have attempted to define mental toughness within the theoretical context of Kobasa's hardiness model.

The relationship between mental toughness and hardiness

The term 'hardiness' has often been used to describe stress-resistant individuals. With its stress-buffering (e.g., Kobasa, 1979; Maddi, Kahn, & Maddi, 1998; Wiebe, 1991), and performance-enhancing (e.g., Atella, 1999; Westman, 1990) functions, the moderating effects of this construct have become associated with those purported of mental toughness (cf. Clough *et al.*, 2002; Golby & Sheard, 2004, 2006; Golby, Sheard, & Lavallee, 2003; Sheard, 2009b; Sheard & Golby, 2006a, 2006b). Further, the environments in which the moderating effects of hardiness have been demonstrated make sport a similarly promising potential source of empirical enquiry for the conceptualisation of mental toughness. Indeed, of the England cricket team's visit to the World War I memorials at Flanders Field and the Menin Gate ahead of the 2009 Ashes series, director Andy Flower attempted to transplant the meaning of heroic deeds into a contextual similarity: 'A lot of the values that the military hold dear apply to us in a sporting context' (as cited in Briggs, 2009c: S14). Thus, it seems plausible that mental toughness and hardiness share the same conceptual space.

Conceptualising hardiness

The hardiness construct, with its roots in existential theory (e.g., Frankl, 1959; Gendlin, 1966; Kierkegaard, 1843/1959), emerged from individual differences research on stress reactions, and has been conceptualised as a combination of the three attitudes (3Cs) of *commitment, control*, and *challenge* (Kobasa, 1979; Maddi, 2006a). Hardiness provides the existential courage that aids the individual in pursuing the future despite its uncertainty (Maddi, 2004; Tillich, 1952). Research has primarily examined the construct as a moderator of stressor–strain relationships (Beehr & Bowling, 2005). Commitment (vs. alienation) epitomises those individuals who are committed to, and feel deeply involved in, the activities of their life domains (e.g., family, friends, work, leisure activities, hobbies). People high in commitment get involved rather than withdraw, seeing this as the best way to turn their environments and whatever they are experiencing into something that seems interesting, worthwhile, and important, regardless of how stressful things become (Maddi, 2006a; Maddi, Khoshaba, Persico, Lu, Harvey, & Bleecker, 2002). Control (vs. powerlessness) reflects people's desire to continue to have an influence on the outcomes going on around them, no matter how difficult and stressful this becomes (Maddi, 2006a). Hardy individuals control the events of their experience in terms of what they choose to do and how they choose to respond to various events (Maddi, 1990). Challenge (vs. security) typifies an expectation that life is unpredictable and that changes will stimulate personal development. Potentially stressful situations are appraised as exciting and stimulating rather than threatening, enabling people to feel positively about life's fluctuations. People high in challenge believe that what improves their lives is growth through learning rather than easy comfort and security (Maddi, 2006a). The conceptualised process whereby hardiness leads to enhanced performance and health is depicted in Figure 3.2.

According to Salvatore Maddi and Deborah Khoshaba, hardy individuals construct meaning in their lives by recognising that: everything they do constitutes a decision; decisions invariably involve pushing towards the future or shrinking into the past; and choosing the future expands meaning, whereas choosing the past contracts it (Maddi & Khoshaba, 2001). Though positive in terms of meaning and possibilities, choosing the future raises anxiety over the unpredictable nature of things not yet experienced. Almost

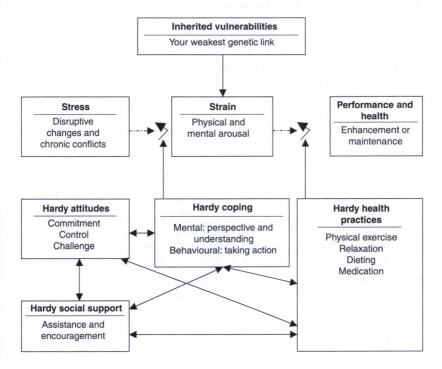

Figure 3.2 The hardiness model for performance and health enhancement.
© 1986–2006, Hardiness Institute, Inc.

Source: Adapted from Maddi (2006), reprinted by permission of Taylor & Francis Ltd, www.
informaworld.com

every decision we make entails predicting the future. To accept this so-called
ontological anxiety and push ahead with choosing the future anyway
requires the courage that is the manifestation of existentialist theory. Adoption of such a philosophy helps us to accept that 'life is full of risks. It is
pretty much all there is to life: it is a ribbon of uncertainty that one day
suddenly runs out' (Joseph, 2008: 3). Ultimately, life unfolds and we have
to do our best to embrace the good parts and endure its challenges. All of
which give texture to life. Substituting courage with hardiness lends precision to the existential formulation by emphasising the three inter-related
beliefs about one's interaction with the world: commitment, control, and
challenge.

As conceptualised, the 3Cs of hardiness are a cognitive/emotional/
behavioural amalgam constituting a learned, growth-oriented, personality
style. Hardiness theory submits that people who feel committed, in control,

and positively challenged by life circumstances have the tendency to perceive events or circumstances as less stressful, seeing them as manageable rather than overwhelming (Khoshaba & Maddi, 1999). Performance of these individuals is enhanced by their active or decisive coping efforts in stressful situations (Soderstrom, Dolbier, Leiferman, & Steinhardt, 2000). As such, hardiness is a pathway to resilience under stress (Beasley, Thompson, & Davidson, 2003; Bonanno, 2004). The positive influence of hardiness on performance has been reported in such diverse samples as given in Note 9. Hardiness has also been identified as an important personality construct within sport-specific situations. To elaborate, research has shown that athletes with high levels of hardiness demonstrate better peripheral vision (Rogers, Alderman, & Landers, 2003), report more facilitative interpretation of anxiety (Hanton, Evans, & Neil, 2003), cope more effectively with stressors (Goss, 1994; Kelley, 1994), and possess a greater ability to withstand burnout (Hendrix, Acevedo, & Hebert, 2000). Hardiness is also related to decreased injury-time loss in high-level sport performers (Ford, Eklund, & Gordon, 2000). Further, research has shown that hardiness, measured before competition, predicted six out of seven indices of male basketball performance excellence (Maddi & Hess, 1992) and female synchronised swimming selection to the US Olympics team in 2000 (Lancer, 2000). Similarly, Golby *et al.* (2003) reported significantly higher levels of hardiness in professional rugby league footballers who had learnt to play the game in Australia, while a subsequent study showed that professional rugby league players operating at international level scored significantly higher in hardiness than their sub-elite counterparts (Golby & Sheard, 2004).

Some people have a 'hardy' personality in the sense that they possess, for example, coping skills that enable them to thrive under adverse circumstances. Kobasa's (1979) hardy personality style serves as a useful theoretical model for the construct validity of mental toughness. Characteristics of the hardy personality are consonant with those of mentally tough performers, identified earlier in Chapter 2. For example, consistent with findings for hardiness (e.g., Benishek & Lopez, 1997; Khoshaba & Maddi, 1999), recent research has shown a positive association between higher levels of mental toughness and problem or approach coping strategies (Kaiseler, Polman, & Nicholls, 2009; Nicholls, Polman, Levy, & Backhouse, 2008). Similarly, the stress-buffering and performance-enhancement benefits derived from possession of a hardy personality style are congruous with those of mentally tough individuals (see Clough *et al.*, 2002; Fourie & Potgieter, 2001; G. Jones *et al.*, 2002; R. E. Smith & Smoll, 1989; R. M. Williams, 1988). Indeed, past research has synonymised mental toughness with cognitive hardiness (e.g., Hollander & Acevedo, 2000; R. E. Smith, 2006). Thus, for some researchers, the relationship with Kobasa's model of hardiness has served as an appropriate theoretical frame of reference for the conceptual-isation of mental toughness.

Conceptualising mental toughness using the hardiness model

Kobasa's (1979) model (i.e., a commitment to be fully involved in one's environment; a sense of control over it; and a view of the future which approaches it with a sense of challenge, rather than with feelings of appre-hension) has been employed to show links between hardiness and mental toughness. For example, Clough *et al.* (2002) provided support for the 3Cs of hardiness, but also revealed the importance of a fourth attitude (confi-dence) to reflect the transposition of the related construct of hardiness into the more sport-specific concept of mental toughness. According to Clough *et al.*, hardiness fails 'to capture the unique nature of the physical and mental demands of competitive sport' (ibid.: 37). However, their transposi-tion of hardiness to mental toughness was not fully justified. In particular, the authors did not provide a rationale as to why mental toughness is a sport-specific form of hardiness. Further, the 3Cs hardiness model assumes confidence to be implicit across the three hardiness attitudes (Maddi & Khoshaba, 2001).

More than a pathway to resilience under stress

Undoubtedly, the mentally tough mindset includes an ability to bounce back from stressful experiences quickly and effectively. Dealing effectively with pressure – that constant sporting currency – 'sorts out the great players from the good' (B. Moore, 2009a). However, if the sole function of mental toughness is as a moderator of the stress response, then the construct is little different to psychological resilience, in that it is the demonstration of effect-ive coping and adaptation in the face of loss, hardship, or adversity (Rutter, 1999; Tugade & Fredrickson, 2004). Refusing to give in is a fine character-istic; but I believe the mental toughness mindset offers more.

It is assumed that many elite performers possess mentally tough qualities such as resilience and an ability to experience stress and cope with it to maintain and to enhance their performance. However, it could also be claimed that athletes are likely to require other mental toughness attributes that need not necessarily manifest exclusively in adversity. Arguably, the most important finding in a study of mental toughness in Australian Rules football was that mental toughness was considered important not only for those situations with negative effects (e.g., injury, de-selection), but also for some situations with positive effects (e.g., good form, previous season champions) (Gucciardi *et al.*, 2008).

Previous conceptualisations of mental toughness have focused too heavily on the notion of adversity and how the key components enable athletes to deal with and overcome such setbacks. Mental toughness involves having to deal with, and overcome, situations with negative effects, but it also enables individuals to flourish in situations where there are positive effects and perceived positive pressure. Defined in this sense, mental toughness can be conceptualised not only as a buffer against adversity, but as a collection of inter-related protective and enabling attributes that promote and maintain adaptation to other positive, though challenging, situations.

Support for this is provided in an investigation of mental toughness and sport performers' goal orientation. A study by Kuan and Roy (2007) that recruited 40 Malaysian athletes revealed that individuals with a high task/ moderate ego goal profile had greater mental toughness in controlling negative energy than athletes with a moderate task/low ego goal profile. High task/moderate ego athletes were also significantly higher in positive energy when compared to moderate task/moderate ego performers. Results also suggest the possibility that athletes with a high task/moderate ego goal profile probably benefit during adversities in competition, due to good control over oneself, leading to greater mental toughness.

A mindset for all situations

At some time in their career, athletes are likely to experience stress and cope with it to maintain and enhance their performance. This notwithstanding, there is more to mental toughness than its function defence mechanism against adversity. Gucciardi *et al.* (2008) suggest that, within Australian Rules football at least, mental toughness is a collection of values, attitudes, behaviours, and emotions that facilitate performers' perseverance in adverse situations. But they added that it is also the ability to maintain concentration and motivation to achieve goals. The athletes interviewed in the Gucciardi *et al.* study stated that thorough preparation made a substantial contribution to their self-belief. In addition, an exceptional work ethic characterised by determination, perseverance, and time-management was considered vital in not only overcoming adversities, but also surmounting them quicker and better than expected (e.g., injury rehabilitation).

Interestingly, professionals operating in rugby league football have conceptualised mental toughness similarly. In addition to performers having the ability to handle pressure and thrive in adverse circumstances, vastly experienced head coach and director of rugby Shaun McRae suggested a good work ethic and collective responsibility are also constitutive of mental toughness (personal communication, November 28, 2007). McRae added:

Mental toughness is the ability of athletes to take themselves out of their comfort zone. Such athletes perform to their ability against adversity, stress, or pressures, when other athletes tend to make mistakes and lose focus. Also, mentally tough athletes generally achieve their goals, hold their nerve, and always lead by action rather than words.

Stressing that mental toughness included possession of an unyielding mindset, he also articulated that mentally tough performers understand the consequences of quitting. Recently retired senior professional Malcolm Alker (personal communication, December 19, 2007) corroborated McRae's conceptualisation:

> Mental toughness is the ability of athletes to take their body and mind to a place where it hurts and where they don't really want to be, but know it's the only way to achieve their goals. Athletes are willing to make sacrifices to overcome adversity and negativity to realise their talent.

Similarly, former New Zealand international Robbie Paul spoke of mental toughness in terms of 'senior players creating a mentally tough environment ... learning from life's experiences ... and a high work ethic' (personal communication, November 28, 2007).

Mental toughness as psychological preparation

Clearly, as conceptualised above, such attributes of mental toughness need not be shown only in adverse circumstances. It is also apparent that mental toughness is a multi-factorial construct, with its constitutive factors manifested behaviourally either singly or in combination in response to the appropriate situation or context. Such a conceptualisation is remarkably similar to the work of the pioneering Soviet sport psychologist Avksenty Cezarevich Puni. He wrote of the psychological preparation of athletes for competition, yet it could so easily be read as a blueprint for mental toughness. Puni (1963) stated that sport performers need a sensible confidence in their abilities, the readiness to overcome all obstacles, including unexpected ones of various degrees of difficulty, the active aspiration to strive passionately to achieve not only the set goal but also the highest result possible, the appropriate level of emotional arousal, and the ability to control one's own thoughts, feelings, and behaviours. Collectively, these components were termed *boevaya gotovnost*, or 'readiness to fight'. An English translation of Puni's theoretical and practical tutorial, and the possible applications of the model for practitioners in preparing athletes for the rigours of competition, has been published (see Ryba, Stambulova, & Wrisberg, 2009).

Mental toughness as a life skill

It has been suggested that the attributes associated with mentally tough performers could facilitate life outside of sport (Connaughton, Wadey, Hanton, & Jones, 2008). As conceptualised, mental toughness could be explored as a life skill. The study's authors suggested that this is particularly relevant if athletes' concerns relate as much to broader life issues as to specific sport performance matters. This supports the S. C. Middleton *et al.* (2004a) model that suggests mental toughness has broad relevance. Indeed, it is difficult to conceive why mental toughness should be a mindset relevant only in sport situations, rather than a personality style that more broadly allows individuals to deal effectively with life's myriad circumstances.

A positive psychological perspective

The aforementioned constitutive characteristics suggest that mental toughness be considered within the framework of 'positive psychology' (Seligman & Csikszentmihalyi, 2000). Psychology has traditionally been characterised by a pathogenic paradigm in what Barnard (1994: 136) called 'an obsessive proclivity for "deficit detecting" to the exclusion of acknowledging strengths and resources'. However, emerging from humanistic theory, positive psychology offers an alternative context that concentrates on positive experiences and positive character or virtues.

Positive psychology

The positive psychology movement suggests that psychology since World War II has been sidetracked by an over-emphasis on mental illness from its other two important missions: making the lives of all people more fulfilling, and identifying and nurturing high talent. The negative has dominated psychology (Rozin & Royzman, 2001). Optimal functioning, such as superior sport performance, cannot be understood within a purely problem-oriented framework. In contrast to the pathological interest in 'what can go wrong', there have also been ongoing attempts to discover 'what can go right' (Basic Behavioral Science Task Force, 1996: 23). Compared to a psychology as 'victimology', the new positive paradigm is turning it into a 'science of strength' (Seligman & Csikszentmihalyi, 2000: 6, 8), 'a fascination with strengths' (Saleeby, 1997: 4), and a 'psychology of survivorship, resiliency, encouragement, and strength' (Abi-Hashem, 2001: 86). In effect, positive psychology is an umbrella term for the theories and research about what makes life most worth living, its aim being 'to catalyse a change in the focus of psychology from preoccupation only with repairing the worst things in life to also building positive qualities' (Seligman & Csikszentmihalyi, 2000: 5).

Martin Seligman and Mihaly Csikszentmihalyi have called for the study of psychology to move beyond psychological disorders and problems, and for greater efforts to be spent on positive psychology; that is, how psychology can be used to facilitate human functioning (Seligman & Csikszentmihalyi, 2000). Facilitating human performance is the primary goal of the sport psychologist, with much research in the field of sport psychology focusing considerable attention on what it takes to be a great athlete. The focus is on what makes individuals (e.g., athletes) and communities (e.g., sports teams/ organisations) thrive and flourish (see Keyes & Haidt, 2003; C. R. Snyder, Lopez, & Pedrotti, 2011). Attention should be given to achieving the typically human goals of feeling good and being psychologically satisfied. A positive psychological approach recognises that a failure to materialise these goals is not a function of deep-seated pathologies, but a lack of skills or knowledge of how to achieve them. The approach is concerned less with the 'curing' (i.e., treatment and correction) of any perceived pathologies, than with training individuals into how to improve their self-control skills and other attributes (i.e., mastering strengths) that will enable them to achieve their goals. Thus, positive psychology is an appropriate theoretical framework within which researchers can explore further the relationship between mental toughness and superior sport performance (D. Gould, 2002).

Indeed, several researchers have conceptualised mental toughness such that it reflects the positive psychology paradigm. G. Jones *et al.* (2007: 244) commented on 'a diverse range of positive psychological characteristics being associated with mental toughness'. One of S. C. Middleton *et al.*'s (2004a) 12 key mental toughness characteristics included 'believing in your own potential and capacity for growth and development'. S. J. Bull *et al.* (2005) also recognised mental toughness as a positive psychological construct. Moreover, their positive psychological framework of mental toughness is now an integral part of the English Cricket Board's (ECB) Level 3 and 4 coaching qualifications. Furthermore, several studies have revealed numerous positive psychological constructs as key correlates of mental toughness; for example: hardiness, dispositional optimism, self-efficacy, self-esteem, and positive/negative affectivity (see Clough *et al.*, 2002; Golby & Sheard, 2006; Nicholls *et al.*, 2008; Sheard & Golby, 2003, 2006a, 2006b).

The study of optimal functioning, human strengths, and positive psychological outcomes is growing rapidly (Kahneman, Diener, & Schwartz, 1999; Seligman & Csikszentmihalyi, 2000). Termed the scientific study of human strengths and happiness (Seligman & Csikszentmihalyi), positive psychology focuses on individuals' resilience, resourcefulness, and capacity for renewal. The subsequent application of this focus is to facilitate optimal functioning (Linley & Joseph, 2004). The belief that, for example, athletes are shaped not by the experience itself, but by their perception of that experience makes positive psychology a particularly appealing theoretical context in which to frame mental toughness. Indeed, the constituent components of mental toughness sit comfortably alongside the classified positive psychological character strengths; namely: wisdom and knowledge, courage, humanity, justice, temperance, and transcendence (see Park, Peterson, & Seligman, 2004; Peterson & Seligman, 2004).

Given that sport performers will face experiences throughout their careers, positive psychology theory implies that personality has the potential to develop and the capacity to improve. For example, some people are better at handling failure than others. Some also are able to recover and find ways of improving, while others feel inhibited and frustrated. A central tenet of the positive psychology paradigm is that stressors, adversity, and other inordinate demands are inherent to the human condition. However, the paradigm assumes that there are also sources of strength, through which this condition can be endured and even transcended. Physical, emotional, and social stressors can stimulate growth and strengthening in many individuals. Such people are often able to tap into previously unknown capacities, perspectives, and virtues. Mental toughness distinguishes people in these behaviours; in effect, reflecting stoicism, a term employed synonymously in one recent study (see Hutchinson, Sherman, Martinovic, & Tenenbaum, 2008). In this context, addressing the question of why some sportspeople are mentally tougher than others is important for both theoretical and practical reasons, and should be a central goal of a comprehensive positive psychology.

The call for psychology to devote more attention to facilitating optimal human functioning (Seligman & Csikszentmihalyi, 2000), and for this to be achieved through the application of positive psychology (Linley & Joseph, 2004), are being increasingly heeded in the sporting domain (see, for example, Allan & McKenna, 2009; Ashfield, McKenna, & Backhouse, 2009; Brady, 2009; Brady, Ashfield, Allan, McKenna, & Duncan, 2009; Duncan, 2009; McCarthy, Mulliner, & Barker, 2009; Salama-Younes, 2011). Indeed, Fabio Capello gave his backing to the movement: 'When players win trophies they are happier, and I believe in positive psychology' (as cited in Winter, 2010g: S5). The positive psychology movement's assertion that 'psychology is not just the study of pathology, weakness, and damage; it is also the study of strength and virtue. Treatment is not just fixing what is broken; it is nurturing what is best' (Seligman & Csikszentmihalyi, 2000: 7), is an obviously desirable theoretical frame of reference within which to carry out further research with regard to the construct validation of mental toughness.

Conclusion

This chapter has conceptualised the term 'mental toughness' and, via its proposed relationship with hardiness, that the behavioural manifestation of the mentally tough mindset incorporates mechanisms that afford resilient individuals the opportunity to overcome stress or adversity. It is assumed that the positive orientation towards life afforded by hardiness helps individuals to stay healthy and to maintain successful performance under stressful circumstances. Moreover, mental toughness involves multiple cognitive and motivational processes that moderate the impact of the objective environment and ameliorate performance (Lyubomirsky, 2001).

The mental toughness mindset advocated in this chapter reflects the model suggested by Loehr (1986) – that mental toughness is predicated on the feeling that one is in control (as a result of good preparation and a high level of commitment) and is able to thrive on the pressure of competition. Similarly, performers interviewed by D. Gould *et al.* (2002) described mental toughness as attending to what one can control, and the demonstration of perseverance, resilience, and persistence in the face of difficulties. Further support may be derived from definitional comments reported by G. Jones *et al.* (2002: 212); for example, 'not getting unsettled by things you didn't expect or can't control; the mentally tough performer is able to compose himself and come back and still win; mental toughness is using the competition pressure to get the best out of yourself'.

The observation of Marcelo Loffreda, ahead of Argentina's debut Rugby World Cup semi-final, that: 'It is in adversity that we are more comfortable, it brings out a lot of mental toughness in our players' (as cited in Gallagher, 2007) is well founded and acknowledged. Yet the key point here is that mental toughness characteristics are not shown exclusively in adverse circumstances. There is more to mental toughness than mere reaction. Mental toughness is as much concerned with the mindset which performers bring to training and competition (and life, in general) as it is with reacting to, and coping with, stressful situations. In addition to having the ability to cope (and thrive) in stressful and adverse circumstances, it is clear from the evidence proffered in this chapter that mentally tough athletes possess self-belief, determination, motivation, competitiveness, and a high work ethic; each of which can be demonstrated long before athletes need to deal with adverse situations. Further, mental toughness is not sport-specific. Rather, it is a core set of attributes constitutive of a positive mindset. Attributes specific to any particular sport are on the periphery.

In a nutshell, mental toughness is a mindset and stable disposition that captures the cognitive, emotional, and behavioural characteristics of top sport performers. I would argue that mental toughness reflects a lived and experienced philosophy, applied to each situation encountered. Therefore, it is a global disposition. And I say this because mental toughness is both an active and a moderating variable. Manifestations of mental toughness in as many contexts as possible are desirable; not only in sport, but in home life, work life, all aspects.

Finally, given the definitional consensus on athletes' resilience, resourcefulness, and capacity for renewal, this chapter proposed that mental toughness be considered within the positive psychology paradigm (Seligman & Csikszentmihalyi, 2000). Moving away from a pathogenic or deficit model, this movement observes positive outcomes in the face of adversity, giving consideration instead to the development processes that lead to both physical and mental health and well-being (Schoon & Bartley, 2008). Clearly, this positive psychology paradigm is an appropriate and desirable theoretical frame of reference within which to consider mental toughness.

Acknowledging the widespread use of the term mental toughness by sport psychologists, coaches, performers, and the media, the present chapter has examined the construct in terms of its conceptualisation. Despite the volume of qualitative research (see Chapter 2), insufficient effort has been devoted to the development of a reliable and valid measure of mental toughness in sport. Indeed, an obstacle in the path of further empirical work on mental toughness has been the apparent lack of suitable inventories. As the following chapter shows, there have been developmental difficulties with inventories purporting to measure mental toughness. However, this is no longer the case. Revealed in Chapter 4, there are, finally, psychometrically acceptable instruments that measure mental toughness.

4 Measuring mental toughness

Accuracy is a duty – not a virtue.

A. E. Housman

Introduction

The general aim of the scientific method is to establish a well-defined theory for a domain of knowledge and, where possible, to be able to measure the construct under examination (Thurstone, 1947). Theory, and the measure it generates, should provide descriptive, explanatory, and predictive power. Such theories are not well developed in psychological science if, indeed, they are possible. As in the examination of the concept of intelligence, it might be easier to devise tests than it is to establish that which is being measured. It is, therefore, both important and necessary that developed measures of mental toughness are subjected to empirical research that has the opportunity to negate or support their conceptual classifications and psychometric properties.

The nature of psychological profiling, and, for example, its potential for predicting potentially successful athletes, has prompted researchers to engage in the design of psychometric instruments capable of measuring the range of skills thought to underlie sport performance (M. Wilkinson & Ashford, 1997). The use of psychometric testing to provide psychological profiles is moving progressively from business into sport (see Forsyth, 2011; Herbert, 2010; Hotten, 2003; Selvey, 2011a; J. Wilson, 2011). However, there is only limited evidence concerning mental toughness predicting success in a variety of competitive sporting environments. Given that the literature dedicated to mental toughness has been characterised by a general lack of conceptual clarity and consensus over its definition, as covered in the previous chapters, there has been difficulty in developing a psychometrically acceptable measure of the construct. Addressing, in particular, Aidan Moran's (2004) critical observation that mental toughness lacks an independent index, this chapter critically appraises previous attempts to develop psychometrically acceptable measures of mental toughness.

Mental toughness as a subscale of more general measures

Research has suggested that athletes tend to be more 'tough-minded' than the average population (Eysenck, Nias, & Cox, 1982; Kirkcaldy, 1985). However, tough-minded in these studies was determined by higher scores on some scales (e.g., dominance, risk taking, psychoticism, sensation seeking), and by greater emotional stability as measured by lower scores on anxiety and neuroticism scales, not by a specifically designed measure of mental toughness itself. Similarly, the phrase 'tough-mindedness' has been used to describe the determination and resolve of high-performance climbers (S. Egan & Stelmack, 2003). Attempts have also been made to measure mental toughness as a bipolar personality style (Shafer, 1999). Researchers using the Comrey Personality Scales (CPS; Comrey, 1994) have described mental toughness as a primary trait loading on to three higher-order factors (namely: extraversion, conscientiousness, empathy) within a general personality factor (Rushton & Irwing, 2009). However, the five variables pertaining to the mental toughness versus sensitivity subscale on the CPS bear no resemblance to the instrument's potential utility in a sport context (e.g., no fear of bugs, no crying, no romantic love, tolerance of blood, and tolerance of vulgarity). As this scale was not designed specifically for sport, the appropriateness of such variables as measurements of mental toughness in a sport environment is questionable (D. L. Gill, Dzewaltowski, & Deeter, 1988). Moreover, given the complexity of the mental toughness construct (as annotated in Chapters 2 and 3), viewing sensitivity as the 'opposite' of mental toughness might be deemed questionable.

Other studies have developed sport-specific questionnaires with the purpose of assessing, among other psychological subscales, mental toughness. For example, Patrick Thomas and co-workers developed the Ten-Pin Bowling Performance Survey (Thomas, Schlinker, & Over, 1996). The substantive section of the questionnaire was designed to obtain information on psychological and psychomotor skills in ten-pin bowling and involvement in the sport. Each item was worded with direct reference to ten-pin bowling; that is, respondents (N = 172 bowlers; 87 males, 85 females) rated their mental toughness within the bowling context. They then rated each item on a 5-point scale, ranging from 'strongly disagree' to 'strongly agree'.

Factor analysis of responses to 37 items in the Ten-Pin Bowling Performance Survey yielded five component measures of psychological skills, accounting for 41 per cent of the variance. The scale's third factor was labelled 'mental toughness', and evaluated concentration and coping with pressure during competitive bowling. Five items were positively worded and six items were negatively worded. The 11 items relating to the mental toughness subscale, along with their factor loadings, are shown in Table 4.1.

The mental toughness subscale had a 0.80 coefficient alpha for internal reliability, and a 0.87 test–retest correlation coefficient. Concurrent validity was demonstrated as skilled bowlers rated themselves significantly higher ($p < 0.001$) on mental toughness than their less-skilled counterparts. The efficacy of mental toughness in helping to establish and maintain optimum performance under adverse circumstances is also evident in statements by elite bowlers such as US PBA champions Dick Weber ('every bowler who wins a lot thrives on pressure') and Carmen Salvino ('I love it when I need a double to win'). Successful players like these report that they perform well under pressure, have no difficulty 'handling the pace', can concentrate for extended periods, and often come from behind to win (Herbst, 1986). Thus, prowess at ten-pin bowling is associated with high levels of mental toughness.

Developed by Gershon Tenenbaum and colleagues, the Running Discomfort Scale (Tenenbaum *et al.*, 1999) sought to elicit feelings and thoughts of people engaged in running activities. The final version of the questionnaire consisted of 32 items divided into eight correlated subscales. Mental toughness was the seventh subscale, consisting of items 30 and 31, and had a coefficient alpha of 0.63. These items had factor loadings of 0.79 and 0.75, respectively, accounting for 3.4 per cent variance out of a total 63.6 per cent

Table 4.1 Ten-Pin Bowling Performance Survey mental toughness items

Mental toughness subscale item	Factor loading
Play best under pressure of competition	0.67
Concentration is easily broken	−0.64
Mentally tough competitor at bowling	0.61
Play better at practice than competition	−0.57
Difficulty 'handling the pace' frames 8, 9, 10	−0.55
Come from behind to win a match	0.52
Difficult to refocus attention after distraction	−0.51
Concentrate for extended periods	0.49
Not easily distracted during delivery	0.42
Unsettled by what other players say and do	−0.40
Self-talk during competition is negative	−0.37

Source: Adapted from Thomas *et al.* (1996) reprinted by permission of Taylor & Francis Ltd, www.informaworld.com

variance. The authors defined mentally tough runners as those who were 'psychologically strong' and were capable of 'intense concentration'.

The motivational-affective second-order dimension yielded by Tenenbaum *et al.* (1999) was associated with motivation during the discomfort state; therefore, the authors suggested that: ' "mental toughness" is conceptually associated with this global dimension' (ibid.: 194). Particularly noteworthy from the findings of this study was the assertion that mental toughness had a strategic role: 'Runners in distance races are more concerned with task completion and mental toughness strategies than with physical discomfort symptoms coming from their legs, respiratory system, proprioceptive systems, and head and stomach' (ibid.: 194). The authors concluded that under such conditions of perceived discomfort, the mechanisms for the regulation of pain are more likely to stem from psychological (i.e., mental toughness) than physical bases.

Questionnaires designed specifically to assess mental toughness

The Sports Performance Inventory

The Sports Performance Inventory (SPI; J. W. Jones *et al.*, 2001) is a sport-specific attitudinal measure. Exploratory factor analysis of data from 274 US university athletes on an 83-item survey yielded six interpretable factors; namely: competitiveness, team orientation, emotional control, positive attitude, safety consciousness, and mental toughness. All subscale reliability estimates were 0.79 or higher. However, no further published psychometric data are available for the SPI, and, crucially, there remains the need for the inventory to be subjected to confirmatory factor analyses. Several of the SPI's 17 mental toughness items share features with Loehr's (1986) blueprint. For example, the item 'I have trouble handling the pressure of important competitions' reflects Loehr's *negative energy control* subscale. However, the SPI mental toughness subscale fails to capture the breadth of the constitutive components of mental toughness.

The Mental Toughness 48

The Mental Toughness 48 (MT48; Clough *et al.*, 2002) was developed by Peter Clough and colleagues to operationalise their own 4Cs model of mental toughness. The scale contains 48 items that are scored on a 5-point Likert scale ranging from 'strongly agree' to 'strongly disagree', with an average completion time between 10 and 15 minutes. The MT48 yields scores for overall mental toughness and on each of the inventory's four subscales; namely:

commitment, control, challenge, and confidence. The first three components of the MT48 reflect the authors' attempt to define mental toughness within the theoretical framework of Kobasa's (1979) hardiness.

The instrument has gained increasing popularity as a measure of mental toughness (e.g., R. J. Simpson, Gray, & Florida-James, 2006; T. B. Walker, Lennemann, McGregor, Mauzy, & Zupan, 2011). However, as only minimal psychometric information is available, its usefulness is questionable. The instrument has an overall test–retest coefficient of 0.90, with the internal consistency of the subscales found to be 0.71, 0.73, 0.71, and 0.80 for commitment, control, challenge, and confidence, respectively. Alongside the MT48, Clough *et al.* (2002) developed the MT18 (a shorter 18-item version), 'to make it more accessible and usable for the end-user (sports people)' (ibid.: 39). The two instruments have shown a strong correlation ($r = 0.87$; Clough *et al.*, 2002). However, the MT18 provides only an overall score for mental toughness and not a profile of subscales, as with the MT48.

The MT48 has recently been refined and relabelled as the MTQ48. The modifications apply to the control and confidence subscales; that is, emotional control and life control, and interpersonal confidence and confidence in abilities. Using the updated instrument on a non-sport sample of 544 participants, an overall coefficient alpha of 0.89 for the scale was reported (Marchant, Clough, Polman, Levy, & Strycharczyk, 2007). In a subsequent study, again utilising a non-sport sample, the responses of 522 employees yielded an overall coefficient alpha of 0.89, with each subscale above 0.70 (Marchant, Polman, Clough, Jackson, Levy, & Nicholls, 2009). Crust (2009) reported a good overall coefficient alpha (0.86) for the scale from a sample of 112 sport participants. Adam Nicholls and co-workers have published separate papers using the same data (Nicholls *et al.*, 2008; Nicholls, Polman, Levy, & Backhouse, 2009). Using a sample of 677 athletes, they reported an overall coefficient alpha of 0.87 for the scale, with individual subscales ranging from 0.58 to 0.71, suggesting only satisfactory reliability (Kline, 2005). Using a sample of 110 male athletes, Crust and Swann (2011) reported an overall coefficient alpha of 0.90, with four subscales ranging between 0.70 and 0.77, but two, emotional control and life control, showed reliability only at 0.45 and 0.50, respectively. The study's authors, however, acknowledged the low sample size. On a sample of 482 athletes, Kaiseler *et al.* (2009) reported an overall coefficient alpha of 0.92, with five subscales ranging between 0.69 and 0.80, but one, emotional control, showing reliability only at 0.55. These researchers recalculated the alpha coefficient for this subscale employing the iterative deletion of items. Two items were removed, resulting in an improved coefficient alpha of 0.68 for the emotional control subscale. Thus, it would appear that the MTQ48 emotional control subscale contains unreliable items and is not yet finalised. Further studies need to show that the scale should retain its 48 items, or, as Kaiseler *et al.* discovered, whether it would be better to delete or re-word some items.

Whether as the original (MT48) or the modified (MTQ48) version, there is little published evidence of the scale's psychometric properties. Although the construct (MT48, Clough *et al.*, 2002; MTQ48, Nicholls *et al.*, 2008, 2009), and criterion (MT48, Clough *et al.*, 2002; Crust & Clough, 2005; MTQ48, Crust & Azadi, 2010; Marchant *et al.*, 2007) validity of both versions appear to have been established, to date, other than reliability analyses, there is scant published independent research examining the instrument's psychometric properties. Its factor structure, in particular, has not been rigorously scrutinised using exploratory and confirmatory techniques. Further, the scale's authors offered comparatively little rationale for the association with hardiness, which, ultimately, is the basis for the instrument's subscales.

The Mental Toughness Inventory

The Mental Toughness Inventory (MTI; S. C. Middleton, Marsh, Martin, Richards, & Perry, 2004b), developed by Cory Middleton and co-workers, is a 67-item instrument that measures 12 components of mental toughness alongside global mental toughness. The authors piloted the questionnaire that operationalised their definition of mental toughness (S. C. Middleton *et al.*, 2004a). S. C. Middleton *et al.* (2004b) recruited 479 elite student athletes to complete the pilot MTI (117 items). A series of confirmatory factor analyses produced the 12-factor 67-item scale. A 5-item-per-factor solution yielded the best fit [RMSEA = 0.065, TLI = 0.973, RNI = 0.975]. The reliability coefficients for each of the factors ranged from 0.87 to 0.95. Each of the 12 factors correlated strongly with global mental toughness, with correlation coefficients ranging from $r = 0.45$ to $r = 0.87$. The MTI appears to have been developed from a sound theoretical base and has been evaluated via a construct validation framework. Researchers have used the scale to examine the relationship between mental toughness attributes and changes in stress-recovery imbalance associated with a competition break (Tibbert, Morris, & Andersen, 2009). However, few other details of the scale are available. Moreover, that the scale has been validated using only elite sport high school athletes with a mean age of just 14 years (range 12 to 19 years) appears to be a limitation. Further testing of the MTI is needed to determine its predictive validity (e.g., elite vs. non-elite athletes).

The Mental Toughness Scale

Designed by Andrew Lane and colleagues, the Mental Toughness Scale (MTS; Lane *et al.*, 2007) was developed from qualitative data from elite athletes and was an attempt to capture the nature of mental toughness as described by G. Jones and co-workers (2002). In addition, the study attempted to pursue Graham Jones' argument that mental toughness hinges on a sophisticated understanding of emotional intelligence, and that 'people who perform to a very high level have acute awareness' (as cited in Wark, 2003). The result was a 27-item measure in which items were rated on a 7-point Likert scale, anchored by 'not at all' and 'very much so'. Forward multiple regression indicated that optimism, social skills, and appraisal of one's own emotions accounted for 60 per cent of the variance in mental toughness, as measured by the MTS. However, only 75 participants completed the inventory. Also, other than correlations with a measure of emotional intelligence, the authors, to date, fail to report any further details of the scale's psychometric properties.

The Australian football Mental Toughness Inventory

Created by Daniel Gucciardi and co-workers, the Australian football Mental Toughness Inventory (AfMTI; Gucciardi, Gordon, & Dimmock, 2009b) is a 24-item scale that measures four components of mental toughness in Australian Rules football; namely: *thrive through challenge* (which relates to dealing with, and thriving when challenged by, external and internal forces), *sport awareness* (which relates to an understanding of individual and team performances), *tough attitude* (which describes attitudes directed towards becoming the best one can be), and *desire success* (which relates to achieving individual and team success). Preliminary data on the factor structure, internal reliability, and construct validity of the scale were encouraging. The authors also found no evidence that the football players sampled were giving socially desirable responses (Gucciardi *et al.*, 2009b).

Further studies of youth-aged Australian Rules footballers reported subscale coefficients alpha greater than 0.70 (Gucciardi, 2010) and, more specifically, ranging from 0.67 to 0.93, with a mean of 0.84 (Gucciardi, Gordon, & Dimmock, 2009c), indicating adequate to good internal consistency. However, confirmatory analysis using a sample of 350 male footballers found no psychometric support for the *a priori* model of the AfMTI (Gucciardi, 2009). Although support was found for a revised version of the AfMTI, the scale's author admits that: 'Further research is required to cross-validate the results of this study with a greater variety of Australian footballers' (ibid.: 988). Clearly, further and more stringent psychometric examinations must be conducted before the revised AfMTI can be considered a useful tool for measuring mental toughness. It must be stressed also that the scale has been designed for use solely in the domain of Australian Rules football.

The Cricket Mental Toughness Inventory

The Cricket Mental Toughness Inventory (CMTI; Gucciardi & Gordon, 2009) is the result of a mixed-method research design involving qualitative and quantitative data collection and analyses. Perceptions of current and retired cricketers generated a qualitative item pool, from which was created a quantitative 15-item instrument scale that measures five factors of mental toughness in cricket; namely: affective intelligence, attentional control, resilience, self-belief, and desire to achieve. The authors conducted confirmatory factor analyses using three independent samples of cricketers from several different countries. Preliminary data on the factor structure, internal reliability, and construct validity of the CMTI are promising. The scale correlated positively with dispositional flow, hardiness, and resilience, and showed a negative relationship with athlete burnout. Further research has lent additional support to the scale's psychometric properties (Gucciardi, 2011). Again, as with the AfMTI, replication and more stringent psychometric examinations must be conducted before the CMTI can be considered a useful tool for measuring mental toughness. It needs reiterating that both the AfMTI (Australian Rules football) and the CMTI (cricket) reflect the authors' attempts to measure mental toughness distinctly in exclusive sports, and, *de facto*, are only applicable as indices of mental toughness measurement solely in those contexts.

The Mental, Emotional, and Bodily Toughness Inventory

The Mental, Emotional, and Bodily Toughness Inventory (MeBTough), developed by Mack and Ragan (2008), is a 43-item scale based entirely on Loehr's (1986) definition of mental toughness. Items are scored on a 7-point Likert scale and include: 'negative emotions are hard to change', 'competitive circumstances affect me', 'I display confidence/energy', and 'I compete fully recovered'. Preliminary Rasch analysis demonstrated a good model–data fit (Mack & Ragan). However, the sample of 261 undergraduate students is below the recommended minimum for such analysis (Tabachnick & Fidell, 2007). In addition, there remains ambiguity as to whom the inventory is targeted. Mack and Ragan intimate that though the instrument is of 'great interest to those helping individuals perform and comply with rehabilitation', future researchers ought to focus on 'developing more specific items that are tailored to the early stages of rehabilitation to better measure and ultimately serve our patients' (Mack & Ragan: 131). The authors need to state clearly whether the MeBTough is an inventory designed solely to measure mental toughness in injury rehabilitation contexts. Moreover, irrespective of context, the instrument needs to be subjected to thorough exploratory and confirmatory analysis techniques before it can be recommended as an index for assessing mental toughness.

Loehr's blueprint revisited

The Psychological Performance Inventory

The above findings reflect the difficulties researchers have encountered in their endeavours to construct a psychometrically sound measurement of mental toughness. As evidenced by the aforementioned efforts of Mack and Ragan (2008), particularly influential in the area of mental toughness research is Jim Loehr's (1986) frequently cited monograph, *Mental toughness training for sports: Achieving athletic excellence*, and his Psychological Performance Inventory (PPI). However, despite its ongoing influence on both research and practice, minimal rigorous evaluation has been conducted on the psychometric properties of the PPI. In trying to define mental toughness, Loehr interviewed hundreds of athletes who gave surprisingly similar accounts of their experiences prior to and during peak performance.

Personality characteristics such as a high level of resolution, a refusal to be intimidated, an ability to stay focused, a capacity for retaining an optimum level of arousal, an eagerness to compete, an unyielding attitude when being beaten, and an inflexible insistence on finishing a contest rather than conceding defeat emerged from the interviews. Subsequent analysis yielded seven subscales of mental toughness; namely: self-confidence, negative energy control, attention control, visualisation and imagery control, motivation, positive energy, and attitude control. The resultant PPI was one of the first instruments to include specific cognitive-behavioural and self-evaluation dimensions.

The inventory was developed to assess 'mental strengths and weaknesses' (Loehr, 1986: 157) and to improve athletes' awareness and understanding of their mental skills. Although Loehr offered a persuasive discussion of the instrument and the rationale for its seven subscales, the conceptual and theoretical basis for the instrument was not strong and, in particular, he presented no psychometric support for its use. In fact, though the PPI remains a promising tool for use in the assessment and potential development of mental toughness and continues to be used in research (e.g., T. W. Allen, 1988; Dongsung & Kang-Heon, 1994; Hanrahan, Grove, & Lockwood, 1990; Kang-Heon, Dongsung, Myung-Woo, & Elisa, 1994; Kuan & Roy, 2007; Nizam, Omar-Fauzee, & Abu Samah, 2009), to date, only limited research has been conducted on its reliability and validity.

Psychometric analyses of the PPI

To date, there are only two published studies which have examined the psychometric properties of Loehr's (1986) PPI (Golby, Sheard, & van Wersch, 2007; S. C. Middleton *et al.*, 2004c). Neither study found support for the instrument's structural validity using exploratory (Golby *et al.*) or confirmatory (S. C. Middleton *et al.*) factor analyses. However, the Middleton *et al.* study should be viewed as preliminary since it contained a number of limitations; namely: the sample size used could only be described as 'fair' (Comrey & Lee, 1992), as fewer participants ($N = 263$) were recruited than are generally recommended for factor analysis (Tabachnick & Fidell, 2007); further, and potentially problematic with regard to external validity, was the young mean age of the participants (14 years); Golby and co-workers recruited 408 sport performers with a mean age of 24 years.

Construction of a revised model

The alternative 5-factor 16-item mental toughness structure suggested by S. C. Middleton *et al.* (2004c) did not include a measure of self-confidence or an appealing measure of control – two mental toughness characteristics identified in earlier chapters. Therefore, Golby *et al.* (2007) extended S. C. Middleton and co-workers' earlier psychometric work on the PPI by successfully developing a multidimensional questionnaire designed to assess mental toughness in the athletic domain. From their exploratory analysis of the PPI, Golby and co-workers ultimately yielded four factors of mental toughness; these were labelled determination, self-belief, positive cognition, and visualisation. The revised instrument was named the PPI-A. Additional analyses beyond those conducted by S. C. Middleton *et al.* were used to investigate the factor structure of the PPI-A.

Golby and co-workers (2007) appear to be the first researchers looking at a psychometrically acceptable measure of mental toughness to employ higher-order factor analysis. This procedure takes into account the reality of correlated factors by allowing the extraction of variance accounted for by the general higher-order factor 'g' (Carretta & Ree, 2001; B. Thompson, 2004). The remaining variance, which is free of all variance present in the g factor (e.g., mental toughness), is then assigned to the already identified first-order factors. This has the benefit of reducing the first-order factors to residual factors uncorrelated with each other and with the higher-order factor. The residualised domain-specific factor loading of each variable can be specified by partialing out the variable's g loading and uniqueness. Therefore, each factor represents the independent contribution of the factor in question. This transformation is achieved by the Schmid–Leiman procedure (Schmid & Leiman, 1957), a technique strongly recommended for higher-order model solutions prior to model solution interpretations (Gignac, 2007). Schmid–Leiman results suggested evidence of both a general mental toughness factor, as well as the four previously mentioned first-order factors (see Figure 4.1). Finally, model fit was assessed using confirmatory factor analysis, and both absolute and incremental fit indices showed good support for the correlated 4-factor PPI-A model. The PPI-A inventory is shown in Table 4.2.

Subsequent research appears to have supported the sound psychometric properties of the PPI-A (Sheard, 2009b). However, a potential limitation of the 4-factor PPI-A is that it does not include a measure of control, a characteristic routinely identified in the mental toughness literature (see Clough *et al.*, 2002; G. Jones *et al.*, 2002; Thelwell *et al.*, 2005). The original PPI negative energy control and attention control subscales were structurally weak and, as a result of rigorous exploratory analysis in the Golby *et al.* (2007) study, did not have a sufficient number of items for confirmatory factor analysis. Given that good attentional control is inextricably linked with good emotional control (Thomas, Murphy, & Hardy, 1999), the next stage was to develop a scale that includes a *control* subscale capable of measuring athletes' anxiety and coping response.

The Sports Mental Toughness Questionnaire

Adopting a mixed-methodology approach, Sheard, Golby, and van Wersch (2009) have developed the first psychometrically acceptable measure of mental toughness (namely, the Sports Mental Toughness Questionnaire [SMTQ]) that includes a *control* subscale. To begin the process of construct validation, the authors of the scale used the raw data themes and quotes from qualitative studies (e.g., S. J. Bull *et al.*, 2005; Clough *et al.*, 2002; Fourie & Potgieter, 2001; D. Gould *et al.*, 2002; G. Jones *et al.*, 2002; Loehr, 1986; Thelwell *et al.*, 2005) to develop a corpus of sport-relevant items. An initial pool of 53 items was administered to five female and five male athletes, and to 10 coaches working in a variety of sports. This panel of experts assessed the initial 53-item pool for comprehensibility by athletes. Using a dichotomous scale (applicable vs. inapplicable), they were instructed to assess the applicability of each item in their respective sport. Using the ratings provided by athletes and coaches, and on their numerous comments, several items were re-written in order to improve their clarity and to broaden their applicability across sports, thus establishing good content validity. Experts involved in previous mental toughness investigations reviewed the resulting bank of items. They retained 18 items.

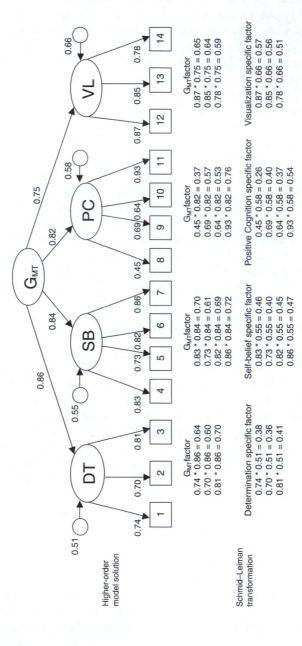

Figure 4.1 The PPI-A model, which includes the higher-order estimates displayed within the figure, as well as the corresponding calculations required for performing the Schmid–Leiman transformation of the higher-order model.

Note: G_{MT} = General Mental Toughness; DT = Determination; SB = Self-belief; PC = Positive Cognition; VL = Visualization.

Source: Adapted from Golby *et al.* (2007).

Table 4.2 PPI-A item wording

		Almost never	Seldom	Sometimes	Often	Almost always
1	The goals I've set for myself as a player keep me working hard	1	2	3	4	5
2	I don't have to be pushed to play or practise hard. I am my own best igniter	1	2	3	4	5
3	I'm willing to give whatever it takes to reach my full potential as a player	1	2	3	4	5
4	I lose my confidence very quickly	5	4	3	2	1
5	I can keep strong positive emotion flowing during competition	1	2	3	4	5
6	I am a positive thinker during competition	1	2	3	4	5
7	My self-talk during competition is negative	5	4	3	2	1
8	I can clear interfering emotion quickly and regain my focus	1	2	3	4	5
9	Playing this sport gives me a genuine sense of joy and fulfilment	1	2	3	4	5
10	I can change negative moods into positive ones by controlling my thinking	1	2	3	4	5
11	I can turn crisis into opportunity	1	2	3	4	5
12	I mentally practise my physical skills	1	2	3	4	5
13	Thinking in pictures about my sport comes easy for me	1	2	3	4	5
14	I visualise working through tough situations prior to competition	1	2	3	4	5

Note: Items 1–3 measure Determination; 4–7 measure Self-belief; 8–11 measure Positive Cognition; 12–14 measure Visualisation.

Determination and Visualisation scores range from 3–15; Self-belief and Positive Cognition scores range from 4–20; Composite scores range from 14–70.

Source: Adapted from Golby *et al.* (2007).

The second stage of construct validation involved 633 performers, with a mean age of 22 years, drawn from 25 sport classifications, and competing at international, national, county and provincial, or club and regional standards, completing the SMTQ during training camps. Principal axis factoring analysis yielded a 3-factor 14-item model, which explained 40.7 per cent of the variance. The factors correspond meaningfully with the definitions of mental toughness within the extant literature: confidence (vs. self-doubt), constancy (vs. irresolute), and control (vs. agitation) are themes, as covered in Chapter 2, encountered frequently in qualitative studies (see S. J. Bull *et al.*, 2005; Clough *et al.*, 2002; Fourie & Potgieter, 2001; D. Gould *et al.*, 2002; G. Jones *et al.*, 2002; Thelwell *et al.*, 2005), and Loehr's (1986) mental toughness blueprint. Moreover, the SMTQ is the only psychometrically acceptable mental toughness instrument that includes a measure of emotional and negative energy control.

The third construct validation stage involved using an independent sample of 509 athletes, with a mean age of 20 years, competing at the aforementioned standards, and representative of 26 sports, to complete the 3-factor 14-item SMTQ. A single factor underlying mental toughness (G_{MT}) was identified with higher-order exploratory factor analysis using the Schmid–Leiman procedure (see Figure 4.2). Further, the three factors extracted in the exploratory analysis exhibited good internal consistency with each independent sample used in this study ($\alpha \geq 0.70$; Coaley, 2010; Furr & Bacharach, 2008; Kline, 2005) – Study 1: Confidence = 0.80, Constancy = 0.74, Control = 0.71; Study 2: Confidence = 0.79, Constancy = 0.76, Control = 0.72).

Confirmatory analysis using structural equation modelling confirmed the overall structure of the SMTQ. The oblique 3-factor model yielded absolute fit indices that indicated a good model fit: χ^2 (74, N = 509) = 182.56, $p < 0.01$, χ^2/df = 2.47, GFI = 0.95, AGFI = 0.93, RMSEA = 0.05, RMR = 0.05. Similarly, the incremental fit indices indicated good support for the model: TLI = 0.91, CFI = 0.92, IFI = 0.93. Divergent validity was demonstrated by the observed pattern of weak to moderate correlations between the SMTQ and the hardiness PVS III-R (Maddi & Khoshaba, 2001; r range = 0.14–0.33), dispositional optimism LOT-R (Scheier, Carver, & Bridges, 1994; r range = 0.23–0.38), and affect PANAS (Watson, Clark, & Tellegen, 1988; Watson, Wiese, Vaidya, & Tellegen, 1999; r range = 0.12–0.49) subscales.

Finally, subgroup differences relative to competitive standard, gender, and age indicated some variation in mental toughness levels, revealing that the SMTQ appears to possess good discriminative power. The implication of these findings is that, first, and subject to further validation, different sets of norms may need to be developed. And, second, in addition to the many attributes requisite to outstanding sport performance, a psychological profile that includes high levels of mental toughness appeared to distinguish

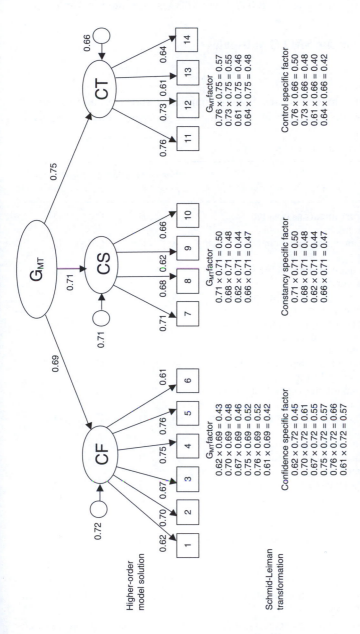

Figure 4.2 The SMTQ model, which includes the higher-order estimates displayed within the figure, as well as the corresponding calculations required for performing the Schmid–Leiman transformation of the higher-order model.

Note: G_{MT} = General Mental Toughness; CF = Confidence; CS = Constancy; CT = Control.

Source: Adapted from Sheard *et al.* (2009).

older, male performers operating at the highest competitive standard (i.e., international) (Sheard *et al.*, 2009). The SMTQ is presented in Table 4.3.

Rationale for the SMTQ subscales

Confidence

That six items loaded on the SMTQ confidence subscale, and explained most of the scale's variance in its development, corroborates the findings of

Table 4.3 SMTQ item wording

		Very true	Mostly true	A little true	Not at all true
1	I interpret threats as positive opportunities	A	B	C	D
2	I have an unshakeable confidence in my ability	A	B	C	D
3	I have qualities that set me apart from other competitors	A	B	C	D
4	I have what it takes to perform well while under pressure	A	B	C	D
5	Under pressure, I am able to make decisions with confidence and commitment	A	B	C	D
6	I can regain my composure if I have momentarily lost it	A	B	C	D
7	I am committed to completing the tasks I have to do	A	B	C	D
8	I take responsibility for setting myself challenging targets	A	B	C	D
9	I give up in difficult situations	A	B	C	D
10	I get distracted easily and lose my concentration	A	B	C	D
11	I worry about performing poorly	A	B	C	D
12	I am overcome by self-doubt	A	B	C	D
13	I get anxious by events I did not expect or cannot control	A	B	C	D
14	I get angry and frustrated when things do not go my way	A	B	C	D

Note: Items 1–6 measure Confidence; 7–10 measure Constancy; 11–14 measure Control.

Confidence scores range from 6–24; Constancy and Control scores range from 4–16; Composite scores range from 14–56.

Items 1–8 are positively scored (i.e., A = 4, B = 3, C = 2, D = 1). Items 9–14 are negatively scored (i.e., A = 1, B = 2, C = 3, D = 4).

Source: Adapted from Sheard *et al.* (2009).

previous research (Gucciardi *et al.*, 2008; G. Jones *et al.*, 2002; Thelwell *et al.*, 2005), which reported the emergence of high self-confidence and self-belief as the most important attributes of mentally tough performers. The six items in this subscale stress the importance of athletes having belief in their ability to achieve their goals and believing that they are different to and, crucially, better than their opponents. SMTQ confidence comprised items tapping similar self-regulatory feelings such as self-belief and staying positive, especially when facing challenging and pressured situations, as highly competitive sport often presents. SMTQ confidence reflects self-efficacy theory in that the subscale is concerned with the independent effects of positive self-perception on real-life outcomes, irrespective of performers' 'actual' competence. Mentally tough athletes have a raging belief in their ability, especially under pressure. Further, SMTQ confidence taps into the suggestion of Cioffi (1991) that though a situation may be viewed as poten-tially difficult, the efficacious individual displays stoic mental toughness and simply persists in the face of it. Thus, confidence is 'an acceptable conceit tailored to a specific end' (Garside, 2010: S21).

Implicit in SMTQ confidence is that athletes high in this attribute have a competitive, authoritative, and commanding presence. In response to Olympic champion Michael Johnson's question – 'Will they only battle for second, go after [Usain] Bolt, or allow Bolt's presence and dominance to shatter their own belief in themselves?' (Johnson, 2009b: S14) – performers high in SMTQ confidence would harness their self-belief and meet the chal-lenge. They would not shy away from expecting to beat the best. Such competitors would possess a mindset that includes an air of confidence, not misplaced arrogance. As Michael Phelps states: 'If you have done the right things in practice, and if you have done them over and over so often they have lodged inside your mind and body, you ought to have complete confi-dence in your abilities' (as cited in Syed, 2009g: 59).

The power of an athlete's presence should not be underestimated. Mentally tough performers have an authoritative demeanour. Opponents can be quick to pick up on submissive body language, such as slumped shoulders or a drop of the head. The projected image is key. Opponents can be unsettled by the confidence emanating from a competitor. The import-ance of confidence and self-belief cannot be overstated (see Barbour & Orlick, 1999: 23–24; Weissensteiner, Abernethy, & Farrow, 2009: 286). About his admiration of Andrew Flintoff, former Australian wicketkeeper Adam Gilchrist stated that: 'He is in your face, but not recklessly so. And he just creates the aura that he's in control' (as cited in Briggs, 2009b: S13). While of the redoubtable former West Indies cricketer Sir Vivian Richards it has been written: 'He would saunter to the wicket like a gladiator entering the arena without a thought of failure' (as cited in Martin-Jenkins, 2009:

60). I can still visualise him stepping across his crease, yet gently, almost effortlessly, easing the final ball – that had been arrowed at the exposed stumps – of the West Indies innings in the 1979 World Cup final high into the Mound Stand at Lord's for yet another six. Majestic!

Thus, as constitutive of mental toughness, confidence is considered a cause, rather than a consequence, of high performance. As Chamorro-Premuzic and Furnham stated: 'The idea that confidence may affect an individual's performance has existed so long that it seems irrelevant to date it' (2006: 769). Mentally tough athletes are awash with a rigorous self-belief. The consequences of their not being so is summed up by Ireland international rugby union footballer Rob Kearney: 'I find I play my best rugby when I'm confident. When I start to doubt myself that's when things start to go wrong' (as cited in Kitson, 2009b: 10). There is a substantial theoretical overlap between the concepts of confidence and self-efficacy, notably the emphasis on the self-fulfilling effects of subjective evaluations – regardless of their accuracy – as determinants of actual performance. As the incomparable Muhammad Ali said: 'I am a great golfer, I just haven't played the game yet' (as cited in Goodbody, 2002: 32). Unshakeable self-belief!

Constancy

This factor reflects athletes' determination to meet the demands of training and competition, willingness to take responsibility for setting training and competition goals, possession of an unyielding attitude, and an ability to concentrate. Mentally tough performers recognise that they must take responsibility for their training and competition performances. They recognise also that, ultimately, in performance, they are on their own. Implicit in SMTQ constancy is the assumption that without ownership there is no responsibility. In comparing Formula One driver Jenson Button with Michael Schumacher, the comments of Ross Brawn, team principal of Brawn GP, resonated with mental toughness constancy: 'What I see in Jenson is the dedication, the commitment, the focus . . . There's also the winning mentality. Michael acquired it and Jenson is getting it' (as cited in Gorman, 2009a: 63). Indeed, Button himself stated: 'Every time you take to the track, it's a non-stop challenge which requires you to maintain absolute focus, concentration and precision' (as cited in Cary, 2009: S16). This attitude of taking ownership of whatever is required to succeed is reflected also in the comments of Olympic and Tour de France cyclist Mark Cavendish: 'Part of what makes me so successful, is that I never settle on anything I've achieved. I always set my next target' (as cited in McRae, 2009c: 6).

SMTQ constancy also taps into athletes' preparedness to focus, to show grit, and to not give up in the face of adversity. These items reflect the association between successful athletes' tendency to keep a more task-oriented focus of concentration and avoid preoccupation with negative outcomes, which may otherwise increase the likelihood of reducing effort or even quitting (J. M. Williams & Krane, 2001). This very much reflects the mental toughness described by former Australia cricket captain Steve Waugh, who stated that: 'The arts of concentration and discipline were a part of my game. These two attributes form the nucleus of mental toughness' (Waugh, 2006: 23–24). Continuous attention is a matter of mental discipline. Unless athletes wish to be at the mercy of every passing distraction, they must learn how to hold the mind to its task. Athletes scoring highly in constancy are predicted to be more able to maintain their focus, particularly when faced with provocation. The deliberate mental disintegration tactic of 'sledging' (i.e., verbally abusing and insulting opponents) has, sadly, become widespread and socially acceptable in sport (see Syed, 2012a), most notably cricket (Barnes, 2008a, 2008b, 2008f). Banter is fine; sledging is puerile, offensive, and unacceptable. Mentally tough athletes high in constancy cope with intimidating bitter invective hurled their way. Moreover, mentally tough sportspeople have no need of it in the first place, supported by former England cricket captain Mike Atherton's belief that: 'Toughness has nothing to do with staring, sledging or ganging up on the opposition. It has everything to do with an ability to execute hard-won skills under maximum pressure' (Atherton, 2009h: 64). An unsavoury and pitiful spokesperson for the modern competitive struggle, sledging is shameful and loathsome. Mentally tough athletes should not feel the need to resort to abuse opponents.

Control

Perceived control, the perception that one can bring about a desired outcome, is regarded by some as a fundamental human need and a central component of psychological health. People who believe they have control over events in their lives feel better about themselves, cope better with adversity and life crises, and perform better on various cognitive tasks, as compared to those who have less feeling of control. The notion of perceived control is reflected in various theoretical constructs, such as locus of control (Rotter, 1954), health locus of control (Wallston, 1989), self-efficacy (Bandura, 1997), and hardiness (Kobasa, 1979).

SMTQ control addresses the omission of a similar subscale in the PPI-A, the only other published psychometrically acceptable measure of mental toughness. Keeping emotions in control and remaining calm and relaxed under pressured situations (Côté, 2002), plus a capacity to regain psychological control following unexpected, uncontrollable events (G. Jones *et al.*, 2002), are consistently reported attributes of mental toughness. The adverse repercussions of failing to do this in both individual (see Sheard, 2003) and team (see Greenwood, 2009a; Dickinson, 2012; Hayward, 2012; Souster, 2012a) sports are well documented.

Performers high in SMTQ control are able to control their emotions and frustrations at not getting everything their own way. Such athletes are also more disposed to let go of things they are less able to control. Here are two examples from tennis – ahead of winning the 2010 US Open, Belgian tennis star Kim Clijsters said: 'I've been improving every match. The pressure is a privilege' (as cited in Mitchell, 2010: 11); and similarly, Roger Federer's admission of the nerves that sometimes afflict him and that athletes' arrangements sometimes do not go to plan, but one must accept this, take it in one's stride, and get on with it: 'It can be a feeling you have deep within yourself. You think "OK, I'm nervous, I don't know why". You can't sleep well, you don't manage to eat well, you feel a bit dizzy, and you don't know exactly why. There are days like that on the tour. That happens' (as cited in Chadband, 2009b: S16). Mentally tough athletes realise that they have to accept the circumstances. It is impossible to beat an opponent and the circumstances. A high level of SMTQ control may very well be the antidote to adrenalin tending to play havoc with discipline.

Recent developments

I have extended previous psychometric work on the PPI-A and the SMTQ (Sheard, 2008b). See Appendix A for this work, which was presented at the 14th European Conference on Personality in Tartu, Estonia.

Conclusion

We are all fellow travellers on the road to enlightenment, searching for the most parsimonious explanation of a complex and elusive concept and, ultimately, a measure of it. After all, it is one thing to measure mental toughness, yet quite another to value it. In the spirit of positive psychology, I advocate the use of the most psychometrically robust measures available to identify not only specific weaknesses, but also strengths, on which sport and exercise psychologists can concentrate. There now exist reliable and valid measures of mental toughness. For example, the widely used sport-general MTQ48, though needing to undergo published rigorous psychometric scrutiny, looks promising (see Clough & Strycharczyk, 2012); while the preliminary findings on the psychometric properties of the sport-specific CMTI (cricket) and the revised AfMTI (Australian Rules football) are very encouraging.

However, at long last, after much conceptual debate, researchers have finally developed what appear to be psychometrically acceptable multi-factorial measures of mental toughness; namely: the PPI-A and the SMTQ. Each is a concise 14-item scale that demonstrably taps into the very characteristics that have been routinely identified in the qualitative literature. Collectively, satisfying confirmatory factor analysis absolute and incremental fit index benchmarks, and showing support for the instruments' reliability, and divergent and differential validity, rigorous psychometric testing has revealed favourable construct validation features of the PPI-A and the SMTQ. Most recently, Crust and Swann (2011) conducted a reliability analysis of the SMTQ. Coefficients alpha for the overall scale (0.81) and the confidence subscale (0.81) were good. The constancy (0.56) and control (0.60) subscales were adequate, given the study's sample size ($N = 110$). Additional studies have also reported supporting data for the psychometric properties of the PPI-A and the SMTQ (Chen & Cheesman, in press; Golby & Meggs, 2011). To date, the PPI-A and the SMTQ are the only published mental toughness instruments that have been subjected to rigorous exploratory and confirmatory analysis techniques, satisfying their stringent criteria. Thus, each instrument has demonstrably acceptable psychometric properties.

Mindful that construct validation is an ongoing process, a number of research projects are in progress using, in particular, the PPI-A and the SMTQ with performers, coaches, and officials across a diverse range of sports. Particularly noteworthy, in collaboration with researchers around the world, work has begun on the translation of each scale into different languages; notably: Afrikaans, French, German, Japanese, Portuguese, and Turkish. These studies aimed at further validation will enhance the efficacy of each scale in practical and research settings. The PPI-A and the SMTQ are strongly advocated as valuable research tools for use in psychological interventions.

As Richard Dawkins (1989) points out, we face a danger of reification in many academic areas. Words are only tools for our use; their mere presence in dictionaries, separate or compounded, like 'mental' and 'toughness', does not mean they necessarily have to refer to something definite in the real world. Karl Popper (1959) advanced the view that all scientific knowledge is conjectural, and that falsifiability rather than verifiability is the test of scientific validity. Ultimately, all psychological measures are theory-laden, and theories, rather than being objective, reflect the integrity of their formulators. In such a spirit, practitioners must await future research to demonstrate weaknesses in the measures.

Of particular note is the burgeoning trend to develop sport-specific measures of mental toughness (e.g., Gucciardi & Gordon, 2009; Gucciardi *et al.*, 2009b). While the PPI-A and the SMTQ are sport-general measures of mental toughness, the CMTI and the AfMTI, for example, are sport-specific instruments to be used exclusively in cricket and Australian Rules football, respectively. Exponents of sport-specific measures have suggested that sport-general measures may not adequately capture context-specific components of mental toughness that reflect shared knowledge within a sport's culture (Gucciardi & Gordon, 2009; Gucciardi *et al.*, 2009b). Sport-specific instruments may be helpful. However, existing sport-general measures of mental toughness (e.g., MTQ48, PPI-A, SMTQ) would appear to reflect sufficiently the core set of attributes constitutive of a mentally tough mindset, and that attributes specific to any particular sport are on the periphery (Sheard, 2009d).

Regardless of a sport-specific or sport-general perspective, it is clear that the mentally tough athlete possesses, and, crucially, can be measured in, determination/constancy, self-belief/confidence, positive thinking (especially in difficult situations), visualisation, and anxiety/emotional control. In view of the breadth of characteristics encapsulated in the mental toughness mindset, it might be, as Gaudreau and Blondin (2002) reported of athletes' use of coping strategies in sport, that, because of their situation-driven nature and multiple determinants, mental toughness characteristics serve different functions for different individuals in different competitive situations. Given this, it could very well be, as Gucciardi and Gordon (2009) suggest, that the development and validation of sport-specific measures of mental toughness may represent a potentially fruitful avenue of future research. At the very least, sport-general and sport-specific instruments can be utilised complementarily.

Mentally tough performers are able to call on the necessary attributes, whether singly or in combination, when faced with the appropriate circumstance. Their ability to do this cannot be wholly innate. Therefore, it must be learnt. The next chapter addresses the question to which every athlete and coach seeks an answer – How is the mentally tough mindset developed?

5 Developing and maintaining mental toughness

If passion drives you, let reason hold the reins.

Benjamin Franklin

Introduction

We live in pressured, stressful times. We live in an era of unprecedented change. Technological innovation is proceeding at a rate with no parallel in human history. Whether living through this period is any more stressful for us than experiencing the Industrial Revolution or either of the last century's World Wars was for previous generations is highly debatable. The challenges today's sports stars face are slight compared with those of, for example, the legendary Australian cricketer Keith Miller who famously remarked: 'When athletes nowadays talk of pressure they only reveal what they don't know of life' (as cited in Parkinson, 2004: 8). Miller had plenty to talk about and his approach to cricket, as well as life, was shaped during the Second World War, when he flew fighter planes over Europe for the Royal Australian Air Force. Having come through such a terrifying experience it is easy to understand why he felt there was more to life than cricket. Indeed, he had the perfect answer when asked if he ever felt under pressure on the cricket field: 'Pressure, I'll tell you what pressure is. Pressure is a Messerschmitt up your arse, playing cricket is not' (as cited in Fraser, 2004: 58). If only we could have measured his level of mental toughness!

The instant-everything culture

Nowadays, I believe most of us would agree that, largely due to the exponential advancement in communication technologies, the 'instant-everything culture' is omnipresent. The benefit of this advance is our tremendous capability, but the trade-off is an escapable pressure to keep up with continual developments. Moreover, such is the breathless insistence of modern sport that instant success, instant results, and, in some cases, instant fame have fuelled a belief in the possibility of achievement with little effort and exacerbated the cult of celebrity and shallow fame: people becoming famous without necessarily having any talent. We live in a celebrity-obsessed age. A generation reared on the instant fame of reality television, brain cells and imagination zapped by the dross of the 10-minute culture and the black and white Twitter world of 140-character instant opinion. This is particularly prevalent in sport, where accusations of too cosy environments and soft, pampered, and self-indulgent athletes have been criticised for failing to inculcate a culture of mental toughness (Ella, 2009b). What are younger squad members doing signing up for ghosted newspaper columns? First you achieve, then you write something of note. We are bombarded with pageantries of celebrity entitlement and the poison of privilege. The sports broadcast media, in particular, pitch sensationalism and have engendered an age of hype, routinely showering performers with underserved superlatives. As Kevin Garside of *The Daily Telegraph* put it: 'Today's heroes inhabit different turf, removed from our orbit by wealth and status. They live life on a pedestal of our making, ordinary folk with extraordinary gifts elevated to a netherworld of managed celebrity' (2009b: S24). They live in a vacuum.

Interestingly, coaches have reported athletes' lack of mental toughness as a source of their own stress (Thelwell, Weston, Greenlees, & Hutchings, 2008). The study's authors reported that athletes' lack of the attributes associated with mental toughness (e.g., determination, resilience) became stressors for the coaches as they realised that their athletes were unable to cope with the demands of the sport. This was reinforced by one of the coaches in the study: 'With some players, you wonder whether they have really got what it takes, you get the softer players, those who don't give 100 per cent, they are not prepared to get in there, they don't guts it out and get the rewards the hard way' (ibid.: 909–910). Too many athletes have reputations, often inflated by their agents, which are inversely proportionate to the length and breadth of their achievements; they have earned their money and their celebrity too cheaply (see Slot, 2012). For some, even instant gratification is not enough! In effect, they are stress-averse, unwilling to invest in something where their fear of failure is sufficiently great that they fail to recognise that their achieving of anything worthwhile should expose them to some degrees of stress. The alternative is to devalue the currency of the achievement itself.

Athletes must take responsibility for their lifestyles. Concomitant with increased money, fame, and prestige is a rise in personal responsibility. This need for focus, rigorous dedication, and self-discipline is summarised concisely by England rugby union World Cup winner and former team manager Martin Johnson:

I understand the need for balance in life but we judge players on what they do on the rugby field and, also, how they interact with the team off it. The world is tempting and they're signing lucrative contracts at a young age. That's fine but they've got to work for it . . . guys have potential lifestyle issues and we need to say, 'Look, you can have that lifestyle . . . but you'll underachieve'.

(as cited in Jenkins, 2009: 7)

Disappointingly, and with not a little irony, England's subsequent quarter-final exit from the 2011 Rugby World Cup was mired as much in off-field player ill-discipline and unacceptable behaviour as poor performances on the pitch (see, for example, Clutton, 2011; Conduct Unbecoming, 2011; Flood, 2011; Lanchester, 2011; Peters, 2011; Slot, 2011b; Souster, 2011b; White, 2011b). The fallout from the debacle included Johnson's resignation, but his valedictory comments identified mental toughness as critical: 'There is a nucleus of young players mentally tough enough to become successful international players. They need to be kept together and the culture of rugby first, hard work, fundamental skill development and responsibility needs to be continued' (as cited in Souster, 2011d: 74). Johnson's successor, Stuart Lancaster, recognised the need for players to be mentally tough: 'If people don't tick the character and talent box then there are 100 other players who want to play for England' (as cited in Kitson, 2012a: 8). His preferred type of player epitomises mental toughness: 'fighters not victims, inspiring leaders, good temperaments, fierce competitors, excellent role models, positive decision-makers' (ibid.: 8). Where England failed, the New Zealand All Blacks finally triumphed. Particularly noteworthy were the findings of a comprehensive external audit of the New Zealand players' shortcomings after their 2007 exit: 'leadership and mental toughness are the two crucial ingredients underpinning success' (as cited in Ackford, 2011c).

There is a strong argument that many performers are 'given' far too much too early in their careers, that they have not yet worked hard enough to have earned the right to such accolades. Indeed, this is the view of veteran Chelsea and England football player Frank Lampard (more than 90 international appearances), who has been critical of the unwarranted comfort zone and easy lifestyles afforded many young footballers (as cited in Winter, 2009a). This viewpoint is reiterated by fellow footballer Nigel Reo-Coker:

The modern game has changed completely . . . A lot of the younger players now, you would have to question why they play football, whether it is to win trophies or just for the lifestyle and the fast cars and showbiz life . . . It was about respect – and that is the main word that is missing nowadays with the younger generation. Kids are coming in and getting it too good too early. They lose track of reality. And reality comes back to bite them on the arse.

(as cited in S. James, 2011c: 5)

Similar observations have been made in elite Australian rugby league, where, of mental toughness, the National Rugby League (NRL) competition 'has exposed how many rugby league players are lacking in this area ... players are recruited younger and younger these days, with most kids earmarked for a club by their early teens, if not before. I wonder whether it all comes a little too easy, before they develop their fight' (P. Kent, 2011). I call this the 'culture of unearned entitlements'. Particularly resonant is that they have yet to achieve anything in their sports, they have merely got a step on the learning curve. And that is the point: a *learning* curve. Just as athletes learn the physical, physiological, mechanical, technical, and tactical components of their sports, so they must devote significant time to their psychological development. As professional footballer Valon Behrami states: 'When you make technical mistakes you can work on them. Easy. You just keep working hard. But the problem is bigger when it is mental. It is very difficult to work on that' (as cited in D. Kent, 2010). It takes years of training in each of the aforementioned components to reach one's potential. The 'finished article' is not born; it must be developed and maintained. For many performers, failings are not physical or technical, but mental. It is important they recognise and understand this. Humility is the first step in mental toughness progression.

Owners and their teams of coaches must be prepared to invest time and money into the development of their athletes. The right culture must be created, if otherwise talented individuals are not to let themselves down (see Harman, 2008; Hodgkinson, 2008). Underachievers squander their talent and chance. Moreover, athletes themselves must recognise this, and practise patience in regard to the development of their sporting abilities. In addition, the mentally tough mindset must be nurtured. It is increasingly recognised also by governing bodies of sports that, just as there is a need to develop technical and physical competence, there is an additional requirement to develop the necessary mental attributes. For example, the British Equestrian Federation has identified the development of mental toughness in its athletes as crucial to the success of its 'Long-Term Rider Development' programme (C. Wilson, Edwards, & Collins, 2005).

Sport performers need to develop the mindset that affords them the opportunities to meet a challenge and to overcome the difficulties that obstruct their progress (Kuehl, Kuehl, & Tefertiller, 2005). They must have resolve, dedication, courage, and perseverance to increase the likelihood of achieving success. This begins with the 'right' attitude; put simply, athletes must train and compete, having accepted personal responsibility for doing everything within their control to optimise their performance. They cannot expect someone else to do it for them. They must do it for themselves. Within their control are strategies such as positive affirmations, making practice and competition behaviours routine, learning to let go of mistakes, and even looking at failure as a stepping stone to future achievement. As Karl Kuehl and his co-authors wrote:

> Mental toughness is the art of taking control of your life, taking charge of the dynamics around you. No one can ever fully or realistically control the elements of luck, fate, and fortune, but all individuals have the ability to take charge of their lives and prepare themselves to face the most difficult challenges. They can all place themselves in a position to succeed.
>
> (ibid.: xiv)

These behaviours reflect the mentally tough mindset and make it far more likely that such performers will 'step up' successfully.

To demonstrate the point, mental toughness attributes (namely: self-confidence, coping with adversity, activation control) distinguished top-ranked under-19 rugby union players from their lower-ranked counterparts (Andrew, Grobbelaar, & Potgieter, 2007). Similarly, professional rugby league footballers operating at the highest level (i.e., international) possess significantly higher levels of mental toughness than their sub-elite counterparts (Golby & Sheard, 2004). If, as Vince Lombardi said, 'mental toughness is an essential key to success' (as cited in Cadigan, 2008), the likelihood of sporting success is, at least to some extent, dependent on a mentally tough mindset. We can also assume that international-level performers were not as mentally tough in the early stages of their career. Rather, they developed the requisite mental toughness characteristics that contributed to their progression to the sporting summit.

The essentials

Athletes' development of their mental toughness is predicated on the supposition that rational thought processes and self-discipline take precedence over emotional reactions. According to Scarnati (2000), enormous self-discipline and willpower are required. Scarnati's essentials for developing mental toughness require individuals to: develop competence; do the 'right' thing; develop the spiritual as well as the physical you; stay steady, resist pressure, and do quality work; develop a positive sense of worth and self-confidence; conquer emotions with rational thinking; develop persistence and resolve when facing problems; develop career goals; learn to say 'no'; and never empower or enable others to mentally cripple you (ibid.: 174–175). Similar attributes were assessed by Marchant *et al.* (2007) who, from their research of managers in the workplace, concluded that mental toughness has a state tendency, suggesting it has the potential to be trained, and develops with age and managerial responsibilities.

A long-term process

Of his struggle in the 2005 Ashes cricket series, Adam Gilchrist, widely acknowledged as the greatest wicketkeeper batsman in the history of the game, admitted to struggling to regain confidence in his batting:

> It was the first hurdle that I came to in my career that I didn't seem able to be able to climb over. I could almost feel the angst and the stomach churning even through the series, but it was only at the end that I started to get the seeds of doubt in my mind . . . I'm glad it happened at that stage of my career, and not a year or two in, because I might not have been equipped to deal with it.
>
> (as cited in Briggs, 2009b: S13)

His words resonate with the wisdom that mental toughness develops during an athlete's career. Just as you don't judge a champion athlete or team by streaks of brilliance, but, rather, by its longevity, so mental toughness is accumulated over time. Mental toughness is for the long haul.

It would be unrealistic to expect the mentally tough performer to possess characteristics, such as those mentioned by Scarnati (2000) above, without proceeding through developmental stages. Athletes, coaches, parents, and administrators need to realise that, like physical and technical skills, the development of mental toughness requires time and practice. For example, cricketers, coaches, and administrators in Australia considered mental toughness to be an essential contributor to successful batting performance, but, crucially, recognised that it is developed through accumulated experience (Weissensteiner *et al.*, 2009). As one experienced cricket administrator put it: 'Mental toughness is by assessment clearly the distinguishing feature of those who ultimately play at the elite level . . . I think mental toughness is something that actually comes as a result of experience, so to be mentally tough at 13 is not appropriate because it's experiential' (ibid.: 287). Interestingly, the coaches interviewed in the study agreed that being resilient in the face of adversity and setbacks stems from, or is built by, mental toughness.

To expect immediate success is to misunderstand the desired enduring effect of mental skills adoption. Gould and co-workers found that mental skills of the elite develop over extended periods of time and are influenced by a wide range of individuals (e.g., teachers, parents, coaches) (D. Gould *et al.*, 2002). Thelwell, Such, Weston, Such, and Greenlees (2010) determined that mental toughness in elite gymnasts was promoted by sport process (training, competition, and club experiences), sport personnel (relationships with coach and team-mates, rivalries with competitors, and psychological skills taught by sport psychologists), non-sport personnel (the encouragement and emotional support of parents and siblings, and the motivation, emotional support, and belief of significant others), and environment (positive training and family environments, being motivated by other athletes' performances, and sport as a component of national identity). Understanding mental toughness in the context of physical demands and fatigue emerged as a finding from a study of elite youth footballers (Cook, Nesti, & Littlewood, 2010). The authors also reported the importance of self-belief, resilience, and the role of parents in the development of mental toughness.

The responses of retired top world-ranked Australian tennis players revealed that male respondents felt that coaches, sport psychologists, and former elite players are those best equipped to teach mental toughness to aspiring players (J. Young & Pearce, 2010). This was consistent with responses from female participants who extended the nominees to also include parents and fitness advisers. The authors' data analyses also revealed that the teaching of mental toughness involved mastering several challenges, including those of being self-confident, and having sound self-awareness skills, a strong work ethic, and a balanced perspective on development (as opposed to winning). To address these challenges, male participants recommended a range of strategies that included the adoption of routines, visualisation, match plans, breathing techniques, and rigorous training focused on developing a player's strengths. The study's female subjects endorsed these approaches, but also highlighted the need for those teaching mental toughness to consider emotional (e.g., concern with one's body image) and support group factors.

Jean Côté and co-workers (Côté, 1999; Côté, Baker, & Abernethy, 2003, 2007; Côté & Hay, 2002), following investigations of the development of elite Australian and Canadian athletes, proposed a pathway towards elite performance that consists of three developmental stages; namely: the sampling years (childhood, 5–12 years), the specialising years (early-adolescence, 13–15 years), and the investment years (late adolescence, 16+ years). The sampling years are characterised by participation in a wide range of sports with the focus on play and enjoyment. The specialising years typically involve competitive engagement in a limited number of sporting activities, while the investment years are when performers have chosen one particular sport and must demonstrate complete commitment to it.

In a similar vein, Declan Connaughton and colleagues conducted a study with regard to the development of mental toughness and whether it requires maintenance (Connaughton *et al.*, 2008). Seven of the sample used originally by G. Jones *et al.* (2002) participated in semi-structured interviews. Findings indicated that the development of mental toughness is a long-term process that encompasses a multitude of underlying mechanisms that operate in a combined, rather than independent, fashion.

Reflecting Bloom's (1985) three career phases (namely: early, middle, and later years), participants in the Connaughton *et al.* (2008) study perceived mental toughness to develop in stages. In the early years, the experience of critical incidents was felt to have a powerful influence in cultivating mental toughness. The athletes' motivational climate should be challenging, rewarding, and enjoyable. This remained important in the middle and later years, but these subsequent stages were also reported to provide their own unique impression in the development of mental toughness. This suggestion corroborates the finding of Thelwell *et al.* (2005), whose professional football participants attached importance to their environment and experience during their formative years in regard to the development of their mental toughness. In particular, parental influence, childhood background, and transition into an appropriate cricket environment were found to be key environmental influences in the development of mental toughness in international cricketers (S. J. Bull *et al.*, 2005).

The middle years were more competitive for performers in the Connaughton *et al.* (2008) study. Opportunities existed for athletes to learn from significant others (e.g., senior athletes, coaches, parents) and to have a heightened determination to succeed. The later years were alleged to develop mental toughness fully through increased competitive experience and the use of basic and advanced psychological skills and strategies. S. J. Bull *et al.* (2005) suggest that more attention should be devoted to creating tough environments so that participants can learn from their experiences, rather than on formal mental skills training. However, much more empirical work is needed to substantiate the claim. An interesting point in the S. J. Bull *et al.* study was that mentally tough performers reported a sense of being an outsider (i.e., playing cricket in a foreign country) to be important in developing mental toughness. This is corroborated anecdotally in a newspaper interview given by England cricketer Stuart Broad who admitted that: 'My life changed forever the first time I went to the southern hemisphere. It was one of those "I went there a boy and came back a man" experiences' (as cited in McRae, 2009e: 6). Broad was 17 when he went to

Melbourne on his own to play district cricket – and work as a labourer, mixing cement and heaving paving stones. He recollects that the back-breaking work he did in Melbourne was the making of him.

It was also reported by Connaughton *et al.* (2008), reiterated in the findings of a subsequent investigation (Connaughton, Hanton, & Jones, 2010), that once mental toughness had been developed, three perceived underlying mechanisms were required to maintain this mindset; namely: a desire and motivation to succeed that were insatiable and internalised; a support network that included sporting and non-sporting personnel; and the effective use of basic and advanced psychological skills. We have already covered desire and motivation as constituent characteristics of mental toughness. The benefits of a support network of significant others are well established in the literature (see Pargman, 1999; Ray & Wiese-Bjornstal, 1999). We shall turn our attention to the third of Connaughton *et al.*'s (2008) underlying mechanisms – the effective use of psychological skills.

Psychological skills training

In their aforementioned examination of the development and maintenance of mental toughness, Connaughton *et al.* (2008) indicated the use of psychological skills training (PST) to be critical for both aspects. In a qualitative study of US college athletes, the teaching of mental toughness and enhancing athletes' psychological skills emerged as important themes (Butt, Weinberg, & Culp, 2010). Encouraging athletes to use psychological skills during their formative years may promote, for example, better coping skills once they mature (Lane, Harwood, Terry, & Karageorghis, 2004). Well-planned PST programmes are an opportunity to nurture positively young athletes' personal development in competitive sport and to facilitate their growth in other areas of their life by generalising the use of mental skills (Tremayne & Tremayne, 2004). However, despite a wealth of literature citing the benefits of PST programme interventions, and the advocacy of mental toughness training programmes (Hanton, 2008), few studies have measured mental toughness empirically as a specific dependent variable.

Notably, Sheard and Golby (2006a) reported a significant ($p < 0.01$) improvement in levels of mental toughness among a group of 36 national-level swimmers following a 7-week PST programme. The majority of participants ($n = 28$) improved their mental toughness scores post-intervention having been exposed to a programme of goal setting, visualisation, relaxation, concentration, and thought-stopping skills. Interestingly, reflecting that mental toughness is related to general well-being as well as performance, all participants reported the PST intervention as useful and that they would continue to practise the skills contained within the programme for competitive performance and life in general. In particular, the swimmers expressed how the skills learned in the PST programme had benefited other areas of their lives (e.g., school, college, relationships).

Gucciardi *et al.* (2009c) reported a significant ($p < 0.001$) improvement in two of the AfMTI components among youth-aged (under-15s) Australian Rules footballers randomly allocated to one of three discrete groups, two of which received intervention programmes delivered via single, two-hour sessions provided once per week over a 6-week period prior to the competitive season. The third group acted as a control. Participants in both the mental toughness training (MTT) and PST groups scored significantly higher ($p < 0.001$) post-test mean levels of *thrive through challenge* than the control group. The MTT group also scored significantly higher ($p < 0.001$) in *tough attitude* than the control group. The MTT programme content included such core themes as personal and team values, work ethic, self-motivation, self-belief, concentration and focus, resilience, emotional intelligence, sport intelligence, and physical toughness. The PST programme contained themes that included self-regulation, arousal regulation, attentional control, self-efficacy, mental rehearsal, and identification of the ideal performance state. Overall, both intervention groups reported more positive changes in subjective ratings of mental toughness than the control group, suggesting evidence for the efficacy of both packages in enhancing mental toughness. A subsequent qualitative follow-up study by the same authors elicited key stakeholders' (i.e., athletes, coaches, parents) perspectives on the goals, procedures, and results of the mental toughness training intervention (Gucciardi, Gordon, & Dimmock, 2009d). Thematic content analysis yielded several identifiable benefits of the programme, including valuing the importance of quality preparation, being more receptive to criticism, team cohesion, an increased work ethic, tougher attitudes, and the identification and development of transferable skills.

It has been suggested that athletes may neglect PST due to their perception that attributes such as mental toughness are inherent rather than developed (Lane, 2008). Sport psychologists need to work with coaches to counter this misunderstanding. This is particularly important in light of research findings, which may very well be indicative of elsewhere, that more than a quarter of sampled young provincial-level South African netball players indicated average, below average, or poor psychological preparation for competitions (Van den Heever, Grobbelaar, & Potgieter, 2007).

A criticism levelled at some intervention programmes has been that they were not designed to examine mental toughness; rather, they were designed as practical approaches, promoting specific mental skills in order to overcome adversity and improve performance (Connaughton *et al.*, 2008).

However, many of the PST techniques advocated by, for example, Jim Loehr (1986) and Alan Goldberg (1998) have been supported empirically. Significant improvements in mental toughness and swimming performance followed PST interventions underpinned by Loehr's and Goldberg's work (see Sheard & Golby, 2006a). Further, the work of Gucciardi and co-workers (2009c, 2009d) also demonstrates the efficacy of theory-driven intervention programmes. Studies have shown that goal setting is associated with increased well-being and represents an individual's striving to achieve personal self-change, enhanced meaning, and purpose in life (Green, Oades, & Grant, 2006; Sheldon, Kasser, Smith, & Share, 2002). Other research has demonstrated the positive effects of visualisation on other outcome variables, which, as covered in earlier chapters, are conceptually constitutive of mental toughness; for example: self-confidence (Garza & Feltz, 1998; Nordin & Cumming, 2008), self-efficacy (Carboni, Burke, Joyner, Hardy, & Blom, 2002), and decreased anxiety (Vadocz, Hall, & Moritz, 1997). Further, research guided by Paivio's (1985) analytic framework has reported the creation of images related specifically to mental toughness (Hall, Mack, Paivio, & Hausenblas, 1998). Indeed, this mental toughness-enhancing motivational general-mastery imagery type has been shown to be both practised widely and particularly effective across a variety of sports (see Abma, Fry, Li, & Relyea, 2002; Arvinen-Barrow, Weigand, Thomas, Hemmings, & Walley, 2007; Callow, Hardy, & Hall, 2001; J. Cumming & Hall, 2002; Hall *et al.*, 1998; Hardy, Hall, & Hardy, 2004; Harwood, Cumming, & Hall, 2003; McCarthy, 2009; O & Hall, 2009).

Particularly noteworthy is the observation that the most successful PST programmes are those in which sessions are conducted on an individual basis. Participants mentioned this during the social validation component of the Sheard and Golby (2006a) swimming study. Interestingly, Puni (1963) stressed that such psychological preparation for a competition must be individualised and that it be based on the athlete's idiosyncrasies (e.g., temperament, character, motivation, and abilities). Individualisation is a must in team sports as well as individual sports. In their efforts to design systematic programmes to develop collective mental toughness, sport psychology practitioners must remain aware of athletes' individual differences. In team sports, individual preparation should be conducted in the context of psychological preparation of the team as a whole. In addition, it has been suggested that sport psychology practitioners may want to offer PST programmes differently according to the gender of their athletes (Maniar, Curry, Sommers-Flanagan, & Walsh, 2001; Martin *et al.*, 2001). Stating explicitly the phrase 'mental toughness strategies' may be particularly attractive to male athletes who participate in sports that emphasise physical contact, risk taking, and masculinity. The term 'mental toughness' may stimulate such athletes to be more open to seek sport psychology services, to learn mental skills, and to adhere to mental skills training (Martin, 2005).

Finally, there is no reason why coaches, rather than just athletes, should not be equipped with the necessary mental skills to manage the competitive environment. Because coaches are performers also, formal PST and the development of mental toughness may very well help them to cope more effectively with the job's demands (Olusoga, Butt, Hays, & Maynard, 2009). This may be particularly beneficial to coaches at higher competitive levels, with the concomitant persistent stressors of media scrutiny and intrusion.

A force for good in injury or illness rehabilitation?

Injuries are the curse of all sport performers, the recovering from which forces athletes to confront directly their sporting mortality. This is especially difficult given that most athletes, especially those at the highest competitive levels, acquire their sense of identity through sport. A lot of what they determine to be their values are assigned to sport. Returning to sport following a serious injury or illness can be a stressful process for athletes (Bianco, 2001). Returning athletes often experience fears associated with re-injury (Kvist, Ek, Sporrstedt, & Good, 2005; N. Walker, Thatcher, Lavallee, & Golby, 2004) and concerns about their ability to perform up to pre-injury/illness levels (Crossman, 1997; Podlog & Eklund, 2006). These worries were summed up by Arsenal FC defender Johan Djourou: 'You are always thinking: "Am I going to come back to my best level?" Some players come back and are never the same' (as cited in McCarra, 2011b: 12). In addition, there are pressures to meet specific return deadlines (Bauman, 2005; Murphy & Waddington, 2007), and difficulties associated with feelings of alienation from team-mates, coaches, and even oneself (Ermler & Thomas, 1990). As worryingly, there has been an increase in the incidence of serious injury at the elite level, with many athletes (e.g., Andrew Flintoff) admitting to having 'played most of my career in discomfort' (as cited in Briggs, 2009f: S3), culminating in the conclusion that 'a string of injuries has worn him down mentally and physically' (as cited in Kidd, 2009a: 68), and, ultimately, precipitating his premature retirement from Test cricket (O. Gibson, 2009).

For many athletes, pain is a fact of life. Mike Atherton admitted taking a high dosage of a non-steroidal inflammatory drug every day to mask the pain of his back injury: 'When I was 22 . . . the choice for me was simple: find something else to do or be prepared to take painkillers to enable me to have a cricket career' (Atherton, 2011b: 66). In addition, the role of the coach is critical. Good coaches will possess a thorough understanding of the stressors (e.g., physical, social, performance) of returning to sport and recognising the importance of assisting athletes with this transition (Podlog & Eklund, 2007).

If athletes have high mental toughness in the domain of their sport, does this mindset transfer to other fields? Though Sheard and Golby (2006a) showed the transference to different situations of the ameliorative effects of increased mental toughness, high levels of mental toughness in one activity domain are not necessarily accompanied by high mental toughness in other spheres of activity (or inactivity). For example, what does mentally tough mean or involve to an athlete who is severely injured or suffering from a serious health condition? The answer could be different than what it means to a performer who is fully fit and focused on other performance criteria. After all, there is only so much treatment and rehabilitation the human spirit can take. No injured or ill athlete can draw from an infinite well of hope. It is not just physical fitness that is hard to maintain during a lay-off, it is also difficult to remain psychologically positive and constructive. Fighting to keep the mind strong while self-doubt and misery shadow rehabilitation can be a Herculean struggle. The psychological trauma of rebounding from injuries or illness can, eventually, become overwhelming. Mental toughness may need to be developed to improve injury and illness rehabilitation outcome probabilities, as well as the more obvious ameliorative effects in training and competition performance.

In the domain of sport injuries, mental toughness may be justifiably associated with pain tolerance. Throughout their careers, many sport performers are confronted with various situations in which the ability to tolerate pain is extremely important. Moreover, athletes with an ability to withstand a high level of pain are expected to achieve a higher level of performance than performers with low levels of pain tolerance (Whitmarsh & Alderman, 1993). For example, in winning the 2008 US Open Golf Championship despite excruciating pain, and claiming his 14th major title, it was reported that Tiger Woods 'displayed tremendous mental toughness' (Elliott, 2008: 9).

Five of the 12 athletes interviewed by Podlog and Eklund (2006) reported that overcoming injuries enhanced their mental toughness. One of the participants was quoted as saying (ibid.: 62):

At this point, I'd say that [the injury] definitely made me mentally tougher. I've overcome all these questionings of myself which happen probably in the first 2 or 3 or 4 months after the injury. I guess now I'll see it as something bad that's happened but I've overcome it and I think it's made me a stronger person.

The same study found that mental toughness was associated with athletes' greater ability to push through the pain barrier, an increased awareness of the necessary steps required to achieve their goals, and an enhanced sense of confidence in their ability to achieve such goals.

Researchers have found that elite swimmers high in mental toughness reported fewer injuries than less mentally tough individuals competing at the same level (Levy, Clough, Polman, Marchant, & Earle, 2005). The same team of researchers investigated the relationship between mental toughness, sport injury beliefs, pain, and adherence towards a sport injury rehabilitation programme. Using a sample of 70 patients undertaking a sport injury rehabilitation programme for a tendonitis-related injury, they found that high mentally tough individuals displayed more positive threat appraisals and were better able to cope with pain than their less mentally tough counterparts (Levy, Polman, Clough, Marchant, & Earle, 2006). The authors also reported a greater attendance at rehabilitation sessions by more mentally tough individuals. However, more positive behaviour during clinic rehabilitation was characterised by low mental toughness. Levy *et al.* (2006: 252) suggested that this might be due to 'high mentally tough individuals appraising their injury to be less severe and less susceptible to reoccur and thereby perceive compliance to clinic based activity to be less important'. Thus, despite the benefits of being mentally tough, a high degree of mental toughness may have negative consequences upon rehabilitation behaviour and, subsequently, recovery outcomes. Though it would appear that they probably cope better and process pain more effectively, injured performers high in mental toughness could also return prematurely to training or competition. Clearly, there is a need for athletes to develop the appropriate mental toughness attributes to deal more effectively with injury and rehabilitation.

Mental toughness as conceptualised by Sheard *et al.* (2009) would predict adherence to clear plans and goals of a programme of injury or illness rehabilitation. Mentally tough athletes would have clear goals and even clearer restrictions. Such performers would also not use injury or illness as a displacement for poor performance. They will reject the notion that they are merely passive recipients of care; rather, they will demonstrate an active engagement with regard to their rehabilitation programme. Mental toughness ought to increase the likelihood of collaboration, commitment, responsibility, and ownership with regard to any injury or illness rehabilitation programme. High mentally tough performers will move away from the culture of 'no pain, no gain'. For such athletes it will be a case of the appropriate pain for the right amount of gain. I suggest that it takes more mental toughness to say 'I'm not ready', than to jump in too soon and conform to pressure from any prevailing 'sport ethic' environment (R. H. Hughes & Coakley, 1991). Such a mindset will also assist injured or ill athletes to maintain their mental toughness post-rehabilitation.

Further, there is no reason why the very skills used in PST interventions to enhance training and competition performance should not be used to achieve the aforementioned mental toughness objectives as an integral part of injury or illness rehabilitation programmes. For example, motivational mastery imagery (Hardy, Gammage, & Hall, 2001) and motivational imagery for goal setting (Driediger, Hall, & Callow, 2006), in particular, have been found to improve injured athletes' levels of mental toughness. Goal setting is also an essential part of any injury or illness rehabilitation programme. Goals need to be specific, measurable, and most of all, achievable. Danish, Petitpas, and Hale (1993) described an educational-developmental model in which injury is not seen as a problem, but as an opportunity for growth and development in and outside of sport. Additional research findings also suggest that mental toughness may have implications for the personal growth and development of athletes in response to adversity in sport, such as injury and rehabilitation (Galli & Vealey, 2008; Podlog, Lochbaum, & Stevens, 2010). Perhaps, mentally tough performers are more likely to respond to injury, illness, and rehabilitation in a way that allows them to achieve personal growth.

One world champion performer who has had more than his fair share of injury setbacks advocates just such a philosophy. England Rugby World Cup winner Jonny Wilkinson wrote of his reaction after injuring knee ligaments at the beginning of the domestic season in September 2006:

> It doesn't take me long, even from the biggest setbacks, to return to my core belief in sport and in life, too. If you want something enough and if it's worth enough to you, then you have to fight, fight, fight and then fight some more. I don't mean physically attacking other people, I mean smashing through challenges, I mean standing tall and believing in myself when others stop doing so. It entails getting up as soon as I physically can after I get knocked down and digging my heels in when it gets too tough for others. It is not time to call it a day until I decide I want to do so.
>
> (J. Wilkinson, 2008: 247–248)

No sooner had he rehabilitated from that injury, two months later Wilkinson sustained a serious kidney injury. Recollecting this time in his autobiography, his mentally tough philosophy is even more apparent:

> When one door closes, another one opens. For the first time since the serious neck injury, which seemed to kick off this bizarre run of setbacks, I considered just how fragile my body (and the human body in general) was. It reinforced my growing understanding that our true strength and power must lie inside rather than in the muscles we build.
>
> (ibid.: 256)

And upon his successful return to top-flight competition in the autumn of 2009, Wilkinson reflected: 'It's been a long road back. There was a time last year when I did doubt that I'd ever see days like this again. But it was a doubt I fought against constantly' (as cited in Cleary, 2009k, S22). These recollections reveal a mentally tough competitor who has had to come to terms with continual injury setbacks as a post-script to World Cup glory. The devastating sequence of injuries that have punctuated Wilkinson's career since 2003 would have finished a less mentally tough individual.

Wilkinson's England team-mate Lewis Moody feared he would never play rugby union again after suffering a broken ankle just two months after battling back from a ruptured Achilles tendon. Though he made a full recovery, Moody recalled: 'There was a time when I considered calling it a day. The thought of going through all the rehab again just got me down. That sort of stuff does break you mentally' (as cited in Mairs, 2009b: S15).

Another high-profile international rugby union star to have suffered several injury setbacks is Wales centre Gavin Henson. Of coming close to quitting the game due to persistent injuries, Henson said:

> I am down and depressed, maybe I am cursed. It has been another difficult year. I get my enjoyment through playing, but I am managing only eight starts a season. It is hard to come back all the time and it is pretty tough off the field. Thoughts about my future run through my head. I would miss rugby, but is it worth it?
>
> (as cited in Clutton, 2009b: S12)

In an earlier newspaper interview, Henson had already intimated that the injuries were sapping his spirit:

> I just can't believe my luck . . . I have to go through another rehab programme and it could be six to eight weeks . . . I find it hard to keep taking those injuries to be honest. It's really knocking me back every time. It is hard to come back, it's tough for me and my family. I do love playing the game, but the other side of things is not so enjoyable as it once was. I still dream of playing good games, but they are few and far between. Last season was the same and the year before and the year before. There is not much enjoyment then . . . It is soul destroying.
>
> (as cited in Clutton, 2009a: S19)

Evidently, injury has dealt a shattering blow to the career aspirations of a hugely talented individual.

Rugby league player Jon Clarke spoke of his frustration when a complicated broken ankle excluded his appearing in the 2009 Challenge Cup final:

'At the time I did not see a light at the end of the tunnel. There were times when I though "Is this it?" But I just had to stay positive' (as cited in Kuzio & Coates, 2010: 5). However, he returned after an 11-month rehabilitation to make a winning appearance for Warrington at Wembley the following year.

But such psychological reactions to injury do not belong solely to those performing in a high-impact collision sport such as rugby. Basketball legend Magic Johnson reflected on his return to competition following an injury-enforced absence: 'I had lost a lot of confidence during the long layoff. And for a long time after I returned, I still held back. All I could think about was protecting my knee from another injury' (as cited in J. Taylor & Taylor, 1997: 273). Speaking of her own injury woes, former world No. 1 tennis player Ana Ivanovic reveals the torment and mental anguish associated with trying to regain her pre-injury level of performance: 'I have had a lot of different experiences in the past two years, having to cope when not feeling great, being injured ... being frustrated, losing patience with myself. Because I am a perfectionist, I had just assumed I would play perfectly all the time' (as cited in Harman, 2009a: 16). However, her mental toughness is apparent: 'But I have learnt that in those times I have to find a way to win ... There are going to be setbacks and real champions adjust to that. You might lose, but you must never lose the belief in yourself' (ibid.: 16). Similarly, England cricketer Katherine Brunt spoke of her despair while rehabilitating from a spiral fracture of her left hand and later the same year the career-threatening agony of a prolapsed disc that required surgery and sidelined her for 15 months: 'There were times when I felt totally helpless. I was determined to get through it, but at my lowest point I did wonder if it was all worth it. Recovering from injury is a tedious, slow process' (as cited in Potter, 2009: 87).

England international footballer Owen Hargreaves spent nearly three years in rehabilitation from career-threatening chronic patellar tendonitis. He had difficulties in coming to terms with such a slow recovery, reflected in the observation that: 'The people closest to Hargreaves say it has been a psychological battle as well as a physical one' (D. Taylor, 2010a: 3). Ultimately released by Manchester United FC, the midfielder's own take on the injury is not untypical of sports performers: 'As an athlete, you think you are invincible. You don't think something of this magnitude will ever happen' (as cited in ibid.: 3). Unfortunately for Hargreaves, it did, and he will need to show considerable mental toughness to get back to where he was.

Of the serious, complicated knee ligament injury, and subsequent re-habilitation, that kept him from competing for 19 months, Czech international footballer Tomas Rosicky emphasised his mental anguish: 'I had to go through a difficult period. I had so many disappointments on this road and it was very difficult for me to handle . . . Of course I thought I might not be back. The mental side is the biggest problem' (as cited in Kay, 2009e: 4). Arsenal FC team-mate and England international Theo Walcott spoke of the positive influence of Rosicky's mentally tough mindset on his own injury rehabilitation: 'I watched Tomas Rosicky out for 18 months, coming in every day, very mentally strong, getting on with his rehab work, always smiling and business-like, and that was an example. I learned to come in, smile every day' (as cited in White, 2010a: S5). He added that he had returned to competition much stronger – mentally as well as physically. And, perhaps Andrew Flintoff's high-profile retirement from Test cricket was precipitated by injury, or rather, injuries. His list of injuries reads like a busy 24 hours in accident and emergency: broken nose, sore back, stress fracture of left foot, four ankle operations, shoulder injuries, side strain, hip tear, double hernia, surgery on a torn meniscus in his right knee. Flintoff admitted that his racked knees could no longer cope with the stresses of Test match cricket: 'I've been thinking about it for a while. My body is telling me to give in for my own sanity. I can't keep going through rehabilitation' (as cited in Kidd & Westerby, 2009: 4). While Croatian footballer Ivan Klasnic's story is one of 'courage, perseverance and one man's quiet but unbreakable resolve' (D. Taylor, 2009b: 7). He not only survived two kidney transplants, but returned to play professional football and establish himself as a star of the Croatia national team.

A final thought on sport injury/illness rehabilitation and mental toughness. Given the perception within the elite sporting community, and society in general, that elite athletes are motivated to use performance-enhancing drugs (Bloodworth & McNamee, 2010; Petróczi, 2007), an interesting line of enquiry for future research in the domain of sport injuries would be the relationship between mental toughness and the use of such substances. Interviews with five elite athletes, who were also 'admitted dopers' (they had either tested positive for banned substances or had admitted to prior drug use after their retirement from competitive sport), revealed interesting findings (Kirby, Moran, & Guerin, 2011). Three of the group felt that athletes high in mental toughness would be more inclined to take performance-enhancing drugs because such individuals would be intensely goal-focused: '. . . if you look at doping as just another step necessary to achieving your goals, then you know, by being mentally tough and goals-focused, then maybe the next rational decision for you is to dope' (ibid.: 212). The other two athletes thought that mental toughness would play a part in helping an athlete to resist doping: 'You've got to be incredibly mentally strong to resist it . . . to believe that it's enough for you, knowing that you've done it on your own steam' (ibid.: 212). In another study, researchers reported that 50 per cent of their sample of 116 elite Australian Rules footballers and soccer players indicated a high likelihood that they would use a performance-enhancing drug for rehabilitation purposes (Strelan & Boeckmann, 2006). The athletes believed that the use of a banned harmful substance was a viable response to a career-threatening situation, and many indicated their willingness to use such drugs if faced with such a threat. It would be interesting to discover if such a belief corresponded with high or low mental toughness.

Coaches' responsibilities for developing athletes' mental toughness

Of the themes to emerge from an investigation of elite coaches' views on effective talent development (Martindale, Collins, & Abraham, 2007), two were particularly prominent: recognising that 'mental toughness is the key to progression' and that athletes must possess the 'mental desire and attitude to improve/succeed'. These findings were corroborated in a study in which coaches felt that it was important that performers possessed a general attribute (they called it 'mental toughness' or 'mental strength') that enabled them to respond positively in the face of adversity and to deal with the demands of high-level sport (Oliver, Hardy, & Markland, 2010). In elaboration, one of the study's coaches stated: 'When you get to the elite level there's such a fine line between winning and losing or being the best or just coming second, and I think a big thing is – not getting beat up upstairs . . . you've got to be really strong upstairs' (ibid.: 438). This has been evidenced in practice where England cricket team director Andy Flower spoke of his player selection criteria: 'We took into account everyone's talent and then their capacity to handle pressure. Mental toughness is a vital component of competitive sport' (as cited in Wilde, 2009a). This has been similarly recognised by the ECB's managing director of cricket partnerships, former England captain Mike Gatting, who, in his 'Playing under Pressure' programme, advocates that: 'The aim is to develop mental toughness and make them appreciate from a younger age what is required at the highest level' (as cited in Westerby, 2009b).

To this end, coaches have a responsibility to model and teach the concepts of mental toughness in the pursuit of sporting excellence. In addition to the attributes identified and discussed previously, other desirable attributes include sportsmanship, fair play, and respect for opponents; needed never more so than now to counter an alarming increase in impenitence (see Kitson, 2009a; P. Wilson, 2011b; Woodcock, 2009). A wonderful example of sportsmanship was demonstrated by England soccer coach Stuart Pearce, whom nobody could ever say lacked mental toughness. After a Swedish player missed a decisive penalty, Pearce immediately went across to console his opposite number. It was noted that: 'It was a sporting gesture from a man who admits the dignity shown to him by the West Germany players, after he had missed in the semi-final defeat at the 1990 Fifa World Cup, provided him with an important lesson in the development that has led him to this successful juncture' (Lansley, 2009a: 14). Coaches need to teach young athletes, in particular, how to behave and conduct themselves properly. Above all, this needs to be conducted in an environment of open and honest communication. Coaches must be mindful not to place primary emphasis on winning. Research suggests that results-obsessed youth coaches often exploit their athletes rather than considering their developmental stages and advancing their psychological and social best interests (Gilbert, Gilbert, & Trudel, 2001a, 2001b).

The overall goal of any coach is the development of the athlete (Côté, Salmela, Trudel, Baria, & Russell, 1995). Of the four higher-order categories identified in a study for building a successful sport programme, 'individual growth' was considered particularly important (Vallée & Bloom, 2005). The study's expert coaches aimed at developing performers into high-level athletes, instilling intrinsic motivation to maximise their potential. Fostering individual growth was accomplished through life skills development and empowerment of each athlete.

As one coach in the Vallée and Bloom (2005) study put it: 'Being a champion is in every part of their life, including how they carry themselves. It affects those decisions they make around eating, sleeping, and hydrating. It is that whole package' (ibid.: 187–188). All coaches mentioned positive reinforcement and persuasion as indispensable tactics to enhance self-confidence in their players. Reflecting this, another coach added (ibid.: 188):

> I think your players very much reflect your attitude as a coach. If someone ever mentioned anything about not being as good as or at a lower level, that was unacceptable. We spoke of ourselves as winners, as successful women, who would have no reason to look back at ourselves. We did everything that we could to give ourselves an opportunity to be successful.

All coaches in the Vallée and Bloom study stated that their ultimate philosophy included more than winning games (see Chapter 1). It involved developing well-rounded individuals who would be successful in life. One coach even explicitly stated that winning the national championship was not the end goal; rather, it was to teach her athletes about life through sport. Clearly, this coach recognises the tremendous opportunity that exists to shape young people and to have a positive influence on their lives. Interestingly, findings from a recent study suggest that coaches working with mentally tough athletes should consider emphasising training and instructive behaviours if they wish for congruence between actual and athletes' preferred leadership behaviours; for example, skill development aimed at improving performance (Crust & Azadi, 2009).

Australian Rules football coaches' perspectives on how they can both facilitate and hinder the development of mental toughness have also been explored (Gucciardi, Gordon, Dimmock, & Mallett, 2009). Four categories emerged that appeared to be central to the coach's role in the facilitation of player mental toughness. The importance of nurturing and being committed to a long-term *coach–athlete relationship* was highlighted by all of the coaches in the study. The following quote captures the essence of this: 'If players don't trust or respect their coach, then they won't be as willing to take on board what they say or do.' The adoption of a holistic development perspective was a *coaching philosophy* typically ascribed to. Those coaches characterised by this philosophy were found to 'view players as a person and athlete, and not just a player on their team . . . acknowledge and accept that players are going to fail at times . . . but focus on helping players learn from their failures so they can do it differently in the future'. There was a consensus that creating challenging *training environments* contributed to the development of player mental toughness. Pushing players' limits by continuously exposing them to tough, adverse situations assists them by affording them the opportunity to identify the processes for dealing effectively with such situations. As one coach remarked: 'Simulating competition scenarios during training sessions so that players can develop the necessary skills to cope with pressure and anxiety during competition.' And, the coaches discussed a number of *specific strategies* for instilling core mental toughness attributes such as self-belief and a strong work ethic among their players. Such techniques included positive reinforcement and encouragement for poor and excellent performances and effort, praising positive behaviours in front of the whole team, encouraging mistakes to be interpreted as opportunities from which to learn, and an egalitarian philosophy among the players (ibid.).

Coaches, in their role as leader, must also be mindful of their own behaviour. Their body language transmits signals that their athletes will be only too quick to interpret. Mental toughness can be developed and maintained vicariously. For example, of Manchester United FC's manager:

[Sir Alex] Ferguson's demeanour in the dugout sets the tone for his players; he will move to the edge of his technical area to encourage greater urgency but he always exudes a belief in his players, a refusal to panic. Ferguson has seen it all before, overcome adversities before

> ... Even in individual games, with the clock running against United, the players never lose their belief because they trust in their manager.
>
> (Winter, 2009c: S6)

While goalkeeper Manuel Almunia clearly benefited from the approach of Arsenal FC's Arsène Wenger: 'Working alongside him makes you feel incredibly relaxed and at peace' (as cited in J. Wilson, 2009b: S3). Similarly, it has been written of the late soccer manager Brian Clough's man-management that: 'The best I ever saw. He asked you to do what you were good at, and made you feel as though you were great at it' (Boycott, 2009b: S9). Under coaches such as these, performers have been willing to give their all and have, subsequently, demonstrably fulfilled their potential and achieved glittering success. A coaching philosophy centred on trusting athletes will empower them to make their own decisions and raise their self-awareness. Coaches are critical in developing athletes' mental toughness. Through their own support, attributes, and practices, they are responsible for creating a positive, but tough, working and practice environment (Butt *et al.*, 2010). Positive values create such a culture – as long as the values are real and not merely corporate spin or platitudes on a dressing room poster.

Challenging experiences

There is a widespread cultural assumption that controlled exposure to challenge can be potentially beneficial (Miles & Priest, 1990; Watts, Webster, Morley, & Cohen, 1992). For example, adventure experiences have gained an enduring reputation for developing desirable personality characteristics in their participants that reflect the currency of mental toughness. Such experiences as rock climbing, canoeing, orienteering, and camping have long been suggested to foster qualities such as initiative, perseverance, determination, self-restraint, co-operation, and resourcefulness (Celebi & Ozen, 2004; Luckner & Nadler, 1997; Schoel, Prouty, & Radcliffe, 1988).

The notion of adventure experiences assisting in the development of mental toughness is intuitively appealing. This is particularly emphasised if the theoretical rationale adopts a 'neo-Hahnian approach'; that is, that adventure experiences build character or have certain therapeutic effects associated with personal characteristics (Brookes, 2003). This approach represents a development-by-challenge philosophy and provides an underlying justification for adventure experiences (Neill & Dias, 2001). A general and a research-based literature exist on the character-building effects of, for example, Outward Bound, outdoor adventure courses, and outdoor adventure education curriculum activities (e.g., Bronson, Gibson, Kichar, & Priest, 1992; Cason & Gillis, 1994; Ewert & Yoshino, 2008; Hattie, Marsh,

Neill, & Richards, 1997; McKenzie, 2000; Neill & Dias, 2001; Sheard & Golby, 2006b).

Recent research has shown a positive association between higher levels of mental toughness and a preparedness to take physical risk (Crust & Keegan, 2010). Adventure experiences can be used as an effective medium for participants to recognise and to understand their own weaknesses, strengths, and personal resources (Nadler, 1993; Taniguchi & Freeman, 2004). Moreover, the skills learned in challenging situations are deemed to be transferable (Priest & Gass, 2005). Adventure experiences have a major enduring impact on the lives, in general, and the psychological development, in particular, of participants. Evidence suggests that the experiences provided by adventure experiences contribute to improvements in self-esteem, self-confidence, locus of control, conflict resolution, problem-solving skills, and group cohesion (Cason & Gillis, 1994; Hans, 2000; Hattie *et al.*, 1997; Neill & Richards, 1998).

Climbing Mount Everest

Psychologist David Fletcher provided scientific support for a group of mountaineers on Everest Base Camp in April 2007. Rather than merely coping with the pressure, the trekkers and climbers had to develop the qualities that would enable them to thrive on the difficulties and raise their performance level. In keeping with previous research on participants attempting to climb the world's highest mountain (e.g., S. Egan & Stelmack, 2003), Fletcher (2007) identified three key attributes that would be crucial in meeting the demands presented by the environment: self-belief, motivation, and focus. A high priority of the training programme was to develop confidence that remained as robust under pressure. Self-belief was also a critical factor at higher altitudes, where the most simple of tasks, such as putting on boots in the morning, can leave the fittest mountaineer breathless. Short-term goal setting was used, and visualisation of the more complex climbing techniques became a particularly salient mental skill higher up the mountain.

With regard to motivation, Fletcher encouraged the trekkers and climbers to reflect on their motives and consider the fundamental reasons for their ambitions. He suggested this is a critical process, since only a small proportion of individuals who attempt to climb Mount Everest actually reach the summit successfully. He emphasised that developing mental toughness is not about creating ruthless and uncaring climbers with nerves of steel. Rather, his programme was designed to develop mentally tough performers who were highly motivated through their self-awareness, internal drive, and knowledge of when to re-group and return another day. Regarding focus, Fletcher's training programme emphasised that when under pressure, it is critical to maintain focus on 'controllables' rather than 'non-controllables', and the present, on processes, positives, and composure. This focus strategy has also been found to be successful in previous mental toughness development programmes (see Goldberg, 1998; Sheard & Golby, 2006a). The strategy also proved beneficial for the England cricket team as the following list was revealed on a dressing room notice board the day after securing victory against Australia in 2009: 'Can control: desire, respect, passion, commitment, patience, discipline, consistency, focus, preparation and trust. Can't control: weather, pitch, umpires, nets, schedule and, last of all, the Ashes' (Atherton, 2009i: 230). Control that which you have the power to influence, let go that which you have not. Thus, challenging environments would appear conducive to the development of mental toughness.

As an interesting footnote, on July 31, 1954, the late Italian mountaineer Achille Compagnoni made the final assault on the summit of Karakoram 2 (K2), the world's second highest mountain, which, according to experts, is a steeper and more dangerous mountain, with more intense weather. Compagnoni, one of the first two men to reach the summit of K2, was invited to head the conquest because of his leadership qualities and hardiness. Expedition organiser Ardito Desio considered Compagnoni a man of iron will, 'endowed with great strength both of body and mind' (as cited in Achille Compagnoni, 2009: 31). Clearly, these are attributes requisite to securing such an achievement.

Cross-cultural/national differences

Most people hold beliefs about personality characteristics typical of members of their own and others' cultures (Peabody, 1985). These perceptions of national character may be generalisations from personal experience, stereotypes with a kernel of truth, or inaccurate stereotypes (Y. T. Lee, Jussim, & McCauley, 1995; Macrae, Stangor, & Hewstone, 1996). Stereotypes are oversimplified judgements. As Formula One's 2010 and 2011 champion driver Sebastian Vettel explained: 'I hear this phrase quite a lot in England – "Oh, he's a typical German". It's normal. In Germany we have the same thing about "a typical Englishman". I think it's quite funny. National stereotypes come about but not every person fits into the scheme' (as cited in McRae, 2010b: 6). I can recommend Raphael Honigstein's *Englischer Fussball* as a perceptive, and generally accurate, attempt to explain English character stereotypes using a football metaphor. (See References for details.) However, if there is some veracity, national character should reflect the average emotional, inter-personal, experiential, attitudinal, and motivational styles of members of the culture.

Reports in the Western media since the shattering earthquakes of 11 March 2011 have emphasised Japanese mental toughness; for example, one reader wrote to the editor of *Time* magazine: 'The comments in your cover story about the resolve and fortitude of the Japanese people are right on the mark ... they can never take away our samurai spirit' (Imamura, 2011: 4); while the chairman and chief executive officer of Renault-Nissan, Carlos Ghosn, was moved to add:

> Japan's resilience in the aftermath of the Tohoku earthquake has reminded the world of this nation's extraordinary capacity to face adversity and pull together ... The social and cultural values demonstrated by Japan's people with such dignity, calm and resolve amid the catastrophe reaffirm my faith in the country's ability to rally in the face of almost any challenge.
>
> (Ghosn, 2011: 40–41)

There was no looting or panic in the aftermath of the earthquake. Nobody barged the queues as the emergency supplies arrived; rather, there was self-control and orderliness – an extraordinary stoic mentality the Japanese call *gaman*. Terracciano and co-workers concluded that their study of personality traits 'offers the best evidence to date that in-group perceptions of national character may be informative about the culture, but they are not descriptive of the people themselves' (Terracciano *et al.*, 2005: 99).

Little is known about the validity of relationships between mental toughness and the effects of culture. This is somewhat surprising since personalities may be shaped by one's cultural niche (Hofstede, 1984). Moving from cross-sectional studies of personality in sport within one country to cross-national studies represents a new and interesting direction in mental toughness research. Examining the effects of contextual variables on culture, and culture's effects on individuals and their personalities, is an accepted framework within cross-cultural studies (Segall, Dasen, Berry, & Poortinga, 1999). Further, it has been suggested that culture may be expressed in terms of culture values, or principles endorsed in a culture (Schwartz, 1994), which subsequently help shape the extent to which people will develop certain personality styles. Given this suggestion, therefore, it would be expected that the magnitude of the relationships between personality and successful sport performance would differ because of cultural influence (Glazer, Stetz, & Izso, 2004) and national differences in sport ideology (Bale, 2002).

To date, cultural differences in coping strategies have been reported between Australian and US (Anshel, Williams, & Hodge, 1997), and Australian and Indonesian (Hoedaya & Anshel, 2003) competitive athletes. Differences have been found also in psychological characteristics between lacrosse players from five English-speaking countries (Heishman & Bunker, 1989), US and Chinese collegiate-level athletes (Cox & Liu, 1993), US and British university soccer players (Mahoney & Todd, 1999), and among

Singaporean, North American, Chinese, and Nigerian professional athletes (Zheng, Smith, & Adegbola, 2004). In particular, Heishman and Bunker reported on the significantly superior psychological attributes of the world champion Australian lacrosse players. Interestingly, Golby *et al.* (2003) reported that World Cup rugby league players who had learnt to play the game and were playing club rugby league in Australia at the time of the study had the highest level of mental toughness, while Sheard (2009b) found that the Australian Universities rugby league team had significantly higher levels of mental toughness in comparison to their Great Britain opponents.

'Advance Australia fair' – the Australian phenomenon

Since the 1980s, and coinciding with the collapse of the former Soviet Union and eastern bloc hegemony, Australia has enjoyed success, and even dominance, in a variety of international sports, including cricket, cycling, hockey, rugby union, rugby league, and swimming (Anthony, 2007; Bierley, 2004; Gallagher, 2011b; Slot, 2011a). A fact similarly recognised by England rugby union international Josh Lewsey: 'They [the Australians] have overachieved for generations. If you look at cricket, rugby union, swimming, tennis or rugby league, they have been outstanding' (Lewsey, 2007: 18). The Australian cricket Test (until recently, ranked No. 1 for more than a decade) and One-Day (1987, 1999, 2003, 2007 World Champions) teams have been the best in the world, appearing to possess 'mental reserves like no other' (Nicholas, 2008: S24). That Australian national cricket teams held the upper hand for two decades reveals a different psychology, of dramatically heightened mental toughness. (When England won the 2009 Ashes, it was only the ninth time they had done so in a home series of more than three Tests.) The national cricket team's star may have fallen recently, but there can be little doubt that it will return in due course to be the sport's absolute marker. Australian cricket has demonstrated the ability to nurture outstanding talent and to house it in a superior psychology. It has been suggested of this pervasive culture of toughness, passed down through generations of cricketers, that mental toughness is *caught* via environmental influences (socialised) and *taught* through training (coached) (S. Gordon, Gucciardi, & Chambers, 2007). In other words, mental toughness is learned and can be developed. Writing of the necessity of developing heightened mental toughness to survive, let alone thrive, in international cricket, the fearsome former Australian fast bowler Dennis Lillee sums it up succinctly: 'What you learn is that there are weak people and there are tough, strong people . . . there are two games going on out there, a mind game as well as a physical game of cricket, and you must never let anyone dominate you. The tough survive and the weak do not' (Lillee, 2003: 30).

Writing of the tough environment of Australia's inter-state competition, The Sheffield Shield, Pakistan cricketing legend Imran Khan (2003) suggests: 'It is this fierce competitiveness that produces Test-match temperament and gives cricketers mental toughness.' The intensity of unyielding competitiveness breeds a firm, deep-rooted, reliable, and enduring mental toughness that transfers effortlessly to the Test arena. The competition also affords Australia the luxury of a talent pool that is sufficiently battle-hardened, exemplified by Dennis Lillee: 'I played because I loved winning, being part of a winning team, victory meant everything to me. I had that in-built win at all costs mentality' (as cited in White, 2009a: S19).

The Australian mindset, in sport at least, has commanded well-earned respect from journalists, competitors, and retired combatants alike. Examples of cricket writers' comments include: 'Here again, we had evidence of the Australian belief that no game is beyond their powers of recovery. All you have to do is dig deep into available resources, and maintain the belief that when it comes to fighting only extremely rarely does anyone do it better' (Lawton, 2009b: 60–61); 'This is what Australians do. They grow an even thicker skin when adversity's boot is pressing at their throats' (Garside, 2009c: S17); 'Australians are like beetles. You cannot get rid of them no matter how hard you bring down the boot' (Garside, 2009f: S6); 'How do Australians manage this? They seem to be able to give a whistle and an organised, ready-made middle order Ayers Rock immediately materialises' (Chadband, 2009g: S5); 'It's the source of their get in, stay in mentality. Even in their tough evening practice sessions, they pride themselves on keeping their wicket intact in the nets' (S. Hughes, 2009a: S7); 'Willow does not wilt quite so easily in Australian hands' (Garside, 2009d: S24); 'Australian toughness under pressure . . . There is still no reverse gear in the Australian cricketing psyche' (Hayward, 2009b: 3); 'Where Australia continue to score heavily is in character' (M. Henderson, 2009b: S6); 'England have suddenly started . . . playing the game like Aussies' (White, 2010b: 26); and 'Australia, who never lose if they can possibly help it, were themselves scarcely able to believe the comeback . . . a team who do not know when they are beaten' (Brenkley, 2010a: 13).

England cricketers, similarly, have acknowledged the mindset of their Australian opponents. For example, captain Andrew Strauss: 'As is always the case with the Aussies, they come back at you' (as cited in Briggs, 2009e: S3); spinner Graeme Swann: 'They batted as Australian teams always do, with that sort of cocksure swagger' (as cited in A. Bull, 2009: 4); and batsman Kevin Pietersen: 'The Australian way is to come out and be fiercely competitive, dominant in what they do, forceful in their approach' (as cited in Hobson, 2009b: 70) has each admiringly recognised desirable psychological attributes in the Australians.

Mike Atherton admitted: 'It takes the kind of mental toughness not granted to everyone to withstand cricketers as fiercely proud, committed and skilful as those of Australia. It was a day for substance over style, for bloody-mindedness over brilliance' (2009d: 3), and: 'They [Australia] almost made it through to the close, showing the kind of resilience that Australia Test cricketers have become renowned for' (2010d: 72). Indeed, Atherton has written at length of the mental toughness of Australian cricketers. The following are examples from his book reflecting on the 2009 Ashes series (Atherton, 2009i): 'Australia are a resilient bunch' (ibid.: 102), 'Australia are nothing if not resilient' (ibid.: 143), 'Australia's resilience has never been in question' (ibid.: 146), 'Competing and producing under pressure is exactly how Australian cricketers are built' (ibid.: 187), and 'There have always been periods of dominance, mostly Australian' (ibid.: 219). Of this Australian mindset phenomenon, perhaps former rugby union international Brian Moore, another proud Englishman able to draw upon his vast experience of Anglo-Australian contests, sums it up best: 'The Ashes as an entity is fortunate that Australia is one of the protagonists because with the Aussies you will never get a side that can be criticised for lack of effort. Their national psyche will not accept teams that are uncompetitive' (B. Moore, 2009e: S17). And this mentally tough sporting culture has been around a fair while. Of Don Bradman's Invincibles 1948 tour of England it was written: 'Australianism means single-minded determination to win – to win within the laws, but, if necessary, to the last limit within them. It means that where the impossible is within the realm of what the human body can do, there are Australians who believe that they can do it – and who have succeeded often enough to make us wonder if anything is impossible to them. It means they have never lost a match – particularly a Test match – until the last run is scored or their last wicket has fallen' (Arlott, 1949).

One particularly interesting footnote about mental toughness and Australian cricketers concerns the players' uniform. The famous baggy green cap – the 'Baggy Green' – favoured by Australian players has achieved iconic status: 'The baggy green cap is not the emblem of Australian cricket but of Australian life. It carries within its DNA a genetic characteristic that compels the wearer to fight to the last follicle to retain all that he has' (Garside, 2009c: S17). There is a symbolism associated with the cap that is seldom seen elsewhere. Indeed, it has been noted that: 'Australian cricket still does symbolism and meaning much better than England' (Atherton, 2009c: 70). For its wearers, the revered Baggy Green symbolises the ultimate achievement: representing Australia. This is not taken lightly. As former captain – a position and role seen as the benchmark of mental strength – Steve Waugh, who was, arguably, the poster-boy for mental toughness in cricket, explains:

I just love wearing it. It makes us feel special and I think it can intimidate the opposition. It gives us strength and it unites us and shows that we're a committed unit. As far as the team is concerned, the traditions we uphold are an important element used to develop a sense of pride, camaraderie and high morale that hopefully will give us a mental toughness when we are challenged.

(as cited in Kidd, 2009c: 4)

The goal of playing for Australia and wearing the coveted Baggy Green is a strong motivator. One cricketer in a recent study stated: 'I remember clearly, Dennis Lillee bowling that last ball at Viv Richards and thinking how great it'd be to play Test cricket, and wear the baggy green cap' (Weissensteiner *et al.*, 2009: 289). This simple piece of kit enjoys iconic status, as Shane Warne states: 'In Australia we have great respect for anybody who has worn the baggy green cap' (Warne, 2007: 207). Such symbolism can help instil mental toughness by recognition of what is required to achieve its award.

The Australian rugby league team, The Kangaroos, is also the world's best (six consecutive World Cup titles between 1975 and 2000). It has been written of their domination that 'belief is a powerful elixir and Australia's rugby league players have it by the bucket-load' (Irvine, 2003: 35). Their greatest strength is their feeling of invincibility. Australian rugby league's domestic competition, the NRL, is the most demanding and, arguably, the most competitive league of any football code worldwide (see A. Wilson, 2011a). The standard of play in the annual State of Origin series between New South Wales and Queensland surpasses anything else anywhere on the planet. The Australian rugby union team, The Wallabies, have appeared in three World Cup finals. They were world champions in 1991 and 1999, and in losing the 2003 final, it was commented 'any side but Australia would have capitulated ... but Australia expect to beat England' (Barnes, 2003: 38). They consistently stand proud atop the Commonwealth Games medals table. Even in a sport considered 'minority' in Australia, its soccer team, The Socceroos, was unlucky to lose to the eventual tournament winners, Italy, in the 2006 Fifa World Cup.

That Australians appear at ease with major sporting events should not be overlooked. As has been intriguingly noted: 'There's a cheerful efficiency that respects the importance of taking part, but never forgets the sustaining ritual of recording the result' (Beard, 2009: 17). The Australian mentally tough mindset has, on many occasions, been a psychological hurdle for, in particular, their English/British sporting counterparts. A failure to raise their game has resulted, all too often, in English/British opponents being swept aside. Examples are numerous in hockey, rugby league, rugby union, and, to which I alluded earlier in this section, cricket, where it has been suggested that: 'When it comes to an Ashes series, Australians seem to grow to fit their national mythology. England always know that in such contests their most assuredly demanding confrontation will be with the opposition's attitude . . . the tourists' fiercely disciplined sense of purpose' (McIlvanney, 2009: 20). The outcome of which has all too often been 'Australia's intensely professional determination to exact a steep price for their wickets and the tendency of England's batsmen to sell theirs cheaply' (ibid.: 20); 'The Australians are masters at getting the upper hand from the start . . . Australians know it does not always take much to bring out the old insecurities in the English. England teams know they usually lose to Australia' (Wilde, 2009c: 4); 'Australia are still Australia and England are, at base, ever so slightly frightened of them. Australia, even in transition, have enough to intimidate England' (Barnes, 2009f: 88); 'The problem is that England can never really believe that they are beating Australia; such a belief seems to be flying in the face of nature. The rule works the other way too: Australia can never really believe that England are beating them . . . Australian cricket teams – at least when playing England – have a level of belief that borders on credulousness' (Barnes, 2009j: 5); and 'It was that whenever pressure was applied by the Australians over less than two days and a half of what was turned into a parody of a Test match, England were found to be wholly inadequate' (Lawton, 2009d: 4).

It has been written of Australian and English cricket that 'a yawning gap exists between them' (Atherton, 2009h: 64). The former England captain added:

> The gulf is nothing to do with talent . . . both teams are matched. But one thing this Australia team have in common with their predecessors is toughness, a soul-deep toughness that, at the critical moment, befriended them again while deserting their opponents . . . competing and producing under pressure is exactly how Australian cricketers are built.

> (ibid.: 64)

It is in the Australian national character to fight when the situation demands. Particularly revealing, it was not the England players' technical shortcomings, but rather their lack of mental toughness, that was noted in a dossier prepared for their Australian counterparts ahead of the 2009 Ashes series. The truth is, Australians, whether players, coaches, or its media, rarely miss an opportunity to heap on the psychological pressure (see, for example, Magnay, 2010b).

There is almost a natural order of things when Australia beat England. It wasn't always thus. And, perhaps, a corner has just been turned. England's retaining of the Ashes (they won the best of five contest 3–1) was their first series victory in Australia since 1986–87. The England rugby union team won in Australia in the summer of 2010, and backed it up with another victory over the Wallabies at Twickenham in the autumn. Yet, these instances aside, it is becoming increasingly inconceivable that England/ Great Britain will win a Test rugby league series in Australia in the foreseeable future. My own view is that victory matters that much more to Australians, or rather, losing matters that much more. Beating England matters. Defeating Great Britain matters. Beaten by England matters more. Defeated by Great Britain matters more. The phenomenon can be explained, to some extent, as a throwback to empire, symbolic of the colonials beating imperial England/Great Britain at its own games (P. Smith, 1996). Australian identity is built largely upon the solid foundation of sporting success, England/ Great Britain less so. Thus, defeat for England/Great Britain should be less of a surprise. A colossal shift in mental toughness is required to redress this power balance.

In the face of seemingly psychologically superior opposition, unsurprisingly, English/British sporting failures have been attributed to the lack of a mentally tough mindset. It has been suggested that 'English and British sport in the past few decades has been one long tale of disappointments, nearlys, what ifs, buts, apologies, explanations and excuses, which together form a deepening psychological accommodation with failure' (Anthony, 2007: 41), and that there exists:

> an absence of 'mental toughness' and resilience of performers from the UK compared with other elite performance nations . . . failing to cope with the demands brought about by competing at the highest level, when deficiencies in ability are more easily exposed and when combined with unrealistic public and media expectations loaded on performers, lead to underachievement, failure or limited success on the world stage.
>
> (Mahoney, 2009: 64)

Accepting defeat despite trying hard (B. Moore, 2010) and an inability to defend titles successfully (R. Williams, 2010) have been put forward as deleterious English/British sporting traits. In addition, there exists a cultural acceptance of worshipping sport performers, who, ultimately, have failed (Reed, 2007).

Similar observations have been made in New Zealand, where yet another Rugby World Cup failure manifested for the pre-tournament favourite All Blacks (Drake, 2007; Loe, 2007). Indeed, the observations of David Kirk, the first All Black captain to lift the Rugby World Cup, and on the eve of their quarter-final exit to France in 2007, were undoubtedly more prescient than he intended:

The time will surely come when the 2007 All Blacks will stand on the edge of the precipice that their 1991, 1995, 1999 and 2003 predecessors have fallen into. There will be a time when the stomach churns, the limbs feel like water and doubt crouches in the hallway. It will be then that we will know just how great this All Black team is. I always look for the signs of mental toughness and resilience in the little things.

(D. Kirk, 2007)

The experience of the defeated New Zealanders was all the worse for the unprecedented hype surrounding, and expectation placed upon, the players. Arguably, they bought in too much to others' expectations. For the World Cup to return to New Zealand, the prescription, according to All Black Aaron Mauger, is clear: 'Test match rugby is a mental exercise; you can be the most gifted team in the world but that counts for nothing if your mind isn't totally focused, and that can only come with experience. We have the gifted players – now we have to acquire the mental toughness' (as cited in Philip, 2004b). New Zealand finally won the Rugby World Cup for a second time in 2011 – again as hosts.

'Deutschland über Alles' – the German phenomenon

The German national soccer team is a product with a proven track record. Germany has won the World Cup three times, has been runners-up on four occasions, semi-finalists in the two most recent tournaments, and has been involved in the decisive match in six out of the last 10 European Champion-ships, winning three of them. They qualified for the 2012 competition with a perfect played 10, won 10 record. Brazil (5) and Italy (4) aside in terms of the number of World Cup triumphs, no other country can match this record. Phillip Lahm, the national team's captain, neatly summarises the expectancy: 'We [Germany] won the World Cup in 1954, 1974, and 1990, and the European Championship in 1972, 1980, and 1996. We've made it through to finals at least as often. So we've grown up with the conviction that Germany are always good enough to reach the final – and more' (as cited in Radnedge, 2012, p. 57). West Germany/Germany are the only side to have played in three consecutive World Cup finals – 1982 (runners-up), 1986 (runners-up), and 1990 (winners), and are also the only side to have reached three succes-sive European Championship finals – 1972 (winners), 1976 (runners-up), and 1980 (winners). They were losing finalists in the 1992 and 2008 competitions. The reason behind this success? The suggestion put forward by Franz Beck-enbauer, and he should know as the only man to have lifted the World Cup on separate occasions as captain (1974) and coach (1990) [not to mention losing final appearances as player (1966) and coach (1986), as mentioned in Chapter

1], is extremely convincing: 'The German mentality is stronger than that of other nations. I can assure you Germany does not have better players, but even when they are under pressure they seem to maintain a winning mentality' (as cited in Cameron, 1995: 109). This 'mentality' is summed up wonderfully, when, interviewed during the 2008 Uefa European Championships, Czech Republic goalkeeper Petr Cech spoke of the mental strength of his German counterpart, Jens Lehmann: '. . . there are doubts about his level of performances after spending most of the season on the bench. That should not influence him and that is his biggest strength – mentally he is very powerful and nothing seems to faze him' (as cited in Balague, 2008: 15). This mental toughness is similarly recognised in the media. Of Germany under-21s going 2–0 up against England [they went on to win 4–0] in the 2009 European Championship final, it was reported that: 'German teams do not throw away such leads and so it proved' (Hytner, 2009b: 9).

As someone who has faced Germany several times in his international career, former England captain Tony Adams is better placed than most to pass comment, and his observations on Germany's surprise progression to the 2002 Fifa World Cup final reflect more than a passing admiration:

> It is remarkable how Germany have recovered from the 5–1 defeat in Munich. I always expected them to qualify but not, I have to admit, fare this well. They learn quickly the lessons of adversity, though. And they have a winning mentality. Not for them the unease of winning when they suspect deep down they don't deserve to, a feeling that they have done as well as they ought to . . . While the history of former great teams, who have brought them three World Cups, can be a burden, it is one they thrive on . . . There is none more resilient than the Germans.
>
> (Adams, 2002)

Evidenced, in particular, by the German national side's unmatched success in penalty shoot-outs: it has not lost one since 1976, begging the question – is there greater steel in the German national character? Imagine my surprise, even astonishment, then, at Bayern Munich's own 'Lost Final' – they lost a penalty shoot-out in the Uefa Champions League final in their own stadium. Germans don't lose penalty shoot-outs! What odds on those same Bayern Munich players redeeming themselves while wearing the German national team shirt in the forthcoming 2012 Uefa European Championships? Consider these two examples. A few months after England defeated Germany 1–0 in Charleroi in the 2000 competition, the score line was reversed in the last ever international football match staged at the old Wembley Stadium. Nine months after they had lost 1–5 to England in the return World Cup qualifying match in Munich's Olympiastadion, Germany were lining up in the World Cup final in Yokohama; while England had exited, somewhat limply, at the quarter-final stage to ten-man Brazil. My point? Germany has the last word.

Of his three highly favourable years at FC Bayern Munich, Germany's most famous and successful club, Scottish international footballer Allan McInally recalled: 'You knew your place and refined your aims and ambitions accordingly. The rules bring a sort of determination with them. The practice games were never 10–8 but more like 2–1. Training was never a laugh. It was your job and you did it right' (as cited in Cameron, 1995: 112). And this was rewarded. 'The players came first . . . The players are always looked after. They receive the most respect,' McInally added (as cited in ibid.: 111). According to goalkeeper Oliver Kahn, who also made 86 appearances for Germany, Bayern Munich's philosophy is to have its players representing the German national team (Kahn, 2010). Could this club–country wisdom ever belong in England? The environment that surrounds Bayern Munich and, in particular, the German national team is conducive to achievement (see Hawkey 2012; Hesse-Lichtenberger, 2003; Jenson, 2012b; Tomlinson & Young, 2006; Winter, 2012c).

Oliver Bierhoff, general manager of the national team, is largely credited with being the architect of instilling discipline, respect, and pride into players before they become established stars: 'A national team is a national icon, the property of the people, and we [the national teams] don't pay our players anywhere near what they get for their clubs, so it is a matter of pride at being selected among the 20–23 best players in the country' (as cited in Ogden, 2011: S5). The recognition and trappings of success come with responsibility. Interestingly, and in stark contrast to England, domestic clubs work with the national team and German players are told that, while they can earn big money and fame in club football, they must succeed at a World Cup to become legends (ibid.)

The Australian and German sporting mindsets share commonalities. They each afford their athletes to build victory upon victory. These mindsets facilitate the outlook that each success is taken as a stepping-stone to a more permanent condition of strength. No consideration is given to premature and spurious self-congratulation. Teams and individuals representing these countries have endured setbacks; for example, losing to England in the 1981 Ashes cricket series seems to have sewn seeds of doubt in Australian minds, whenever in future years they have had to face a low total in the fourth innings. Australian cricket teams, trying to get a comparatively small number of runs to win a Test match, have been known to crumble under the pressure (e.g., versus England in 1981 and 2009). And few observers are surprised when the German national soccer team, having negotiated a passage through to the deciding match of a major tournament, falls short at the final hurdle. As West Germany (1982 and 1986) or as Germany (2002), they have lost three Fifa World Cup finals in recent memory, and lost two Uefa European Championships finals (as Germany, in 1992 and 2008). Yet, they bounce back (Australia the uninterrupted holders of the Ashes from 1989 to 2005; West Germany the Fifa world champions in 1990 and Uefa European champions [as Germany] in 1996). And for this, they remain the most consistently feared and respected opponents. For example, when the draw was made for the group stages of the 2010 Fifa World Cup, the English/British media made a great deal of the possibility that England were highly likely to meet Germany in the first knockout round. (They did – Germany won 4–1.) That's a big monkey on the back, or a large looming shadow. Either way, it reflects an inferiority mindset. Australia and Germany, whose sporting accomplishments are magnificent, have a history of fielding teams across a variety of sports consisting of players sufficiently virtuous to be willing to subsume their individual identity for the greater good. They are instilled with the virtues of discipline, hard work, and meticulous planning. This is the lived philosophy of the mentally tough performer.

Tilfreds

An interesting comparison can be drawn with Denmark. Surveys over 30 years have shown that the Danes score higher than any other Western country on measures of life satisfaction (Layard, 2006; Turner, 2007). There is a valuable lesson to be learned from the Danes' celebration of ordinariness: an ease and contentment with oneself, a quiet competence, and a confidence borne out of exclusivity. This is summed up in the Danish word *tilfreds*, meaning, literally, 'at peace'. Parallels can be drawn between an appropriate mindset for sport and contentment. Contentment is having a comfortable lifestyle without being swept up by competitive consumption. It is a feeling of belonging, of knowing and accepting the rules of the club. The development of mental toughness involves athletes and coaches realising that sport is to be enjoyed and that winning is not the sole purpose of sport (Barnes, 2008c). An all-consuming ambition with coming out top is unhealthy and does not develop mental toughness. Moreover, such ambition in the absence of mental toughness is wholly unrealistic. Indeed, wanting to win more than anyone else can become obsessive and the inevitable letdown, when it happens, is palpable. Rather, the obsession should not be with winning, but with putting everything in place that increases the likelihood of victory; in particular, the development of athletes' mental toughness, which, unless it is natural, can be gained only from experience (B. Moore, 2009a). For example, supportive home environments; motivational, rewarding, and enjoyable

training environments; challenging experiences; exposure to realistic competition; and PST programmes all have a vital role.

Athletes ought to have *tilfreds*: an inner peace and calm that come from
doing all one can to secure victory. Possession of an inner calm and mental
toughness are perfectly compatible bedfellows, operating harmoniously to
result in higher subjective well-being. As Michael Johnson reflected of one
particular group's underperformance in the 2008 Beijing Olympics: 'British
athletes must train harder and smarter . . . and develop a tougher attitude to
compete with the American, Caribbean and African athletes who generally
approach competition with a tougher attitude and approach' (Johnson,
2008: V5). Commitment to mental toughness development from the
aforementioned sources would address the concern that 'we want to win.
We want to win as much if not more than anyone else. We just do not want
to do what is necessary to win' (Anthony, 2007: 41).

Conclusion

Of central importance in the development of mental toughness is the ability
to problem-solve and to take personal responsibility. Athletes should be
exposed gradually to demanding situations in competition and training.
Learning environments should be challenging, yet supportive, thus
facilitating the nurturing of effective coping strategies. As part of their
physical and emotional maturity, athletes should also be empowered to
make decisions regarding their own development. Further, all situations
should be viewed as potential learning opportunities.

Not only is it crucial for athletes to develop their mental toughness in
order to increase the likelihood of their reaching the highest competitive
standards, but they must also identify what it takes to stay there. Researchers
have stated that 'there should be equal concern over what it takes to retain
that expertise' (Starkes, Weir, Singh, Hodges, & Kerr, 1999: 284). Indeed,
it is often considered that to be a true champion, one must be able to retain
excellence (Abbott & Collins, 2004). The development and maintenance of
a mentally tough mindset will facilitate the necessary adjustments.

On their way to the sporting summit, athletes will encounter confronta-
tions, setbacks, mistakes, and unavoidable failures, along with successes
and satisfactions. They are part of life's ebb and flow. Obstacles are an
inevitable part of the developmental process. Sustained success comes from
training and performing well over the long term rather than winning in the
short term (Balyi & Hamilton, 2004). Just as there is no shortcut to success
in athletic preparation, so the development of mental toughness is a long-
term process. In particular, understanding of this will facilitate successful
PST programme outcomes.

The more we invest in something, the more commitment we feel towards it. This is not to confuse investment with expenditure. Investment implies a return of significant personal value from a particular outlay. Surely, more athletes would invest in appropriate PST programmes if, in return, they develop into psychologically complete performers with highly developed levels of mental toughness. Such athletes would possess a competitive mind; be assertive, forceful, dominant; display commitment, eagerness, passion; have a high level of game intelligence; be focused, tremendously disciplined; and supremely self-confident.

In a newspaper interview, former England international cricketer Graeme Hick reflected on whether he ought to have been mentally tougher during his test career: 'At school in Zim [Zimbabwe] I was taught to play sport to your best, to respect opponents and play it in the right spirit. Only when I played here [England] did it start to get an "edge" and that's got more intense in the last few years' (as cited in S. Hughes, 2008a: S13). It is illuminating that the player he most admires is Steve Waugh, mentioned earlier in this chapter. Noted for his game intelligence, in particular his perception, reasoning, and decision-making, Waugh was a consummate tactician who visualised options, responded to changes in the pattern of play, and modified his team to suit environmental conditions. Yet, Waugh openly confessed to experiencing negative emotions just as strongly as other players. The crucial moderator, however, was his mental toughness that facilitated the appropriate response. He was much admired by many of his contemporaries, including Hick, who spoke of Waugh's mental toughness: '. . . his patience and discipline were amazing. He was one of the hardest characters in the game' (as cited in ibid.: S13).

Clearly, Steve Waugh's mental toughness elevated fellow cricketers' respect for him, particularly from his compatriots; evidenced when a despondent Michael Hussey, suffering a form trough, wrote to Waugh pleading for mental toughness insights into how to turn his fortunes around (Haigh, 2009). England's Paul Collingwood admitted to being overwhelmed by Waugh's presence: 'I was coming out to bat for my first one-day international against Australia at Old Trafford and Waugh was standing in my place at the crease setting the field, putting in slips and gullies . . . I had to stand out of the way and wait until he'd finished to take guard. It was typical of him. He had this amazing aura' (as cited in S. Hughes, 2010b: S23). Former Australian Test captain and broadcaster Richie Benaud wrote: 'Australia needs cricketers like Steve Waugh, players who excel when the going is hard and who improve as it becomes tougher and tougher' (Benaud, 1995: 195). Even Australia's national rugby league coach Tim Sheens, ahead of the 2009 Four Nations tournament, consulted Waugh on how to handle the pressure of being overwhelming favourites (A. Wilson, 2009c). Waugh's on-field persona corroborates observations of other highly successful crick-eters, such as Sachin Tendulkar, the highest run-scorer in international cricket: 'Cricket is not just about physical ability, it is also about mental ability, adapting to different conditions and situations' (as cited in Viner, 2009: 54), and Andrew Strauss: 'Cricket tests your character, and provides vital lessons to learn about yourself. People live the majority of life in their comfort zone; cricket forces you out of that' (as cited in Wheatley, 2009: 4). Similarly, England's national selector, Geoff Miller, stated that: 'Cricket is a game of mental toughness and psychology, as well as capability and tech-nique' (as cited in Booth & Rae, 2009), and that, as mentioned earlier in this chapter, the selectors, in consideration of player preference, were 'looking at mental toughness' (as cited in Hayter, 2009). Fittingly, and with typical insightfulness, the former Australian captain's shall be the final words on the benefits of developing a mentally tough mindset: 'Having a reputation for being mentally tough can have enormous advantages, because opponents respect and admire that trait and will put you on a pedestal, while teammates also hold you in higher esteem' (Waugh, 2006: 645).

6 Concluding mental toughness

> To live is to change, and to be perfect is to have changed often.
>
> Cardinal John Henry Newman

Concluding commentary

This has been a considerable journey: we now know what is constitutive of mental toughness, how it has been conceptualised, that it can be measured with reliable and valid instruments, and, crucially, how it can be developed and maintained. Mental toughness is an attribute that can be learned. The complex nature of mental toughness has been discussed throughout this book. To conclude, I would like to proffer the possibility that an element of mental toughness may be genetic. Indeed, such a suggestion has been advanced previously by international sport performers: 'Mental toughness is having the natural or developed psychological edge that enables you to . . .' (G. Jones *et al.*, 2002: 209). By 'natural', these athletes were suggesting that such an attribute might be innate as well as developed over many years of experience. I hasten to emphasise the 'as well as', and the absence of 'rather than'.

Inheriting mental toughness

Sir Francis Galton, best known for his early studies on genetic influences on intelligence (1865, 1869, 1874, 1875, 1884), is credited with the phrase 'nature or nurture', yet it is possible he was borrowing from William Shakespeare (1623/1998); specifically, Prospero's description of Caliban as 'A devil, a born devil, on whose nature/Nurture can never stick' (*The Tempest*, Act IV, scene 1). Perspectives on explaining successful sport performance vary, considering hereditary contributors (Bouchard & Malina, 1984; Bouchard, Malina, & Pérusse, 1997), and the role of dedicated practice over many years (Ericsson & Charness, 1994; Ericsson, Krampe, & Tesch-Römer, 1993). Because the attainment of the highest levels of performance in sport depends on so many variables, it is not easy to partial out the role of heredity. The premise that genetic determinants are as powerful as experiences and environments in life is not new. (For a succinct explanation, while at the same time enjoying an extremely funny motion picture, watch *Trading Places* [Folsey & Landis, 1983], and, specifically, the conversation, early in the film, held in the members-only Heritage Club between the commodity-trading brothers Randolph and Mortimer Duke.) However, though research has begun to claim links between genes and performance (Pérusse, Rankinen, Rauramaa, Rivera, Wolfarth, & Bouchard, 2003), little has been discussed in relation to how this information might be used to modify specific sporting performance.

It is commonly believed that highly successful performers are talented individuals. Their success is often attributed to complex, domain-specific cognitive structures and skills that are acquired as a consequence of attaining a sequence of increasingly challenging goals over extended periods of time (Ericsson, 1996; Ericsson & Charness, 1994; Ericsson *et al.*, 1993). On the basis of such research, Ericsson and Lehmann (1996), and later Ericsson (2003), argued that expert performance is attributable to prolonged periods of deliberate practice, rather than the presence of any innate talent.

An alternative view is that athletic talent is based, at least in some part, on a genetic predisposition that is responsive to training intervention. There is evidence to suggest that these theoretical positions are not mutually exclusive, and that both environmental and genetic factors interact in contributing to successful sport performance. We behave not as a result of nature versus nurture, but rather as 'their sum, their product and their expression' (Bell, 2009: 565). No one with any understanding of genetics believes that genes entirely explain behavioural traits, accepting, as Matt Ridley put it, that nature works via nurture (M. Ridley, 2003).

Personality characteristics are moderately heritable (Rushton, Bons, & Hur, 2008; Zuckerman, 2005), and we know that certain genetic combinations leave people more susceptible to environmental triggers. Yet, little is known about the potential inheritance of mental toughness or mental toughness as phenotype. Using the MTQ48 scale, mental toughness subscale heritability estimates of between 0.36 and 0.56 were reported in a sample of 219 pairs of adult twins (Horsburgh, Schermer, Veselka, & Vernon, 2009). The authors reported that 52 per cent of the variation in total mental toughness was due to genetic factors. The results also revealed that the more extravert a person was, the more mentally tough they were. In contrast, those who tended to be anxious or neurotic were less likely to be mentally tough. Interestingly, given the differences observed in MTQ48 subscale heritability estimates, and that the attributes influenced by environmental triggers may be more malleable than those influenced by genetic factors (Cloninger, 2000; Cloninger, Svrakic, & Przybeck, 1993), Horsburgh *et al.*

suggested that it may be easier to develop specific mental toughness attributes rather than mental toughness as a whole.

Hunting down the genes that influence personality remains a dauntingly difficult business. To date, research has examined genetic variability underlying brain neurotransmitter systems (namely: glutamate, γ-aminobutyric acid, norepinephrine, dopamine, and serotonin) (e.g., Caspi 2004; Caspi *et al.*, 2003; Grigorenko, 2002; Kalia, 2005; Kendler, Kuhn, Vittum, Prescott, & Riley, 2005; Krishnan *et al.*, 2007; Wilhelm *et al.*, 2006; Xie *et al.*, 2009). In sport, researchers have just begun to explore the relationship between genetic make-up and personality. For example, the relationship between the specific genotype of the serotonin transporter 5-hydroxytryptamine (5-HTT) gene, which is proposed to moderate reactions to stress (the 5-HTT polymorphism has regulatory properties within the serotonergic system), and positive psychological characteristics in young swimmers has been examined (Golby & Sheard, 2006). While no significant associations were observed, possibly as a result of the small sample size and that the participants had not yet specialised in a single competitive stroke or distance, the relationship between genotype and psychological characteristics in sport performers remains a particularly intriguing area for further research.

Genetics was voted the most important scientific advance of the first decade of the 21st century in a vote at the 2011 Cheltenham Science Festival. Genes would appear to have a bigger influence on our lives than we previously thought. People's DNA sequence is a barcode of their genetic origins, their gender, and many of their personal characteristics. Undoubtedly, they are a powerful force whose influence necessitates considerable effort on the part of those individuals wishing to overcome an undesirable trait in the natural programming of their personalities. However, I am not for one moment suggesting that there are direct causal relationships between genes and, for example, mental toughness. Specifically, genetic influences do not imply that personality is both biological and unchangeable (Caspi, Roberts, & Shiner, 2005; Kagan, 1999; Plomin, DeFries, McClearn, & McGuffin, 2001). Nobody inherits an unalterable capacity for mental toughness. What would be the point of PST programmes if people's levels of mental toughness, or even constituent parts, were genetically predetermined? Genes are not destiny. Biological heritage is not fate. We are not prisoners of our genes. That our personalities are influenced by genetics does not mean immutable; moreover, it does not mean that our environment is irrelevant. To ignore nurture would handicap the capacity to make new discoveries about nature. Environment is crucial. The brain is 'plastic', adapting and sharpening according to the experiences it has (LeDoux, 2002). Individuals vary in developmental plasticity, with some being more susceptible than others to good and bad environmental effects. More probable is that the quality of exceptional sport performers arises from a unique combination of inherited traits and capacities developed through training, experience, and exposure to challenging, yet supportive, environments; that is, an interaction. I believe Lance Armstrong summarises this interaction succinctly: 'It takes a lot of hard work, a lot of natural talent' (Armstrong, 2008: 2), environment being the former, and heredity accounting for the latter.

Particularly noteworthy, is the belief of a number of world-class athletes that they were born with some innate psychological attributes that facilitated their sporting success (Hays, Maynard, Thomas, & Bawden, 2007). Such attributes as an analytical personality, natural competitiveness, confidence, and mental strength were deemed by seven of the 14 athletes interviewed as being at least partly inherent. One judo world champion elaborated:

> I think I had the ability to block things out and that's important. I would be more nervous two to three weeks before a major event than I was the day before or the day of, something used to click and I could cope with it. There's not many people who can do it . . . I think it's something you can train, I think it's something you can develop and improve, but I think it's something that you are born with, I think it's a gift, I really believe that . . . some people have just got that mindset to be stronger, mentally.
>
> (ibid.: 445)

Though recent studies involving pairs of twins have suggested, for example, an inherited 'reserve' of happiness ($N = 900$ pairs; Weiss, Bates, & Luciano, 2009), and that self-confidence not only predicted better performance at school, but also that it is genetically influenced ($N = {>}3{,}700$ pairs; Greven, Harlaar, Kovas, Chamorro-Premuzic, & Plomin, 2009), any genetic component of mental toughness is, for now, speculation. Behavioural genetic research has shown that genetics and the environment are important throughout psychology. However, despite methods becoming available that can identify specific genes, it has been difficult to find them. Similarly, explaining why children growing up in the same family (i.e., shared environment) are so different has proven difficult. Most likely is that many genes are involved and each gene has a small effect in the nature–nurture interface. Having the genes is not enough; most likely, the environment or culture is needed to flip the switch. Much more 'genetic × environment interaction' research, adhering to rigorous methodologies (Moffitt, Caspi, & Rutter, 2005), needs to be conducted in the sporting domain.

It was not the aim of this section to demonstrate an interaction between genetic and environmental factors. Compelling research evidence shows this already. Rather, the model depicted in Figure 6.1 shows the interaction between genetic and environmental factors, their contribution to a combination of

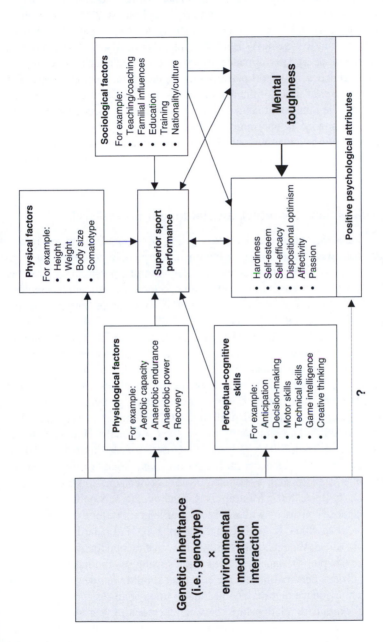

Figure 6.1 The position of mental toughness as a contributor to superior sport performance.

physical (e.g., Malina, Peña Reyes, Eisenmann, Horta, Rodrigues, & Miller, 2000), physiological (e.g., Reilly, Bangsbo, & Franks, 2000), perceptual-cognitive (e.g., A. M. Williams & Davids, 1995), and sociological factors (e.g., J. Baker, Horton, Robertson-Wilson, & Wall, 2003; Carlson, 1993), and their contribution to superior performance. Any potential association between mental toughness, genetics, and sport performance is, therefore, a complex one. The absence, to date, of proof of the association is not proof of the absence of an association. The number of candidate genes that may influence variability in human performance is enormous. A map showing all the links could be the answer; but it is a long way off. Despite a popular trend of 'neuro-hubris', this is a science still in its infancy. Moreover, genetics and brain imaging alone are unlikely to explain fully something as complex and human as personality.

Other directions for future mental toughness research

Future studies may also consider investigating how mental toughness relates to other constructs contributing to the positive psychology movement (e.g., flow, happiness, hope). Other constructs, for example, passion (Vallerand *et al.*, 2003), whose recent exploration relative to the sport domain has yielded promising findings (e.g., Amiot, Vallerand, & Blanchard, 2006; Donahue, Rip, & Vallerand, 2009; Lafrenière, Jowett, Vallerand, & Carbonneau, 2011; Sheard & Golby, 2009; Vallerand & Miquelon, 2007), offers opportunities to assess further the construct validation of mental toughness. Given the physical and psychological demands of sport, especially at higher competitive levels, research ought to examine how mental toughness relates to other psychological phenomena with an extant literature germane to sport; for example, burnout (see Cresswell & Eklund, 2007; Goodger, Gorely, Lavallee, & Harwood, 2007; D. Gould & Whitley, 2009; Lonsdale, Hodge, & Rose, 2009; Quested & Duda, 2011; A. L. Smith, Gustafsson, & Hassmén, 2010; A. L. Smith, Lemyre, & Raedeke, 2007), positive and negative components of perfectionism (see Anshel, Weatherby, Kang, & Watson, 2009; S. J. Egan, Piek, Dyck, & Rees, 2007; Mouratidis & Michou, 2011; Stoeber & Stoeber, 2009), and those constructs with a nascent profile in sport, for example, mindfulness (see Baer, 2003; K. W. Brown & Ryan, 2003; F. L. Gardner & Moore, 2004, 2006; Kee & Wang, 2008). Further, now that mental toughness is measurable (see Chapter 4), once sufficient studies using psychometrically sound instruments have been published, the construct should provide a critical mass of empirical evidence that may contribute to meta-analyses, similar to those that have examined relationships between personality variables and, for example, burnout (Alarcon, Eschleman, & Bowling, 2009). Longitudinal studies would afford the possibility of, for example, examining further the effects of PST interventions and outdoor adventure education activities on levels of mental toughness, related positive psychological attributes, and performance. Research should also consider the moderating role of mental toughness in the development of high-quality interpersonal relationships (e.g., coach–athlete, parent–athlete), and, presciently (see D. James, 2012), the sports career termination process. Identifying potential relationships between mental toughness and self-reported exercise and physical activity would also be an interesting, and worthwhile, research departure.

In addition, given the increasing prevalence and severity of injury in, for example, high-impact collision sports such as those given in Note 10, longitudinal research would allow the recording and monitoring of athletes' mental toughness and positive psychological profile during the rehabilitation process. The implementation of injury surveillance studies at major sporting events such as the Olympic Games (Junge *et al.*, 2006, 2009), World Athletics Championships (Alonso, Junge, Renström, Engebretsen, Mountjoy, & Dvorak, 2009), and Fifa World Cup tournaments (Dvorak, Junge, Grimm, & Kirkendall, 2007; Junge, Dvorak, & Graf-Baumann, 2004), affords sport psychology practitioners similar opportunities, ideally adhering to recommended theoretically informed methodology (see Podlog & Eklund, 2006; Podlog, Dimmock, & Miller, 2011).

Given the ever-increasing media scrutiny and game-related pressures facing sport referees and umpires (i.e., the culture of dogmatic instant judgement aped from reality television and toxic radio show phone-ins and tweets), consideration should be given also to how mental toughness manifests in sports officiating. A recent mixed methods study reported that performance pressures and expectations, environmental tensions, and full-time commitment pressures were consistent stressors of professional elite-level rugby league referees (Sheard & Golby, 2008). See Appendix B for this work, which was presented at the 14th World Congress of Psychiatry in Prague, Czech Republic.

This research needs to be extended across a variety of sports, and should consider how mental toughness may be placed within theoretical officiating contexts; for example, the 'four cornerstones' model (Mascarenhas, 2002). Interesting work has been conducted in the domain of sportsmanship (see, for example, Chantal, Robin, Vernat, & Bernache-Assollant, 2005; Vallerand, Deshaies, Cuerrier, Brière, & Pelletier, 1996). How mental toughness relates empirically to athletes' sportsmanship and sense of fair play (see, for example, Davidson, 2009a, 2009b; Kidd, 2009b; McLachlan, 2010; Norman, 2011; Reason, 2009c), and, in turn, how officials (see, for example, Parks, 2010; Winter, 2010k) and performers (see, for example, Aylwin, 2009; Briggs, 2010c; Lawton, 2009c; Winter, 2010m) respond to being on the receiving end of gamesmanship behaviours should also be addressed. A particularly recent phenomenon is the call for officials to toughen up under criticism. For example, Celtic FC assistant manager Johan Mjallby suggested that referees should be able to take criticism: 'It's a hard job and I understand that, but at the same time, if you want to be a referee you need to be mentally tough . . . I think most of them are competent enough, but maybe they should be mentally tougher' (as cited in Murray, 2011a). This clamouring for greater mental toughness exists at a time when many officials, across many sports, are being found guilty in the 'court of video analysis'. Clearly, this is not only topical, but also highly relevant, and there is much work that can be done in the sports officiating domain. An extension of such work could include an examination of how officials respond to athletes' behaviour influenced by the 'assistance' or 'strain' afforded by the home advantage phenomenon (see, for example, Bray & Widmeyer, 2000; Cashmore, 2008; Nevill, Balmer, & Williams, 2002; H. M. Wallace, Baumeister, Roy, & Vohs, 2005; Woodward, 2012).

The worldwide nurturing of positive psychology, and mental toughness specifically, offers great potential for cross-cultural research. As mentioned in Chapter 4, work has begun on the translation of the PPI-A and the SMTQ into other languages. This will enable their utilisation by non-English-speaking sport performers. Establishing each of the scale's psychometric properties in other languages will afford the opportunity to examine further how mental toughness may be influenced by cultural factors; the results of which should be interpreted according to local culture. Further empirical study ought to be devoted to advancing the preliminary research (see Golby & Meggs, 2011) which has shown a relationship between prenatal testosterone and levels of mental toughness. Finally, with increased participation in sport by athletes with disabilities, researchers should seek to recruit these exceptional performers as volunteers for further studies into the construct validation of mental toughness (see Coakley & Pike, 2009, Chapters 1, 8, and 11; LeUnes, 2008, Chapter 19).

Conclusion

Mental toughness has been criticised for being a potentially revealing measure that has devolved, rather than evolved, and for its being a misused and abused term 'thrown about with impunity' (Carlstadt, 2004: 225). This book has been a response to such observations, and has shown mental toughness to be a potent construct with instruments sufficiently sensitive to measure psychological performance. Indeed, the psychometrically robust PPI-A and SMTQ, and promising AfMTI, CMTI, and MTQ48, inventories presented in Chapter 4 refute the assertion that 'a personality inventory does not exist to measure the trait of mental toughness independent of other personality traits' (Cox, 2007: 31).

Sporting events are often won or lost between the ears. The exercise to summon the ultimate effort begins in the mind. Mental toughness elevates those athletes who have it above the rest. A hardened, disciplined mindset differentiates between the good and the great, facilitating the execution of skills consistently under pressure, especially at the highest standards of competition. Such are the margins at this level. Being mentally tough reflects positive values: responsibility, self-reliance, self-belief, and positivity to challenge. Mentally tough athletes have confidence, a 'can-do/anything is possible' attitude, and a winning mentality. Theirs is a ferocious work ethic. They recognise that sporting success is determined by incremental differences, the small per cent improvements that increase the likelihood of achievement, and that only through hard work, grit, and determination should success be expected. They are prepared to exert the effort that entails tackling challenges that lie just beyond their competence. To become good, they realise that they must extend themselves. They have strength of character and are able to bounce back from the inevitable mistakes and setbacks lurking around the corner. In sport, as in life, there are always checks and balances. Failure and success are only relative; it is how athletes handle both that matters. With an acquired sense of perspective and humility, mentally tough athletes remain honest and humble. They should reject any notion of their being reduced to the level of a celebrity. They adapt to adversity and with a fighter's heart and a winner's mind, they are steadfast, persistent, and have a conviction about their purpose.

Mentally tough performers also have presence – a hugely powerful force in any sporting contest. Mental toughness is the 'edge', the 'X factor', if you like. I prefer the 'A factor': 'A' for achievement. A high level of mental toughness gives individuals and teams an overwhelming advantage. If physical and technical skills are matched, and environmental conditions do not favour inequitably an individual or team, it is those who are mentally stronger that prevail. In training and competition situations that are pivotal to success, athletes with heightened mental toughness are able to perform to their best when it counts the most. The commitment, which produces the mentally tough mindset that generates the achievement, is worth all the labour. Mentally tough athletes are able to combine striving for personal excellence with competitive success. They do not get fazed by big occasions. They have a determination to work for the moment and then seize it. At the same time, they are also able to encourage fairness and respect for the rules/laws of their sport and opponents. These are the exceptional individuals, the leaders who rise to the moment, the champions who possess the virtues to excel, and the victors who win with integrity and thrill us with their mental toughness – 'the Achievers'.

Successful sport performance is, ultimately, about ability and mental toughness. Without denying the crucial role of talent, though which by itself is insufficient, I have tried to present a case that it is something else that separates the hugely talented from the very best and, in turn, distinguishes the greatest athletes – an achievement mindset. The determination, commitment, self-belief, positive cognition, emotional discipline, self-sufficiency, and perseverance necessary for success are each constitutive of the achievement mindset that I call mental toughness. This mindset, complementary to talent, lends performers a moral authority. It confers upon them psychological wealth. In the absence of mental toughness you are left with 'ability without confidence, talent without aura' (Barnes, 2009k: 2), demonstrated by the England rugby union team in the 2010 Six Nations Championship, as full-back Delon Armitage acknowledged: 'We've got the talent . . . But we've talked too much about it. We've got to go out and do it' (as cited in Cleary, 2010b: S12). Similarly, Duncan Fletcher stressed the crucial role of a mentally tough personality: 'I have seen so many talented players who lacked character, and you just know that they are never going to get near fulfilling their potential. That is why you should select a side on personality as much as on talent . . . England selected on character, not just talent' (Fletcher, 2010: 1, 7).

That's why I conclude that it is mental toughness that makes someone a supremely talented sport performer. Mental toughness helps to ensure that athletes look back on their careers with trophies, medals, and titles – not regrets. Mentally tough athletes trust their ability. But it is not just a question of talent. As Great Britain Davis Cup tennis player Jamie Baker quite rightly observed: 'Talent isn't just in the hands, but in the mind' (J. Baker, 2010: S15). Mental toughness prevents talent being squandered. Only the strongest – mentally, as well as physically – survive and flourish. Athletes may possess ability, but that of the very best is buttressed by mental toughness. Decisive and winning behavioural manifestations of talent come down to mental toughness. Talent can only take an athlete to a certain point. Mental toughness makes up the deficit between talent and performance. Only athletes of exceptional ability and acute mental toughness advance. Winners are distinguished by their mental and behavioural toughness: the ones who, on any given day, are mentally tougher. They know how to employ a range of self-ameliorative strategies and confidence techniques, and are able to manage emotions such as anxiety and anger. They are able to command their bodies and maintain outstanding technical skill levels in the face of adversities such as danger, pain, fatigue, and potentiality of defeat.

History never forgets those performers who demonstrate that the real barriers to sporting achievement are in the mind. In the spirit of which, I leave the last word to a sporting great – Michael Phelps (as cited in Syed, 2009g: 59):

> If I have an ambition in my mind, whatever it is, nothing will stop me. Nothing . . . People say that I have great talent, but in my opinion excellence has nothing to do with talent. It is about what you choose to believe and how determined you are to get there. The mind is more powerful than anything else.

Appendix A
Measuring mental toughness

Construct validation of the alternative
Psychological Performance Inventory
(PPI-A) and the Sports Mental
Toughness Questionnaire (SMTQ)

Introduction

Research has identified 'mental toughness' as a crucial attribute to success in competitive sport and the development of champion sport performers (Durand-Bush & Salmela, 2002; Gould *et al.*, 2002). Yet, despite a general definitional consensus reflecting the cognitive-behavioural multi-variate nature of the construct (Sheard, 2009d), insufficient effort has been devoted to the development of a reliable and valid measure of mental toughness in sport. Thus, there is ambiguity in how mental toughness can be measured. Consequently, the present study examined the construct validity of two multi-dimensional measures of mental toughness in sport, which, to date, have demonstrated encouraging psychometric properties: The alternative Psychological Performance Inventory (PPI-A; Golby *et al.*, 2007), and the Sports Mental Toughness Questionnaire (SMTQ; Sheard *et al.*, 2009).

A theory-based model of mental toughness

The construct validation of mental toughness undertaken in this research is in the spirit of what has been baptised 'positive psychology' (Seligman & Csikszentmihalyi, 2000). A central tenet of the positive psychology paradigm is that stressors, adversity, and other inordinate demands are inherent to the human condition. However, the paradigm assumes that there are also sources of strength, through which this condition can be endured and even transcended. Physical, emotional, and social stressors can stimulate growth and strengthening in many individuals. Such people are often able to tap into previously unknown capacities, perspectives, and virtues. Thus, positive psychology is an obviously desirable frame of reference within which to examine the construct validation of mental toughness.

Mentally tough performers have the ability to bounce back from stressful experiences, such as competitive sport, quickly and effectively. Such an outcome is likely to be facilitated by athletes' possession of relatively enduring characteristics; for example, optimism, hardiness, and positive affectivity are highly desirable dispositional tendencies that can predispose a situation-specific response. When confronting a challenge, individuals high in optimism, hardiness, and positive affectivity tend to approach it with confidence and persistence (Golby & Sheard, 2004; Sheard & Golby, 2006). Such persons feel engaged in, and influential over, whatever they are doing, and thus derive positive emotions from their involvement (Forgas, 2006; Maddi, 2006a, 2006b). This perspective facilitates adaptive solution-focused behaviours, resulting in people concluding that the challenges facing them can be overcome. Studies have revealed relationships, but also distinctions, between mental toughness and hardiness (Golby *et al.*, 2003; Sheard, 2009b), optimism (Nicholls *et al.*, 2008), and positive affectivity (Sheard & Golby, 2006a).

Methods

Participants

Volunteers ($N = 455$; M age $= 21.8$ years; $SD = 4.15$) were drawn from 19 sport classifications (Table A.1) and were presently competing either at elite (i.e., international, national) or sub-elite (i.e., county, club) representative standards. Institutional ethics approval was obtained, and ethical procedures conforming to recognised standards were adhered to throughout the research process (British Psychological Society, 2006). All participants provided informed consent and were assured confidentiality. They were also naïve to the research hypotheses.

In addition to the PPI-A and SMTQ, participants also completed the Personal Views Survey III-R (PVS III-R; Maddi & Khoshaba, 2001), the revised Life Orientation Test (LOT-R; Scheier et al., 1994), and the Positive and Negative Affect Schedule (PANAS; Watson et al., 1988). These instruments were chosen as the divergent validity criterion on the basis of their acceptable psychometric properties, and their conceptual relatedness to, but hypothesised independence and distinction from, mental toughness, as mentioned previously. Participants completed the questionnaires in their respective training camps, and the average completion time was less than 15 minutes. No volunteers refused to complete the questionnaires.

Table A.1 Summary of participants' demographic characteristics

	n	♂	Elite		Sub-elite		♀	Elite		Sub-elite	
			I	N	C	c		I	N	C	c
Contact team sports											
Field hockey	24	6	–	–	3	3	18	–	1	12	5
Rugby league football	179	179	45	50	84	–	–	–	–	–	–
Rugby union football	24	24	2	5	17	–	–	–	–	–	–
Soccer	98	82	–	2	39	41	16	–	2	5	9
Total n	325	291	47	57	143	44	34	–	3	17	14
Contact individual sports											
Martial arts	4	4	1	2	1	–	–	–	–	–	–
Total n	4	4	1	2	1	–	–	–	–	–	–
Non-contact team sports											
Basketball	13	13	–	2	5	6	–	–	–	–	–
Cricket	10	10	–	–	5	5	–	–	–	–	–
Netball	28	–	–	–	–	–	28	2	–	14	12
Total n	51	23	–	2	10	11	28	2	–	14	12
Non-contact individual sports											
Bowls	1	1	1	–	–	–	–	–	–	–	–
Canoeing/kayaking/ rowing	3	3	2	–	1	–	–	–	–	–	–
Climbing/mountaineering/ orienteering	4	1	–	–	–	1	3	–	–	–	3
Cycling	2	2	–	2	–	–	–	–	–	–	–
Equestrianism	5	–	–	–	–	–	5	1	–	2	2
Golf	8	8	–	2	–	6	–	–	–	–	–
Gymnastics	14	–	–	–	–	–	14	1	2	3	8
Racquet sports	11	3	–	–	3	–	8	–	1	2	5
Swimming	17	5	1	1	3	–	12	1	2	2	7
Track and field	4	1	–	1	–	–	3	1	–	2	–
Triathlon	6	2	–	1	1	–	4	–	1	1	2
Total n	75	26	4	7	8	7	49	4	6	12	27
Grand total N	455	344	52	68	162	62	111	6	9	43	53

Note: ♂ = Male; ♀ = Female.
I = International; N = National [Elite]; C = County; c = Club [Sub-elite].

Results

Schmid–Leiman analyses

The respective inter-correlations for the PPI-A and SMTQ items are shown in Table A.2. Higher-order factor analysis takes into account the reality of

Table A.2 Intercorrelations among PPI-A, SMTQ, and criterion positive psychological scales

	1DT	2SB	3PC	4VL	5Total PPI-A	6CF	7CS	8CT	9Total SMTQ	10Com	11Con	12Cha	13Total PVS III-R	14LOT-R	15PANAS (+)	16PANAS (−)
1		0.44	0.51	0.45	0.75	0.29	0.32	0.15	0.33	0.38	0.24	0.09	0.31	0.16	0.39	−0.06
2			0.54	0.32	0.75	0.42	0.36	0.33	0.49	0.41	0.34	0.38	0.48	0.40	0.39	−0.33
3				0.47	0.81	0.47	0.38	0.25	0.49	0.41	0.26	0.31	0.42	0.33	0.43	−0.23
4					0.76	0.30	0.27	0.12	0.31	0.28	0.18	0.13	0.25	0.10	0.33	0.00
5						0.48	0.43	0.28	0.52	0.48	0.33	0.30	0.47	0.32	0.50	−0.20
6							0.49	0.33	0.85	0.42	0.38	0.37	0.49	0.44	0.46	−0.27
7								0.38	0.77	0.43	0.37	0.25	0.45	0.27	0.41	−0.25
8									0.69	0.32	0.32	0.29	0.39	0.38	0.33	−0.42
9										0.51	0.46	0.40	0.58	0.48	0.52	−0.39
10											0.49	0.44	0.84	0.49	0.56	−0.36
11												0.38	0.78	0.48	0.40	−0.31
12													0.75	0.43	0.36	−0.31
13														0.59	0.56	−0.42
14															0.45	−0.42
15																−0.24

Note: DT = Determination; SB = Self-belief; PC = Positive Cognition; VL = Visualization; Total PPI-A = Mental toughness composite score [PPI-A]; CF = Confidence; CS = Constancy; CT = Control; Total SMTQ = Mental toughness composite score [SMTQ]; Com = Commitment; Con = Control; Cha = Challenge; Total PVS III-R = Hardiness composite score [PVS III-R]; LOT-R = Dispositional optimism; PANAS (+) = Positive Affect; PANAS (−) = Negative Affect.

Correlation coefficients: ($p < 0.01$) are in bold; ($p < 0.05$) are underlined; ($p > 0.05$) are in roman.

correlated factors by allowing for the extraction of variance accounted for by the general factor (B. Thompson, 2004). The remaining variance, which is free of all variance present in the general factor (e.g., mental toughness), is then assigned to the lower-order factors. The residualised domain-specific factor loading of each variable can then be specified by partialling out the variable's 'g' loading and uniqueness. Therefore, each factor represents the independent contribution of the factor in question. This transformation is achieved by the Schmid–Leiman procedure (Schmid & Leiman, 1957). Within each scale, there was evidence to suggest the plausibility of both a general mental toughness (G_{MT}) factor, and unique and orthogonal first-order factors (see Figs A.1 and A.2 for calculations).

Confirmatory factor analysis (CFA)

CFA was conducted using LISREL 8.14 (Jöreskog & Sörbom, 1993). Factor loadings and error variances for each scale are shown in Table A.3. Absolute and incremental fit indices indicated good model fits for each scale. The equivalent higher-order models, with four first-order and three first-order factors (for the PPI-A and SMTQ, respectively), and one second-order general factor yielded the same degree of model fit as the preceding models (as expected). Each factor also demonstrated acceptable internal consistency (Table A.3) (Kline, 2005).

Divergent validity

Divergent validity was demonstrated by the observed pattern of weak to moderate correlations among the mental toughness and PVS III-R, LOT-R, and PANAS subscales (Table A.2).

Differential validity

To reduce the variance attributable to demographic variables, multivariate analysis of covariance (MANCOVA) was used to analyse the data (Tabach-nick & Fidell, 2007). Because G_{MT} is a composite of the scores of each scale's factors, a separate MANCOVA was employed to identify significant composite differences. Alpha (α) was set at 0.05. When necessary, *post hoc* comparisons were made using the Dunn-Sidak method, which accounted for the inflated Type I error rate (R. C. Kirk, 1995). α was adjusted to 0.008. These analyses were conducted using SPSS v14.0 (SPSS Inc, Chicago, IL).

Means and standard deviations of all variables are presented in Table A.4. Subscale MANCOVA revealed a significant multivariate effect for competitive standard, Wilks' $\lambda = 0.73$, $F(21, 1,267) = 7.16$, $p < 0.001$,

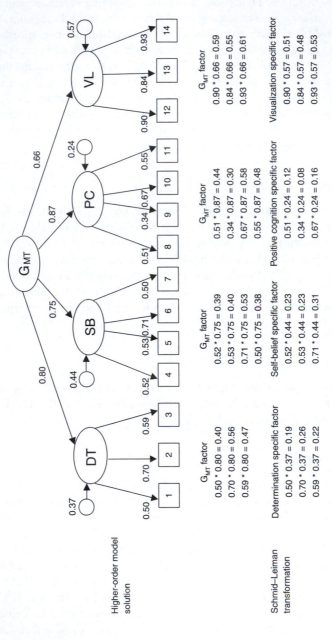

Figure A.1 The PPI-A model tested in this investigation, which includes the higher-order estimates displayed within the figure, as well as the corresponding calculations required for performing the Schmid–Leiman transformation of the higher-order model.

Note: G_{MT} = General Mental Toughness; DT = Determination; SB = Self-belief; PC = Positive Cognition; VL = Visualisation.

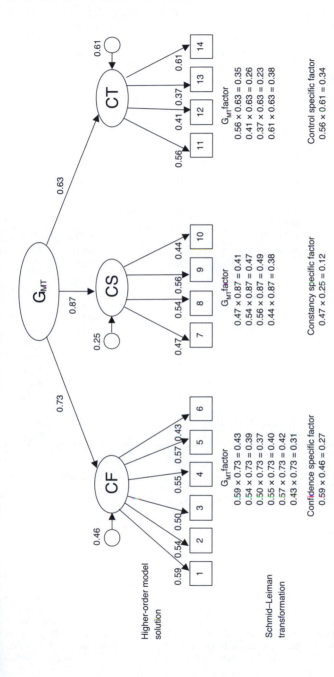

Figure A.2 The SMTQ model tested in this investigation, which includes the higher-order estimates displayed within the figure, as well as the corresponding calculations required for performing the Schmid–Leiman transformation of the higher-order model.

Note: G_{MT} = General Mental Toughness; CF = Confidence; CS = Constancy; CT = Control.

Table A.3 CFA factor loadings, error variance, fit indices, and reliability

PPI-A item	PPI-A CFA factor loadings and error variance				SMTQ item	SMTQ CFA factor loadings and error variance		
	DT	SB	PC	VL		CF	CS	CT
1	0.66				1	0.64		
	0.56					*0.59*		
2	0.76				2	0.72		
	0.42					*0.48*		
3	0.69				3	0.64		
	0.52					*0.59*		
4		0.50			4	0.65		
		0.75				*0.58*		
5		0.65			5	0.75		
		0.58				*0.44*		
6		0.81			6	0.60		
		0.34				*0.64*		
7		0.51			7		0.61	
		0.74					*0.63*	
8			0.59		8		0.66	
			0.65				*0.56*	
9			0.51		9		0.62	
			0.73				*0.61*	
10			0.74		10		0.61	
			0.45				*0.63*	
11			0.67		11			0.75
			0.55					*0.44*
12				0.76	12			0.59
				0.42				*0.65*
13				0.75	13			0.50
				0.44				*0.75*
14				0.81	14			0.72
				0.35				*0.48*

χ^2(df:71)					χ^2(df:74)			
	284.90 ($p < 0.01$)					236.16 ($p < 0.01$)		
GFI	0.93				GFI	0.93		
AGFI	0.91				AGFI	0.91		
RMR	0.07				RMR	0.05		
RMSEA	0.05				RMSEA	0.05		
NFI	0.91				NFI	0.91		
TLI	0.91				TLI	0.91		
CFI	0.90				CFI	0.91		
α	0.75	0.70	0.71	0.82	α	0.82	0.72	0.74

Note: DT = Determination; SB = Self-belief; PC = Positive Cognition; VL = Visualisation [PPI-A]; CF = Confidence; CS = Constancy; CT = Control [SMTQ]; GFI = Goodness-of-Fit Index; AGFI = Adjusted Goodness-of-Fit Index; RMR = Root Mean Square Residual; RMSEA = Root Mean Square of Approximation [absolute fit indices]; NFI = Normed Fit Index; TLI = Tucker-Lewis Index; CFI = Comparative Fit Index [incremental fit indices]; α = Cronbach coefficient alpha.

CFA error variances are *italicised*.

Table A.4 Means and standard deviations of the PPI-A and SMTQ

Competitive standard	PPI-A										SMTQ							
	DT		SB		PC		VL		Total		CF		CS		CT		Total	
	M	SD	M	SD	M	SD	M	SD	M	SD	M	SD	M	SD	M	SD	M	SD
International	12.8	2.0	16.3	2.4	16.4	2.1	12.3	2.3	57.9	6.4	20.0	3.0	14.3	1.9	12.6	2.3	46.9	5.6
National	12.5	1.9	15.9	2.2	16.1	2.0	11.0	2.9	55.5	6.3	18.5	3.1	13.8	1.8	11.4	2.3	43.7	5.7
County	12.1	2.1	14.8	2.7	15.2	2.3	10.7	2.8	52.7	7.4	16.5	2.9	12.4	2.1	10.3	2.0	39.2	4.8
Club	11.4	2.1	13.6	2.6	13.8	2.3	9.2	3.0	47.9	7.3	14.7	2.8	11.6	2.1	10.1	2.0	36.3	4.7

Note: DT = Determination; SB = Self-belief; PC = Positive Cognition; VL = Visualisation [PPI-A]; CF = Confidence; CS = Constancy; CT = Control [SMTQ].

Entered covariates: Age; Sport Type [individual, team]; Sport Category [i.e., contact, non-contact]; Gender [i.e., male, female].

partial $\eta^2 = 0.10$. Specifically, there were significant effects for *Determination, F*(3, 447) = 5.69, $p < 0.001$, partial $\eta^2 = 0.04$ [international and national performers scored significantly higher than club athletes], *Self-belief, F*(3, 447) = 11.38, $p < 0.001$, partial $\eta^2 = 0.07$ [international athletes scored significantly higher than county and club performers; national competitors scored significantly higher than club athletes], *Positive Cognition, F*(3, 447) = 14.04, $p < 0.001$, partial $\eta^2 = 0.09$ [national and county athletes scored significantly higher than club counterparts], *Visualisation, F*(3, 447) = 10.07, $p < 0.001$, partial $\eta^2 = 0.06$ [club performers scored significantly lower than all other levels; international athletes scored significantly higher than county performers], *Confidence, F*(3, 447) = 26.29, $p < 0.001$, partial $\eta^2 = 0.15$ [international and national athletes scored significantly higher than county and club competitors], *Constancy, F*(3, 447) = 18.80, $p < 0.001$, partial $\eta^2 = 0.11$ [international and national competitors scored significantly higher than their county and club counterparts], *Control, F*(3, 447) = 16.70, $p < 0.001$, partial $\eta^2 = 0.10$ [international athletes scored significantly higher than all other levels; national competitors scored significantly higher than county and club performers].

Composite MANCOVA also revealed a significant effect for competitive standard, Wilks' $\lambda = 0.76$, F(6, 892) = 21.97, $p < 0.001$, partial $\eta^2 = 0.13$. Specifically, there were significant effects for total *PPI-A, F*(3, 447) = 18.19, $p < 0.001$, partial $\eta^2 = 0.11$ [club athletes scored significantly lower than all other groups; international competitors scored significantly higher than county performers], and total *SMTQ, F*(3, 447) = 39.97, $p < 0.001$, partial $\eta^2 = 0.21$ [international and national performers scored significantly higher than their county and club counterparts] (Table A.4).

Discussion

The aim of this study was to extend the previous psychometric work on the PPI-A and SMTQ (Golby *et al.*, 2007; Sheard *et al.*, 2009). Higher-order factor analyses suggested evidence of a G_{MT} factor in each scale, as well as their respective first-order factors. Absolute and incremental CFA fit indices showed good support for each model. All factors in each scale showed good reliability. Divergent validity was established by a pattern of correlations between each mental toughness scale and positive psychological measures. Finally, further evidence of each scale's discriminative power was observed; specifically, international level competitors were characterised by the highest levels of mental toughness when adjustments were made for covariates.

This research offers support for the PPI-A and SMTQ as valid measures of mental toughness. The instruments possess encouraging psychometric integrity. As construct validation is an ongoing process (Anastasi & Urbina, 1997), meaningful comparisons should now be made on PPI-A and SMTQ data collected over time, with the recommendation that practitioners use changes in PPI-A and SMTQ scores as indices for evaluating the impact of psychological skills training. This would fulfil the ultimate construct validation criterion of application in research and practice (Marsh, 2002).

Appendix B
Resisting stress
in sports officiating
The moderating role of positive psychology

Introduction

While research has considered the decision-making of elite-level officials of collision sports (Mascarenhas, Collins, & Mortimer, 2005; Mascarenhas, Collins, Mortimer, & Morris, 2005), little is known about how these individuals respond to stress. This is somewhat surprising given the attention devoted to understanding the stress encountered by the performers whom they are officiating. In particular, though recent research has reported on the stress-buffering role of desirable positive psychological attributes in elite-level rugby league footballers (Golby & Sheard, 2004; Golby et al., 2003), similarly high-achieving rugby league officials have been previously overlooked.

The award of full-time professional status in December 2006 has brought with it new challenges for this elite group of officials. Rugby league referees must make difficult judgements in front of large, noisy, and sometimes hostile crowds. Cognitive, emotional, and behavioural responses can each contribute to stress when, for example, officials believe they have lost control of a contest or when they, or significant others, assess their performance as inadequate. The accompanying media scrutiny, criticism by coaches, and increased levels of accountability have the potential to be sources of considerable stress.

The present study is timely given recent high-exposure media coverage of officiating in rugby league (Irvine, 2007a; Ledger, 2008; Shepherd, 2007). Thus, the purpose of this research was to examine the sources of stress encountered by professional rugby league football referees and how they resist these stressors.

Methods

Participants

Participants were six male professional referees officiating in Super League, European rugby league's highest competitive standard. Institutional ethics approval was obtained, and ethical procedures conforming to recognised standards were adhered to throughout the research process (British Psychological Society, 2006). Permission for the referees to participate was obtained from the Rugby Football League (RFL) Match Officials Director. The participants ranged in age from 25 to 41 years, with a mean age of 32.5 years ($SD =$ 6.2). Their experience refereeing Grade I rugby league (the highest) ranged from 3 to 12 years, with a mean of 6.8 years ($SD = 3.4$). Their total officiating experience ranged from 8 to 17 years, with a mean of 12.8 years ($SD = 3.3$).

Data collection

To strengthen any potential research claims, a mixed methods approach was adopted (Gorard & Taylor, 2004). The first stage involved participants completing a battery of positive psychological questionnaires and stress-specific instruments (see Table B.1). Each of the referees subsequently participated in qualitative semi-structured interviews (Stage 2). The authors conducted one 20-minute semi-structured interview with each participant. A list of open-ended questions guided the interview (see Table B.2). Semi-structured questions were designed to provide a consistent framework in which to operate across the participants, but also to allow opportunities to explore participant responses when appropriate. With the permission of the participants, the interviews were audiotaped. The first author transcribed the tapes. The second author checked the transcriptions. The transcriptions were returned to the participants for checking of their accuracy. Both stages were conducted in private rooms at RFL headquarters.

Data analysis procedures

Quantitative measures were analysed using SPSS for Windows v.14.0 (SPSS Inc., Chicago, IL). With regard to the qualitative methods, the authors and two additional trained researchers independently reviewed the raw data (i.e., quotes) taken from the verbatim transcriptions. Seventeen pages of single-spaced text were transcribed from the six tape-recorded interviews. Hierarchical content analysis was employed in this study (Côté, Salmela, Trudel, Baria, & Russell, 1993). Each researcher independently identified raw data themes. These reflected a particular abstraction or concept that emerged. After the independent content analysis, the four researchers discussed the identified themes. Triangular consensus was employed to ensure which raw data themes would be used in the analysis. Disagreements were resolved by further reviews of the transcripts. An inductive analysis was conducted to identify more general themes, which were identified from first- and second-order themes. The highest level represented the most general themes. Three major themes were identified as general dimensions and each was considered to be distinct. Triangular consensus was reached on all the identified higher-order themes. The identified raw data, first-order, second-order, and general dimensions are presented in Figure B.1.

Results

Quantitative measures found all volunteers to be high in stress-buffering positive psychological attributes (Table B.1). However, a wide range of scores was found relative to the stress-specific PSS measure (*viz.*, 22–40).

Qualitative findings corroborated these results. The referees rated themselves between 75–95 per cent on how well they thought they had done. Inductive analyses revealed several major themes associated with combating the stressors faced by professional rugby league football referees: (a) they possess high levels of positive psychological attributes; (b) they have a strong refereeing identity; and (c) they try to work as a cohesive team despite an apparent tension between satisfying individual official's ambitions and working as a harmonious group. Table B.2 shows illustrative quotations from the participants.

Conclusion

The present study revealed some interesting insights into the thoughts, feelings, and behaviours of professional rugby league referees operating at the highest level. In addition to high levels of physical fitness and an ability to apply a consistently accurate interpretation of the laws of the game, these referees also have the desirable positive psychological attributes to deal effectively with the increased scrutiny concomitant with the professional status of their role. Identifying strongly with their officiating role, each of the referees in the present study has a broad repertoire of stress management skills, facilitating appropriate handling of potentially stressful situations. Particularly noteworthy is that scores of officials in the present study compare favourably with the elite-level players they are refereeing (Golby & Sheard 2004; Golby *et al.*, 2003). Given the high level of competition among the referees for being appointed to the limited number of top matches, it is unsurprising that a 'cooperation versus competition tension' exists among the referees in their efforts to appear the most appropriate nomination in the opinion of those ultimately making such appointments.

Raw data themes	1st-order themes	2nd-order themes	General dimensions
Improving performance Performing well Perform well each week Setting high standard Performance environment	**Performance**	**TAKING RESPONSIBILITY**	**POSITIVE PSYCHOLOGY**
Focused No outside distractions	**Focus**		
Specific aims (extrinsic) Non-specific aims (intrinsic)	**Determination**		
Good technical ability Ability to read game Understanding of the game Increased learning	**Game intelligence**	**AUTHORITATIVE SELF-BELIEF**	
Confidence Confidence in decision-making Self-assurance	**Confidence**		
Communication Delivery of message Refereeing style	**Self-presentation**		
Good attitude Attitude to training Attitude to job Enjoy job	**Positive cognition**		
Dealing with disappointment Capricious fortunes Handling criticism	**Coping**	**EMOTIONAL CONTROL**	

Figure B.1 Elite-level rugby league referees' inductive analysis results.

(Continued opposite)

Raw data themes	1st-order themes	2nd-order themes	General dimensions
Preparation More time to train Relaxed preparation/reviewing Work/life balance	**Full-time benefits**	**PROFESSIONAL ENVIRONMENT**	**STRONG REFEREEING IDENTITY**
Inability to get away from rugby No break Always thinking 'what's next'	**Full-time pressures**		
More critical analysis needed More coaching at lower level	**Development**		
Not worrying about other issues Money Job easier	**Rewards**		
Bosses not dealing with issues Abuse from players Abuse from spectators	**Conflict**	**EARNED RECOGNITION**	
Player man-management Player and colleagues' respect Rapport with players	**Social recognition**		
Getting big games Missing out on big games Being on television Stress of being dropped	**Media perception**		
Solid relationships Good group atmosphere	**Social**	**SUPPORTIVE ENVIRONMENT**	**GROUP TENSION**
Cooperation	**Cooperation**		
Competitive environment	**Competition**	**STRESSFUL ENVIRONMENT**	
Keep own counsel Distance oneself Concern about being outspoken Officials being favoured Frustrating group atmosphere Stressful group atmosphere	**Anxiety**		
Atmosphere could be better Interpersonal criticism Moaning colleagues	**Comments**	**STRESSFUL COMMENTS**	

Table B.1 Means and standard deviations of positive psychological measures

Positive psychological measures	Scores		
	Desired score	M	SD
Confidence	24	21.3	2.5
Constancy	16	14.5	1.5
Control	16	12.2	2.6
Total mental toughness [SMTQ] (Sheard, Golby, & van Wersch, 2009)	56	48.0	5.4
Determination	15	14.6	0.5
Self-belief	20	18.2	1.6
Positive cognition	20	18.0	2.0
Visualisation	15	12.8	2.2
Total mental toughness [PPI-A] (Golby, Sheard, & van Wersch, 2007)	70	63.6	5.5
Commitment		17.8	5.5
Control		11.0	3.7
Challenge		13.5	3.0
Total hardiness [PVS III-R] (Maddi & Khoshaba, 2001)		42.3	8.0
Dispositional optimism [LOT-R] (Scheier, Carver, & Bridges, 1994)	30	24.3	4.7
Positive affect [PANAS] (Watson, Clark, & Tellegen, 1988)	50	45.0	8.6
Negative affect [PANAS] (Watson, Clark, & Tellegen, 1988)[†]	10	14.2	2.1
Self-esteem [RSES] (Rosenberg, 1965)	40	36.2	5.2
Self-efficacy [GSES] (Schwarzer & Jerusalem, 1993)	40	34.2	4.7
Self-perception of quality of performance [SPQPQ] (Ebbeck & Weiss, 1988)	35	31.3	2.4
Perceived stress [PSS] (Cohen, Kamarck, & Mermelstein, 1983)	40	30.7	7.2
Group climate [GCS] (Kanas & Ziegler, 1984)	20	14.8	3.0

[†] = lower score desirable.

Table B.2 Illustrative quotes elicited from the semi-structured interviews

---

Q1   How well do you think you have done so far? Give a percentage.
'It's been like a roller-coaster. You have your highs and you have your lows.'
75 per cent.
'There have been a few distractions, just making little mistakes in games.'
95 per cent.

Q2   What were the best moments for you so far this season?
'Probably last week. That was definitely the biggest game of the year. The most personal pressure for me.'
'Definitely the Test match.'

Q3   What were the worst? Why?
'Without a shadow of doubt, when I was taken to the office to hear that because of a decision I had made the week before, I wouldn't be on the Super League list the following week. Horrendous in terms of my career.'
'I can't understand why I haven't been on television [since the beginning of the season]. The perception of things by everybody outside of this office is that if you are not refereeing on television, you are probably not refereeing well.'

Q4   What are your strengths as a referee?
'Fitness, ability to read the game, man-management with the players, the communication, identification of the tackle area.'
'I'm clear in what needs to be done. I've built a good standard for myself.'

Q5   Your weaknesses?
'Sometimes, I am a little bit too sure of myself.'
'A little of mental weakness. Sometimes, you don't feel you are getting the games that you should.'

Q6   Have you suffered from stress recently? If so, when, where, how, and how often?
'When I was dropped. You start to question your ability to do this job. We are in a performance environment.'
'Yes, definitely. A lot of it is created by employers, by not dealing with things that they should. A lot of things that get put on internet sites about you, your family. External pressures. Actually, the stress of the game is manageable.'

Q7   Have you any comments on the group atmosphere?
'It could be better. It can be a source of stress.'
'The group atmosphere does get frustrating at times.'

Q8   What do you think are the main differences between professional/full-time and amateur/part-time referees?
'Now, I've got time to spend with my family, which alleviates that external pressure.'
'You don't really get away from rugby. Sometimes, that can be difficult, because there's no break from it.'

Q9   What are your aims for the rest of the season?
'Challenge Cup Final, Play-offs, Grand Final, Referee of the Year, World Cup.'
'Just referee to the best of my ability, and what will be, will be.'

Notes

1 For literature intimating that desirable psychological attributes contribute significantly to superior sport performance, see: M. S. Allen, Greenlees, & Jones, 2011; Cohn, 1991; Eklund, 1994, 1996; V. Evans & Quarterman, 1983; Gee, Marshall, & King, 2010; D. Gould, Guinan, Greenleaf, Medbery, & Peterson, 1999; Greenleaf, Gould, & Dieffenbach, 2001; Hanton & Jones, 1999; Holt & Dunn, 2004; S. A. Jackson, 1995; S. A. Jackson, Mayocchi, & Dover, 1998; G. Jones, Hanton, & Swain, 1994; A. W. Meyers, Whelan, & Murphy, 1995; M. C. Meyers, Bourgeois, LeUnes, & Murray, 1998; M. C. Meyers, LeUnes, & Bourgeois, 1996; W. P. Morgan & Johnson, 1978; Orlick, 1992, 1996; Piedmont, Hill, & Blanco, 1999; Privette & Bundrick, 1997; Scanlan, Russell, Beals, & Scanlan, 2003; Schaubhut, Donnay, & Thompson, 2006; Stanimirovic & Hanrahan, 2010; Thomas & Over, 1994; Vealey, 1994.

2 Reports where the term 'mental toughness' has been used to explain preparation, performances, and results in a variety of sports include: American football (e.g., Berkow, 2006; Hutton, 2007; J. Reid, 2010; Reiss, 2006; Shpigel, 2011; J.-J. Taylor, 2011; Tomase, 2007), athletics (e.g., Broadbent, 2009c), Australian Rules football (Malthouse, 2010), badminton (e.g., Emms, 2009), baseball (e.g., Connolly, 2011; Shpigel, 2008), basketball (e.g., Galluzzo, 2011; Goodwill, 2007), boxing (e.g., G. A. Davies, 2009; McRae, 2008), cricket (e.g., Atherton, 2009h; D. Berry, 2012; S. Berry, 2008; Brenkley, 2009e; Coverdale, 2011; G. A. Davies, 2010b; Hobson, 2009a; Hopps, 2009b; Lyles, 2008; A. Wilson, 2011c), cycling (e.g., Barnett, 2009), diving (e.g., Jeffries, 2012), Formula One (e.g., Gorman, 2008a), golf (e.g., Dixon, 2009a, 2010b; Duckworth, 2002; Hoult, 2009c; Reason, 2009a; Sweeney, 2009), gymnastics (e.g., Barnes, 2009; Hart, 2009b), horse racing (e.g., J. A. McGrath, 2010; McRae, 2009a), mixed martial arts (e.g., G. A. Davies, 2010a), rowing (e.g., Goodbody, 2004a), rugby league (e.g., Crawley, 2012; Irvine, 2008a, 2009a; P. Kent, 2011; McDonald, 2011; A. Wilson, 2009b), rugby union (e.g., Ashton, 2010; Cain, 2008; Cleary, 2009a; Ella, 2008; S. Jones, 2008; Lewsey, 2009; Mairs, 2006, 2010b; P. Morgan, 2011; Rees, 2010, 2011e; Slot, 2007b; Souster, 2009b, 2012b; L. Stuart, 2009a; Walsh, 2007, 2009a; Westerby, 2008), soccer (e.g., Adams, 2002; Doyle, 2010; T. Evans, 2011; P. Gordon, 2009, 2010; Grahame, 2012; Gunn, 2010; M. Hughes, 2011b; Hytner, 2008, 2009a, 2010c, 2011b, 2012; Jardine, 2008; Kay, 2008; Marcotti, 2010; McLintock, 2005; McVay, 2009; Murray, 2009; Powell, 2010; Rowan, 2009, 2012; Spiers, 2008a; Stone, 2010; Walsh, 2008b, 2009b; J. Wilson, 2010b; Winter, 2006, 2010b), swimming (e.g., Gilmour, 2010; Maese, 2008),

Notes

table tennis (e.g., Jago, 2002), and tennis (e.g., Bierley, 2007, 2009a; Cash, 2008, 2009; Eaton, 2009; Flatman, 2010; Kidd, 2010; Mulvenney, 2007; Newman, 2010a).

3 Examples of memorable encounters, where the determinant of success has been attributed anecdotally to performers' 'mental strength' include: Ackford, 2011b; Adams, 2002; Atherton, 2003, 2009b, 2009i; Barnes, 2003, 2005, 2011a; Best, 2005; Boycott, 2010b; Briggs, 2009a, 2009g; Broadbent, 2009a; Burt, 2009; Cambers, 2011; Cascarino, 2010; Champagne cricket, 2011; Coe, 2004; Conquering Heroes, 2003; Corry, 2007; Coward, 2006; G. Davies, 2007; Dickinson, 2011b; Dixon, 2010a, 2010c; Doyle, 2011; L. Ellis, 2011; T. Evans, 2012; D. Faulkner, 2012; Fletcher, 2011b; R. Gould, 2011; Greenwood, 2010a, 2010b; Harman, 2012; Hayward, 2003, 2005; Hill, 2008; Hussain, 2010; S. James, 2010b; Kay, 2009f; Kessel, 2009; Kitson, 2010a; Magnay, 2010a; Mairs, 2010a; Marcotti, 2012; McRae, 2009b, 2009f; G. Moore, 2012; Nicholas, 2007; Norrish, 2008; Padgett, 2012a; Pearce, 2012; Rej, 2011; Richards, 2012; Smyth, 2009; Syed, 2009d, 2010; D. Taylor, 2009a; Tongue, 2008; Warne, 2008, 2009; R. Williams, 2009a; Willstrop, 2010; A. Wilson, 2012b; J. Wilson, 2010a; Winter, 2005, 2009h, 2010n.

4 Examples of memorable encounters, where the determinant of performance failure is blamed, anecdotally, on the absence of 'mental strength' include: Bolton, 2008; Ella, 2009a; M. Hughes, 2011b; S. Hughes, 2008a; Kay, 2011e; Randall, 2008; Rich, 2008; L. Stuart, 2009b; Vickers, 2010; Winter, 2007.

5 For additional examples of phrases used synonymously to infer mental toughness, see: 'positive mental state' (Hopps, 2010), 'mental capability' (Donegan, 2011c), 'mental capacity' (Rees, 2012), 'robust of mind' (S. James, 2010d), 'tough of mind' (G. Davies, 2010), 'mentally strong' (S. Berry, 2011a; Boycott, 2009a, 2011a; M. Hughes, 2010d; Keohane, 2006; P. Wilson, 2012), 'mentally stout' (Slot, 2009), 'mental attitude' (Boycott, 2010b; Vaughan, 2010c), 'mental solidity' (Pringle, 2011a; Willstrop, 2010), 'refusal to yield' (R. Williams, 2012; Winter, 2012d), 'guts' (Cleary, 2012e; Padgett, 2012b), 'mindset' (Butler, 2012a), 'greatness of will' (Lawton, 2012a), 'bloody-minded defiance' (Kay, 2012b), 'spirit of togetherness' (D. Taylor, 2012), 'moxie' (Lawton, 2012a), 'never-say-die attitude' (Hytner, 2009d; Walrond, 2012), 'never-say-die mindset' (R. Gould, 2011), 'never-say-die spirit' (J. Jackson, 2012b; E. Smith, 2011b), 'iron constitution' (Atherton, 2010c), 'iron will' (Pilger, 2010), 'resilient' (Adams, 2002; Atherton, 2009f, 2009g, 2009i; Chadband, 2009h; Cleary, 2009c; Corrigan, 2009; Dallaglio, 2010; Dickinson, 2009; Doyle, 2010; Glanville, 2010; Hadfield, 2005; Hands, 2008b; Hunter, 2009b; Jago, 2009; Kitson, 2008; Lacey, 2011a; McCarra, 2010a; McRae, 2009f, 2010c; Pringle, 2010c; I. Ridley, 2009; Roebuck, 2009c; D. Taylor, 2010b; R. Williams, 2011a; A. Wilson, 2008, 2009a), 'resilient attitude' (O. Brown, 2010), 'resilient mind' (S. Hughes, 2011a), 'mentally resilient' (Booth, 2008; McRae, 2009b), 'psychological resilience' (Hart, 2012), 'mental resilience' (Ackford, 2010a; Campbell, 2010; Flatman, 2011; Fletcher, 2009; Haigh, 2010; Kitson, 2004; Lansley, 2010c; Whittell, 2012), 'mental hardness' (Rees, 2011c), 'mentality' (Cross, 2010; Dallaglio, 2011; Ella, 2009a; Hansen, 2011; Heppenstall, 2009; S. James, 2011a; Kay, 2010; Lawton, 2011a; Murray, 2011b; Ogden, 2010; Selvey, 2011a; D. Taylor, 2011b; Vaughan, 2010b; Wilde, 2010a; R. Williams, 2011b; World Cup 2010), 'indomitable mentality' (Harman, 2010a), 'mental indomitability' (Hodgkinson, 2011b), 'perseverance' (McCarra, 2012; Winter, 2012d),

'stubborness' (Kitson, 2012b), 'indomitability' (Syed, 2012d), 'mettle' (Atherton, 2009i; Booth, 2009; Broadbent, 2009b; Cleary, 2011a, 2012a; Fifield, 2010; Gower, 2010; Hytner, 2009b; Newman, 2010b; Pringle, 2010b; J. Reid, 2010; Selvey, 2011d; Stern, 2009; Winter, 2010o, 2011a), 'bottle' (Boycott, 2011a; Lawton, 2012a; Marks, 2011a), 'heart' (Atherton, 2011a; Boycott, 2011a; Cascarino, 2012; Hewett, 2011; Mitchell, 2011), 'fighting heart' (Lawton, 2010d), 'temperament' (Boycott, 2011b; Brenkley, 2011; Chadband, 2011; Dean, 2009a; Pringle, 2011a; Selvey, 2011a), 'spirit' (Atherton, 2011c; Briggs, 2011; Cleary, 2010d; Cross, 2010; Dart, 2010; Ducker, 2011b; Harman, 2009d; Hayward, 2011a; Kay, 2010, 2011b; Lawton, 2010c; Marks, 2011a; McCarra, 2011d; Mitchell, 2011, 2012; Pringle, 2010b; Rutherford, 2012; R. Smith, 2012a; Trainis, 2009; Winter, 2010e, 2010l, 2011b, 2012b), 'indomitable spirit' (Harman, 2010b; Selvey, 2011c), 'fighting spirit' (Hayward, 2012; Rudd, 2011; P. Wilson, 2011a), 'stickability' (Souster, 2011c), 'forbearance' (Brenkley, 2010b; Cleary, 2010e), 'resolve' (Barnes, 2010a; Boycott, 2010a; O. Brown, 2011b; Butler, 2011b; Chadband, 2009d, 2009e, 2009f, 2009i; Cleary, 2010f, 2011b, 2011f, 2012c; Conn, 2009; Dart, 2009a; Fifield, 2009b, 2012; P. Gardner, 2010; Harman, 2011; Hoult, 2009a; M. Hughes, 2008; S. Hughes, 2010a, 2010d, 2011b; Hytner, 2009d; Irvine, 2009d, 2011; Jacob, 2009b, 2010b; Kay, 2012a; Lawrenson, 2010b; Lawton, 2012a; Ley, 2010, 2011; Liew, 2010; Mairs, 2011; Marks, 2011b; Rees, 2011a, 2012a; R. Smith, 2012a; Souster, 2009a; Syed, 2009f; G. Walker, 2011; Weaver, 2012; White, 2012; Winter, 2009b), 'mental resolve' (Kay, 2010; McRae, 2009b; Smithies, 2007; White, 2009c), 'steely resolve' (Hytner, 2010b), 'resolute' (A. Bull, 2011; Butler, 2012b; Caulkin, 2011; Ducker, 2011a; Eason, 2010; Lacey, 2011b; Lawrenson, 2010a; Vickers, 2011b; Weeks, 2010), 'resoluteness' (McLintock, 2005), 'resolutely determined' (Irvine, 2008c), 'resolution' (S. Hughes, 2008b; Lansley, 2010b; Lawton, 2011b; Macaskill, 2009), 'mental discipline' (Trott, 2010), 'toughness' (Hansen, 2010), 'psychological toughness' (T. Evans, 2012; McRae, 2009b), 'hardy' (McRae, 2010c), 'redoubtable' (Ducker, 2010b; Hopps, 2009a), 'backbone' (O. Brown, 2008b; Cleary, 2009d; S. Hughes, 2010a), 'spine' (Ogden, 2008; Wilde, 2010b; R. Williams, 2011c), 'steel' (Aylwin, 2011; S. Berry, 2011b; Butler, 2011a; Rees, 2012b; Vickers, 2011b), 'inner steel' (Dean, 2009b), 'steeliness' (Donegan, 2011b; D. Lewis, 2008; McCarra, 2009; McRae, 2009f), 'obduracy' (Barclay, 2010b; Chadband, 2010c; Irvine, 2009e; McRae, 2010a; Pringle, 2009b; White, 2012), 'obdurate' (O. Brown, 2011a; Caulkin, 2011; Forsythe, 2010; Irvine, 2010; Lacey, 2010; Lawton, 2010b, 2010e; Selvey, 2011b), 'steadfastness' (Hayward, 2011b), 'doggedness' (S. Berry, 2011a; Brenkley, 2009c, 2011; Cleary, 2010d; Rees, 2011b), 'sturdiness' (McCarra, 2010c), 'bloody-mindedness' (Atherton, 2009d, 2010a; Aylwin, 2011; Greenwood, 2011; Hodgkinson, 2011b; Hopps, 2009a; Mitchell, 2009b; S. Wallace, 2011; White, 2012), 'tough-mindedness' (Lawton, 2010d), 'stoic' (Lawton, 2009a; Rudd, 2010), 'stoicism' (Brenkley, 2009c; Cleary, 2009i; Hayward, 2009c; S. Hughes, 2008b; C. McGrath, 2009; Winter, 2010h), 'doughty' (Brenkley, 2010d; Gallagher, 2011a; Marks, 2010), 'strength of mind' (Collomosse, 2012; Macaskill, 2011; Parkinson, 2005; Westerby, 2009a), 'mental effort' (Johnson, 2009c), 'mental sharpness' (Herbert, 2012; Murray, 2010b), 'mental aptitude' (Newman, 2010b), 'obstinacy' (Butler, 2011b; Latham, 2009), 'cussedness' (Ackford, 2011a; Brenkley, 2009a; Cleary, 2012e; Edwards, 2011), 'grit' (Cleary, 2010f; Hussain, 2011; McLintock, 2005; Pearce, 2012; Pringle, 2010b;

R. Smith, 2012a), 'gritty' (Barnes, 2011b; Brenkley, 2009b; Gallagher & Willis, 2011; G. Walker, 2011), 'combativeness' (McCarra, 2011c), 'character' (Atherton, 2009a; Averis, 2011; Bagchi, 2012; Barclay, 2010a; Barnes, 2009h; S. Berry, 2012; Beyond the Ashes, 2010; Boycott, 2011a; Briggs, 2010a, 2011; Chadband, 2010a; Cleary, 2009b, 2011d, 2011f, 2012c, 2012e; Fletcher, 2010; Garside, 2011; Hansen, 2009; Harman, 2009c, 2009g; M. Henderson, 2009a; Hobson, 2010a; M. Hughes, 2011a; Kay, 2011d; King, 2009; Lawton, 2010e, 2012a, 2012b; Martin-Jenkins, 2010; McRae, 2009g; Montgomerie, 2011; B. Moore, 2009g; Pitt-Brooke, 2012; Pringle, 2009a, 2010a, 2011b; Roebuck, 2009b; Selvey, 2011a; Souster, 2009c; Spiers, 2009; Syed, 2009c; D. Taylor, 2011a; Trott, 2010; Vaughan, 2010a; Vickers, 2011a; Walsh, 2012; Westerby, 2011; Wilde, 2009b; J. Wilson, 2010c; Winter, 2009f, 2010a, 2010f, 2011b), 'tougher character' (Atherton, 2008), 'strength of character' (Atherton, 2010b; Bagchi, 2012; Hoult, 2010; Kitson, 2011a, 2011b; P. Wilson, 2011c), 'character in adversity' (Massie, 2010), 'strength of personality' (Winter, 2010l), 'stronger attitude' (Lacey, 2009a), 'fortitude' (Bagchi, 2011; Brenkley, 2009d, 2010b; O. Brown, 2011b; Caplan, 2010; Cleary, 2009e, 2012b, 2012e; Harman, 2009c; Hart, 2011b; Irvine, 2009c; Johnson, 2009a; Kay, 2011a; A. Lee, 2011; C. McGrath, 2009; Newman, 2010b; Souster, 2009a, 2009e; Winter, 2010j), 'mental fortitude' (Boycott, 2010b; Burt, 2009; Hart, 2010c; Hayward, 2009a; Hodgkinson, 2010, 2011a; Hopkins, 2011; Hoult, 2009b; S. James, 2010a; Kay, 2012c; Macaskill, 2009; Mitchell, 2009a; Murray, 2010a; The Secret Footballer, 2012; White, 2011a; Winter, 2010m), 'strong nerve' (Briggs, 2010a), 'will and conviction' (Cleary, 2010g), 'tenacity' (Cleary, 2012e; Craven, 2012; Dickinson, 2011a; Fletcher, 2011a; S. Jones, 2010; Macaskill, 2010; Marks, 2011c; McCarra, 2010e; Roebuck, 2009b), 'competitive tenacity' (Lynam, 2011), 'valour' (Kitson, 2010b; R. Lewis, 2011), 'valiant' (A. Bull, 2011), 'mental impregnability' (S. Hughes, 2011c), and, in particular, 'resilience' (Adams, 2002; Atherton, 2010d; Bagchi, 2012; Barnes, 2009a, 2009g, 2010b; 2012b; Bolton, 2011; Brenkley, 2010c, 2010d; Briggs, 2010a, 2010b; O. Brown, 2007, 2008a; Caulkin, 2010; Chadband, 2009a, 2010b; Craven, 2012; Dallaglio, 2012; Dart, 2010; Dart & Jacob, 2010; Fifield, 2009a, 2012; Fletcher, 2011a; Gallagher, 2007; R. Gibson, 2010; Hansen, 2008, 2010; Harman, 2009e; Harris, 2012; Hayward, 2010a; Hobson, 2010b; Hodgson, 2009; M. Hughes, 2010a, 2010e, 2012b; S. Hughes, 2010d; Hunter, 2009b, 2012; Inverdale, 2007; Jacob, 2010a; S. James, 2011b; Jenson, 2012a; John, 2010; Kay, 2012d, 2012e; Kempson, 2012; Kitson, 2011e, 2012b; Lansley, 2010a, 2010d; Lawrence, 2009; Lawton, 2010a; Ley, 2007; Mahoney, 2006; Martin-Jenkins, 2010; Mason, 2012; McCarra, 2010b, 2010d, 2011a, 2011c; McRae, 2009d, 2011; Pitt, 2012; Rich, 2011; Roper, 2007; Rudd, 2012; E. Smith, 2009, 2010, 2011a, 2011b; R. Smith, 2012b; Souster, 2009c; Stewart, 2010; Syed, 2009a, 2009e, 2009f; The England Cricket Team, 2005; Vickers, 2011a; R. Williams, 2011b; A. Wilson, 2010, 2011b, 2012a; J. Wilson, 2009a; Winter, 2009i, 2010c, 2010h, 2012a, 2012b, 2012d).

6 For methods of cheating, in any guise, which are shown not to belong with mental toughness, see: Averis, 2009; Barnes, 2012a; Broadbent, 2012; L. Davies, 2009; Ducker, 2012; Eason, 2009; Fifield, 2009c; Francis & Francis, 2009; Gallagher, 2009a, 2009b; Gorman, 2009c; Hands, 2009b; Hart, 2010b; J. Jackson, 2012a; S. James, 2012; S. Jones, 2009; Kelso, 2009a, 2009b, 2009c, 2012a, 2012b; Kempson, 2010; Keown, 2012; Kessel, 2012; Lacey, 2009b; Lanchester, 2011;

Mairs, 2009a; McEvoy, 2012a, 2012b; B. Moore, 2009f; O'Briain, 2009; Ogden, 2012; Rich, 2012; Scott-Elliot, 2011; Souster, 2009d; Syed, 2012b, 2012c; Winter, 2009j.

7 Literary examples highlighting the struggle to give a definitional consensus whereby mental toughness has been viewed as a state of mind: an ability to cope with pressure, stress, and adversity (e.g., S. J. Bull *et al.*, 2005; Cashmore, 2010; Clough *et al.*, 2002; Fourie & Potgieter, 2001; D. Gould *et al.*, 1987; G. Jones *et al.*, 2002; S. C. Middleton *et al.*, 2004a; Parkes & Mallett, 2011; R. E. Smith & Smoll, 1989; Thelwell *et al.*, 2005; R. M. Williams, 1988); an ability to overcome or rebound from setbacks (e.g., Dennis, 1981; D. Gould *et al.*, 1987; G. Jones *et al.*, 2002; Loehr, 1995; J. Taylor, 1989; Tutko & Richards, 1976); an ability to persist or a refusal to quit (e.g., Cashmore, 2002, 2010; Dennis, 1981; Fourie & Potgieter, 2001; Goldberg, 1998; D. Gould *et al.*, 1987; G. Jones *et al.*, 2002; Loehr, 1995); an ability to withstand strong criticism and to avoid becoming upset when losing or performing poorly (e.g., Clough *et al.*, 2002; Loehr, 1995; Tutko & Richards, 1972); an insensitivity or resilience (e.g., Alderman, 1974; Clough *et al.*, 2002; Goldberg, 1998; Loehr, 1995; Parkes & Mallett, 2011); an ability to maintain an optimal mindset throughout a sporting event (e.g., Cashmore, 2002, 2010; J. W. Jones *et al.*, 2001); a willingness to take personal responsibility (e.g., S. J. Bull *et al.*, 2005; Fourie & Potgieter, 2001); an ability to show dedication and commitment (e.g., S. J. Bull *et al.*, 2005; Fourie & Potgieter, 2001); an ability to believe in self (e.g., S. J. Bull *et al.*, 2005; Clough *et al.*, 2002; Thelwell *et al.*, 2005); an ability to subordinate emotions to the greater requirements of winning competitions (e.g., Cashmore, 2010); qualities of mind or intellect (e.g., Cashmore, 2005, 2010); and the possession of superior mental skills (e.g., S. J. Bull, Albinson, & Shambrook, 1996; Fourie & Potgieter, 2001; Golby & Sheard, 2004; Golby *et al.*, 2003; Loehr, 1986, 1995).

8 Examples of the proposed characteristics of mentally tough performers in the extant literature have been wide ranging, e.g.: confidence, optimism, self-belief, and self-esteem (e.g., S. J. Bull *et al.*, 1996, 2005; Cashmore, 2002; Favret & Benzel, 1997; Fourie & Potgieter, 2001; Goldberg, 1998; D. Gould *et al.*, 1987; Graham & Yocom, 1990; Hodge, 1994; G. Jones *et al.*, 2002; Loehr, 1986, 1995; Luszki, 1982; Pankey, 1993; Parkes & Mallett, 2011; J. Taylor, 1989; Thelwell *et al.*, 2005; Woods *et al.*, 1995); achieving consistency (e.g., Clough *et al.*, 2002; Fourie & Potgieter, 2001; D. Gould *et al.*, 1987; Graham & Yocom, 1990; Loehr, 1986; R. M. Williams, 1988); commitment, desire, and determination (e.g., S. J. Bull *et al.*, 1996, 2005; Cashmore, 2002; Clough *et al.*, 2002; Fourie & Potgieter, 2001; Goldberg, 1998; Hodge, 1994; G. Jones *et al.*, 2002; Loehr, 1986; Luszki, 1982; S. C. Middleton *et al.*, 2004a; Thelwell *et al.*, 2005; Tunney, 1987; R. M. Williams, 1988); concentration and focus (e.g., Cashmore, 2002, 2010; Fourie & Potgieter, 2001; Goldberg, 1998; Graham & Yocom, 1990; C. M. Jones, 1982; G. Jones *et al.*, 2002; Loehr, 1986; Luszki, 1982; S. C. Middleton *et al.*, 2004a; Thelwell *et al.*, 2005; Tunney, 1987); and control, courage, motivation, and willpower (e.g., S. J. Bull *et al.*, 1996; Cashmore, 2002; Favret & Benzel, 1997; D. Gould *et al.*, 1987; Graham & Yocom, 1990; Hodge, 1994; G. Jones *et al.*, 2002; Loehr, 1986; Thelwell *et al.*, 2005; Tunney, 1987; Tutko & Richards, 1976; Woods *et al.*, 1995).

9 The positive influence of hardiness on performance has been reported in such diverse samples as: athletes (Golby & Sheard, 2004; Golby *et al.*, 2003; Rezae,

Ghaffari, & Zolfalifam, 2009; Sheard, 2008a, 2009b; Sheard & Golby, 2006a; Sheard & Golby, 2007a, Sheard & Golby, 2010; C. Thomson & Morris, 2009), college students (Lifton, Seay, & Bushke, 2000; Maddi, Harvey, Khoshaba, Fazel, & Resurreccion, 2009), student teachers (W. C. Thomson & Wendt, 2010), human resource consultants (Maddi, Harvey, Khoshaba, Lu, Persico, & Brow, 2006), military personnel (Bartone, 1999; Bartone, Roland, Picano, & Williams, 2008; Bartone & Snook, 1999; Delahaij, Gaillard, & van Dam, 2010; Dolan & Adler, 2006; Zakin, Solomon, & Neria, 2003), healthcare professionals (Judkins & Rind, 2005), and university undergraduates (Hystad, Eid, Laberg, Johnsen, & Bartone, 2009; Maddi, Khoshaba, Jensen, Carter, Lu, & Harvey, 2002; Maddi, Wadhwa, & Haier, 1996; Mathis & Lecce, 1999; Sheard, 2009a; Sheard & Golby, 2007b; Zhang, 2011).

10 Examples of high-impact collision sports include: American football (Boden, Tacchetti, Cantu, Knowles, & Mueller, 2007; Carlisle, Goldfarb, Mall, Powell, & Matava, 2008; Feeley, Powell, Muller, Barnes, Warren, & Kelly, 2008; S. S. Gill & Boden, 2008; Gladwell, 2009; Langer, Fadale, & Palumbo, 2008; Mall, Carlisle, Matava, Powell, & Goldfarb, 2008; Nack, 2001; Ramirez, Schaffer, Shen, Kashani, & Kraus, 2006; C. Ryan, 2009; M. J. Stuart, 2005; Whittell, 2010), Australian Rules football (McIntosh, McCrory, & Comerford, 2000; Orchard & Seward, 2002; Seward, Orchard, Hazard, & Collinson, 1993), rugby league (Fisher, 2009; Gabbett, 2000; Gabbett & Godbolt, 2010; Gabbett, Jenkins, & Abernethy, 2010; Irvine, 2009b; Killen, Gabbett, & Jenkins, 2010; McIntosh *et al.*, 2000; Meir, McDonald, & Russell, 1997; D. M. O'Connor, 2004; Seward *et al.*, 1993), and rugby union (Ackford, 2010b; A. Bull, 2010; Cleary, 2005a, 2010a, 2011c, 2012d; G. Davies, 2012; Gallagher, 2005; Hands, 2009c, 2010; Hewett, 2010; McIntosh *et al.*, 2000; Quarrie & Hopkins, 2008; Reason, 2009d, 2010; Seward *et al.*, 1993; Slot, 2005; Warburton, 2012; R. Williams, 2009b), and contact sports, such as soccer (Dickinson, 2010; Junge, Dvorak, Graf-Baumann, & Peterson, 2004; Kofotolis, Kellis, & Vlachopoulos, 2007; Le Gall, Carling, Reilly, Vandewalle, Church, & Rochcongar, 2006; L. Taylor, 2010; Volz, 2009; Winter, 2010d),

References

Abbott, A., & Collins, D. (2004). Eliminating the dichotomy between theory and practice in talent identification and development: Considering the role of psychology. *Journal of Sports Sciences*, *22*, 395–408.

Abi-Hashem, N. (2001). Rediscovering hope in American psychology. *American Psychologist*, *56*, 85–86.

Abma, C. L., Fry, M. D., Li, Y., & Relyea, G. (2002). Differences in imagery content and imagery ability between high and low confident track and field athletes. *Journal of Applied Sport Psychology*, *14*, 67–75.

Achille Compagnoni. (2009, May 14). *The Daily Telegraph*, p. 31 (Obituary).

Ackford, P. (2007, December 30). 2008 duel: England v Wales Feb 2. *The Daily Telegraph*. Retrieved April 27, 2009, from http://www.telegraph.co.uk/sport.

Ackford, P. (2009, April 26). Ian McGeechan prepares Lions for a power struggle against Springboks. *The Daily Telegraph*. Retrieved April 27, 2009, from http://www.telegraph.co.uk/sport.

Ackford, P. (2010a, March 27). Steve Borthwick is no longer England's untouchable. *The Daily Telegraph*. Retrieved March 29, 2010, from http://www.telegraph.co.uk/sport.

Ackford, P. (2010b, April 11). Scrums 'putting lives at risk'. *The Sunday Telegraph*, p. S13 (Sport).

Ackford, P. (2011a, February 27). England show true grit to march on towards title glory. *The Sunday Telegraph*, pp. S2–S3 (Sport).

Ackford, P. (2011b, October 5). Only defeat will throw spotlight on manager's conservatism. *The Daily Telegraph*, pp. S2–S3 (Sport).

Ackford, P. (2011c, November 13). How New Zealand built a team of champions after World Cup quarter-final failure. *The Daily Telegraph*. Retrieved November 14, 2011, from http://www.telegraph.co.uk/sport.

Adams, T. (2002, June 30). It's tough to call but the defender in me goes for Germany. *The Observer*. Retrieved July 30, 2009, from http://www.guardian.co.uk/sport.

Aidman, E., & Schofield, G. (2004). Personality and individual differences in sport. In T. Morris & J. Summers (Eds.), *Sport psychology: Theory, applications and issues* (2nd edn, pp. 22–47). Milton, Australia: Wiley.

Alarcon, G., Eschleman, K. J., & Bowling, N. A. (2009). Relationships between personality variables and burnout: A meta-analysis. *Work & Stress*, *23*, 244–263.

Alderman, R. B. (1974). *Psychological behavior in sport*. Toronto, Ontario, Canada: W.B. Saunders Company.

Allan, J., & McKenna, J. (2009). Presentation 3: Positive psychology – resilience and adventure programmes for young people in higher education. *Journal of Sports Sciences*, *27*, S7–S8.

Allen, J. (2007). *Michael Schumacher: The edge of greatness*. London: Headline.

Allen, M. S., Greenlees, I., & Jones, M. (2011). An investigation of the five-factor model of personality and coping behaviour in sport. *Journal of Sports Sciences*, *29*, 841–850.

Allen, T. W. (1988). The cognitive bases of peak performance: A classroom intervention with student athletes. *Journal of Counseling and Development*, *67*, 202–204.

Alonso, J. M., Junge, A., Renström, P., Engebretsen, L., Mountjoy, M., & Dvorak, J. (2009). Sports injury surveillance during the 2007 IAAF World Athletics Championships. *Clinical Journal of Sports Medicine*, *19*, 26–32.

Amiot, C. E., Vallerand, R. J., & Blanchard, C. M. (2006). Passion and psychological adjustment: A test of the person-environment fit hypothesis. *Personality and Social Psychology Bulletin*, *32*, 220–229.

Anastasi, A., & Urbina, S. (1997). *Psychological testing* (7th edn). New York: Prentice-Hall.

Andrew, M., Grobbelaar, H. W., & Potgieter, J. C. (2007). Sport psychological skill levels and related psycho-social factors that distinguish between rugby union players of different participation levels. *South African Journal for Research in Sport, Physical Education and Recreation*, *29*, 1–15.

Anshel, M. H. (2001). Qualitative validation of a model for coping with acute stress in sport. *Journal of Sport Behavior*, *24*, 223–246.

Anshel, M. H., Weatherby, N. L., Kang, M., & Watson, T. (2009). Rasch calibration of a unidimensional perfectionism inventory for sport. *Psychology of Sport and Exercise*, *10*, 210–216.

Anshel, M. H., Williams, L. R. T., & Hodge, K. (1997). Cross-cultural and gender differences on coping style in sport. *International Journal of Sport Psychology*, *28*, 141–156.

Anthony, A. (2007, November 25). Born to lose. *Observer Sports Monthly*, pp. 36–46.

Arlott, J. (1949). *Concerning cricket*. London: Longmans, Green.

Armstrong, L. (2008, October). To raise cancer awareness, the cyclist is returning to the road. *Time*, p. 2 (10 Questions).

Arvinen-Barrow, M., Weigand, D. A., Thomas, S., Hemmings, B., & Walley, M. (2007). Elite and novice athletes' imagery use in open and closed sports. *Journal of Applied Sport Psychology*, *19*, 93–104.

Ashfield, A., McKenna, J., & Backhouse, S. (2009). Presentation 2: Flourishing: The need for conceptual clarity and an initial attempt to achieve it. *Journal of Sports Sciences*, *27*, S7.

Ashton, B. (2010, May 22). How Sarries pushed back boundaries by abandoning position. *The Independent*, p. 17 (Sport).

Atella, M. D. (1999). Case studies in the development of organizational hardiness: From theory to practice. *Consulting Psychology Journal: Practice and Research*, *51*, 125–134.

Atherton, M. (2003, July 21). Two souls laid bare in the ultimate of tests. *The Times*, pp. 20–21 (The Game).

Atherton, M. (2008, September 29). Shah should be beneficiary from Vaughan's absence for India tour. *The Times*, p. 68 (Sport).

Atherton, M. (2009a, February 12). Stand by Bell? It's an open-and-shut case. *The Times*, p. 75 (Sport).

Atherton, M. (2009b, July 6). Renaissance man aware that first impressions last. *The Times*, pp. 10–11 (The Ashes).

Atherton, M. (2009c, July 8). Balancing act offers Panesar chance to be star turn again. *The Times*, pp. 70–71 (Sport).

Atherton, M. (2009d, July 13). It was torture – but worth it. *The Times*, pp. 2–3 (The Ashes).

Atherton, M. (2009e, July 13). Changes of gear needed for Lord's. *The Times*, p. 3 (The Ashes).

Atherton, M. (2009f, July 18). Ponting in search of Lord's prayer as England bowlers show their potential. *The Times*, pp. 4–5 (Sport).

Atherton, M. (2009g, July 20). A cliffhanger in the making. *The Times*, pp. 2–3 (The Ashes).

Atherton, M. (2009h, August 13). Tough talk no match for tough tradition. *The Times*, p. 64 (Sport).

Atherton, M. (2009i). *Atherton's ashes: How England won the 2009 Ashes*. London: Simon & Schuster.

Atherton, M. (2010a, January 8). Concentration, discipline and application: Why saving the day is all in the mind. *The Times*, pp. 100–101 (Sport).

Atherton, M. (2010b, February 25). Time to end depressing culture of failure. *The Times*, p. 87 (Sport).

Atherton, M. (2010c, November 29). England pair remorselessly expose home frailties as Johnson toils. *The Times*, pp. 62–63 (Sport).

Atherton, M. (2010d, December 7). Ponting's men left on ropes as Pietersen strikes sucker punch. *The Times*, pp. 72–73 (Sport).

Atherton, M. (2011a, January 3). New captain but familiar dark clouds spell peril for Australia. *The Times*, pp. 60–61 (Sport).

Atherton, M. (2011b, March 10). Pills, pain and the problem with Pietersen. *The Times*, p. 66 (Sport).

Atherton, M. (2011c, March 28). England are given harsh lesson by the masters of their subject. *The Times*, pp. 62–63 (Sport).

Averis, M. (2009, August 10). Quins face new inquiry in fake blood case. *The Guardian*, p. 13 (Sport).

Averis, M. (2011, March 14). Lièvremont rails at French 'cowards' and axes six players. *The Guardian*, p. 4 (Sport).

Aylwin, M. (2009, November 15). De Villiers angered by poorly sung anthem. *The Observer*, p. 15 (Sport).

Aylwin, M. (2011, February 2). Robinson steps up the fear factor to put steel into Scotland. *The Guardian*, pp. 6–7 (Sport).

Baer, R. A. (2003). Mindfulness training as a clinical intervention: A conceptual and empirical review. *Clinical Psychology: Science and Practice, 10*, 125–143.

Bagchi, R. (2011, February 2). Despite his travails, Morgan is a one-day master. *The Guardian*, p. 10 (Sport).

Bagchi, R. (2012, February 8). Azhar follows the Barnacle and Boycott as new kid with the block. *The Guardian*, p. 41 (Sport).

Baillie, M. (2011, January 11). Lennon tells players to silence boo boys. *The Daily Express*. Retrieved January 11, 2011, from http://www.express.co.uk/sport.

Baker, A. (2008, July 5). Laura Robson proves she is real deal. *The Daily Telegraph*, p. S5 (Sport).

Baker, A. (2009, July 6). Henman: Murray needs fans' patience. *The Daily Telegraph*, p. S7 (Sport).

Baker, J. (2010, March 10). Be patient, we have young talent coming up. *The Daily Telegraph*, p. S15 (Sport).

Baker, J., Horton, S., Robertson-Wilson, J., & Wall, M. (2003). Nurturing sport expertise: Factors influencing the development of the elite athlete. *Journal of Sports Science and Medicine, 2*, 1–9.

Balague, G. (2008, June 9). Buffon is best of breed but Casillas could be top dog. *The Times*, p. 15 (The Game).

Bale, J. (2002). *Sports geography*. London: Spon.

Balyi, I., & Hamilton, A. (2003, Issue 20). Long-term athlete development update: Trainability in childhood and adolescence. *Faster Higher Stronger*, pp. 6–8.

Balyi, I., & Hamilton, A. (2004, Spring). Long term athlete development: Trainability in childhood and adolescence. *Olympic Coach*, pp. 4–8.

Bandura, A. (1997). *Self-efficacy: The exercise of control*. New York: Freeman.

Barbour, S., & Orlick, T. (1999). Mental skills of National Hockey League players. *Journal of Excellence, 2*, 16–36.

Barclay, P. (2010a, April 26). Selection dilemmas dominate Capello's World Cup roulette. *The Times*, p. 8 (The Game).

Barclay, P. (2010b, May 3). Warner's forgotten men of 2006 still awaiting pay day. *The Times*, p. 9 (The Game.)

Barlow, C. (2006, December 22). Fletcher and his team's mindset was all wrong [Letter to the editor]. *The Daily Telegraph*, p. S17 (Sport).

Barnard, C. P. (1994). Resilience: A shift in our perception? *American Journal of Family Therapy, 22*, 135–144.

Barnes, S. (2003, November 24). Where our rugby boys have led, the rest can follow. *The Times*, p. 38 (Sport).

Barnes, S. (2005, May 26). The miracle of Istanbul. *The Times*, p. 96 (Sport).

Barnes, S. (2008a, January 7). Let he who has never sledged complain about others sledging. *The Times*, p. 61 (Sport).

Barnes, S. (2008b, January 8). Sledging was always going to put the game on slippery slope. *The Times*, p. 65 (Sport).

Barnes, S. (2008c, January 11). The ten commandments to remind us that sport was always meant to be fun. *The Times*, p. 94 (Sport).

Barnes, S. (2008d, January 14). Winning is not everything. *The Times*, p. 66 (Sport).

Barnes, S. (2008e, January 21). Federer shows qualities that go into making true champion. *The Times*, p. 71 (Sport).

Barnes, S. (2008f, March 24). How swearing became a national sport. *The Times*, p. 23.

Barnes, S. (2009a, February 23). Cautious Strauss helps rebirth of a cricketing force. *The Times*, p. 63 (Sport).

Barnes, S. (2009b, June 26). Murray's show of authority suggests he can succeed where Henman failed. *The Times*, p. 84 (Sport).

Barnes, S. (2009c, June 27). Henmaniacal traits give Federer brief worry but he soon regains control. *The Times*, p. 10 (Sport).

Barnes, S. (2009d, June 30). Andy, don't take it personally but everybody really does hate you. *The Times*, p. 64 (Sport).

Barnes, S. (2009e, July 4). This is no time for despair: All the greatest players benefit from defeat. *The Times*, pp. 1, 4.

Barnes, S. (2009f, July 10). Flintoff venom unleashed in one short burst is enough to stir memories. *The Times*, p. 88 (Sport).

Barnes, S. (2009g, July 13). Team of Collies would add bite. *The Times*, p. 5 (The Ashes).

Barnes, S. (2009h, July 17). Endangered species well worth protecting. *The Times*, p. 89 (Sport).

Barnes, S. (2009i, July 17). Captain quick to seize the day off his own bat. *The Times*, p. 92 (Sport).

Barnes, S. (2009j, July 20). Forsaking false idols I believe in Freddie. *The Times*, p. 5 (The Ashes).

Barnes, S. (2009k, August 8). In search of a hero at Headingley. *The Times*, p. 2 (Sport).

Barnes, S. (2009l, October 19). Beth Tweddle wins gold for Britain at World Gymnastics Championships. *The Times*. Retrieved October 20, 2009, from http://www.timesonline.co.uk/tol/sport.

Barnes, S. (2010a, February 1). Mystery of a champion in the making. *The Times*, p. 61 (Sport).

Barnes, S. (2010b, July 30). So Ferrari, so good in grand scheme of things. *The Times*, p. 79 (Sport).

Barnes, S. (2011a, March 14). Fragile England out on an emotional limb. *The Times*, p. 67 (Sport).

Barnes, S. (2011b, June 30). López taken apart by clinical display from new Mr Cool. *The Times*, pp. 86–87 (Sport).

Barnes, S. (2012a, April 16). Referees just victims of players who cry foul. *The Times*. Retrieved April 16, 2012, from http://www.timesonline.co.uk/tol/sport.

Barnes, S. (2012b, May 21). How villains satisfy our deep-seated needs. *The Times*. Retrieved May 22, 2012, from http://www.timesonline.co.uk/tol/sport.

Barnett, C. (2009, July 28). Bradley Wiggins eyes Olympic and Tour de France double in 2012. *The Daily Telegraph*. Retrieved August 4, 2009, from http://www.telegraph.co.uk/sport.

168   *References*

Bartone, P. T. (1999). Hardiness protects against war-related stress in army reserve forces. *Consulting Psychology Journal*, *51*, 72–83.

Bartone, P. T., Roland, R. R., Picano, J. J., & Williams, T. J. (2008). Psychological hardiness predicts success in US army special forces candidates. *International Journal of Selection and Assessment*, *16*, 78–81.

Bartone, P. T., & Snook, S. A. (1999, May). Cognitive and personality factors predict leader development in US Army cadets. In: Paper presented at 35th International Applied Military Psychology Symposium (IAMPS), Florence, Italy.

Basic Behavioral Science Task Force of the National Advisory Mental Health Council. (1996). Basic behavioral science research for mental health: Vulnerability and resilience. *American Psychologist*, *51*, 22–28.

Bauman, J. (2005). Returning to play: The mind does matter. *Journal of Clinical Sport Medicine*, *15*, 432–435.

Beard, R. (2009, July 4). Down Under, but right on top. *The Daily Telegraph*, p. 17 (News Review & Comment).

Beasley, M., Thompson, T., & Davidson, J. (2003). Resilience in response to life stress: The effects of coping style and cognitive hardiness. *Personality and Individual Differences*, *34*, 77–95.

Becker, B. (2009, July 6). Roddick stopped believing when the crucial points were there for the taking. *The Daily Telegraph*, p. S3 (Sport).

Beehr, T. A., & Bowling, N. A. (2005). Hardy personality, stress, and health. In C.L. Cooper (Ed.), *Handbook of stress, medicine, and health* (2nd edn, pp. 193–211). London: CRC Press.

Bell, V. (2009, July). Forum beyond boundaries. *The Psychologist*, 565.

Benaud, R. (1995). *The appeal of cricket: The modern game*. London: Hodder and Stoughton.

Benishek, L. A., & Lopez, F. G. (1997). Critical evaluation of hardiness theory: Gender differences, perception of life events, and neuroticism. *Work & Stress*, *11*, 33–45.

Berkow, I. (2006, September 30). Fragile quarterback shows some mental toughness. *The New York Times*. Retrieved October 2, 2006, from http://www.nytimes.com.

Berry, D. (2012, February 12). Mental toughness sorts the best from the rest. *The Age*. Retrieved February 15, 2012, from http://www.theage.com.au/sport.

Berry, S. (2008, September 28). Durham grit secures maiden County Championship title. *The Daily Telegraph*. Retrieved September 29, 2008, from http://www.telegraph.co.uk/sport.

Berry, S. (2011a, March 29). Sri Lanka sweat on Muralitharan. *The Daily Telegraph*, p. S10 (Sport).

Berry, S. (2011b, March 30). Sri Lanka's steel gives Muralitharan one last chance to bamboozle. *The Daily Telegraph*, p. S11 (Sport).

Berry, S. (2012, April 15). Hamilton-Brown sets up thrilling finale. *The Sunday Telegraph*, p. S14 (Sport).

Best, D. (2005, June 30). Key areas where tourists must improve. *The Daily Telegraph*. Retrieved April 7, 2009, from http://www.telegraph.co.uk/sport.

Beyond the Ashes. (2010, December 30). *The Times*, p. 2.

Bianco, T. (2001). Social support and recovery from sport injury: Elite skiers share their experiences. *Research Quarterly for Exercise and Sport*, *72*, 376–388.

Bierley, S. (2001, September 3). Henman's mental frailty exposed. *The Guardian*. Retrieved January 12, 2011, from http://www.guardian.co.uk/sport.

Bierley, S. (2004, August 24). Awesome Aussies continue to exert their sporting dominance. *The Guardian*, pp. 6–7 (Sport).

Bierley, S. (2007, February 20). Murray stands apart in shot variety and mental toughness. *The Guardian*. Retrieved January 12, 2011, from http://www.guardian.co.uk/sport.

Bierley, S. (2009a, March 23). Nadal replaces Federer as the standard setter for Murray. *The Guardian*. Retrieved March 23, 2009, from http://www.guardian.co.uk/sport.

Bierley, S. (2009b, June 30). Dogged Murray raises the roof after battling back to win epic tussle. *The Guardian*, p. 1 (Sport).

Bingham, J. (2009, April 21). Children copying sportsmen's dirty tricks. *The Daily Telegraph*, p. 14.

Bloodworth, A., & McNamee, M. (2010). Clean Olympians? Doping and anti-doping: The views of talented young British athletes. *International Journal of Drug Policy, 21*, 276–282.

Bloom, B. S. (Ed.). (1985). *Developing talent in young people*. New York: Ballantine.

Boden, B. P., Tacchetti, R. L., Cantu, R. C., Knowles, S. B., & Mueller, F. O. (2007). Catastrophic head injuries in high school and college football players. *American Journal of Sports Medicine, 35*, 1075–1081.

Bolton, P. (2008, May 12). Jones to start Sale inquest. *The Daily Telegraph*, p. S27 (Sport).

Bolton, P. (2011, April 3). Foden keeps it clean to inspire Saints. *The Sunday Telegraph*, p. S14 (Sport).

Bonanno, G. (2004). Loss, trauma, and human resilience: Have we underestimated the human capacity to thrive after extremely aversive events? *American Psychologist, 59*, 20–28.

Booth, L. (2008, October 7). England opt for army boot camp in readiness for Stanford. *The Guardian*, p. 8 (Sport).

Booth, L. (2009, July 17). A good day for England, but a better one for me, says Strauss. *The Guardian*, p. 4 (Sport).

Booth, L. (2010). In search of his aura. In E. Craig (Ed.), *Cricket 2010: The story of the year as told by The Wisden Cricketer* (pp. 22–23). London: Wisden Cricketer Publishing Ltd.

Booth, L., & Rae, R. (2009, July 13). England fear for Flintoff future as knee injury flares up again. *The Guardian*. Retrieved July 27, 2009, from http://www.guardian.co.uk/sport.

Bott, R. (2010, April 24). New England coach Steve McNamara marshals his troops. *The Daily Mail*. Retrieved January 12, 2011, from http://www.dailymail.co.uk/sport.

Bouchard, C., & Malina, R. M. (1984). Genetics and Olympic athletes: A discussion of methods and issues. In J. E. L. Carter (Ed.), *Kinanthropology of Olympic athletes* (pp. 28–38). Basel, Switzerland: Karger.

Bouchard, C., Malina, R. M., & Pérusse, L. (1997). *Genetics of fitness and physical performance*. Champaign, IL: Human Kinetics.

Boycott, G. (2005, September 13). Warne lets the urn slip from his grasp. *The Daily Telegraph*, p. S6 (Sport).

Boycott, G. (2009a, February 23). I fear Flintoff Test days numbered. *The Daily Telegraph*, p. S21 (Sport).

Boycott, G. (2009b, May 13). England miss a trick by leaving out Panesar. *The Daily Telegraph*, p. S9 (Sport).

Boycott, G. (2009c, August 20). This match is about who wants it more. *The Daily Telegraph*, p. S4 (Sport).

Boycott, G. (2010a, January 19). Pietersen should not be untouchable – if you can't score runs you make way. *The Daily Telegraph*, p. S14 (Sport).

Boycott, G. (2010b, July 29). Pietersen and Morgan must be leading men, not cameo artists. *The Daily Telegraph*, p. S7 (Sport).

Boycott, G. (2011a, March 19). Improve quick or luck will run out. *The Daily Telegraph*, p. S3 (Sport).

Boycott, G. (2011b, April 3). Victory was fitting reward for a team effort. *The Sunday Telegraph*, p. S9 (Sport).

Boycott, G. (2011c, June 1). Batsman may be one-paced, but his mental toughness is invaluable. *The Daily Telegraph*, pp. S10–S11 (Sport).

Braddock, J. H., Royster, D. A., Winfield, L. F., & Hawkins, R. (1991). Bouncing back: Sports and academic resilience among African-American males. *Education and Urban Society*, *24*, 113–131.

Brady, A. (2009). Presentation 1: Research publication trends associated with deficit and abundance concepts in sport psychology. *Journal of Sports Sciences*, *27*, S6.

Brady, A., Ashfield, A., Allan, J., McKenna, J., & Duncan, E. (2009). Enriching sport psychology: Engaging with positive psychology. *Journal of Sports Sciences*, *27*, S6.

Bray, S. R., & Widmeyer, W. N. (2000). Athlete's perception of home advantage: An investigation of perceived causal factors. *Journal of Sport Behavior*, *23*, 1–10.

Brenkley, S. (2009a, July 10). Home fires extinguished by dogged Australian duo. *The Independent*, pp. 62–63 (Sport).

Brenkley, S. (2009b, July 13). Ponting fury as England pull off the great escape. *The Independent*, pp. 1, 3 (Sport).

Brenkley, S. (2009c, July 13). England's final pair defiant to the bitter end. *The Independent*, pp. 2–3 (Sport).

Brenkley, S. (2009d, July 14). England hit by familiar Flintoff fear. *The Independent*, p. 52 (Sport).

Brenkley, S. (2009e, December 16). Strauss calls on team to thrive as pressure builds. *The Independent*, p. 52 (Sport).

Brenkley, S. (2010a, May 15). Australia's amazing comeback fashioned by stunning Hussey. *The Independent*, p. 13 (Sport).

Brenkley, S. (2010b, July 16). Reborn Katich leaves Pakistan praying for a miracle at Lord's. *The Independent*, p. 50 (Sport).

Brenkley, S. (2010c, July 27). 'Pakistan has so much talent but we don't channel it properly'. *The Independent*, pp. 52–53 (Sport).

Brenkley, S. (2010d, December 20). Perth's in the past, but there are five areas England must fix. *i*, p. 45 (Sport).

Brenkley, S. (2011, January 6). 'I couldn't hit the middle of the bat six months ago'. *i*, p. 42 (Sport).

Brewer, J., & Davis, J. (1995). Applied physiology of rugby league. *Sports Medicine*, *13*, 129–135.

Briggs, S. (2009a, March 29). Unsung heroes key to beating Australia. *The Daily Telegraph*. Retrieved July 30, 2009, from http://www.telegraph.co.uk/sport.

Briggs, S. (2009b, June 24). Flintoff paid big price for 2005, says Gilchrist. *The Daily Telegraph*, p. S13 (Sport).

Briggs, S. (2009c, June 29). England learn real lessons of leadership. *The Daily Telegraph*, p. S14 (Sport).

Briggs, S. (2009d, July 13). Collingwood the iron man enters legend. *The Daily Telegraph*, p. S4 (Sport).

Briggs, S. (2009e, July 17). Indomitable leader sets sights on a Test best. *The Daily Telegraph*, p. S3 (Sport).

Briggs, S. (2009f, July 21). 'It's said I'm retiring as I'm getting better as a bowler'. *The Daily Telegraph*, p. S3 (Sport).

Briggs, S. (2009g, December 29). Centurion saved by technology – and his own hard work. *The Daily Telegraph*, p. S13 (Sport).

Briggs, S. (2010a, January 8). Onions shows he's no tail-end Charlie. *The Daily Telegraph*, p. S7 (Sport).

Briggs, S. (2010b, April 11). Grant drinks deep from Cup of cheer. *The Sunday Telegraph*, p. S6 (Sport).

Briggs, S. (2010c, December 7). Australian attitude hardened by Lance incident. *The Daily Telegraph*, p. S13 (Sport).

Briggs, S. (2011, January 7). The loyal lieutenant who had substance over style. *The Daily Telegraph*, p. S6 (Sport).

British Psychological Society (2006, March). *Code of ethics and conduct*. Leicester, UK: Author.

Broadbent, R. (2009a, June 15). Ohuruogu looking to stay at head of the class. *The Times*, p. 60 (Sport).

Broadbent, R. (2009b, July 23). Spirited Idowu has mettle to handle great expectations. *The Times*, p. 61 (Sport).

Broadbent, R. (2009c, November 2). Radcliffe facing the mother of all battles to land elusive Olympic gold. *The Times*, p. 78 (Sport).

Broadbent, R. (2012, April 30). Four-year global ban would bring muscle to drugs war. *The Times*, pp. 62–63 (Sport).

Bronson, J., Gibson, S., Kichar, R., & Priest, S. (1992). Evaluation of team development in a corporate adventure training program. *Journal of Experiential Education*, *15*, 50–53.

Brookes, A. (2003). A critique of neo-Hahnian outdoor education theory. Part one: Challenges to the concept of 'character building'. *Journal of Adventure Education and Outdoor Learning*, *3*, 49–62.

Brown, K. W., & Ryan, R. M. (2003). The benefits of being present: Mindfulness and its role in psychological well-being. *Journal of Personality and Social Psychology*, *84*, 822–848.

Brown, O. (2007, December 3). Villa and United renew rivalry. *The Daily Telegraph*, p. S1 (Sport).

Brown, O. (2008a, October 6). Brown's stock on the rise. *The Daily Telegraph*, p. S2 (Sport).

Brown, O. (2008b, November 3). Benitez stunned at reversal. *The Daily Telegraph*, p. S13 (Sport).

Brown, O. (2010, July 18). 'Jin and Yang' keep Koreans in the mix. *The Sunday Telegraph*, p. S5 (Sport).

Brown, O. (2011a, April 3). Insipid display leaves Arsenal stuck on the road to nowhere. *The Sunday Telegraph*, p. S2 (Sport).

Brown, O. (2011b, June 12). Calm during the storm steered McDowell to victory. *The Sunday Telegraph*, pp. S6–S7 (Sport).

Bull, A. (2009, July 14). Swann sees nothing but brightness after 'getting out of jail'. *The Guardian*, p. 4 (Sport).

Bull, A. (2010, February 15). Evans out for season but set to return from neck injury. *The Guardian*, p. 11 (Sport).

Bull, A. (2011, March 26). Kiwis add final chapter to Smith's tales of woe. *The Guardian*, p. S9 (Sport).

Bull, S. J., Albinson, J. G., & Shambrook, C. J. (1996). *The mental game plan: Getting psyched for sport*. Eastbourne, England: Sports Dynamics.

Bull, S. J., Shambrook, C. J., James, W., & Brooks, J. E. (2005). Towards an understanding of mental toughness in elite English cricketers. *Journal of Applied Sport Psychology*, *17*, 209–227.

Bullock, N., Gulbin, J. P., Martin, D. T., Ross, A., Holland T., & Marino, F. (2009). Talent identification and deliberate programming in skeleton: Ice novice to Winter Olympian in 14 months. *Journal of Sports Sciences*, *27*, 397–404.

Burt, S. (2009, September 8). Frank Lampard: I have never known an England team to be so confident. *The Daily Telegraph*. Retrieved September 9, 2009, from http://www.telegraph.co.uk/sport.

Burt, S. (2010, May 20). King's fitness coach joins backroom team. *The Daily Telegraph*, p. S3 (Sport).

Butler, E. (2011a, February 27). France fail to summon whiff of the exotic but still rattle their great rival. *The Observer*, p. 3 (Sport).

Butler, E. (2011b, October 10). Weepu sticks boot in but Kiwis count cost of victory. *The Guardian*, p. 5 (Sport).

Butler, E. (2012a, March 18). Tenacious Wales dig deep and deliver a grand slam to order. *The Observer*, pp. 1, 3 (Sport).

Butler, E. (2012b, April 18). Lancaster unshackles England to tie up loose ends in job application. *The Observer*, p. 6 (Sport).

Butt, J., Weinberg, R., & Culp, B. (2010). Exploring mental toughness in NCAA athletes. *Journal of Intercollegiate Sport*, *3*, 316–322.

Byers, T. (2004). Managing sport operations, quality and performance. In J. Beech & S. Chadwick (Eds.), *The business of sport management* (pp. 240–267). London: Pearson.

Cadigan, N. (2008, April 18). Jack Gibson: Played strong, done good. *The Daily Telegraph (Australia)*. Retrieved August 30, 2008, from http://www.dailytelegraph.com.au/sport.

Cain, N. (2008, March 30). Where there's life, there's hope for Leeds. *The Times*, p. 16 (Sport).

Callow, N., Hardy, L., & Hall, C. (2001). The effect of motivational general-mastery imagery intervention on the sport confidence of high-level badminton players. *Research Quarterly for Exercise and Sport, 72*, 389–400.

Cambers, S. (2011, June 26). Wimbledon 2011: Serena Williams's advance sends shudder through rivals. *The Guardian*. Retrieved June 27, 2011, from http://www.guardian.co.uk/sport.

Cameron, C. (1995). *Football, Fussball, Voetbal: The European Game 1955–Euro96*. London: BBC Books.

Campbell, D. (2010, October 9). Commonwealth Games 2010: British athletes gaining vital experience for London 2012. *The Daily Telegraph*. Retrieved October 11, 2010, from http://www.telegraph.co.uk/sport.

Caplan, P. (2010, September 27). Warriors jump the final hurdle. *Rugby Leaguer & League Express*, pp. 18–19.

Carboni, J., Burke, K. L., Joyner, A. B., Hardy, C. J., & Blom, L. C. (2002). The effects of brief imagery on free throw shooting performance and concentrational style of intercollegiate basketball players: A single-subject design. *International Sports Journal, 6*, 60–67.

Carlisle, J. C., Goldfarb, C. A., Mall, N., Powell, J. W., & Matava, M. J. (2008). Upper extremity injuries in the National Football League. Part II: Elbow, forearm, and wrist injuries. *American Journal of Sports Medicine, 36*, 1945–1952.

Carlson, R. (1993). The path to the national level in sports in Sweden. *Scandinavian Journal of Medicine and Science in Sports, 3*, 170–177.

Carlstadt, R. A. (2004). *Critical moments during competition: A mind–body model of sport performance when it counts the most*. New York: Psychology Press.

Carretta, T. R., & Ree, M. J. (2001). Pitfalls of ability research. *International Journal of Selection and Assessment, 9*, 325–335.

Cary, T. (2009, May 20). Button in credit but crunch time for Monte Carlo. *The Daily Telegraph*, p. S16 (Sport).

Cascarino, T. (2009, August 3). Keane drive set to ensure promotion. *The Times*, p. 14 (The Game).

Cascarino, T. (2010, May 1). Ultimate football weekend: Lower-league lowdown. *The Times*, pp. 12–13 (Sport).

Cascarino, T. (2012, April 25). Manner of victory does not reflect well on English football. *The Times*, p. 70 (Sport).

Cash, P. (2008, June 22). Federer's case for the defence. *The Sunday Times*, pp. 6–7 (Sport).

Cash, P. (2009, June 14). If you want to win, learn to play football. *The Sunday Times*, p. 6 (Sport).

Cashmore, E. (2002). *Sport psychology: The key concepts*. London: Routledge.

Cashmore, E. (2005). *Making sense of sports* (4th edn). London: Routledge.

Cashmore, E. (2008). *Sport and exercise psychology: The key concepts* (2nd edn). London: Routledge.

Cashmore, E. (2010). *Making sense of sports* (5th edn). London: Routledge.

Cason, D., & Gillis, H. L. (1994). A meta-analysis of outdoor adventure programming with adolescents. *Journal of Experiential Education, 17*, 40–47.

Caspi, A. (2004, November). Life events and 5HTT promoters: The long and the
short of it. In M. Gill (Chair), *Affective disorders*. Symposium conducted at the
meeting of the Beyond Nature and Nurture: Genes, Environment and their Inter-
play in Psychiatry Conference, London.

Caspi, A., Roberts, B. W., & Shiner, R. L. (2005). Personality development: Stability
and change. *Annual Review of Psychology, 56*, 453–484.

Caspi, A., Sugden, K., Moffitt, T. E., Taylor, A., Craig, I. W., Harrington, H., *et al.*
(2003). Influence of life stress on depression: Moderation by a polymorphism in
the 5-HTT gene. *Science, 301*, 386–389.

Cattell, R. B. (1957). *Personality and motivation structure and measurement*. New
York: Harcourt, Brace, and World.

Cattell, R. B., Blewett, D. B., & Beloff, J. R. (1955). The inheritance of personality.
A multiple variance analysis determination of approximate nature-nurture ratios
for primary personality factors in Q data. *American Journal of Human Genetics,
7*, 122–146.

Caulkin, G. (2010, September 20). Arsenal showing familiar frailties. *The Times*,
pp. 10–11 (Sport).

Caulkin, G. (2011, April 20). Newcastle pull out the stops to slow down United title
charge. *The Times*, pp. 86–87 (Sport).

Celebi, M., & Ozen, G. (2004, March). University students and adventure education
programmes: A study of meanings and experience of adventure training activities. In
W. Krause (Chair), *Outdoor and adventure education – developments and
programmes*. Symposium conducted at the meeting of the International Conference
on Leisure, Tourism & Sport – Education, Integration, Innovation, Cologne, Germany.

Chadband, I. (2009a, February 21). Return of the messiah. *The Daily Telegraph*,
p. S24 (Sport).

Chadband, I. (2009b, June 5). Federer feels weight of destiny. *The Daily Telegraph*,
p. S16 (Sport).

Chadband, I. (2009c, June 9). 'Sun King' plans a stroll on the grass. *The Daily
Telegraph*, p. S10 (Sport).

Chadband, I. (2009d, July 6). Swiss warrior forced to find new reserves. *The Daily
Telegraph*, p. S4 (Sport).

Chadband, I. (2009e, July 9). Blue-collar attack puts in hard yards. *The Daily Telegraph*, pp. S4–S5 (Sport).

Chadband, I. (2009f, July 10). Captain picks moment with perfect timing. *The Daily
Telegraph*, p. S4 (Sport).

Chadband, I. (2009g, July 11). Clarke's in mood to seize the day. *The Daily Telegraph*, pp. S4–S5 (Sport).

Chadband, I. (2009h, July 20). Old Tom's story was too good to be true. *The Daily
Telegraph*, pp. S4–S5 (Sport).

Chadband, I. (2009i, August 8). Ponting takes brutal revenge. *The Daily Telegraph*,
p. S4 (Sport).

Chadband, I. (2009j, August 10). Broad and Swann prove they are no pussycats. *The
Daily Telegraph*, pp. S4–S5 (Sport).

Chadband, I. (2010a, July 18). Casey makes his Open charge. *The Sunday Telegraph*, p. S1 (Sport).

Chadband, I. (2010b, July 29). New kid on the blocks set for the big time. *The Daily Telegraph*, pp. S2–S3 (Sport).

Chadband, I. (2010c, November 8). All Blacks upset by rare lapses from perfection. *The Daily Telegraph*, p. S14 (Sport).

Chadband, I. (2011, February 28). Wenger's callow side crying out for leaders. *The Daily Telegraph*, p. S4 (Sport).

Chamorro-Premuzic, T., & Furnham, A. (2006). Self-assessed intelligence and academic performance. *Educational Psychology*, *26*, 769–779.

Champagne cricket. (2011, January 8). *The Times*, p. 27.

Chantal, Y., Robin, P., Vernat, J.-P., & Bernache-Assollant, I. (2005). Motivation, sportspersonship, and athletic aggression: A mediational analysis. *Psychology of Sport and Exercise*, *6*, 233–249.

Chen, M. A., & Cheesman, D. (in press). Mental toughness at different levels of competitive mixed martial arts. *Perceptual and Motor Skills*.

Cioffi, D. (1991). Beyond attentional strategies: A cognitive-perceptual model of somatic interpretation. *Psychological Bulletin*, *109*, 25–41.

Clayton, J. (2009, July 1). Boks' attitude is one in the eye for fans. *The Times*, p. 22 (Opinion).

Cleary, M. (2005a, January 11). Injury crisis is sending game to intensive care. *The Daily Telegraph*, p. S6 (Sport).

Cleary, M. (2005b, February 8). Tales of the unexpected are talk of the town. *The Daily Telegraph*, p. S6 (Sport).

Cleary, M. (2007, October 15). England heroes defy odds and logic for one final fling. *The Daily Telegraph*, pp. S2–S3 (Sport).

Cleary, M. (2008, September 5). World's top players can raise bar again in Guinness Premiership. *The Daily Telegraph*, p. S12 (Sport).

Cleary, M. (2009a, February 13). Shaun Edwards is a man close to Wales' heart. *The Daily Telegraph*. Retrieved February 13, 2009, from http://www.telegraph.co.uk/sport.

Cleary, M. (2009b, February 23). Gritty Wasps steal contentious win. *The Daily Telegraph*, pp. S14–S15 (Sport).

Cleary, M. (2009c, May 18). Hard-nosed Tigers focused on Leinster. *The Daily Telegraph*, pp. S16–S17 (Sport).

Cleary, M. (2009d, June 1). Wounded Lions' unity put to the test. *The Daily Telegraph*, pp. S8–S9 (Sport).

Cleary, M. (2009e, June 2). O'Driscoll back as Lions look for inspiration. *The Daily Telegraph*, p. S14 (Sport).

Cleary, M. (2009f, June 15). Lions feast on grit and real confidence. *The Daily Telegraph*, pp. S12–S13 (Sport).

Cleary, M. (2009g, June 29). Lions have to live with reality of defeat. *The Daily Telegraph*, pp. S8–S9 (Sport).

Cleary, M. (2009h, July 3). Lions inject fresh blood. *The Daily Telegraph*, p. S15 (Sport).

Cleary, M. (2009i, July 4). Vickery looks for perfect exit line. *The Daily Telegraph*, p. S16 (Sport).

Cleary, M. (2009j, July 6). Lions win battle for hearts and minds. *The Daily Telegraph*, pp. S16–S17 (Sport).

Cleary, M. (2009k, September 21). Wilkinson of old conquers French hearts. *The Daily Telegraph*, pp. S22–S23 (Sport).

Cleary, M. (2010a, January 21). Hopley: Injury toll threatens game. *The Daily Telegraph*, p. S13 (Sport).

Cleary, M. (2010b, March 10). Armitage given reprieve but Moody is dropped. *The Daily Telegraph*, p. S12 (Sport).

Cleary, M. (2010c, May 15). Brits the Saracens joy giver. *The Daily Telegraph*, pp. S20–S21 (Sport).

Cleary, M. (2010d, September 20). Languishing Leeds left adrift at foot of the table after dispiriting defeat. *The Daily Telegraph*, pp. S16–S17 (Sport).

Cleary, M. (2010e, November 5). Hodgson tackles painful memory. *The Daily Telegraph*, p. S11 (Sport).

Cleary, M. (2010f, November 6). Johnson and new England enter the toughest of proving grounds. *The Daily Telegraph*, p. S3 (Sport).

Cleary, M. (2010g, December 21). There's no substitute for fine selection. *The Daily Telegraph*, p. S14 (Sport).

Cleary, M. (2011a, February 28). Johnson takes one step at a time on the rocky road to a Slam. *The Daily Telegraph*, pp. S18–S19 (Sport).

Cleary, M. (2011b, April 12). Clout of their clubs should stiffen Irish spines at World Cup. *The Daily Telegraph*, p. S13 (Sport).

Cleary, M. (2011c, April 13). Barnes retires in face of serious injury risk. *The Daily Telegraph*, p. S12 (Sport).

Cleary, M. (2011d, October 3). England finding ways to survive the siege. *The Daily Telegraph*, pp. S4–S5 (Sport).

Cleary, M. (2011e, October 6). 'I hated Dallaglio the most. I wanted to smash him'. *The Daily Telegraph*, pp. S6–S7 (Sport).

Cleary, M. (2011f, October 10). Weepu rescues All Blacks from Puma ambush. *The Daily Telegraph*, p. S11 (Sport).

Cleary, M. (2011g, October 11). Evergreen Williams buoyed by Wales' squad of ages. *The Daily Telegraph*, p. S7 (Sport).

Cleary, M. (2012a, February 8). Parisse lying in wait to test Morgan's mettle. *The Daily Telegraph*, pp. S10–S11 (Sport).

Cleary, M. (2012b, February 11). England prepare to win ugly in scrum battle. *The Daily Telegraph*, pp. S12–S13 (Sport).

Cleary, M. (2012c, February 13). Lancaster looks to widen England's attacking horizons. *The Daily Telegraph*, p. S18 (Sport).

Cleary, M. (2012d, March 13). Stricken Rees forced to call time on career. *The Daily Telegraph*, p. S15 (Sport).

Cleary, M. (2012e, April 30). Leinster dig deep to seal all-Irish final. *The Daily Telegraph*, p. S20 (Sport).

Cloninger, C. R. (2000). Biology of personality dimensions. *Current Opinions in Psychiatry*, *13*, 611–616.

Cloninger, C. R., Svrakic, D. M., & Przybeck, T. R. (1993). A psychobiological model of temperament and character. *Archives of General Psychiatry, 50*, 975–990.

Clough, P., Earle, K., & Sewell, D. (2002). Mental toughness: The concept and its measurement. In I. Cockerill (Ed.), *Solutions in sport psychology* (pp. 32–45). London: Thomson.

Clough, P. J., & Strycharczyk, D. (2012). *Developing mental toughness: Improving performance, wellbeing and positive behaviour in others.* London: Kogan Page.

Clutton, G. (2009a, April 2). Henson casts future into doubt. *The Daily Telegraph*, p. S19 (Sport).

Clutton, G. (2009b, July 14). Henson denies talk of quitting game. *The Daily Telegraph*, p. S12 (Sport).

Clutton, G. (2011, October 4). Guscott blasts unacceptable player antics. *The Daily Telegraph*, p. S2 (Sport).

Coakley, J., & Pike, E. (2009). *Sports in society: Issues and controversies.* Maidenhead, England: McGraw-Hill.

Coaley, K. (2010). *An introduction to psychological assessment and psychometrics.* London: Sage.

Coe, S. (2004, August 30). Mental strength the key to an Olympic double to savour. *The Daily Telegraph*, p. S3 (Sport).

Cohen, S., Kamarck, T., & Mermelstein, R. (1983). A global measure of perceived stress. *Journal of Health and Social Behavior, 24*, 386–396.

Cohn, P. J. (1990). An exploratory study on sources of stress and athlete burnout in youth golf. *The Sport Psychologist, 4*, 95–106.

Cohn, P. J. (1991). An exploratory study on peak performance in golf. *The Sport Psychologist, 5*, 1–14.

Collomosse, T. (2012, May 28). Bairstow falls short as Windies pacemen find weakness. *i*, p. 48 (Sport).

Comrey, A. L. (1994). *Revised manual and handbook for the Comrey Personality Scales.* San Diego, CA: Educational and Industrial Testing Services.

Comrey, A. L., & Lee, H. B. (1992). *A first course in factor analysis* (2nd edn). Mahwah, NJ: Erlbaum.

Conduct Unbecoming: England's rugby players need to show a discipline that has so far been absent. (2011, October 3). *The Times*, p. 2.

Conn, M. (2009, July 12). Kevin Pietersen's struggles are in his head. *The Australian*. Retrieved July 13, 2009, from http://www.theaustralian.com.au/sport.

Connaughton, D., Hanton, S., & Jones, G. (2010). The development and maintenance of mental toughness in the world's best performers. *The Sport Psychologist, 24*, 168–193.

Connaughton, D., Wadey, R., Hanton, S., & Jones, G. (2008). The development and maintenance of mental toughness: Perceptions of elite performers. *Journal of Sports Sciences, 26*, 83–95.

Connolly, D. (2011, August 23). Britton turns in solid outing in Orioles' 4-1 win over Twins. *The Baltimore Sun*. Retrieved October 4, 2011, from http://www.baltimoresun.com/sports.

Conquering Heroes. (2003, November 24). *The Guardian*, p. 21.

Conroy, D. E. (2001). Fear of failure: An exemplar for social development research in sport. *Quest*, *53*, 165–183.

Conroy, D. E., & Coatsworth, J. D. (2006). Coach training as a strategy for promoting youth social development. *The Sport Psychologist*, *20*, 128–144.

Cook, C., Nesti, M., & Littlewood, M. (2010). A multidisciplinary approach to understanding mental toughness at an elite professional soccer academy. *Journal of Sports Sciences*, *27*, S120–S121.

Corrigan, J. (2009, October 5). Ruddock defends his resilient Worcester. *The Independent*, p. 15 (Sport).

Corry, M. (2007, October 15). Now we're the rugby version of Jamaica's bobsleigh team. *The Guardian*, p. 3 (Sport).

Côté, J. (1999). The influence of the family in the development of talent in sport. *The Sport Psychologist*, *13*, 395–417.

Côté, J. (2002). Coach and peer influence on children's development through sport. In J. M. Silva & D. E. Stevens (Eds.), *Psychological foundations of sport* (pp. 520–540). Boston, MA: Allyn & Bacon.

Côté, J., Baker, J., & Abernethy, B. (2003). From play to practice: A developmental framework for the acquisition of expertise in team sports. In J. Starkes & K. A. Ericsson (Eds.), *Expert performance in sports: Advances in research on sport expertise* (pp. 89–110). Champaign, IL: Human Kinetics.

Côté, J., Baker, J., & Abernethy, B. (2007). Practice and play in the development of sport expertise. In G. Tenenbaum & R. C. Eklund (Eds.), *Handbook of sport psychology* (3rd edn, pp. 184–202). Hoboken, NJ: Wiley.

Côté, J., & Fraser-Thomas, J. (2007). Youth involvement in sport. In P. R. E. Crocker (Ed.), *Introduction to sport psychology: A Canadian perspective* (pp. 266–294). Toronto, Ontario, Canada: Pearson/Prentice Hall.

Côté, J., & Hay, J. (2002). Children's involvement in sport: A developmental perspective. In J. Silva & D. Stevens (Eds.), *Psychological foundations of sport* (pp. 484–502). Boston, MA: Allyn & Bacon.

Côté, J., Salmela, J., Trudel, P., Baria, A., & Russell, S. (1993). Organising and interpreting unstructured qualitative data. *The Sport Psychologist*, *7*, 127–137.

Côté, J., Salmela, J. H., Trudel, P., Baria, A., & Russell, S. J. (1995). The coaching model: A grounded assessment of expert gymnastic coaches' knowledge. *Journal of Sport and Exercise Psychology*, *17*, 1–17.

Coulter, T. J., Mallett, C. J., & Gucciardi, D. F. (2010). Understanding mental toughness in Australian soccer: Perceptions of players, parents, and coaches. *Journal of Sports Sciences*, *28*, 699–716.

Coverdale, B. (2011, November 10). Where's the mental toughness? Australia's batsmen cannot blame the pitch for their lowest total in 109 years. *ESPN*. Retrieved November 11, 2011, from http://www.espncricinfo.com.

Coward, M. (2006, November, 27). Mental toughness is essential. *The Australian*. Retrieved August 30, 2008, from http://www.theaustralian.com.au/sport.

Cox, R. H. (2007). *Sport psychology: Concepts and applications* (6th edn). New York: McGraw-Hill.

Cox, R. H., & Liu, Z. (1993). Psychological skills: A cross-cultural investigation. *Journal of Sport and Exercise Psychology*, *16*, 135–149.

Craven, D. (2012, April 16). Derby win evokes Wembley memories for Rovers. *Yorkshire Post*, p. 6 (Sport).

Crawley, P. (2012, February 9). Maguire brings mental toughness, discipline and attitude to South Sydney: Crocker. *The Daily Telegraph (Australia)*. Retrieved February 11, 2012, from http://www.dailytelegraph.com.au/sport.

Cresswell, S. L., & Eklund, R. C. (2007). Athlete burnout: A longitudinal qualitative study. *The Sport Psychologist*, *21*, 1–20.

Cross, J. (2010, September 20). Time to forget Hughes era and build for future, says Samba. *The Independent*, p. 9 (Sport).

Crossman, J. (1997). Psychological rehabilitation from sports injuries. *Sports Medicine*, *23*, 333–339.

Crust, L. (2009). The relationship between mental toughness and affect intensity. *Personality and Individual Differences*, *47*, 959–963.

Crust, L., & Azadi, K. (2009). Leadership preferences of mentally tough athletes. *Personality and Individual Differences*, *47*, 326–330.

Crust, L., & Azadi, K. (2010). Mental toughness and athletes' use of psychological strategies. *European Journal of Sport Science*, *10*, 43–51.

Crust, L., & Clough, P. J. (2005). Relationship between mental toughness and physical endurance, *Perceptual and Motor Skills*, *100*, 192–194.

Crust, L., & Keegan, R. (2010). Mental toughness and attitudes to risk-taking. *Personality and Individual Differences*, *49*, 164–168.

Crust, L., & Swann, C. (2011). Comparing two measures of mental toughness. *Personality and Individual Differences*, *50*, 217–221.

Cumming, J., & Hall, C. (2002). Athletes' use of imagery in the off-season. *The Sport Psychologist*, *16*, 160–172.

Cumming, S. P., Smoll, F. L., Smith, R. E., & Grossbard, J. R. (2007). Is winning everything? The relative contributions of motivational climate and won-lost percentage in youth sports. *Journal of Applied Sport Psychology*, *19*, 322–336.

Curtis Management Group. (1998). *Motivation Lombardi style*. Lombard, IL: Celebrating Excellence Publishing.

Dall, J. (2007, December 19). Wenger proud of passion. *Sky Sports News*. Retrieved December 19, 2007, from http://www.skysports.com.

Dallaglio, L. (2007). *In the blood*. London: Headline.

Dallaglio, L. (2010, February 7). England have given themselves a platform to deliver a championship. *The Sunday Times*, p. 2 (Sport).

Dallaglio, L. (2011, February 13). Winning mentality gives France plenty to ponder. *The Sunday Times*, p. 3 (Sport).

Dallaglio, L. (2012, April 15). Wasps can break away from cycle of decline. *The Sunday Times*, p. 11 (Sport).

Danish, S. J., Petitpas, A. J., & Hale, B. D. (1993). Life development intervention for athletes: Life skills through sports. *The Counseling Psychologist*, *21*, 352–385.

Dart, T. (2009a, August 13). Defoe spares England's blushes. *The Times*, p. 72 (Sport).

Dart, T. (2009b, October 23). 60-second interview: Stephen Gostkowski. *The Times*. Retrieved November 4, 2009, from http://www.timesonline.co.uk/tol/sport.

Dart, T. (2010, June 28). Milovan Rajevac's side closer to an historic goal. *The Times*. Retrieved June 29, 2010, from http://www.thetimes.co.uk/tto/sport.

Dart, T., & Jacob, G. (2010, September 29). Fabianski keeps nerve as Arsenal bounce back. *The Times*, p. 84 (Sport).

Davidson, M. (2009a, July 11). Good losers make the game worth the candle. *The Daily Telegraph*, pp. W1–W2 (Weekend).

Davidson, M. (2009b). *It's not the winning that counts*. London: Little, Brown.

Davies, G. (2003, November 24). Europe can benefit from shift in balance of power. *The Times*, p. 36 (Sport).

Davies, G. (2007, October 19). While there is more than one way to play the game, there is only one objective for the defending champions tomorrow after their return to core values. *The Times*, p. 19 (The Final).

Davies, G. (2009, November 9). Gatland's men impress but must learn from the All Blacks. *The Times*, p. 72 (Sport).

Davies, G. (2010, November 5). Time for Henson to let hands and feet do the talking and recover lost ground. *The Times*, p. 93 (Sport).

Davies, G. (2012, February 10). Authorities need to acknowledge the danger signs over 'tip tackle' saga. *The Times*, p. 82 (Sport).

Davies, G. A. (2009, April 30). Boxer Manny Pacquiao looks beyond the ring to politics after Ricky Hatton fight. *The Daily Telegraph*. Retrieved May 22, 2009, from http://www.telegraph.co.uk/sport.

Davies, G. A. (2010a, March 27). Underdog Hardy looking for stand-up fight. *The Daily Telegraph*, p. S16 (Sport).

Davies, G. A. (2010b, December 22). The cagefighter who put Bell through hell. *The Daily Telegraph*, p. S4 (Sport).

Davies, J. (2008, June 15). Decisions made the difference. *The Independent on Sunday*, p. 86 (Sport).

Davies, L. (2009, November 21). Red faces for supporters of les Bleus: How hand of Henry took shine off a golden generation. *The Guardian*, p. 27.

Dawkins, R. (1989). *The selfish gene*. Oxford, England: Oxford University Press.

Dean, G. (2009a, December 29). Hard work is paying off for Essex openers past and present. *The Times*, p. 60 (Sport).

Dean, G. (2009b, December 30). Bell displaying lower middle class at No 6 with return to top Test form. *The Times*, pp. 76–77 (Sport).

Deaner, H., & Silva, J. M. (2002). Personality and sport performance. In J. M. Silva & D. E. Stevens (Eds.), *Psychological foundations of sport* (pp. 48–65). Boston, MA: Allyn & Bacon.

Delahaij, R., Gaillard, A. W. K., & van Dam, K. (2010). Hardiness and the response to stressful situations: Investigating mediating processes. *Personality and Individual Differences, 49*, 386–390.

Dennis, P. W. (1981). Mental toughness and the athlete. *Ontario Physical and Health Education Association, 7*, 37–40.

Devonport, T. J. (2006). Perceptions of the contribution of psychology to success in elite kickboxing. *Journal of Sports Science and Medicine, 5*, 99–107.

DeWiggins, S., Hite, B., & Alston, V. (2010). Personal performance plan: Application of mental skills training to real-world military tasks. *Journal of Applied Sport Psychology, 22*, 458–473.

Dickinson, M. (2009, February 23). Special event. *The Times*, p. 9 (The Game).

Dickinson, M. (2010, March 2). Wenger right to question physical culture. *The Times*, p. 71 (Sport).

Dickinson, M. (2011a, March 7). Ferguson applies silent treatment. *The Times*, pp. 4–5 (The Game).

Dickinson, M. (2011b, April 12). Choker can still have his share of last laughs. *The Times*, p. 57 (Sport).

Dickinson, M. (2012, April 26). Sympathy in short supply as toxic Terry faces the role of outsider. *The Times*, pp. 76–77 (Sport).

Dixon, P. (2009a, April 6). Guru's gadgetry helps Padraig Harrington prepare for Augusta. *The Times*. Retrieved April 6, 2009, from http://www.timesonline.co.uk/tol/sport.

Dixon, P. (2009b, November 2). Steady Fisher nets big prize as he defeats potential Ryder Cup rival. *The Times*, p. 79 (Sport).

Dixon, P. (2010a, July 15). Conditions may enable Harrington to blow his rivals away. *The Times*, p. 74 (Sport).

Dixon, P. (2010b, September 13). Martin Kaymer hits cruise control to raise hopes of being on song for Europe. *The Times*. Retrieved October 11, 2010, from http://www.timesonline.co.uk/tol/sport.

Dixon, P. (2010c, November 29). Winless Woods is a shadow of his former self this year. *The Times*, pp. 56–57 (Sport).

Dixon, P. (2011, April 12). McIlroy facing difficult road back from sorry last-round tale of ifs and putts. *The Times*, p. 56 (Sport).

Dolan, C. A., & Adler, A. B. (2006). Military hardiness as a buffer of psychological health on return from deployment. *Military Medicine, 171*, 93–98.

Donahue, E. G., Rip, B., & Vallerand, R. J. (2009). When winning is everything: On passion, identity, and aggression in sport. *Psychology of Sport and Exercise, 10*, 526–534.

Donegan, L. (2011a, April 5). Graeme McDowell: 'I don't want to win one major and then disappear.' *The Guardian*, pp. 6–7 (Sport).

Donegan, L. (2011b, April 10). McIlroy leads charge of the new power generation. *The Observer*, pp. 12–13 (Sport).

Donegan, L. (2011c, April 12). McIlroy faces long haul to recovery after final-day tailspin. *The Guardian*, pp. 6–7 (Sport).

Dongsung, S. S., & Kang-Heon, L. (1994). A comparative study of mental toughness between elite and non-elite female athletes. *Korean Journal of Sport Science, 6*, 85–102.

Dorfman, H. A. (2003). *Coaching the mental game.* Lanham, MD: Taylor Trade.

Doyle, P. (2010, April 24). Rednapp says new resilience can spur Tottenham on in race for fourth. *The Guardian*, p. 4 (Sport).

Doyle, P. (2011, April 24). Wenger retains trust in Arsenal's self-belief. *The Observer*, p. 8 (Sport).

Drake, J. (2007, October 8). Pressure cooker once again proves too hot for All Blacks. *New Zealand Herald*. Retrieved December 15, 2007, from http://www.nzherald.co.nz.

Driediger, M., Hall, C., & Callow, N. (2006). Imagery use by injured athletes: A qualitative analysis. *Journal of Sports Sciences, 24*, 261–271.

182   *References*

Ducker, J. (2010a, February 27). Fletcher received message loud and clear from Keane. *The Times*, p. 9 (Sport).
Ducker, J. (2010b, April 26). Berbatov finally turns on the style. *The Times*, pp. 6–7 (The Game).
Ducker, J. (2011a, April 20). Doubts linger over Ferguson's midfield as tougher tests await. *The Times*, p. 86 (Sport).
Ducker, J. (2011b, November 28). Pardew praises stars in stripes. *The Times*, pp. 10–11 (Sport).
Ducker, J. (2012, April 16). Ashley Young at risk of earning diver label, Sir Alex Ferguson warns. *The Times*. Retrieved April 16, 2012, from http://www.timesonline.co.uk/tol/sport.
Duckworth, K. (2002, November 18). Archer shows his mental toughness to increase lead. *The Daily Telegraph*. Retrieved April 9, 2009, from http://www.telegraph.co.uk/sport.
Duncan, E. (2009). Presentation 4: Evaluation of the positive coaching scheme, Scotland. *Journal of Sports Sciences, 27*, S8.
Durand-Bush, N., & Salmela, J. H. (2002). The development and maintenance of expert athletic performance: Perceptions of World and Olympic champions. *Journal of Applied Sport Psychology, 14*, 154–171.
Dvorak, J., Junge, A., Grimm, K., & Kirkendall, D. (2007). Medical report from the 2006 Fifa World Cup Germany. *British Journal of Sports Medicine, 41*, 578–581.
Dweck, C. (2006). *Mindset: The psychology of success*. New York: Random House.
Eason, K. (2009, September 17). 'Young drivers may buckle under pressure from desperate owners'. *The Times*, p. 85 (Sport).
Eason, K. (2010, June 23). Uruguay starting to live the dream. *The Times*, p. 12 (The Game).
Eaton, R. (2009, June 28). Teenage Brit raises game. *The Times*, p. 8 (Sport).
Ebbeck, V., & Weiss, M. R. (1988). The arousal-performance relationship: Task characteristics and performance measures in track and field athletes. *The Sport Psychologist, 2*, 13–27.
Edwards, S. (2008, February 29). Cipriani too good to be sitting out games on England's bench. *The Guardian*, p. 9 (Sport).
Edwards, S. (2011, March 18). Ireland will show their ugly side in bid to ruin England's grand plan. *The Guardian*, p. 5 (Sport).
Egan, S., & Stelmack, R. M. (2003). A personality profile of Mount Everest climbers. *Personality and Individual Differences, 34*, 1491–1494.
Egan, S. J., Piek, J. P., Dyck, M. J., & Rees, C. S. (2007). The role of dichotomous thinking and rigidity in perfectionism. *Behaviour Research and Therapy, 45*, 1813–1822.
Eklund, R. C. (1994). A season-long investigation of competitive cognition in collegiate wrestlers. *Research Quarterly for Exercise and Sport, 65*, 169–183.
Eklund, R. C. (1996). Preparing to compete: A season-long investigation with collegiate wrestlers. *The Sport Psychologist, 10*, 111–131.
Ella, M. (2008, July 27). Robbie Deans' men did us proud. *The Australian*. Retrieved July 13, 2009, from http://www.theaustralian.com.au/sport.
Ella, M. (2009a, February 21). On-field success starts in the mind. *The Australian*. Retrieved July 27, 2009, from http://www.theaustralian.com.au/sport.

Ella, M. (2009b, June 6). No kid gloves as Robbie eyes World Cup. *The Australian*. Retrieved July 27, 2009, from http://www.theaustralian.com.au/sport.

Elliott, B. (2008, June 22). Tiger's genuine gesture makes him the all-time sporting great. *The Observer*, p. 9 (Sport).

Ellis, C. (2005, September 13). Pietersen walks tall as the nation celebrates. *The Daily Telegraph*, pp. IV–V (The Ashes 2005).

Ellis, L. (2011, April 12). How to avoid another 'choke'. *The Guardian*, p. 7 (Sport).

Emms, G. (2009, April 10). My chance to inspire self-confidence in the young. *The Times*. Retrieved April 10, 2009, from http://www.timesonline.co.uk/tol/sport.

Epic of sportsmanship. (2009, July 6). *The Daily Telegraph*, p. 19.

Ericsson, K. A. (Ed.). (1996). *The road to excellence: The acquisition of expert performance in the arts and sciences, sports and games*. Mahwah, NJ: Erlbaum.

Ericsson, K. A. (2003). Development of elite performance and deliberate practice: An update from the perspective of the expert performance approach. In J. L. Starkes & K. A. Ericsson (Eds.), *Expert performance in sports: Advances in research on sport expertise* (pp. 49–83). Champaign, IL: Human Kinetics.

Ericsson, K. A., & Charness, N. (1994). Expert performance: Its structure and acquisition. *American Psychologist, 49*, 725–747.

Ericsson, K. A., Krampe, R. T., & Tesch-Römer, C. (1993). The role of deliberate practice in the acquisition of expert performance. *Psychological Review, 100*, 363–406.

Ericsson, K. A., & Lehmann, A. C. (1996). Expert and exceptional performance: Evidence on maximal adaptations on task constraints. *Annual Review of Psychology, 47*, 273–305.

Ermler, K. L., & Thomas, C. E. (1990). Interventions for the alienating effect of injury. *Athletic Training, 25*, 269–271.

Evans, T. (2011, January 10). A shaft of light finally breaks through at end of long tunnel. *The Times*, pp. 4–5 (The Game).

Evans, T. (2012, May 19). How Liverpool put out home fires in Rome. *The Times*. Retrieved May 22, 2012, from http://www.timesonline.co.uk/tol/sport.

Evans, V., & Quarterman, J. (1983). Personality characteristics of successful and unsuccessful black female basketball players. *International Journal of Sport Psychology, 14*, 105–115.

Ewert, A., & Yoshino, A. (2008). An initial exploration of the influence of short-term adventure-based experiences on levels of resilience. In A. B. Young & J. Sibthorp (Eds.), *Abstracts from the Coalition for Education in the Outdoors Ninth Biennial Research Symposium* (pp. 18–19). Cortland, NY: Coalition for Education in the Outdoors.

Eysenck, H. J., Nias, D. K. B., & Cox, D. N. (1982). Sport and personality. *Advances in Behavior Research and Therapy, 4*, 1–56.

Faulkner, D. (2012, May 29).'When Sherwani scored ... I knew I had my Olympic gold'. *i*, p. 45 (Sport).

Faulkner, G. (2006, September 30). Who's a clever boy? *New Scientist*, p. 27 (Letter to the Editor).

Favret, B., & Benzel, D. (1997). *Complete guide to water skiing*. Champaign, IL: Human Kinetics.

Feeley, B. T., Powell, J. W., Muller, M. S., Barnes, R. P., Warren, R. F., & Kelly, B. T. (2008). Hip injuries and labral tears in the National Football League. *American Journal of Sports Medicine, 36*, 2187–2195.

Fifield, D. (2009a, April 2). Hats off to Capello as steely England show new-found strength. *The Guardian.* Retrieved April 2, 2009, from http://www.guardian.co.uk/sport.

Fifield, D. (2009b, October 26). My 'pathetic' players aren't good enough, fumes Allardyce. *The Guardian*, pp. 8–9 (Sport).

Fifield, D. (2009c, November 21). Henry says replay with Ireland would be 'the fairest solution'. *The Guardian*, p. 3 (Sport).

Fifield, D. (2010, March 8). Terry reasserts himself with a display of mettle and the armband. *The Guardian*, p. 3 (Sport).

Fifield, D. (2012a, April 15). A calm head at the Bridge. *The Observer*, pp. 6–7 (Sport).

Fifield, D. (2012b, April 25). Terry's foolishness denies captain the chance to make amends for Moscow. *The Guardian*, p. 51 (Sport).

Fisher, M. (2009, April 20). Westerman collapse puts Saints' rout in shade. *The Daily Telegraph*, p. S27 (Sport).

Fitzgerald, G. (2011, December 16). 'Fantastic talent' Farrell is true heir to Wilkinson, Goode insists. *The Times*, p. 94 (Sport).

Flatman, B. (2010, February 19). Venus Williams overcomes Shahar Peer's noble effort. *The Sunday Times.* Retrieved February 23, 2010, from http://www.timesonline.co.uk/tol/sport.

Flatman, B. (2011, July 3). Winning Grand Slam is all in the mind for despondent Scot. *The Sunday Times*, p. 7 (Sport).

Fletcher, D. (2005). 'Mental toughness' and human performance: Definitional, conceptual and theoretical issues. *Journal of Sports Sciences, 23*, 1246–1247.

Fletcher, D. (2007, December). Toughness training on the world's highest mountain. *The Sport and Exercise Scientist*, pp. 10–11.

Fletcher, D. (2008, September 30). Vaughan still has qualities to do a job for England. *The Guardian*, p. 9 (Sport).

Fletcher, D. (2009, October 31). Smith's work ethic guarantees England will be tested to their limits. *The Guardian*, pp. 8–9 (Sport).

Fletcher, D. (2010, May 18). Character and hard work. Put the two together and you get Collingwood. *The Guardian*, pp. 1, 7 (Sport).

Fletcher, D. (2011a, March 19). Trott and Kallis owe it to brain not brawn. *The Guardian*, p. 11 (Sport).

Fletcher, D. (2011b, March 26). Sweep shot spell can counter the magic of Murali. *The Guardian*, pp. 8–9 (Sport).

Fletcher, D., & Fletcher, J. (2005). A meta-model of stress, emotions and performance: Conceptual foundations, theoretical framework, and research directions. *Journal of Sports Sciences, 23*, 157–158.

Flood, T. (2011, October 11). We got our just deserts. We weren't professional enough. *The Daily Telegraph*, p. S4 (Sport).

Folsey, G. (Executive producer), & Landis, J. (Director). (1983). *Trading Places* [Motion picture]. United States: Paramount Pictures.

Ford, I. W., Eklund, R. C., & Gordon, S. (2000). An examination of psychosocial variables moderating the relationship between life stress and injury time-loss among athletes of a high standard. *Journal of Sports Sciences*, *18*, 301–312.

Forgas, J. P. (Ed.) (2006). *Affect in social thinking and behavior*. New York: Psychology Press.

Forsyth, P. (2011, November 26). Scottish football can learn from the coach who could buy a win. *The Scotsman*, p. 17 (Sport).

Forsythe, R. (2010, September 29). Smith calls for Rangers to steam ahead and convert plaudits into points. *The Daily Telegraph*, p. S6 (Sport).

Foster, C. (2011, September 5). Quarterback controversies still the rage, at UCLA and in LA. *Chicago Tribune*. Retrieved October 4, 2011, from http://www.chicagotribune.com/sports.

Fotheringham, A. (2010, July 19). Schleck left with work to do after cat-and-mouse act with Contador. *The Independent*, p. 15 (Sport).

Fourie, S., & Potgieter, J. R. (2001). The nature of mental toughness in sport. *South African Journal for Research in Sport, Physical Education and Recreation*, *23*, 63–72.

Francis, D., & Francis, F. (2009, September 21). Dodgier than fiction. *The Guardian*, p. 31 (Comment & Debate).

Frankl, V. E. (1959). *Man's search for meaning: An introduction to logotherapy*. Boston, MA: Beacon Press.

Fraser, A. (2004, October 12). Miller, 'invincible' who defied Messerschmitts, dies in Melbourne at 84. *The Independent*, p. 58 (Sport).

Fraser-Thomas, J., Côté, J., & Deakin, J. (2005). Youth sport programs: An avenue to foster positive youth development. *Physical Education and Sport Pedagogy*, *10*, 19–40.

Furr, R. M., & Bacharach, V. R. (2008). *Psychometrics: An introduction*. Thousand Oaks, CA: Sage.

Gabbett, T. J. (2000). Incidence, site, and nature of injuries in amateur rugby league over three consecutive seasons. *British Journal of Sports Medicine*, *34*, 98–103.

Gabbett, T. J., & Godbolt, R. J. B. (2010). Training injuries in professional rugby league. *Journal of Strength & Conditioning Research*, *24*, 1948–1953.

Gabbett, T., Jenkins, D., & Abernethy, B. (2010). Physical collisions and injury during professional rugby league skills training. *Journal of Science and Medicine in Sport*, *13*, 578–583.

Gallagher, B. (2005, June 27). Video footage supports emotional O'Driscoll. *The Daily Telegraph*, p. S1 (Sport).

Gallagher, B. (2007, October 13). South Africa must be wary of Argentina. *The Daily Telegraph*. Retrieved July 30, 2009, from http://www.telegraph.co.uk/sport.

Gallagher, B. (2009a, June 3). Threat of a drug culture must not be ignored. *The Daily Telegraph*, p. S9 (Sport).

Gallagher, B. (2009b, August 10). Harlequins feel heat over ruse. *The Daily Telegraph*, p. S18 (Sport).

Gallagher, B. (2011a, February 27). Chabal at No. 8 was a shambolic choice. *The Sunday Telegraph*, p. S3 (Sport).

Gallagher, B. (2011b, March 23). Australia are back on track with new golden generation. *The Daily Telegraph*, p. S15 (Sport).

Gallagher, B., & Willis, A. (2011, June 13). Baltacha benefits from belated move indoors to claim Aegon outdoor title. *The Daily Telegraph*, p. S8 (Sport).

Galli, N., & Vealey, R. S. (2008). 'Bouncing back' from adversity: Athletes' experiences of resilience. *The Sport Psychologist, 22*, 316–335.

Galluzzo, S. (2011, March 2). Orange Lutheran beats Los Angeles Windward, 78–71, for Southern Section Division 4AA title. *Los Angeles Times*. Retrieved June 1, 2011, from http://www.latimes.com.

Galton, F. (1865). Hereditary talent and character. *Macmillan's Magazine, 12*, 157–166, 318–327.

Galton, F. (1869). *Hereditary genius: An inquiry into its laws and consequences.* London: Macmillan.

Galton, F. (1874). *English men of science: Their nature and nurture.* New York: Appleton.

Galton, F. (1875). The history of twins, as a criterion of the relative powers of nature and nurture. *Fraser's Magazine, 92*, 566–576.

Galton, F. (1884). Measurement of character. *Fortnightly Review, 36*, 179–185.

Gardner, F. L. & Moore, Z. E. (2004). A mindfulness–acceptance–commitment-based approach to athletic performance: Theoretical considerations. *Behavior Therapy, 35*, 707–723.

Gardner, F. L., & Moore, Z. E. (2006). *Clinical sport psychology*. Champaign, IL: Human Kinetics.

Gardner, P. (2010, January 20). Wednesday winning again. *The Daily Telegraph*, p. S9 (Sport).

Garside, K. (2008, March 2). Fitter means faster. *The Sunday Times*, p. 15 (Sport).

Garside, K. (2009a, May 6). Heavy-handed attempts to hype the style issue. *The Daily Telegraph*, p. S7 (Sport).

Garside, K. (2009b, June 22). Mickelson, a true sportsman, shows guts on fairways of life. *The Daily Telegraph*, p. S24 (Sport).

Garside, K. (2009c, June 29). Ponting survives because his is still just about the last face bowlers want to see. *The Daily Telegraph*, p. S17 (Sport).

Garside, K. (2009d, July 13). Flintoff must reprise his superhero act to inspire England to Ashes glory. *The Daily Telegraph*, p. S24 (Sport).

Garside, K. (2009e, July 20). Flintoff defies injury's toll in opening burst. *The Daily Telegraph*, pp. S10–S11 (Sport).

Garside, K. (2009f, July 21). Sweet, sweet taste of home victory. *The Daily Telegraph*, pp. S6–S7 (Sport).

Garside, K. (2010, May 3). Mourinho has offered hope to all underdogs – and that includes England. *The Daily Telegraph*, p. S21 (Sport).

Garside, K. (2011, April 12). 'Something wrong with McIlroy,' say his team. *The Daily Telegraph*, pp. S10–S11 (Sport).

Garza, D. L., & Feltz, D. L. (1998). Effects of selected mental practice techniques on performance ratings, self-efficacy, and state anxiety of competitive figure skaters. *The Sport Psychologist, 12*, 1–15.

Gaudreau, P., & Blondin, J-P. (2002). Development of a questionnaire for the assessment of coping strategies employed by athletes in competitive sport settings. *Psychology of Sport and Exercise, 3*, 1–34.

Gee, C. J., Marshall, J. C., & King, J. F. (2010). Should coaches use personality assessments in the talent identification process? A 15-year predictive study on professional hockey players. *International Journal of Coaching Science, 4*, 25–34.

Gendlin, E. T. (1966). Existentialism and experiential psychotherapy. In C. Moustakas (Ed.), *The child's discovery of himself* (pp. 196–236). New York: Basic Books.

George Steinbrenner. (2010, July 14). *The Times*, p. 55 (Obituaries).

Ghosn, C. (2011, July 4). Rebuilding Japan: How to drive change. *Time*, pp. 40–41.

Giacobbi, P. R., Foore, B., & Weinberg, R. S. (2004). Broken clubs and expletives: The sources of stress and coping responses of skilled and moderately skilled golfers. *Journal of Applied Sport Psychology, 16*, 166–182.

Giacobbi, P. R., Lynn, T. K., Wetherington, J. M., Jenkins, J., Bodendorf, M., & Langley, B. (2004). Stress and coping during the transition to university for first-year female athletes. *The Sport Psychologist, 18*, 1–20.

Gibson, A. (1998). *Mental toughness*. New York: Vantage Press.

Gibson, O. (2009, July 16). Superstar Freddie calls time on Test cricket. *The Guardian*, p. 5.

Gibson, R. (2010, September 20). Fulham survive Rovers wrestling match. *The Guardian*, p. 6 (Sport).

Gignac, G. E. (2007). Multifactor modeling in individual differences research: Some recommendations and suggestions. *Personality and Individual Differences, 42*, 37–48.

Gilbert, W. D., Gilbert, J. N., & Trudel, P. (2001a). Coaching strategies for youth sports. Part 1: Athlete behavior and athlete performance. *Journal of Physical Education, Recreation, and Dance, 72*, 29–33.

Gilbert, W. D., Gilbert, J. N., & Trudel, P. (2001b). Coaching strategies for youth sports. Part 2: Personal characteristics, parental influence, and team organization. *Journal of Physical Education, Recreation, and Dance, 72*, 41–46.

Gill, D. L., Dzewaltowski, D. A., & Deeter, T. E. (1988). The relationship of competitiveness and achievement orientation to participation in sport and nonsport activities. *Journal of Sport and Exercise Psychology, 10*, 139–150.

Gill, S. S., & Boden, B. P. (2008). The epidemiology of catastrophic spine injuries in high school and college football. *Sports Medicine and Arthroscopy Review, 16*, 2–6.

Gilmour, R. (2010, May 28). British swimming set to 'swim tough' at Budapest's European Championships. *The Daily Telegraph*. Retrieved June 29, 2010, from http://www.telegraph.co.uk/sport.

Gladwell, M. (2009, October 16). Offensive play. *The New Yorker*. Retrieved November 18, 2009, from http://www.newyorker.com.

Glanville, B. (2010, October 24). Kalou leaves it late. *The Sunday Times*, p. 2 (Sport).

Glazer, S., Stetz, T. A., & Izso, L. (2004). Effects of personality on subjective job stress: A cultural analysis. *Personality and Individual Differences, 37*, 645–658.

Golby, J., & Meggs, J. (2011). Exploring the organizational effect of prenatal testosterone upon the sporting brain. *Journal of Sports Science and Medicine, 10*, 445–451.

Golby, J., & Sheard, M. (2004). Mental toughness and hardiness at different levels of rugby league. *Personality and Individual Differences*, *37*, 933–942.

Golby, J., & Sheard, M. (2006). The relationship between genotype and positive psychological development in national-level swimmers. *European Psychologist*, *11*, 143–148.

Golby, J., Sheard, M., & Lavallee, D. (2003). A cognitive-behavioural analysis of mental toughness in national rugby league football teams. *Perceptual and Motor Skills*, *96*, 455–462.

Golby, J., Sheard, M., & van Wersch, A. (2007). Evaluating the factor structure of the Psychological Performance Inventory. *Perceptual and Motor Skills*, *105*, 309–325.

Goldberg, A. S. (1998). *Sports slump busting: 10 steps to mental toughness and peak performance*. Champaign, IL: Human Kinetics.

Goodbody, J. (2002, May 18). Achieving greatness is all in the mind. *The Times*, p. 32 (Sport).

Goodbody, J. (2004a, August 20). Grobler demands toughness. *The Times*, p. 40 (Sport).

Goodbody, J. (2004b, August 27). Professional temptations kept away from Khan by protective Edwards. *The Times*, p. 50 (Sport).

Goodger, K., Gorely, T., Lavallee, D., & Harwood, C. (2007). Burnout in sport: A systematic review. *The Sport Psychologist*, *21*, 127–151.

Goodwill, V. (2007, January 24). Learning from mistakes is key to winning. *The Eastern Echo*. Retrieved January 24, 2007, from http://www.easternecho.com.

Gorard, S., & Taylor, C. (2004). *Combining methods in educational and social research*. Maidenhead, England: Open University Press.

Gordon, P. (2007, October 19). Scotland can profit from Italian fear, says Strachan. *The Times*, p. 96 (Sport).

Gordon, P. (2009, February 7). Trent McClenahan in search of gold. *The Times*. Retrieved February 7, 2009, from http://www.timesonline.co.uk/tol/sport.

Gordon, P. (2010, June 10). Neil Lennon feels the weight of Celtic history as he moves into hotseat. *The Times*. Retrieved June 29, 2010, from http://www.thetimes.co.uk/tto/sport.

Gordon, S., Gucciardi, D., & Chambers, T. (2007). A personal construct theory perspective on sport and exercise psychology research: The example of mental toughness. In T. Morris, P. Terry, & S. Gordon (Eds.), *Sport psychology and exercise psychology: International perspectives* (pp. 43–55). Morgantown, WV: Fitness Information Technology.

Gorman, E. (2008a, March 15). Massa determined to give the flying Finn a run for his money. *The Times*, p. 8 (Formula One 2008).

Gorman, E. (2008b, November 3). Hamilton's lap of the gods. *The Times*, p. 76 (Sport).

Gorman, E. (2009a, June 9). Brawn sees shades of Schumacher in Button. *The Times*, p. 63 (Sport).

Gorman, E. (2009b, October 5). Champion in waiting driving critics to distraction. *The Times*, p. 77 (Sport).

Gorman, E. (2009c, October 5). Piquet: 'I did a service to the sport but have ended up the biggest victim.' *The Times*, p. 78 (Sport).

Goss, J. (1994). Hardiness and mood disturbances in swimmers while overtraining. *Journal of Sport and Exercise Psychology*, *16*, 135–149.

Gould, D. (2002). Sport psychology in the new millennium: The psychology of athletic excellence and beyond. *Journal of Applied Sport Psychology*, *14*, 137–139.

Gould, D., Dieffenbach, K., & Moffett, A. (2002). Psychological characteristics and their development in Olympic champions. *Journal of Applied Sport Psychology*, *14*, 172–204.

Gould, D., Guinan, D., Greenleaf, C., Medbery, R., & Peterson, K. (1999). Factors affecting Olympic performance: Perceptions of athletes and coaches from more and less successful teams. *The Sport Psychologist*, *13*, 371–394.

Gould, D., Hodge, K., Peterson, K., & Petlichkoff, L. (1987). Psychological foundations of coaching: Similarities and differences among intercollegiate wrestling coaches. *The Sport Psychologist*, *1*, 293–308.

Gould, D., & Whitley, M. A. (2009). Sources and consequences of athletic burnout among college athletes. *Journal of Intercollegiate Sports*, *2*, 16–30.

Gould, R. (2011, August 3). Mental edge builds Melbourne Storm's belief. *Herald Sun*. Retrieved October 4, 2011, from http://www.heraldsun.com.au/sport.

Gower, D. (2010, December 19). Have tourists been unmasked as flat-track bullies? *The Sunday Times*, p. 9 (Sport).

Graham, D., & Yocom, G. (1990). *Mental toughness training for golf*. Lexington, MA: Stephen Greene Press.

Grahame, E. (2012, April 16). Celtic manager Neil Lennon must wait to learn fate after Scottish Cup referee rant. *The Daily Telegraph*. Retrieved April 16, 2012, from http://www.telegraph.co.uk/sport.

Gray, M. (2009, September 13). Jack Kramer: Wimbledon and US tennis champion – and a promoter with a decisive influence on the modern game. *The Guardian*. Retrieved September 24, 2009, from http://www.guardian.co.uk/sport.

Grayling, A. C. (2001). *The meaning of things: Applying philosophy to life*. London: Weidenfeld & Nicolson.

Green, L. S., Oades, L. G., & Grant, A. M. (2006). Cognitive-behavioral, solution focused life coaching: Enhancing goal striving, well-being, and hope. *Journal of Positive Psychology*, *1*, 142–149.

Greenleaf, C. A., Gould, D., & Dieffenbach, K. (2001). Factors influencing Olympic performance: Interviews with Atlanta and Nagano US Olympians. *Journal of Applied Sport Psychology*, *13*, 179–209.

Greenwood, W. (2007, October 23). Springboks show real style. *The Daily Telegraph*, p. S14 (Sport).

Greenwood, W. (2009a, February 21). England must grasp meaning of teamship. *The Daily Telegraph*, p. S16 (Sport).

Greenwood, W. (2009b, June 27). Lords of the dance can still outrun Boks. *The Daily Telegraph*, pp. S4–S5 (Sport).

Greenwood, W. (2010a, March 6). Time for change, England – and lots of it. *The Daily Telegraph*, p. S14 (Sport).

Greenwood, W. (2010b, November 6). The All Blacks' secret? Do everything and do it better. *The Daily Telegraph*, pp. S2–S3 (Sport).

Greenwood, W. (2011, January 8). Help me eradicate collapsing scrums. *The Daily Telegraph*, p. S13 (Sport).

Gregory, S. (2010, April 5). Tiger at the Masters: An ultimate test of toughness. *Time*. Retrieved June 29, 2010, from http://www.time.com.

Greven, C. U., Harlaar, N., Kovas, Y., Chamorro-Premuzic, T., & Plomin, R. (2009). More than just IQ: School achievement is predicted by self-perceived abilities – but for genetic rather than environmental reasons. *Psychological Science, 20*, 753–762.

Griffith, C. R. (1926). *Psychology of coaching*. New York: Scribner.

Griffith, C. R. (1928). *Psychology and athletics*. New York: Scribner.

Grigorenko, E. L. (2002). In search of the genetic engram of personality. In D. Cervone & W. Mischel (Eds.), *Advances in personality science* (pp. 29–82). New York: Guilford.

Gucciardi, D. F. (2009). Do developmental differences in mental toughness exist between specialized and invested Australian footballers? *Personality and Individual Differences, 47*, 985–989.

Gucciardi, D. F. (2010). Mental toughness profiles and their relations with achievement goals and sport motivation in adolescent Australian footballers. *Journal of Sports Sciences, 28*, 615–625.

Gucciardi, D. F. (2011). The relationship between developmental experiences and mental toughness in adolescent cricketers. *Journal of Sport and Exercise Psychology, 33*, 370–393.

Gucciardi, D. F., & Gordon, S. (2009). Development and preliminary validation of the Cricket Mental Toughness Inventory (CMTI). *Journal of Sports Sciences, 27*, 1293–1310.

Gucciardi, D. F., Gordon, S., & Dimmock, J. A. (2008). Towards an understanding of mental toughness in Australian football. *Journal of Applied Sport Psychology, 20*, 261–281.

Gucciardi, D. F., Gordon, S., & Dimmock, J. A. (2009a). Advancing mental toughness research and theory using personal construct psychology. *International Review of Sport and Exercise Psychology, 2*, 54–72.

Gucciardi, D. F., Gordon, S., & Dimmock, J. A. (2009b). Development and preliminary validation of a mental toughness inventory for Australian football. *Psychology of Sport and Exercise, 10*, 201–209.

Gucciardi, D. F., Gordon, S., & Dimmock, J. A. (2009c). Evaluation of a mental toughness training program for youth-aged Australian footballers: I. A quantitative analysis. *Journal of Applied Sport Psychology, 21*, 307–323.

Gucciardi, D. F., Gordon, S., & Dimmock, J. A. (2009d). Evaluation of a mental toughness training program for youth-aged Australian footballers: II. A qualitative analysis. *Journal of Applied Sport Psychology, 21*, 324–339.

Gucciardi, D. F., Gordon, S., Dimmock, J. A., & Mallett, C. J. (2009). Understanding the coach's role in the development of mental toughness: Perspectives of elite Australian football coaches. *Journal of Sports Sciences, 27*, 1483–1496.

Gunn, B. (2010, June 14). 'I hope he gets another chance': The keepers' view. *The Guardian*, p. 6 (Sport).

Hadfield, D. (2005, April 3). Burrow keeps Wolves from Leeds' door. *The Independent on Sunday*, p. 13 (Sport).

Haigh, G. (2009, August 1). Tormented Michael Hussey left needing return to Steve Waugh and peace. *The Times*. Retrieved August 4, 2009, from http://www.timesonline.co.uk/tol/sport.

Haigh, G. (2010, December 8). Broad's bravado makes him hard man to replace. *The Times*, p. 81 (Sport).

Hall, C. R., Mack, D., Paivio, A., & Hausenblas, H. A. (1998). Imagery use by athletes: Development of the Sport Imagery Questionnaire. *International Journal of Sport Psychology*, *29*, 73–89.

Halliday, S. (2010, July 24). 'Believe me, I am going to be a world champion again'. *The Scotsman*, pp. 10–11 (Sport).

Hands, D. (2008a, May 7). Loffreda pleads for time to turn round Leicester from season of disappointment. *The Times*, p. 68 (Sport).

Hands, D. (2008b, November 3). Hook's nerveless kicking sneaks resilient Ospreys into semi-finals. *The Times*, p. 62 (Sport).

Hands, D. (2009a, June 12). Lions may miss out on chance to get their teeth into unfit Burger. *The Times*, p. 81 (Sport).

Hands, D. (2009b, June 29). Outrage caused by Springbok coach's attitude to the gouging incident. *The Times*, p. 64 (Sport).

Hands, D. (2009c, July 6). Ever-growing list of injuries puts emphasis on menace of incredible bulk. *The Times*, p. 60 (Sport).

Hands, D. (2010, January 21). RFU out to add insight to injuries. *The Times*, p. 81 (Sport).

Hannon, E. (2010, May 31). Field of schemes? Lalit Modi created a hugely successful cricket league, but corruption charges may undo him. *Time*, pp. 47–48.

Hanrahan, S., Grove, J. R., & Lockwood, R. J. (1990). Psychological skills training for the blind athlete: A pilot program. *Adapted Physical Activity Quarterly*, *7*, 143–155.

Hans, T. (2000). A meta-analysis of the effects of adventure programming on locus of control. *Journal of Contemporary Psychotherapy*, *30*, 33–60.

Hansen, A. (2008, November 3). Gomes is one of worst I've seen. *The Daily Telegraph*, p. S13 (Sport).

Hansen, A. (2009, December 28). United's tremendous character makes them title favourites. *The Daily Telegraph*, pp. S4–S5 (Sport).

Hansen, A. (2010, September 27). Goalkeeper is only the start of Wenger troubles. *The Daily Telegraph*, p. S5 (Sport).

Hansen, A. (2011, February 21). Mentality of champions has all but faded. *The Daily Telegraph*, p. S5 (Sport).

Hanton, S. (2008). Using competition anxiety to optimise swimming performance. *Journal of Sports Sciences*, *26(S1)*, 3–21.

Hanton, S., Evans, L., & Neil, R. (2003). Hardiness and the competitive trait anxiety response. *Anxiety, Stress, and Coping*, *16*, 167–184.

Hanton, S., & Jones, G. (1999). The acquisition and development of cognitive skills and strategies: I. Making the butterflies fly in formation. *The Sport Psychologist, 13*, 1–21.

Hardie, D. (2010, March 24). Hibs boss slams players for lack of mental toughness. *The Scotsman*. Retrieved March 26, 2010, from http://www.scotsman.com/sport.

Hardy, J., Gammage, K., & Hall, C. R. (2001). A description of athlete self-talk. *The Sport Psychologist, 15*, 306–318.

Hardy, J., Hall, C. R., & Hardy, L. (2004). A note on athletes' use of self-talk. *Journal of Applied Sport Psychology, 16*, 251–257.

Harman, N. (2008, January 21). Young Briton sent home for flagrant lapses of discipline. *The Times*, p. 69 (Sport).

Harman, N. (2009a, May 9). Former world No. 1 seeking perfection back in the ranks. *The Times*, pp. 16–17 (Sport).

Harman, N. (2009b, June 9). Blue Monday for LTA at Queen's. *The Times*, p. 63 (Sport).

Harman, N. (2009c, July 4). Chance that went begging will return again. *The Times*, p. 7 (Sport).

Harman, N. (2009d, July 6). No slice, but lots of spirit from Serena. *The Times*, p. 65 (Sport).

Harman, N. (2009e, July 6). Crazy Sunday afternoon leaves heroic Roddick a broken man. *The Times*, p. 66 (Sport).

Harman, N. (2009f, July 6). Federer seals his place in history as the greatest. *The Times*, p. 68 (Sport).

Harman, N. (2009g, September 16). Rivals face tall order over stopping Del Potro. *The Times*, p. 74 (Sport).

Harman, N. (2010a, November 29). Hungry Federer feasts at the top table and sends tired Nadal away empty-handed. *The Times*, p. 60 (Sport).

Harman, N. (2010b, December 8). Baltacha's courage wins recognition. *The Times*, p. 71 (Sport).

Harman, N. (2011, March 7). Ward succeeds at last but Britain's prospects remain open to question. *The Times*, p. 64 (Sport).

Harman, N. (2012, January 31). Secret is all in the mind: How Djokovic has learnt to make waves. *The Times*, pp. 56–57 (Sport).

Harrell, E. (2010, June 28). The comedown kid. *Time*, pp. 42–43.

Harris, C. (2012, May 19). Lancashire only prolonging inevitable. *The Times*. Retrieved May 22, 2012, from http://www.timesonline.co.uk/tol/sport.

Hart, S. (2009a, July 4). Murray: I'll be better in 2010. *The Daily Telegraph*, p. S1 (Sport).

Hart, S. (2009b, October 15). Daniel Keatings claims historic medal at the World Gymnastics Championships. *The Daily Telegraph*. Retrieved October 16, 2009, from http://www.telegraph.co.uk/sport.

Hart, S. (2010a, February 18). Grim skaters need fairytale ending. *The Daily Telegraph*, p. S17 (Sport).

Hart, S. (2010b, May 5). Bad behaviour rubbing off on amateurs. *The Daily Telegraph*, p. S11 (Sport).

Hart, S. (2010c, October 11). Party time at last as India humble old foes Pakistan. *The Daily Telegraph*, pp. S14–S15 (Sport).

Hart, S. (2011a, June 11). Bolt will strike form soon, says Gay. *The Daily Telegraph*, p. S13 (Sport).

Hart, S. (2011b, June 12). Daley puts the focus on fun, not despair, as he returns to action. *The Sunday Telegraph*, p. S13 (Sport).

Hart, S. (2012, February 9). School's out for Daley in his bid for gold. *The Daily Telegraph*, pp. S14–S15 (Sport).

Harwood, C., Cumming, J. C., & Hall, C. (2003). Imagery use in elite youth sport participants: Reinforcing the applied significance of achievement goal theory. *Research Quarterly for Exercise and Sport, 74*, 292–300.

Hattie, J., Marsh, H. W., Neill, J. T., & Richards, G. E. (1997). Adventure education and outward bound: Out-of-class experiences that make a lasting difference. *Review of Educational Research, 67*, 43–87.

Hawkey, I. (2012, April 29). Bayern power surge. *The Sunday Times*, p. 10 (Sport).

Hays, K., Maynard, I., Thomas, O., & Bawden, M. (2007). Sources and types of confidence identified by world class sport performers. *Journal of Applied Sport Psychology, 19*, 434–456.

Hayter, P. (2009, May 3). England get tough as new recruits say they have the strength to down the Aussies. *The Daily Mail*. Retrieved January 10, 2011, from http://www.dailymail.co.uk/sport.

Hayward, P. (2003, November 24). England's heroes keep their feet on the ground. *The Daily Telegraph*, p. S2 (Sport).

Hayward, P. (2005, May 26). Bold Liverpool rise from the ashes. *The Daily Telegraph*, p. S3 (Sport).

Hayward, P. (2009a, July 17). England haunted by history as fine start goes to waste. *The Guardian*, pp. 2–3 (Sport).

Hayward, P. (2009b, August 10). Australia's no-names strike a blow for team ethic. *The Guardian*, pp. 2–3 (Sport).

Hayward, P. (2009c, November 7). Wilkinson the returning king restores calm to a team in need of therapy. *The Guardian*, p. 8 (Sport).

Hayward, P. (2010a, January 23). Owen: England exile has left me numb. *The Guardian*, pp. 1, 3 (Sport).

Hayward, P. (2010b, September 14). Dimitar Berbatov reborn after adding labour to love of deft touches. *The Guardian*. Retrieved September 16, 2010, from http://www.guardian.co.uk/sport.

Hayward, P. (2011a, February 27). England's audacity earns stunning reward. *The Observer*, p. 1 (Sport).

Hayward, P. (2011b, July 18). Mickelson's new love for links ends halfway through a regal round. *The Guardian*, p. 4 (Sport).

Hayward, P. (2012, April 25). Terry surrenders to dark side with low-grade thuggery. *The Daily Telegraph*, pp. 54–55 (Sport).

Heishman, M. F., & Bunker, L. (1989). Use of mental preparation strategies by inter-national elite female lacrosse players from five countries. *The Sport Psychologist, 3*, 14–22.

Henderson, J. (2009, June 30). Hewitt keeps on scrapping to set up Roddick show-down. *The Guardian*, p. 5 (Sport).

Henderson, M. (2009a, July 17). Captain must rein in frazzled Pietersen. *The Daily Telegraph*, pp. S6–S7 (Sport).

Henderson, M. (2009b, August 10). The hollow men are exposed. *The Daily Telegraph*, p. S6 (Sport).

Hendrix, A. E., Acevedo, E. O., & Hebert, E. (2000). An examination of stress and burnout in certified athletic trainers at Division I-A universities. *Journal of Athletic Training, 35*, 139–144.

Hensley, J. (2010, October 10). Game 5: Ravens pound Broncos in 31–17 win. *The Baltimore Sun*. Retrieved October 4, 2011, from http://www.baltimoresun.com/sports.

Heppenstall, R. (2009, September 21). Booth delighted as Irish show their ruthless side. *The Daily Telegraph*, p. S20 (Sport).

Herbert, I. (2010, November 19). Secret to Beane's success: Study of data that no one else had thought to study. *The Independent*, p. 71 (Sport).

Herbert, I. (2012, April 16). Dalglish struggles to handle the good times. *The Independent*, pp. 4–5 (Sport).

Herbst, D. (1986). Nobody escapes pressure's clutches. *Bowlers Journal, 73*, 90–94.

Hesse-Lichtenberger, U. (2003). *Tor! The story of German football*. London: WSC Books Ltd.

Hewett, C. (2010, December 8). Torn Achilles forces Powell to call time on his career. *i*, p. 47 (Sport).

Hewett, C. (2011, April 11). Saints use power to squeeze past Ulster. *i*, p. 47 (Sport).

Hill, D. (2008, November 3). It takes mental strength to win a world title. *The Guardian*, p. 3 (Sport).

Hingis, M. (2011, May 21). Williams sisters have made Paris an open goal for Sharapova. *The Daily Telegraph*, p. F6 (French Open).

Hirshey, D., & Bennett, R. (2010, June 14). The World Cup as big business. *Time*, pp. 70–72.

Hobson, R. (2009a, June 20). Sri Lanka into World Twenty20 final. *The Times*. Retrieved July 9, 2009, from http://www.timesonline.co.uk/tol/sport.

Hobson, R. (2009b, July 7). Pietersen warns England they are in no position to pull any punches. *The Times*, p. 70 (Sport).

Hobson, R. (2010a, January 8). Australians must be asking now why heroic Collingwood is but a mere MBE. *The Times*, p. 101 (Sport).

Hobson, R. (2010b, December 20). Flower keen to avoid two on the bounce. *The Times*, p. 64 (Sport).

Hodge, K. (1994). Mental toughness in sport: Lessons for life. The pursuit of personal excellence. *Journal of Physical Education New Zealand, 27*, 12–16.

Hodgkinson, M. (2008, January 21). British No. 2 junior sent home. *The Daily Telegraph*, p. S16 (Sport).

Hodgkinson, M. (2009, June 2). Federer fights back from brink. *The Daily Telegraph*, p. S20 (Sport).

Hodgkinson, M. (2010, March 29). Unhappy Murray looks inside his head to understand his slump. *The Daily Telegraph*, p. S25 (Sport).

Hodgkinson, M. (2011a, March 29). Becker insists Lendl would help Murray to solve 'crisis'. *The Daily Telegraph*, p. S11 (Sport).

Hodgkinson, M. (2011b, June 19). Wimbledon 2011: Serena Williams must scale new heights to defend her singles crown as seventh seed. *The Daily Telegraph*. Retrieved June 19, 2011, from http://www.telegraph.co.uk/sport.

Hodgson, M. (2009, July 20). Dogged resistance may lead England to rue declaration. *Yorkshire Post*, p. 5 (Sport).

Hoedaya, D., & Anshel, M. H. (2003). Use and effectiveness of coping with stress in sport among Australian and Indonesian athletes. *Australian Journal of Psychology*, *55*, 159–165.

Hofstede, G. (1984). *Culture's consequences: International differences in work related values*. Beverly Hills, CA: Sage.

Hoggard, M. (2007, December 24). Why we failed to get ourselves out of sticky situations when the heat was on. *The Times*, p. 62 (Sport).

Holland, M. J. G., Woodcock, C., Cumming, J., & Duda, J. L. (2010). Mental qualities and employed mental techniques of young elite team sport athletes. *Journal of Clinical Sport Psychology*, *4*, 19–38.

Hollander, D. B., & Acevedo, E. O. (2000). Successful English Channel swimming: The peak experience. *The Sport Psychologist*, *14*, 1–16.

Holt, N. L., & Dunn, J. G. H. (2004). Toward a grounded theory of the psychological competencies and environmental conditions associated with soccer success. *Journal of Applied Sport Psychology*, *16*, 199–219.

Holt, N. L., & Hogg, J. M. (2002). Perceptions of stress and coping during preparations for the 1999 women's soccer world cup finals. *The Sport Psychologist*, *16*, 251–271.

Honigstein, R. (2009). *Englischer Fussball: A German view of our beautiful game*. London: Yellow Jersey Press.

Hopkins, J. (2011, July 18). Popular triumph of an 'ordinary bloke' who has overcome deep personal sorrow. *The Times*, pp. 62–63 (Sport).

Hopps, D. (2006, July 12). Wessels backs Panesar's mental toughness to overturn comic image. *The Guardian*. Retrieved January 5, 2011, from http://www.guardian.co.uk/sport.

Hopps, D. (2009a, July 13). Nothing like a good old Colly dog for dragging it out to safety. *The Guardian*, pp. 4–5 (Sport).

Hopps, D. (2009b, September 18). I won't quit, says Andrew Strauss after another batting calamity. *The Guardian*. Retrieved September 24, 2009, from http://www.guardian.co.uk/sport.

Hopps, D. (2010, February 13). The not-so-sheepish captain Cook backs up opening partner Strauss. *The Guardian*, p. 12 (Sport).

Horsburgh, V. A., Schermer, J. A., Veselka, L., & Vernon, P. A. (2009). A behavioural genetic study of mental toughness and personality. *Personality and Individual Differences*, *46*, 100–105.

Hotten, R. (2003, September 5). Football champs must learn mind games. *The Times*, p. 9.

Hoult, N. (2005, September 13). Head-to-head drives Flintoff and Warne to superstardom. *The Daily Telegraph*, p. S5 (Sport).

Hoult, N. (2008, August 21). Prior playing for keeps on England return. *The Daily Telegraph*, p. S20 (Sport).

Hoult, N. (2009a, July 10). Flintoff call to arms, says Swann. *The Daily Telegraph*, p. S3 (Sport).

Hoult, N. (2009b, July 11). Australia's Mr Cricket struggles to find mojo. *The Daily Telegraph*, p. S8 (Sport).

Hoult, N. (2009c, July 20). The Open 2009: Cink in synch with Twitter. *The Daily Telegraph*, p. S5 (Sport).

Hoult, N. (2009d, November 18). Bell in a fight for his future. *The Daily Telegraph*, p. S9 (Sport).

Hoult, N. (2010, December 20). Captain demands batsmen bounce back at Melbourne. *The Daily Telegraph*, pp. S2–S3 (Sport).

Hughes, M. (2008, November 3). Search for perfect goal failing at final hurdle. *The Times*, p. 94 (Sport).

Hughes, M. (2010a, January 18). Fàbregas fabulous on return. *The Times*, pp. 4–5 (The Game).

Hughes, M. (2010b, March 6). Wenger: 'The player who jumps out of tackles gets a bollocking.' *The Times*, p. 4 (Sport).

Hughes, M. (2010c, March 27). Contenders or pretenders? I'll know Chelsea's destiny by 5pm, says Ancelotti. *The Times*, p. 3 (Sport).

Hughes, M. (2010d, June 26). German mould broken by Löw. *The Times*, p. 9 (The Game).

Hughes, M. (2010e, June 29). Masterful Brazil warm to their task. *The Times*, p. 9 (The Game).

Hughes, M. (2011a, April 20). Wenger backs players to pass character test in derby clash. *The Times*, p. 84 (Sport).

Hughes, M. (2011b, November 25). The old guard must step up to mask frailties, warns Ballack. *The Times*, p. 114 (Sport).

Hughes, M. (2012a, February 9). Trouble with Terry ruined hard man's reputation. *The Times*, p. 72 (Sport).

Hughes, M. (2012b, May 21). Long days in store for man who delivered greatest night. *The Times*. Retrieved May 22, 2012, from http://www.timesonline.co.uk/tol/sport.

Hughes, R. H., & Coakley, J. (1991). Positive deviance among athletes: The implications of overconformity to the sport ethic. *Sociology of Sport Journal*, *8*, 307–325.

Hughes, S. (2005a, September 13). Centurion Vaughan fulfils promise. *The Daily Telegraph*, p. VI (The Ashes 2005).

Hughes, S. (2005b, September 13). The day Trent Bridge held its breath. *The Daily Telegraph*, p. VII (The Ashes 2005).

Hughes, S. (2008a, October 4). I lacked cut-throat edge for the big Test. *The Daily Telegraph*, pp. S12–S13 (Sport).

Hughes, S. (2008b, December 15). England play huge part in restoring Indian public's interest in Test cricket. *The Daily Telegraph*. Retrieved May 22, 2009, from http://www.telegraph.co.uk/sport.

Hughes, S. (2009a, July 13). Australians treasure their wickets. *The Daily Telegraph*, p. S7 (Sport).

Hughes, S. (2009b, July 21). Australia get it wrong from the start. *The Daily Telegraph*, p. S8 (Sport).

Hughes, S. (2010a, January 8). Collingwood the new Barnacle stymies Steyn. *The Daily Telegraph*, p. S4 (Sport).

Hughes, S. (2010b, March 20). Collingwood on the Waugh path. *The Daily Telegraph*, p. S23 (Sport).

Hughes, S. (2010c, July 26). Power break may come back to haunt Finn. *The Daily Telegraph*, p. S15 (Sport).

Hughes, S. (2010d, December 6). Fielding proves the fifth member of Strauss's attack. *The Daily Telegraph*, p. S7 (Sport).

Hughes, S. (2010e, December 17). Decline of a great batsman is all in the mind. *The Daily Telegraph*, p. S6 (Sport).

Hughes, S. (2011a, January 1). Collingwood faces his final curtain. *The Daily Telegraph*, p. S17 (Sport).

Hughes, S. (2011b, March 18). 'Big Brother' saves the day for persistent bowlers. *The Daily Telegraph*, pp. S2–S3 (Sport).

Hughes, S. (2011c, August 22). Dravid deserves our respect after frustrating England. *The Daily Telegraph*, p. S16 (Sport).

Hunter, A. (2009a, November 30). Tim Cahill admits Everton 'couldn't hit a barn door at the moment'. *The Guardian*. Retrieved January 5, 2011, from http://www.guardian.co.uk/sport.

Hunter, A. (2009b, December 21). Birmingham rising but wary of great expectations. *The Guardian*, p. 2 (Sport).

Hunter, A. (2012, February 8). Parker takes on Gerrard in battle to lead England at Euro 2012. *The Guardian*, pp. 46–47 (Sport).

Hussain, N. (2010, November 30). Cook's simple recipe makes Aussies stew. *Daily Mail*, p. 79 (Sport).

Hussain, N. (2011, January 1). Hit Clarke and grind Australia deep into the dirt. *Daily Mail*, pp. 106–107 (Sport).

Hutchinson, J. C., Sherman, T., Martinovic, N., & Tenenbaum, G. (2008). The effect of manipulated self-efficacy on perceived and sustained effort. *Journal of Applied Sport Psychology, 20*, 457–472.

Hutton, T. (2007, February 2). Nice guys finish first. *The Sun Sentinel*. Retrieved February 2, 2007, from http://www.sun-sentinel.com.

Hystad, S. W., Eid, J., Laberg, J. C., Johnsen, B. H., & Bartone, P. T. (2009). Academic stress and health: Exploring the moderating role of personality hardiness. *Scandinavian Journal of Educational Research, 53*, 421–429.

Hytner, D. (2008, August 8). Wenger underlines his faith in the young Gunners. *The Guardian*, p. 5 (Sport).

Hytner, D. (2009a, March 14). Wenger's men scent victory in the battle for fourth. *The Guardian*, p. 5 (Sport).

Hytner, D. (2009b, June 30). England suffer final indignity as Loach loses bearings. *The Guardian*, p. 9 (Sport).

Hytner, D. (2009c, October 4). Trapattoni wants Irish to draw on Juventus winning spirit. *The Guardian*, p. 4 (Sport).

Hytner, D. (2009d, November 19). Henry handball ruins Ireland's World Cup dream. *The Guardian*, p. 1 (Sport).

Hytner, D. (2010a, March 6). Why hardened Arsenal will not fall apart this time. *The Guardian*, p. 7 (Sport).

Hytner, D. (2010b, June 27). World Cup 2010: Slovakia stand in the way of hopeful Holland. *The Guardian*. Retrieved June 29, 2010, from http://guardian.co.uk/sport.

Hytner, D. (2010c, September 9). Rafael van der Vaart ready to enjoy his best years at Tottenham. *The Guardian*. Retrieved September 13, 2010, from http://guardian.co.uk/sport.

Hytner, D. (2011a, April 19). Five major reasons Arsenal's season is collapsing. *The Guardian*, pp. 4–5 (Sport).

Hytner, D. (2011b, August 25). Wojciech Szczesny savours Arsenal's mental toughness against Udinese. *The Guardian*. Retrieved August 25, 2011, from http://guardian.co.uk/sport.

Hytner, D. (2012, April 16). Scott Parker says Tottenham will have 'failed' if they don't make fourth. *The Guardian*. Retrieved April 17, 2012, from http://www.guardian.co.uk/sport.

Imamura, G. (2011, April 18). Japan: Grace in the ruins. *Time*, p. 4 (Inbox).

Inverdale, J. (2007, November 21). 'Blade runner' ruling should be heartless, not gutless. *The Daily Telegraph*, p. S13 (Sport).

Irvine, C. (2003, November 24). Ashes whitewash leaves Australia with something to crow about. *The Times*, p. 35 (Sport).

Irvine, C. (2007a, May 12). Controversy puts officials under spotlight. *The Times*. Retrieved May 12, 2007, from http://www.timesonline.co.uk/tol/sport.

Irvine, C. (2007b, October 11). Rhinos look to wild man to end St Helens streak. *The Times*, p. 79 (Sport).

Irvine, C. (2008a, July 5). Hanley's final mission is to turn tables for Doncaster. *The Times*, p. 102 (Sport).

Irvine, C. (2008b, October 5). Rhinos rule in the rain as Leeds win back to back titles. *The Times*. Retrieved October 5, 2008, from http://www.timesonline.co.uk/tol/sport.

Irvine, C. (2008c, October 6). Fierce Rhinos steamroller over farewell party for Anderson. *The Times*, p. 62 (Sport).

Irvine, C. (2009a, April 10). Leon Pryce makes Wigan pay for letting lead slip. *The Times*, p. 78 (Sport).

Irvine, C. (2009b, April 20). Westerman emergency adds to Castleford's problems. *The Times*, p. 61 (Sport).

Irvine, C. (2009c, May 18). Crusaders storm Bradford citadel. *The Times*, p. 59 (Sport).

Irvine, C. (2009d, July 13). Hapless Hull easy prey for famished Tigers. *The Times*, p. 55 (Sport).

Irvine, C. (2009e, September 26). Fiery Dragons put Huddersfield to flight. *The Times*, p. 21 (Sport).

Irvine, C. (2010, July 10). Rovers refuse to buckle as Rhinos run into brick wall. *The Times*, p. 6 (Sport).

Irvine, C. (2011, October 10). McDermott plots triumph from the verge of disaster. *The Times*, p. 64 (Sport).

Jacob, G. (2009a, May 25). Southgate vows to stay amid exodus. *The Times*, p. 8 (The Game).

Jacob, G. (2009b, December 28). Parker provides suitors with a timely reminder of his gifts. *The Times*, p. 12 (The Game).

Jacob, G. (2010a, February 15). Savage hits back with extra fizz. *The Times*, p. 6 (The Game).

Jacob, G. (2010b, May 3). Palace lose Hart but not resolve. *The Times*, p. 12 (The Game).

Jackson, J. (2012a, April 15). Ashley Young fell dramatically to win penalty, says Sir Alex Ferguson. *The Guardian*. Retrieved April 15, 2012, from http://www.guardian.co.uk/sport.

Jackson, J. (2012b, May 12). How Mancini managed to get his offbeat squad to dance to the same tune. *The Guardian*, p. 4 (Sport).

Jackson, S. A. (1995). Factors influencing the occurrence of flow states in elite athletes. *Journal of Applied Sport Psychology*, 7, 138–166.

Jackson, S. A., Mayocchi, L., & Dover, J. (1998). Life after winning gold: II. Coping with change as an Olympic gold medallist. *The Sport Psychologist*, 12, 137–155.

Jago, R. (2002, July 29). Syed shows mental toughness to secure team medal. *The Guardian*. Retrieved June 1, 2011, from http://www.guardian.co.uk/sport.

Jago, R. (2009, August 17). Murray works to rule as he shows resilience to clinch fourth Masters. *The Guardian*, p. 13 (Sport).

James, D. (2012, March 11). High-pressure game without a net. *The Observer*, p. 20 (Sport).

James, S. (2010a, January 8). Day when Bell the boy wonderer became a man. *The Daily Telegraph*, p. S5 (Sport).

James, S. (2010b, April 26). Penalty gaffe gives O'Neill a reason to cheer at last. *The Guardian*, pp. 4–5 (Sport).

James, S. (2010c, November 15). North shines but Wales lose direction. *The Daily Telegraph*, p. S19 (Sport).

James, S. (2010d, December 17). Mr Nice Guy throws off shackles to prove he is genuine article. *The Daily Telegraph*, pp. S2–S3 (Sport).

James, S. (2011a, January 11). England leadership made vision a reality. *The Daily Telegraph*, p. S20 (Sport).

James, S. (2011b, February 28). The sky is blue for Birmingham after years of dark days. *The Guardian*, p. 4 (Sport).

James, S. (2011c, April 9). Reo-Coker happy for now but keeping options open at Villa. *The Guardian*, p. 5 (Sport).

James, S. (2012, April 16). Has Ashley Young finally taken one dive too far? *The Guardian*. Retrieved April 16, 2012, from http://www.guardian.co.uk/sport.

Jardine, P. (2008, December 27). Walter Smith knew Kenny Miller had the mental toughness to succeed at Rangers. *The Daily Mail*. Retrieved June 1, 2011, from http://www.dailymail.co.uk/sport.

Jeffries, S. (2012, May 23). London 2012: 'I dream of doing my best dive,' says Tom Daley. *The Guardian*. Retrieved May 24, 2012, from http://guardian.co.uk/sport.

Jenkins, T. (2009, May 12). 'You can have that lifestyle but you'll underachieve'. *The Guardian*, pp. 6–7 (Sport).

Jenson, P. (2007, November 26). Capello swipe at McClaren. *The Times*, p. 2 (The Game).

Jenson, P. (2012a, April 20). Messi and Co taken to task, but 'Nou Camp will have last word'. *The Independent*, p. 76 (Sport).

Jenson, P. (2012b, April 27). Home comforts boost Bayern's soaring self-belief. *i*, pp. 60–61 (Sport).

John, J. (2010, October 20). Bothroyd affirms Cardiff resolve. *The Times*, p. 74 (Sport).

Johnson, M. (2008, October 1). Battle on track will be even more intense in London. *The Daily Telegraph*, p. V5 (London 2012).

Johnson, M. (2009, June 7). Some critics make me wonder if we should bother turning up. *The Sunday Times*, p. 16 (Sport).

Johnson, M. (2009a, April 9). Tiger Woods has attributes to be No. 1 in any sport. *The Daily Telegraph*, p. S13 (Sport).

Johnson, M. (2009b, May 8). Bolt is going to find this season much tougher. *The Daily Telegraph*, p. S14 (Sport).

Johnson, M. (2009c, August 13). British athletes unprepared for the big stage. *The Daily Telegraph*, p. S20 (Sport).

Jones, C. M. (1982, November). Mental toughness. *World Bowls*, pp. 30–31.

Jones, G., Hanton, S., & Connaughton, D. (2002). What is this thing called mental toughness? An investigation of elite sport performers. *Journal of Applied Sport Psychology, 14*, 205–218.

Jones, G., Hanton, S., & Connaughton, D. (2007). A framework of mental toughness in the world's best performers. *The Sport Psychologist, 21*, 243–264.

Jones, G., Hanton, S., & Swain, A. B. J. (1994). Intensity and interpretation of anxiety symptoms in elite and non-elite performers. *Personality and Individual Differences, 17*, 657–663.

Jones, J. W., Neuman, G., Altmann, R., & Dreschler, B. (2001). Development of the Sports Performance Inventory: A psychological measure of athletic potential. *Journal of Business and Psychology, 15*, 491–503.

Jones, S. (2008, March 9). Next step Grand Slam, then the world. *The Sunday Times*, p. 4 (Sport).

Jones, S. (2009, September 6). Fake injury probe deepens. *The Sunday Times*, p. 9 (Sport).

Jones, S. (2010, February 7). England get up and running at last. *The Sunday Times*, pp. 2–3 (Sport).

Jöreskog, K. G., & Sörbom, D. (1993). *LISREL 8: Structural equation modeling with the SIMPLIS command language*. Hillsdale, NJ: Erlbaum.

Joseph, J. (2008, January 29). Modern morals. *The Times*, p. 3 (Times2).

Judkins, S., & Rind, R. (2005). Hardiness, job satisfaction, and stress among home health nurses. *Home Health Care Management & Practice, 17*, 113–118.

Junge, A., Dvorak, J., & Graf-Baumann, T. (2004). Football injuries during the World Cup 2002. *American Journal of Sports Medicine, 32*(Suppl. 1), 23S–27S.

Junge, A., Dvorak, J., Graf-Baumann, T., & Peterson, L. (2004). Football injuries during Fifa tournaments and the Olympic Games, 1998–2001. *American Journal of Sports Medicine, 32*(Suppl. 1), 80S–89S.

Junge, A., Engebretsen, L., Mountjoy, M. L., Alonso, J. M., Renström, P. A. F. H., Aubry, M. J., *et al.* (2009). Sports injuries during the summer Olympic Games 2008. *American Journal of Sports Medicine, 37*, 2165–2172.

Junge, A., Langevoort, G., Pipe, A., Peytavin, A., Wong, F., Mountjoy, M., *et al.* (2006). Injuries in team sport tournaments during the 2004 Olympic Games. *American Journal of Sports Medicine, 34*, 565–576.

Kagan, J. (1999). Born to be shy? In R. Conlan (Ed.), *States of mind* (pp. 29–51). New York: Wiley.

Kahn, O. (2010, June 27). England will pay the price if they focus on the past. *The Sunday Times*, p. 5 (Sport).

Kahneman, D., Diener, E., & Schwartz, N. (Eds.). (1999). *Well-being: The foundations of hedonic psychology*. New York: Russell Sage.

Kaiseler, M., Polman, R., & Nicholls, A. (2009). Mental toughness, stress, stress appraisal, coping and coping effectiveness in sport. *Personality and Individual Differences, 47*, 728–733.

Kalia, M. (2005). Neurobiological basis of depression: An update. *Metabolism Clinical and Experimental, 54*(Suppl. 1), 24–27.

Kanas, N., & Ziegler, J. (1984). Group climate in a stress discussion group for medical interns. *Behavioral Science, 8*, 35–38.

Kang-Heon, L., Dongsung, S. S., Myung-Woo, H., & Elisa, L. (1994). Developing the norm of Korean table tennis players' mental toughness. *Korean Journal of Sport Science, 6*, 103–120.

Kay, O. (2008, December 30). Oliver Kay Q&A: Steven Gerrard has the mental strength to cope. *The Times*. Retrieved December 30, 2008, from http://www. timesonline.co.uk/tol/sport.

Kay, O. (2009a, May 6). Men united by a lust for glory. *The Times*, p. 2 (Sport).

Kay, O. (2009b, May 18). Little fizz but the party still begins. *The Times*, pp. 4–5 (The Game).

Kay, O. (2009c, May 20). Panic in the seats on Tyneside . . . Teesside, Wearside, Humberside. United team-sheet may hold key to who shares West Brom's fate. *The Times*, pp. 74–75 (Sport).

Kay, O. (2009d, May 25). Shearer's men leave quietly. *The Times*, pp. 2–3 (The Game).

Kay, O. (2009e, November 28). Rosicky's faith in the beautiful game undimmed by bleak days. *The Times*, p. 4 (Sport).

Kay, O. (2009f, December 28). Ten years on, it is time for Terry to be made into an example. *The Times*, p. 20 (The Game).

Kay, O. (2010, October 4). Drogba performs same old routine. *The Times*, pp. 4–5 (The Game).

Kay, O. (2011a, March 15). Ferguson has to confront May of reckoning before thoughts turn to T-word. *The Times*, pp. 70–71 (Sport).

Kay, O. (2011b, April 13). Abramovich's dream bites the dust as Hernández shines. *The Times*, pp. 62–63 (Sport).

Kay, O. (2011c, April 20). Arsenal lack the bottle required to win trophies. *The Times*, pp. 84–85 (Sport).

Kay, O. (2011d, June 13). Welbeck's late strike adds final touch to England fightback. *The Times*, pp. 60–61 (Sport).

Kay, O. (2011e, August 25). Szczesny is the saviour as Arsenal's young guns fight back. *The Times*, pp. 94–95 (Sport).

Kay, O. (2011f, October 6). Capello set to give youngsters his blessing. *The Times*, p. 96 (Sport).

Kay, O. (2012a, April 20). Chelsea can be conquerors in Nou Camp if they keep their heads. *The Times*, p. 77 (Sport).

Kay, O. (2012b, April 25). Torres adds the finishing touch to perfect ten's heroics. *The Times*, pp. 70–71 (Sport).

Kay, O. (2012c, April 26). Galácticos misfire as Bayern hold their nerve in shoot-out. *The Times*, pp. 78–79 (Sport).

Kay, O. (2012d, May 14). Manchester City 3 QPR 2: Miracle at the Etihad sees City reign supreme. *The Times*. Retrieved May 22, 2012, from http://www.timesonline.co.uk/tol/sport.

Kay, O. (2012e, May 21). Bayern Munich 1 Chelsea 1 (aet; Chelsea win 4–3 on penalties): 'You feel that your name is on the cup'. *The Times*. Retrieved May 22, 2012, from http://www.timesonline.co.uk/tol/sport.

Kee, Y. H., & Wang, C. K. J. (2008). Relationships between mindfulness, flow dispositions and mental skills adoption: A cluster analytic approach. *Psychology of Sport and Exercise, 9*, 393–411.

Kelley, B. C. (1994). A model of stress and burnout in collegiate coaches: Effects of gender and time of season. *Research Quarterly for Exercise and Sport, 65*, 48–58.

Kelly, G. A. (1991). *The psychology of personal constructs: A theory of personality* (Vol. 1). London: Routledge. (Original work published 1955)

Kelso, P. (2009a, August 19). RFU to investigate four more matches: Governing body to look into other incidents of cheating at Harlequins. *The Daily Telegraph*, p. S2 (Sport).

Kelso, P. (2009b, August 19). Worst still to come: ERC's full judgment will bury whatever vestige of credibility Harlequins and Richards retain over systemic cheating. *The Daily Telegraph*, p. S3 (Sport).

Kelso, P. (2009c, August 20). Richards: Williams asked for cut. Harlequins' former director of rugby says the player wanted to cover up scandal. *The Daily Telegraph*, p. S20 (Sport).

Kelso, P. (2012a, April 25). UK chief issues drugs ban warning. *The Daily Telegraph*, p. S12 (Sport).

Kelso, P. (2012b, April 30). Chambers and Millar given Games all-clear. *The Daily Telegraph*, pp. S16–S17 (Sport).

Kempson, R. (2010, July 14). Webb insists players must take blame. *The Times*, p. 66 (Sport).

Kempson, R. (2012, April 16). Tevez adds to confusion of City's on-off title chase. *The Independent*, p. 7 (Sport).

Kendler, K. S., Kuhn, J. W., Vittum, J., Prescott, C. A., & Riley, B. (2005). The interaction of stressful life events and a serotonin transporter polymorphism in the prediction of episodes of major depression: A replication. *Archives of General Psychiatry, 62*, S29–S35.

Kent, D. (2010, March 9). West Ham star Valon Behrami calls for mental change at Upton Park. *The Daily Mail*. Retrieved January 7, 2011, from http://www.dailymail.co.uk/sport.

Kent, P. (2011, March 31). League stars lack mental toughness. *The Daily Telegraph (Australia)*. Retrieved October 1, 2011, from http://www.news.com.au/dailytelegraph.html.

Keohane, M. (2006, September 6). Losing is never a good habit. *News 24*. Retrieved September 7, 2006, from http://www.news24.com.

Keown, M. (2012, April 20). Match Drogba at his power play and then watch him fall. *The Daily Mail*, p. 85 (Sport).

Kerr, J. H., Wilson, G. V., Bowling, A., & Sheahan, J. P. (2005). Game outcome and elite Japanese women's field hockey players' experience of emotions and stress. *Psychology of Sport and Exercise, 6*, 251–263.

Kervin, A. (2003, November 24). Woodward finds right answers on his day of judgment. *The Times*, p. 36 (Sport).

Kessel, A. (2009, November 15). Jessica Ennis: Sheffield steel. *Observer Sports Monthly*, pp. 34–37.

Kessel, A. (2012, April 30). From pariah to mentor – how tide of opinion turned for Chambers. *The Guardian*, pp. 10–11 (Sport).

Keyes, C. L. M., & Haidt, J. (Ed.). (2003). *Flourishing: Positive psychology and the life well-lived*. Washington, DC: American Psychological Association.

Khan, I. (2003, March 26). Australia's grass roots take firm hold. *The Daily Telegraph*. Retrieved April 7, 2009, from http://www.telegraph.co.uk/sport.

Khoshaba, D. M., & Maddi, S. R. (1999). Early experiences in hardiness development. *Consulting Psychology Journal: Practice and Research, 51*, 106–116.

Kidd, P. (2009a, July 22). Flintoff told he will 'have to guarantee fitness' for Ashes duty. *The Times*, p. 68 (Sport).

Kidd, P. (2009b, July 24). Gilchrist preaches fair play gospel. *The Times*, p. 68 (Sport).

Kidd, P. (2009c, July 27). Brotherhood of the Baggy Green. *The Times*, p. 4 (The Ashes).

Kidd, P. (2010, June 20). Elena Baltacha ready to come out fighting. *The Times*. Retrieved June 29, 2010, from http://www.thetimes.co.uk/tto/sport.

Kidd, P., & Westerby, J. (2009, July 16). Five-day cricket too tough on the knees as Freddie gives up Tests for Twenty20. *The Times*, p. 4.

Kierkegaard, S. (1959). *Either/Or* (D. F. Swenson & L. M. Swenson, Trans.) Garden City, NY: Doubleday. (Original work published 1843)

Killen, N. M., Gabbett, T. J., & Jenkins, D. G. (2010). Training loads and incidence of injury during the pre-season in professional rugby league players. *Journal of Strength & Conditioning Research, 24*, 2079–2084.

Kimmage, P. (2008, May 18). Talking with a straight bat. *The Sunday Times*, p. 19 (Sport).

King, D. (2009, October 4). Hart salutes 'great' battlers as they finally break the victory drought. *The Mail on Sunday*, pp. 4–5 (Football).

Kirby, K., Moran, A., & Guerin, S. (2011). A qualitative analysis of the experiences of elite athletes who have admitted to doping for performance enhancement. *International Journal of Sport Policy and Politics, 3*, 205–224.

Kirk, D. (2007, September 30). All Blacks are ready to rumble. *The Daily Telegraph*. Retrieved July 30, 2009, from http://www.telegraph.co.uk/sport.

Kirk, R. C. (1995). *Experimental design* (3rd edn). Pacific Grove, CA: Brooks/Cole.

Kirkcaldy, B. D. (1985). The values of traits in sport. In B. D. Kirkcaldy (Ed.), *Individual differences in movement* (pp. 257–277). Lancaster, England: MTP Press.

Kitson, R. (2004, February 9). O'Sullivan aims for English mentality to beat inferiority complex. *The Guardian*. Retrieved January 7, 2011, from http://www.guardian.co.uk/sport.

Kitson, R. (2008, November 17). Johnson's men fall well short of Wallabies when push comes to shove. *The Guardian*, pp. 10–11 (Sport).

Kitson, R. (2009a, June 30). One-eyed De Villiers sees no problem in standing by Burger. *The Guardian*, p. 10 (Sport).

Kitson, R. (2009b, November 28). Kearney primes Ireland for one giant leap. *The Guardian*, p. 10 (Sport).

Kitson, R. (2010a, January 23). Hodgson's glass half full as Exiles search for a hangover cure. *The Guardian*, p. 11 (Sport).

Kitson, R. (2010b, September 6). Heartbroken England rue missed opportunities as New Zealand rule again. *The Guardian*, p. 8 (Sport).

Kitson, R. (2011a, February 28). Johnson calls on buoyant England to forget grand slam and focus on Scots. *The Guardian*, p. 10 (Sport).

Kitson, R. (2011b, March 19). A grand slam game in Dublin, a team on the up. Is it 2003 again? *The Guardian*, pp. 8–9 (Sport).

Kitson, R. (2011c, October 6). Foden calls for smash and grab rather than wait and see. *The Guardian*, pp. 2–3 (Sport).

Kitson, R. (2012a, March 10). Two weekends to decide whether caretaker gets the keys. *The Guardian*, pp. 8–9 (Sport).

Kitson, R. (2012b, April 30). Leinster's compelling resistance keeps Clermont at bay and sets up all-Irish final. *The Guardian*, p. 12 (Sport).

Kline, R. B. (2005). *Principles and practice of structural equation modelling* (2nd edn). New York: Guilford.

Kobasa, S. C. (1979). Stressful life events, personality and health: An inquiry into hardiness. *Journal of Personality and Social Psychology*, *37*, 1–11.

Kofotolis, N. D., Kellis, E., & Vlachopoulos, S. P. (2007). Ankle sprain injuries and risk factors in amateur soccer players during a 2-year period. *American Journal of Sports Medicine*, *35*, 458–466.

Krishnan, V., Han, M-H., Graham, D., Berton, O., Renthal, W., Reister, S. J., *et al.* (2007). Molecular adaptations underlying susceptibility and resistance to social defeat in brain reward regions. *Cell*, *131*, 391–404.

Kroll, W. (1967). Sixteen personality factor profiles of collegiate wrestlers. *Research Quarterly*, *38*, 49–57.

Kuan, G., & Roy, J. (2007). Goal profiles, mental toughness and its influence on performance outcomes among Wushu athletes. *Journal of Sports Science & Medicine*, *6*, 28–33.

Kuehl, K., Kuehl, J., & Tefertiller, C. (2005). *Mental toughness: A champion's state of mind*. Chicago, IL: Ivan R. Dee.

Kuzio, D., & Coates, T. (2010, August 30). The nightmare was worth it, says Clarke. *Rugby Leaguer & League Express*, p. 5.

Kvist, J., Ek, A., Sporrstedt, K., & Good, L. (2005). Fear of re-injury: A hindrance for returning to sports after anterior cruciate ligament reconstruction. *Knee Surgery, Sports Traumatology, Arthroscopy*, *13*, 393–397.

Lacey, D. (2009a, November 14). England's chance to measure against the finest yardstick. *The Guardian*, p. 7 (Sport).

Lacey, D. (2009b, November 21). He bit the hand that fed his good name. *The Guardian*, p. 3 (Sport).

Lacey, D. (2010, February 15). Three flashes of Birmingham's class leave Clough forlorn. *The Guardian*, p. 4 (Sport).

Lacey, D. (2011a, March 21). Spurs off pace in fourth-place race. *The Guardian*, p. 6 (Sport).

Lacey, D. (2011b, March 26). Beware the Welsh corgi underdogs with bite. *The Guardian*, p. 4 (Sport).

Lafrenière, M.-A. K., Jowett, S., Vallerand, R. J., & Carbonneau, N. (2011). Passion for coaching and the quality of the coach-athlete relationship. *Psychology of Sport and Exercise*, *12*, 144–152.

Lage, L. (2011, October 2). No.12 Michigan set to hit the road for 1st time. *Chicago Tribune*. Retrieved October 4, 2011, from http://www.chicagotribune.com/sports.

Lancer, K. (2000). *Hardiness and Olympic women's synchronized swim team*. Paper presented at the Improving Performance in Sport Conference, University of Nevada, Las Vegas, NV.

Lanchester, J. (2011, October 20). Short cuts. *London Review of Books*, p. 22.

Lane, A. M. (2008). *Sport and exercise psychology*. London: Hodder Education.

Lane, A. M., Harwood, C., Terry, P. C., & Karageorghis, C. I. (2004). Confirmatory factor analysis of the Test of Performance Strategies (TOPS) among adolescent athletes. *Journal of Sports Sciences*, *22*, 803–812.

Lane, A. M., Thelwell, R., & Gill, G. (2007). Relationship between emotional intelligence and mental toughness. *Journal of Sports Sciences*, *25*, 312–313.

Langer, P. R., Fadale, P. D., & Palumbo, M. A. (2008). Catastrophic neck injuries in the collision sport athlete. *Sports Medicine and Arthroscopy Review*, *16*, 7–15.

Lansley, P. (2009a, June 27). Heroic Hart puts Pearce on course for final glory. *The Times*, p. 14 (Sport).

Lansley, P. (2009b, June 27). Goalkeeper shrugs off his spot of bother. *The Times*, p. 15 (Sport).

Lansley, P. (2010a, January 11). McLeish believes 'big four' will become a magnificent seven. *The Times*, p. 9 (The Game).

Lansley, P. (2010b, January 18). Zola given new hope by team's resolution. *The Times*, p. 7 (The Game).

Lansley, P. (2010c, March 6). Hart set on proving a fit successor to hero James. *The Times*, p. 11 (Sport).

Lansley, P. (2010d, April 26). Carr trouble as gestures upset crowd. *The Times*, p. 4 (The Game).

Latham, R. (2009, July 14). Crawley digs in to thwart Somerset. *The Daily Telegraph*, p. S14 (Sport).

Lawrence, A. (2009, April 26). Bitter rivalry threatens to reignite. *The Observer*, p. 7 (Sport).

Lawrence, A. (2010, March 27). Streetwise Nasri helping Arsenal navigate the road to success. *The Guardian*, pp. 4–5 (Sport).

Lawrenson, D. (2010a, April 3). Resolute Wigan have the last laugh. *The Daily Telegraph*, p. S24 (Sport).

Lawrenson, D. (2010b, April 13). New improved Westwood . . . but same old sad outcome. *The Daily Mail*, p. 73 (Sport).

Lawson, G. (2009, July 20). Bookies stumped as form fluctuates. *The Daily Telegraph*, p. S14 (Sport).

Lawton, J. (2009a, June 26). Ruthless display from a champion in the making. *The Independent*, pp. 62–63 (Sport).

Lawton, J. (2009b, July 10). Flintoff shows shades of 2005 but England are taught a lesson. *The Independent*, pp. 60–61 (Sport).

Lawton, J. (2009c, July 14). Gamesmanship is just not cricket, no matter which sport is being played. *The Independent*, p. 50 (Sport).

Lawton, J. (2009d, August 10). Ill-tempered rabble whose flaws go right to the top. *The Independent*, pp. 4–5 (Sport).

Lawton, J. (2010a, September 20). Bulgarian displays the touch of an executioner. *The Independent*, p. 4 (Sport).

Lawton, J. (2010b, December 7). A comeback for Warne? Why not call Lillee as well? *i*, p. 50 (Sport).

Lawton, J. (2010c, December 8). Pietersen happy to buy back into the team ethic. *i*, p. 53 (Sport).

Lawton, J. (2010d, December 20). Australia stood up to be counted. It's about respect. *i*, p. 45 (Sport).

Lawton, J. (2010e, December 30). The greatest goal in sport is perfection and rarely has a team come so close. *i*, p. 43 (Sport).

Lawton, J. (2011a, February 14). United's winning attitude highlights City's lack of belief. *i*, p. 53 (Sport).

Lawton, J. (2011b, April 12). Golden generation has lost its lustre – and any claims it's about to inherit world. *i*, p. 46 (Sport).

Lawton, J. (2012a, April 25). After Terry atrocity, Chelsea heroes produce performance of their lives. *The Independent*, pp. 76–77 (Sport).

Lawton, J. (2012b, April 26). Mourinho's men play their part but Bayern win rapier duel. *The Independent*, p. 75 (Sport).

Layard, R. (2006). *Happiness: Lessons from a new science*. London: Penguin.

LeDoux, J. (2002, August). The self and the brain. *Prospect*, *77*, 50–53.

Le Gall, F., Carling, C., Reilly, T., Vandewalle, H., Church, J., & Rochcongar, P. (2006). Incidence of injuries in elite French youth soccer players. *American Journal of Sports Medicine*, *34*, 928–938.

Ledger, J. (2008, June 20). Ganson's steely resolve deserves to whistle up reward. *Yorkshire Post*, p. 23 (Sport).

Lee, A. (2011, June 13). Cecil finds strength in adversity. *The Times*, p. 50 (Sport).

Lee, Y. T., Jussim, L., & McCauley, C. (1995). *Stereotype accuracy: Toward appreciating group differences*. Washington, DC: American Psychological Association.

LeUnes, A. (2008). *Sport psychology* (4th edn). New York: Psychology Press.

Levy, A., Clough, P., Polman, R., Marchant, D., & Earle, K. (2005). Mental toughness and injury occurrence in elite swimming. *Journal of Sports Sciences, 11,* 1256–1257.

Levy, A., Polman, R. C. J., Clough, P. J., Marchant, D., & Earle, K. (2006). Mental toughness as a determinant of beliefs, pain, and adherence in sport injury rehabilitation. *Journal of Sport Rehabilitation, 15,* 246–254.

Lewis, D. (2008, August 20). Christine Ohuruogu's life will never be the same after this. *The Daily Telegraph,* p. S5 (Sport).

Lewis, D. (2009, July 1). Lions exclusive: We will win third Test, insists fiery Welsh dragon Shane Williams. *The Daily Mail.* Retrieved January 8, 2011, from http://www.dailymail.co.uk/sport.

Lewis, R. (2011, March 7). Hatton steps out of his brother's shadow despite emphatic defeat. *The Times,* p. 72 (Sport).

Lewsey, J. (2007, September 30). Colonial rant won't wilt the Red Rose. *The Sunday Times,* p. 18 (Sport).

Lewsey, J. (2009, January 31). Josh Lewsey's guide to the Six Nations teams. *The Daily Telegraph.* Retrieved January 31, 2009, from http://www.telegraph.co.uk/sport.

Ley, J. (2007, December 5). Wenger calls for reality check. *The Daily Telegraph,* p. S3 (Sport).

Ley, J. (2010, March 1). Tottenham push marred by latest injury. *The Daily Telegraph,* p. S7 (Sport).

Ley, J. (2011, March 21). Redknapp: Title is there for the taking. *The Daily Telegraph,* pp. S8–S9 (Sport).

Liew, J. (2010, July 26). England 'must believe to succeed'. *The Daily Telegraph,* pp. S8–S9 (Sport).

Lifton, D., Seay, S., & Bushke, A. (2000, Summer). Can student hardiness serve as an indicator of likely persistence to graduation? Baseline results from a longitudinal study. *Academic Exchange Quarterly,* 73–81.

Lillee, D. (2003). *Lillee: An autobiography.* Sydney: Hodder.

Linley, P. A., & Joseph, S. (2004). Applied positive psychology: A new perspective for professional practice. In P. A. Linley & S. Joseph (Eds.), *Positive psychology in practice* (pp. 3–12). Hoboken, NJ: Wiley.

Lloyd, C. (2007, October 25). Lloyd orders restoration of work ethic after West Indies' fall from greatness. *The Times,* p. 90 (Sport).

Loe, R. (2007, October 14). Top two inches on missing list as Cup hopes buried. *New Zealand Herald.* Retrieved December 15, 2007, from http://www.nzherald.co.nz.

Loehr, J. E. (1986). *Mental toughness training for sports: Achieving athletic excellence.* Lexington, MA: Stephen Greene Press.

Loehr, J. E. (1995). *The new toughness training for sports.* New York: Plume.

Lonsdale, C., Hodge, K., & Rose, E. (2009). Athlete burnout in elite sport: A self determination perspective. *Journal of Sports Sciences, 27,* 785–795.

Lord, C. (2007, November 19). All that glitters is gold for America's man on a mission: Phelps's formula for greatness in the pool. *The Times,* p. 70 (Sport).

208   *References*

Lowe, A. (2009, May 18). Ugly win beautiful for the Tigers. *Yorkshire Post*, p. 11 (Sport).

Lucas, G. (2011, February 14). Rodgers proud after Swansea show their mettle. *i*, p. 49 (Sport).

Luckner, J. L., & Nadler, R. S. (1997). *Processing the experience: Strategies to enhance and generalize learning*. Dubuque, IA: Kendall Hunt.

Lustig, B., Payne, J., Ellzey, L. (Executive producers), & Scott, R. (Director). (2007). *A good year* [Motion picture]. United States: Twentieth Century Fox.

Luszki, W. A. (1982). *Winning tennis through mental toughness*. New York: Everest House.

Lyles, C. (2008, August 3). Ramps in hundred club at last. *The Observer*, p. 4 (Sport).

Lynam, D. (2011, June 11). Can Murray at last find Perry's killer instinct? *The Daily Telegraph*, p. S20 (Sport).

Lynch, R. (2008, November 19). Robinson lashes out at 'unprepared' England. *The Guardian*. Retrieved November 19, 2008, from http://www.guardian.co.uk/sport.

Lyubomirsky, S. (2001). Why are some people happier than others? The role of cognitive and motivational processes in well-being. *American Psychologist, 56*, 239–249.

Macaskill, S. (2009, May 11). All of Albion aiming for a Great Escape reprise. *The Daily Telegraph*, p. S8 (Sport).

Macaskill, S. (2010, April 27). Bayern 'can beat great sides'. *The Daily Telegraph*, p. S7 (Sport).

Macaskill, S. (2011, March 21). Arsenal have started to doubt themselves, admits Wenger. *The Daily Telegraph*, p. S7 (Sport).

Mack, M. G., & Ragan, B. G. (2008). Development of the mental, emotional, and bodily toughness inventory in collegiate athletes and nonathletes. *Journal of Athletic Training, 43*, 125–132.

Macrae, C. N., Stangor, C., & Hewstone, M. (1996). *Stereotypes and stereotyping*. New York: Guilford.

Maddi, S. R. (1990). Issues and interventions in stress mastery. In H. S. Friedman (Ed.), *Personality and disease* (pp. 121–154). New York: Wiley.

Maddi, S. R. (2004). Hardiness: An operationalization of existential courage. *Journal of Humanistic Psychology, 44*, 279–298.

Maddi, S. R. (2006a). Hardiness: The courage to grow from stresses. *Journal of Positive Psychology, 1*, 160–168.

Maddi, S. R. (2006b). Building an integrated positive psychology. *Journal of Positive Psychology, 1*, 226–229.

Maddi, S. R., Harvey, R. H., Khoshaba, D. M., Fazel, M., & Resurreccion, N. (2009). Hardiness training facilitates performance in college. *Journal of Positive Psychology, 4*, 566–577.

Maddi, S. R., Harvey, R. H., Khoshaba, D. M., Lu, J. L., Persico, M., & Brow, M. (2006). The personality construct of hardiness: III. Relationships with repression, innovativeness, authoritarianism, and performance. *Journal of Personality, 74*, 575–597.

Maddi, S. R., & Hess, M. J. (1992). Personality hardiness and success in basketball. *International Journal of Sport Psychology, 23*, 360–368.

Maddi, S. R., Kahn, S., & Maddi, K. L. (1998). The effectiveness of hardiness training. *Consulting Psychology Journal: Practice and Research, 50,* 78–86.

Maddi, S. R., & Khoshaba, D. M. (2001). *Personal Views Survey* (3rd edn, rev.). Newport Beach, CA: The Hardiness Institute.

Maddi, S. R., Khoshaba, D. M., Jensen, K., Carter, E., Lu, J. L., & Harvey R. H. (2002). Hardiness training for high risk undergraduates. *NACADA Journal, 22,* 45–55.

Maddi, S. R., Khoshaba, D. M., Persico, M., Lu, J., Harvey, R., & Bleecker, F. (2002). The personality construct of hardiness: II. Relationships with comprehensive tests of personality and psychopathology. *Journal of Research in Personality, 36,* 72–85.

Maddi, S. R., Wadhwa, P., & Haier, R. J. (1996). Relationship of hardiness to alcohol and drug use in adolescents. *American Journal of Drug and Alcohol Abuse, 22,* 247–257.

Maese, R. (2008, August 14). Phelps' home schooling. *The Baltimore Sun.* Retrieved October 4, 2011, from http://www.baltimoresun.com/sports.

Magnay, J. (2010a April 15). Ayton puts own glory at risk for a happy family. *The Daily Telegraph,* p. S17 (Sport).

Magnay, J. (2010b, September 29). England calm as Australia start the mind games. *The Daily Telegraph,* p. S8 (Sport).

Mahoney, C. (2006, July 10). Body language holds key to sorting winners from also-rans. *The Guardian.* Retrieved January 10, 2011, from http://www.guardian.co.uk/sport.

Mahoney, C. (2009, August). Cultural underachievement and sport psychology – policy and practice. *Sport & Exercise Psychology Review, 5,* 64–66.

Mahoney, C. A., & Todd, M. K. (1999). Cross-cultural comparison of psychological skills in college-aged soccer players. *Journal of Sports Sciences, 17,* 59–60.

Mairs, G. (2006, October 6). Harrison's the head man. *The Belfast Telegraph,* p. 1 (Sport).

Mairs, G. (2009a, June 29). Gouging incident 'disgusts' the Lions. *The Daily Telegraph,* p. S1 (Sport).

Mairs, G. (2009b, December 29). Moody: I almost quit over injuries. *The Daily Telegraph,* p. S15 (Sport).

Mairs, G. (2010a, March 8). Leeds scrum their way up the Premiership. *The Daily Telegraph,* p. S18 (Sport).

Mairs, G. (2010b, August 28). Aviva Premiership 2010–11: Club-by-club guide. *The Daily Telegraph.* Retrieved September 3, 2010, from http://www.telegraph.co.uk/sport.

Mairs, G. (2010c, October 11). Irish withstand the Munster onslaught – now for the hard bit. *The Daily Telegraph,* pp. S20–S21 (Sport).

Mairs, G. (2011, January 19). Easter ready to rise up and captain England in Moody's absence. *The Daily Telegraph,* pp. S10–S11 (Sport).

Malin, I. (2008, September 1). Tributes and tears for Sculthorpe, man of fractured steel. *The Guardian,* p. 14 (Sport).

Malina, R. M., Peña Reyes, M. E., Eisenmann, J. C., Horta, L., Rodrigues, J., & Miller, R. (2000). Height, mass and skeletal maturity of elite Portuguese soccer players aged 11–16 years. *Journal of Sports Sciences, 18,* 685–693.

Mall, N. A., Carlisle, J. C., Matava, M. J., Powell, J. W., & Goldfarb, C. A. (2008). Upper extremity injuries in the National Football League. Part I: Hand and digital injuries. *American Journal of Sports Medicine, 36*, 1938–1944.

Malthouse, M. (2008, May 23). Retirement plays out in the mind before body surrenders. *The Australian.* Retrieved August 30, 2008, from http://www.theaustralian.com.au/sport.

Malthouse, M. (2010, October 2). Mental toughness will decide premiership. *The Australian.* Retrieved October 1, 2011, from http://www.theaustralian.com.au/sport.

Maniar, S. D., Curry, L. A., Sommers-Flanagan, J., & Walsh, J. A. (2001). Student athlete preferences in seeking help when confronted with performance problems. *The Sport Psychologist, 15*, 205–223.

Marchant, D., Clough, P., Polman, R., Levy, A., & Strycharczyk, D. (2007, March). Employees' mental toughness is associated with their managerial position and age. Poster session presented at the annual meeting of the British Psychological Society, York, England.

Marchant, D. C., Polman, R. C. J., Clough, P. J., Jackson, J. G., Levy, A. R., & Nicholls, A. R. (2009). Mental toughness: Managerial and age differences. *Journal of Managerial Psychology, 24*, 428–437.

Marcotti, G. (2010, January 1). Scouting key to clubs in search of potential bargains. *The Times*, pp. 64–65 (Sport).

Marcotti, G. (2012, May 19). Jupp Heynckes' side no strangers to fun of the flair. *The Times.* Retrieved May 22, 2012, from http://www.timesonline.co.uk/tol/sport.

Marks, V. (2010, December 7). Slow-burn Swann deserves more but claims top prize for outwitting Ponting. *The Guardian*, p. 4 (Sport).

Marks, V. (2011a, March 18). Man on the margins helps England extend their passage in India. *The Guardian*, p. 6 (Sport).

Marks, V. (2011b, March 19). Tredwell thrives in spotlight after long winter in the wings. *The Guardian*, p. 11 (Sport).

Marks, V. (2011c, March 20). England combine frailty with fight. *The Observer*, p. 15 (Sport).

Marsh, H. W. (2002). A multidimensional physical self-concept: A construct validity approach to theory, measurement, and research. *The Journal of the Hellenic Psychological Society, 9*, 459–493.

Martens, R. (2004). *Successful coaching* (3rd edn). Champaign, IL: Human Kinetics.

Martin, S. B. (2005). High school and college athletes' attitude toward sport psychology consulting. *Journal of Applied Sport Psychology, 17*, 127–139.

Martin, S. B., Akers, A., Jackson, A. W., Wrisberg, C. A., Nelson, L., Leslie, P. J., *et al.* (2001). Male and female athletes' and non-athletes' expectations about sport psychology consulting. *Journal of Applied Sport Psychology, 13*, 19–40.

Martindale, R. J. J., Collins, D., & Abraham, A. (2007). Effective talent development: The elite coach perspective in UK sport. *Journal of Applied Sport Psychology, 19*, 187–206.

Martin-Jenkins, C. (2009, May 18). Man apart whose qualities have sparkled during any era of the game. *The Times*, p. 60 (Sport).

Martin-Jenkins, C. (2010, January 11). England must win series to put any fear into Australia. *The Times*, pp. 64–65 (Sport).

Mascarenhas, D. (2002, April). The 'four cornerstones' model. *Referee*, p. 38.

Mascarenhas, D. R. D., Collins, D., & Mortimer, P. (2005). Assessing the accuracy and coherence of decision making in rugby union officials. *Journal of Sport Behavior, 28*, 253–271.

Mascarenhas, D. R. D., Collins, D., Mortimer, P. W., & Morris, B. (2005). Training accurate and coherent decision making in rugby union referees. *The Sport Psychologist, 19*, 131–147.

Mason, R. (2012, March 13). Bouncing back key for skipper Bates. *The Northern Echo*, p. 46 (Sport).

Massie, A. (2010, July 24). Muralitharan's landmark may well stand the test of time. *The Scotsman*, p. 17 (Sport).

Mathis, M., & Lecce, L. (1999). Hardiness and college adjustment: Identifying students in need of services. *Journal of College Student Development, 40*, 305–309.

McCarra, K. (2009, October 5). Drogba lays down title marker for Chelsea. *The Guardian*, p. 1 (Sport).

McCarra, K. (2010a, February 25). Inter leave Chelsea bruised but breathing. *The Guardian*, p. 1 (Sport).

McCarra, K. (2010b, March 2). Capello can take Hart to be the new No. 1 and end England's goalkeeping malaise. *The Guardian*, p. 4 (Sport).

McCarra, K. (2010c, March 8). Terry's goal and a lot of elbow grease sink Stoke. *The Guardian*, p. 3 (Sport).

McCarra, K. (2010d, April 26). Kalou hits treble as Chelsea show Stoke no mercy. *The Guardian*, p. 2 (Sport).

McCarra, K. (2010e, September 20). Magnificence of Berbatov makes the difference. *The Guardian*, pp. 2–3 (Sport).

McCarra, K. (2011a, February 2). Koscielny keeps Arsenal on title trail after defender turns the tables on Saha. *The Guardian*, p. 2 (Sport).

McCarra, K. (2011b, February 27). Revitalised Djourou strengthens Wenger's case for defence. *The Observer*, p. 12 (Sport).

McCarra, K. (2011c, March 23). Impregnable self-belief puts Terry back in command. *The Guardian*, pp. 2–3 (Sport).

McCarra, K. (2011d, April 13). United prove a class apart. *The Guardian*, p. 1 (Sport).

McCarra, K. (2012, April 15). Liverpool head into final after Distin's dire gift. *The Observer*, pp. 2–3 (Sport).

McCarthy, P. J. (2009, February). Putting imagery to good affect: A case study among youth swimmers. *Sport & Exercise Psychology Review, 5*, 27–38.

McCarthy, P. J., Mulliner, L., & Barker, J. B. (2009). Could positive emotions help us concentrate better? *Journal of Sports Sciences, 27*, S113.

McDonald, M. (2008, August 5). Knights make bid for finals. *The Australian*. Retrieved August 30, 2008, from http://www.theaustralian.com.au/sport.

McDonald, M. (2011, May 18). Queensland coach Mal Meninga wary of Wayne Bennett's influence on New South Wales. *The Australian*. Retrieved October 4, 2011, from http://www.theaustralian.com.au/sport.

McEvoy, J. (2012a, April 20). Return of the cheat. *The Daily Mail*, pp. 86, 88 (Sport).

McEvoy, J. (2012b, April 20). A betrayal of our Games. *The Daily Mail*, pp. 86–87 (Sport).

McGinn, C. (2008). *The art of living: Sport*. Stocksfield, England: Acumen.

McGrath, C. (2009, July 17). Historic first stand fails to rule the day. *The Independent*, p. 57 (Sport).

McGrath, J. A. (2010, March 13). Imperial assignment no sweat for Qaspal. *The Daily Telegraph*, p. S22 (Sport).

McGrath, J. A. (2011, June 1). Injury fear for Queen's Derby hope. *The Daily Telegraph*, p. S18 (Sport).

McIlvanney, H. (2009, July 12). Ponting can dare to dream. *The Sunday Times*, p. 20 (Sport).

McIntosh, A. S., McCrory, P., & Comerford, J. (2000). The dynamics of concussive head impacts in rugby and Australian rules football. *Medicine and Science in Sports and Exercise*, *32*, 1980–1984.

McKay, J., Niven, A. G., Lavallee, D., & White, A. (2008). Sources of strain among elite UK track athletes. *The Sport Psychologist*, *22*, 143–163.

McKenzie, M. D. (2000). How are adventure education program outcomes achieved? *Australian Journal of Outdoor Education*, *5*, 19–28.

McLachlan, H. (2010, July 24). Why we trust in golf and not in fouling football cheats. *The Scotsman*, p. 30 (Opinion).

McLintock, F. (2005, October 23). Gunners can solve their problems at a stroke – pick me. *The Observer*. Retrieved June 1, 2011, from http://www.guardian.co.uk/sport.

McLoughlin, B. (2011, November 24). McLeish wants senior players to stand up and be counted. *The Times*, p. 105 (Sport).

McRae, D. (2008, January 19). Humble heavyweight Skelton aims for the shock of all ages. *The Guardian*, p. 8 (Sport).

McRae, D. (2009a, January 27). I dream up things and then convince myself they're possible. *The Guardian*. Retrieved January 27, 2009, from http://www.guardian.co.uk/sport.

McRae, D. (2009b, June 2). A low-key approach to being the best in the world. *The Guardian*, pp. 6–7 (Sport).

McRae, D. (2009c, June 30). 'It gets boring beating the other guys all the time.' *The Guardian*, pp. 6–7 (Sport).

McRae, D. (2009d, October 27). 'I'm addicted to it. It's in my blood to be a gymnast.' *The Guardian*, pp. 6–7 (Sport).

McRae, D. (2009e, November 10). Heading south can be making of England's workaholic. *The Guardian*, pp. 6–7 (Sport).

McRae, D. (2009f, November 14). 'People want to stare at me, to touch me . . . I don't like being famous.' *The Guardian*, pp. 2–3 (Sport).

McRae, D. (2009g, November 17). 'Everybody has tough moments. Mine came this year.' *The Guardian*, pp. 6–7 (Sport).

McRae, D. (2009h, November 21). Carter ready to live up to his superhero billing. *The Guardian*, pp. 10–11 (Sport).

McRae, D. (2010a, February 16). Batting anchor weighs a future where the best is still to come. *The Guardian*, pp. 6–7 (Sport).

McRae, D. (2010b, March 9). 'They called me Baby Schumi. I didn't like it but I understood.' *The Guardian*, pp. 6–7 (Sport).

McRae, D. (2010c, April 6). 'You either lie down or get up. I got up.' *The Guardian*, p. 8 (Sport).

McRae, D. (2010d, April 27). 'When I played with men they'd bowl it short. I didn't mind.' *The Guardian*, pp. 6–7 (Sport).

McRae, D. (2011, October 11). 'Who wouldn't want to captain England's Test team?' *The Guardian*, pp. 6–7 (Sport).

McVay, D. (2009, February 15). Uninspired Birmingham still well placed. *The Daily Telegraph*. Retrieved February 16, 2009, from http://www.telegraph.co.uk/sport.

Meir, R. A., McDonald, K. N., & Russell, R. (1997). Injury consequences from participation in professional rugby league: A preliminary investigation. *British Journal of Sports Medicine*, *31*, 132–134.

Meyers, A. W., Whelan, J., & Murphy, S. (1995). Cognitive behavioral strategies in athletic performance enhancement. In A. Meyers, J. Whelan, & S. Murphy (Eds.), *Progress in behavior modification* (pp. 137–164). Pacific Grove, CA: Brooks/Cole.

Meyers, M. C., Bourgeois, A. E., LeUnes, A., & Murray, N. G. (1998). Mood and psychological skills of elite and sub-elite equestrian athletes. *Journal of Sport Behavior*, *22*, 399–409.

Meyers, M. C., LeUnes, A., & Bourgeois, A. E. (1996). Psychological skills assessments and athletic performance in collegiate rodeo athletes. *Journal of Sport Behavior*, *19*, 132–146.

Middleton, C. (2003, September 11). Scottish Hockey: Simpson bemoans fragility. *The Daily Telegraph*. Retrieved April 7, 2009, from http://www.telegraph.co.uk/sport.

Middleton, S. C., Marsh, H. W., Martin, A. J., Richards, G. E., & Perry, C. (2004a, July). Discovering mental toughness: A qualitative study of mental toughness in elite athletes. In G. E. Richards (Chair), *High performing athletes: Self-concept and achievement goals*. Symposium conducted at the meeting of the International Conference on Self-concept, Motivation and Identity: Where to go from here? Berlin, Germany.

Middleton, S. C., Marsh, H. W., Martin, A. J., Richards, G. E., & Perry, C. (2004b, July). Developing the Mental Toughness Inventory (MTI). Poster session presented at the meeting of the International Conference on Self-concept, Motivation and Identity: Where to go from here? Berlin, Germany.

Middleton, S. C., Marsh, H. W., Martin, A. J., Richards, G. E., Savis, J., Perry, C., *et al.* (2004c). The Psychological Performance Inventory: Is the mental toughness test tough enough? *International Journal of Sport Psychology*, *35*, 91–108.

Miles, J. C., & Priest, S. (Eds.). (1990). *Adventure education*. State College, PA: Venture.

Miller, L. (2008). Stress and resilience in law enforcement training and practice. *International Journal of Emergency Mental Health*, *10*, 109–124.

Miller, P. S., & Kerr, G. A. (2002). Conceptualizing excellence: Past, present, and future. *Journal of Applied Sport Psychology*, *14*, 140–153.

Mischel, W., & Shoda, Y. (1995). A cognitive-affective system theory of personality: Reconceptualizing situations, dispositions, dynamics, and invariance in personality structure. *Psychological Review*, *102*, 246–268.

Mitchell, K. (2009a, May 3). The Lion Kings. *Observer Sports Monthly*, pp. 38–49.

Mitchell, K. (2009b, July 14). Lord's will tell if Strauss is officer class or just a mess. *The Guardian*, p. 10 (Sport).

Mitchell, K. (2010, September 6). Old heads Williams and Clijsters make case for experience. *The Guardian*, p. 11 (Sport).

Mitchell, K. (2011, April 24). Hatton needs to ignore siren call of the Golden Boy and stay out of the ring. *The Observer*, p. 7 (Sport).

Mitchell, K. (2012, March 18). Dickson goes backwards but his team go surging forwards. *The Observer*, p. 5 (Sport).

Moffitt, T. E., Caspi, A., & Rutter, M. (2005). Strategy for investigating interactions between measured genes and measured environments. *Archives of General Psychiatry*, *62*, 473–481.

Montgomerie, C. (2011, April 12). Rory's tactics were misguided – but he will learn. *The Daily Telegraph*, pp. S10–S11 (Sport).

Moore, B. (2007, October 15). World-class Wilkinson thrives under pressure. *The Daily Telegraph*, p. S3 (Sport).

Moore, B. (2009a, April 13). Heineken Cup pressure can shred biggest reputations. *The Daily Telegraph*. Retrieved April 13, 2009, from http://www.telegraph.co.uk/sport.

Moore, B. (2009b, April 13). Pressure zone shows the real winners. *The Daily Telegraph*, p. S17 (Sport).

Moore, B. (2009c, May 7). Give Barton a break or football circus will just make him worse. *The Daily Telegraph*, p. S15 (Sport).

Moore, B. (2009d, June 29). Lousy Lawrence is not fit to officiate. *The Daily Telegraph*, p. S9 (Sport).

Moore, B. (2009e, July 9). Ashes stands out without star names. *The Daily Telegraph*, p. S17 (Sport).

Moore, B. (2009f, August 10). 'Bloodgate' puts rugby on slippery slope. *The Daily Telegraph*, p. S19 (Sport).

Moore, B. (2009g, October 5). Quins start to repay faith of fearful fans. *The Daily Telegraph*, p. S21 (Sport).

Moore, B. (2010, November 8). Beaten, yes, but this was a coherent display. *The Daily Telegraph*, p. S15 (Sport).

Moore, B. (2011, April 14). Stars behaving badly is true reality. *The Daily Telegraph*, p. S11 (Sport).

Moore, G. (2012, April 16). Atkinson's guessing game trumps confident refereeing. *The Independent*, p. 4 (Sport).

Moran, A. (2004). *Sport and exercise psychology: A critical introduction*. Hove, England: Routledge.

Morgan, P. (2011, April 23). Gloucester coach Redpath playing mind games ahead of clash with Saracens. *The Daily Mail*. Retrieved April 24, 2011, from http://www.dailymail.co.uk/sport.

Morgan, W. P., & Johnson, R. W. (1978). Personality characteristics of successful and unsuccessful oarsmen. *International Journal of Sport Psychology*, *9*, 119–133.

Mouratidis, A., & Michou, A. (2011). Perfectionism, self-determined motivation, and coping among adolescent athletes. *Psychology of Sport and Exercise*, *12*, 355–367.

Mulvenney, N. (2007, January 23). Defeat raises more questions about Li's mental toughness. *The Guardian*. Retrieved January 23, 2007, from http://www.guardian.co.uk/sport.

Murphy, P., & Waddington, I. (2007). Are elite athletes exploited? *Journal of Sport and Social Issues*, *10*, 239–255.

Murray, E. (2009, February 13). 'Farcical assumptions made after Old Firm matches,' says Smith. Retrieved February 13, 2009, from http://www.guardian.co.uk/sport.

Murray, E. (2010a, March 27). Lennon demands new mental fortitude from Celtic and wants to make a name for himself as manager. *The Guardian*, pp. 8–9 (Sport).

Murray, E. (2010b, April 26). Rangers secure Scottish title. *The Guardian*, p. 6 (Sport).

Murray, E. (2011a, January 14). Scottish referees need to toughen up, says Celtic's Johan Mjallby. *The Guardian*. Retrieved January 15, 2011, from http://guardian.co.uk/sport.

Murray, E. (2011b, April 24). Lennon warns of 'powder-keg' Old Firm match. *The Observer*, p. 6 (Sport).

Murray, E. (2011c, October 3). Lennon feels the heat as Celtic go cold. *The Guardian*, p. 7 (Sport).

Nack, W. (2001, May 7). The wrecking yard. *Sports Illustrated*, pp. 60–75.

Nadler, R. S. (1993). Therapeutic process of change. In M. A. Gass (Ed.), *Adventure therapy: Therapeutic applications of adventure programming* (pp. 57–69). Dubuque, IA: Kendall Hunt.

Neill, J. T., & Dias, K. L. (2001). Adventure education and resilience: The double edged sword. *Journal of Adventure Education and Outdoor Learning*, *1*, 35–42.

Neill, J. T., & Richards, G. E. (1998). Does outdoor education really work? A summary of recent meta-analyses. *Australian Journal of Outdoor Education*, *3*, 2–9.

Nevill, A. M., Balmer, N. J., & Williams, A. M. (2002). The influence of crowd noise and experience upon refereeing decisions in football. *Psychology of Sport and Exercise*, *2*, 261–272.

Newman, P. (2010a, January 28). Murray: I'm six sets from my first Slam. *The Independent*, p. 60–61 (Sport).

Newman, P. (2010b, November 30). England's day of domination. *Daily Mail*, p. 78 (Sport).

Nicholas, M. (2005, September 13). Centurion Vaughan fulfils promise. *The Daily Telegraph*, p. VI (The Ashes 2005).

Nicholas, M. (2007, December 24). India need strength of mind and body. *The Daily Telegraph*, p. S31 (Sport).

Nicholas, M. (2008, January 21). Sharma magic casts a spell. *The Daily Telegraph*, p. S24 (Sport).

Nicholls, A. R., Holt, N. L., & Polman, R. C. J. (2005). A phenomenological analysis of coping effectiveness in golf. *The Sport Psychologist*, *19*, 111–130.

Nicholls, A. R., Holt, N. L., Polman, R. C. J., & Bloomfield, J. (2006). Stressors, coping, and coping effectiveness among professional rugby union players. *The Sport Psychologist*, *20*, 314–329.

Nicholls, A. R., Polman, R. C. J., Levy, A. R., & Backhouse, S. H. (2008). Mental toughness, optimism, pessimism, and coping among athletes. *Personality and Individual Differences*, *44*, 1182–1192.

216   *References*

Nicholls, A. R., Polman, R. C. J., Levy, A. R., & Backhouse, S. H. (2009). Mental toughness in sport: Achievement level, gender, age, experience, and sport type differences. *Personality and Individual Differences*, *47*, 73–75.

Nizam, A., Omar-Fauzee, M. S., & Abu Samah, B. (2009). The effect of higher score of mental toughness in the early stage of the league towards winning among Malaysian football players. *Research Journal of International Studies*, *12*, 67–78.

Noblet, A. J., & Gifford, S. M. (2002). The sources of stress experienced by professional Australian footballers. *Journal of Applied Sport Psychology*, *14*, 1–13.

Noblet, A., Rodwell, J., & McWilliams, J. (2003). Predictors of the strain experienced by professional Australian footballers. *Journal of Applied Sport Psychology*, *15*, 184–193.

Nordin, S. M., & Cumming, J. (2008). Exploring common ground: Comparing the imagery of dancers and aesthetic sport performers. *Journal of Applied Sport Psychology*, *20*, 375–391.

Norman, M. (2011, March 25). Flying Scotsman hits the jackpot. *The Daily Telegraph*, p. S20 (Sport).

Norris, E. K. (1999). *Epistemologies of champions: A discoursive analysis of champions' retrospective attributions. Looking back and looking within.* Michigan, MI: Michigan University Microfilms International.

Norrish, M. (2008, September 17). Steven Gerrard says Liverpool 'stopped playing' in Marseilles. *The Daily Telegraph*. Retrieved September 18, 2008, from http://www.telegraph.co.uk/sport.

Northcroft, J. (2010, March 7). Who's on the plane? *The Sunday Times*, p. 8 (Sport).

O, J., & Hall, C. (2009). A quantitative analysis of athletes' voluntary use of slow motion, real time, and fast motion images. *Journal of Applied Sport Psychology*, *21*, 15–30.

O'Briain, D. (2009, November 21). Just what is the French for blatant handball? *The Guardian*, p. 16 (Sport).

O Captain, our Captain. (2009, June 29). *The Times*, p. 2.

O'Connor, A. (2003, November 24). Serial winners finally learn how to become good losers. *The Times*, p. 39 (Sport).

O'Connor, D. M. (2004). Groin injuries in professional rugby league players: A prospective study. *Journal of Sports Sciences*, *22*, 629–636.

Ogden, M. (2008, November 3). Arsenal 'lack spine' for title chase. *The Daily Telegraph*, p. S14 (Sport).

Ogden, M. (2009, February 20). Sir Alex Ferguson challenges Manchester United to become the 'Invincibles'. *The Daily Telegraph*. Retrieved February 21, 2009, from http://www.telegraph.co.uk/sport.

Ogden, M. (2010, November 6). Mancini limping towards first anniversary with misfiring City. *The Daily Telegraph*, p. S11 (Sport).

Ogden, M. (2011, April 1). 'England the new Germany? Dream on.' *The Daily Telegraph*, p. S5 (Sport).

Ogden, M. (2012, April 16). Young keeps United tumbling to the title. *The Daily Telegraph*, pp. 58–59 (Sport).

Old, J. (2004). Organisational behaviour in sport organisations. In J. Beech & S. Chadwick (Eds.), *The business of sport management* (pp. 69–92). London: Pearson.

Oliver, E. J., Hardy, J., & Markland, D. (2010). Identifying important practice behaviors for the development of high-level young athletes: Exploring the perspectives of elite coaches. *Psychology of Sport and Exercise, 11*, 433–443.

Olusoga, P., Butt, J., Hays, K., & Maynard, I. (2009). Stress in elite sports coaching: Identifying stressors. *Journal of Applied Sport Psychology, 21*, 442–459.

Orchard, J., & Seward, H. (2002). Epidemiology of injuries in the Australian Football League, seasons 1997–2000. *British Journal of Sports Medicine, 36*, 39–44.

O'Reilly, P. (2011, March 20). Sexton comes of age to make No. 10 shirt his own. *The Sunday Times*, p. 2 (Sport).

Orlick, T. (1992). The psychology of personal excellence. *Contemporary Thought on Performance Enhancement, 1*, 109–122.

Orlick, T. (1996). The wheel of excellence. *Journal of Performance Education, 1*, 3–18.

Orlick, T., & Partington, J. (1988). Mental links to excellence. *The Sport Psychologist, 2*, 105–130.

Padgett, M. (2012a, April 13). Wigan and QPR give themselves timely boost. *The Independent*. Retrieved April 17, 2012, from http://www.independent.co.uk/sport.

Padgett, M. (2012b, April 25). Cech: we tried to survive – and we survived well. *The Independent*, p. 79 (Sport).

Pain, M. A., & Harwood, C. G. (2004). Knowledge and perceptions of sport psychology within English soccer. *Journal of Sports Sciences, 22*, 813–826.

Paivio, A. (1985). Cognitive and motivational functions of imagery in human performance. *Canadian Journal of Applied Sport Sciences, 10*, 22–28.

Pankey, B. (1993). Presence of mind: Five ways to lower your class drop-out rate with mental toughness. *American Fitness, 11*, 18–19.

Pargman, D. (Ed.). (1999). *Psychological bases of sport injuries*. Morgantown, WV: Fitness Information Technology, Inc.

Park, N., Peterson, C., & Seligman, M. E. P. (2004). Strengths of character and well being. *Journal of Social and Clinical Psychology, 23*, 603–619.

Parkes, J. F., & Mallett, C. J. (2011). Developing mental toughness: Attributional style retraining in rugby. *The Sport Psychologist, 25*, 269–287.

Parkinson, M. (2004, October 12). Courage of our favourite Aussie. Tribute to Keith Miller: Wartime hero adored in England was ranked with the best all-rounders of all-time. *The Daily Telegraph*, p. 8 (Sport).

Parkinson, M. (2005). In *England's Ashes* (p. 7). London: HarperSport.

Parks, T. (2010, August 19). The shame of the World Cup. *The New York Review of Books*, pp. 44–49.

Patrick, H. (2008, October 5). Leeds beat St Helens to win Super League Grand Final at Old Trafford. Retrieved October 5, 2008, from http://www.telegraph.co.uk/sport.

Peabody, D. (1985). *National characteristics*. New York: Cambridge University Press.

Pearce, N. (2009, June 2). Lions 2009: Confident Hines lauds mental strength of Lions. Retrieved July 27, 2009, from http://www.telegraph.co.uk/sport.

Pearce, N. (2012, April 15). Holmes: I believe girls train harder than guys. *The Sunday Telegraph*, p. 7 (Sports Life).

Pearson, A. (2011, November 25). Sky Sports deal won't solve SPL's problems. *The Scotsman*, pp. 34–35.

Perry, S. (2008, July 11). MotoGP preview. *The Daily Telegraph*. Retrieved July 13, 2009, from http://www.telegraph.co.uk/sport.

Pérusse, L., Rankinen, T., Rauramaa, R., Rivera, M. A., Wolfarth, B., & Bouchard, C. (2003). The human gene map for performance and health-related fitness phenotypes: The 2002 update. *Medicine and Science in Sports and Exercise, 35,* 1248–1264.

Peters, S. (2011, October 3). Judgment flaw harms Haskell. *The Times*, p. 69 (Sport).

Peterson, C., & Seligman, M. E. P. (2004). *Character strengths and virtues: A handbook and classification.* Washington, DC: American Psychological Association.

Petróczi, A. (2007). Attitudes and doping: A structural equation analysis of the relationship between athletes' attitudes, sport orientation and doping behaviour. *Substance Abuse, Treatment, Prevention, and Policy, 2,* 34.

Philip, R. (2004a, August 30). Kelly sprints to pre-eminence. *The Daily Telegraph*, p. S5 (Sport).

Philip, R. (2004b, December 7). Mauger reasons for the All Blacks to be cheerful. *The Daily Telegraph*. Retrieved April 7, 2009, from http://www.telegraph.co.uk/sport.

Piedmont, R. L., Hill, D.C., & Blanco, S. (1999). Predicting athletic performance using the five-factor model of personality. *Personality and Individual Differences, 27,* 769–777.

Pilger, S. (2010). *The official ITV Sport guide to the FA Cup 2010–2011.* London: Boston Hannah International.

Pinsent, M. (2009, May 18). Achievements of Pistorius a tale that is set to run and run. *The Times*, p. 62 (Sport).

Pitt, N. (2009, June 7). Favourite Safina loses her focus and temper in second Paris defeat. *The Sunday Times*, p. 11 (Sport).

Pitt, N. (2012, May 20). Garcia pays price as putting woes return. *The Sunday Times*. Retrieved May 22, 2012, from http://www.timesonline.co.uk/tol/sport.

Pitt-Brooke, J. (2012, April 16). Redknapp: referee knows that he has made a big mistake. *The Independent*, p. 3 (Sport).

Plomin, R., DeFries, J. C., McClearn, G. E., & McGuffin, P. (2001). *Behavioral genetics* (4th edn). New York: Worth.

Podlog, L., Dimmock, J., & Miller, J. (2011). A review of return to sport concerns following injury rehabilitation: Practitioner strategies for enhancing recovery outcomes. *Physical Therapy in Sport, 12,* 36–42.

Podlog, L., & Eklund, R. C. (2006). A longitudinal investigation of competitive athletes' return to sport following serious injury. *Journal of Applied Sport Psychology, 18,* 44–68.

Podlog, L., & Eklund, R. C. (2007). Professional coaches' perspectives on the return to sport following serious injury. *Journal of Applied Sport Psychology, 19,* 207–225.

Podlog, L., Lochbaum, M., & Stevens, T. (2010). Need satisfaction, well-being and perceived return-to-sport outcomes among injured athletes. *Journal of Applied Sport Psychology, 22,* 167–182.

Popper, K. R. (1959). *The logic of scientific discovery.* London: Hutchinson.

Potter, S. (2009, July 10). Brunt back at happy hunting ground. *The Times*, p. 87 (Sport).

Powell, H. (2010, June 16). Strength and spirit off the pitch can help build a successful team on it. *The Guardian*, p. 7 (Sport).

Preston, E. (2008, July, 8). It's tough, it's lonely and it's ruthless as you move up, Robson warned. *The Guardian*, p. 5 (Sport).

Priest, S., & Gass, M. A. (2005). *Effective leadership in adventure programming* (2nd edn). Champaign, IL: Human Kinetics.

Pringle, D. (2005, September 13). It's business as usual at HQ. *The Daily Telegraph*, p. II (The Ashes 2005).

Pringle, D. (2009a, February 16). Strauss century leads revival. *The Daily Telegraph*, p. S1 (Sport).

Pringle, D. (2009b, July 13). Cool Collingwood leads England escape. *The Daily Telegraph*, pp. S2–S3 (Sport).

Pringle, D. (2009c, August 10). Character and nerve desert woeful England. *The Daily Telegraph*, pp. S2–S3 (Sport).

Pringle, D. (2010a, January 8). England stagger to safety. *The Daily Telegraph*, pp. S2–S3 (Sport).

Pringle, D. (2010b, July 30). England breathe sigh of relief at Morgan's fortitude. *The Daily Telegraph*, pp. S2–S3 (Sport).

Pringle, D. (2010c, December 20). England resolve in doubt as bad old days return. *The Daily Telegraph*, pp. S2–S3 (Sport).

Pringle, D. (2011a, January 7). England keep clear head as Australia go into meltdown. *The Daily Telegraph*, pp. S2–S3 (Sport).

Pringle, D. (2011b, March 18). England on the cusp of quarter-final place as bold selection pays off. *The Daily Telegraph*, p. S2 (Sport).

Privette, G., & Bundrick, C. M. (1997). Psychological processes of peak, average, and failing performance in sport. *International Journal of Sport Psychology*, *28*, 323–334.

Puni, A. C. (1963). Psihologicheskaya podgotovka sportsmena k sorevnovaniyu [Psychological preparation of athletes for a competition]. *Theory and Practice of Physical Culture*, *2*, 52–56.

Quarrie, K. L., & Hopkins, W. G. (2008). Tackle injuries in professional rugby union. *American Journal of Sports Medicine*, *36*, 1705–1716.

Quested, E., & Duda, J. L. (2011). Antecedents of burnout among elite dancers: A longitudinal test of basic needs theory. *Psychology of Sport and Exercise*, *12*, 159–167.

Radnedge, K. (2012). *The European Championship 2012 preview: Poland–Ukraine*. London: Carlton Books.

Rae, R. (2011, April 9). Benkenstein stays in the comfort zone for Durham. *The Guardian*, p. 12 (Sport).

Ramirez, M., Schaffer, K. B., Shen, H., Kashani, S., & Kraus, J. F. (2006). Injuries to high school football athletes in California. *American Journal of Sports Medicine*, *34*, 1147–1158.

Randall, C. (2008, January 21). England lacking grit indoors. *The Daily Telegraph*, p. S27 (Sport).

Ray, R., & Wiese-Bjornstal, D. M. (1999). *Counseling in sports medicine*. Champaign, IL: Human Kinetics.

Reason, M. (2009a, April 5). Padraig Harrington's major success is mainly in the mind. *The Daily Telegraph*. Retrieved April 5, 2009, from http://www.telegraph.co.uk/sport.

Reason, M. (2009b, April 14). In the agony of defeat, Perry proves himself a real winner. *The Daily Telegraph*, p. S13 (Sport).

Reason, M. (2009c, July 14). What place is there now for sportsmen like Nicklaus? *The Daily Telegraph*, p. S9 (Sport).

Reason, M. (2009d, October 27). 'I don't want my son to play rugby . . . it's too violent.' *The Daily Telegraph*, pp. S10–S11 (Sport).

Reason, M. (2010, February 16). Increasingly violent hits are risking a fatal impact. *The Daily Telegraph*, p. S13 (Sport).

Redgrave, S. (2011, October 5). Double glory brings shock and awe. *The Daily Telegraph*, pp. T2–T3 (Great Olympic moments).

Reed, T. (2007, December 13). Every loser wins. *MSN UK News*. Retrieved December 13, 2007, from http://www.news.uk.msn.com.

Rees, P. (2007, October 15). So now the best preparation is not to prepare at all. *The Guardian*, p. 4 (Sport).

Rees, P. (2008, March 13). Gatland brings best out of new-model Henson. *The Guardian*, p. 11 (Sport).

Rees, P. (2010, February 13). Gatland demands Welsh discipline as Scots provide pivotal test. *The Guardian*, p. 11 (Sport).

Rees, P. (2011a, March 14). Ireland to receive IRB apology for the try that wasn't. *The Guardian*, p. 5 (Sport).

Rees, P. (2011b, April 11). Saints seize on Ulster errors to book place in last four. *The Guardian*, p. 11 (Sport).

Rees, P. (2011c, October 3). Gatland ends long wait for no-hopers to become contenders. *The Guardian*, pp. 8–9 (Sport).

Rees, P. (2011d, October 3). Lièvremont gets serious as France become the butt of jokes. *The Guardian*, pp. 10–11 (Sport).

Rees, P. (2011e, October 10). Gatland's hard-working band puts days of hard drinking behind them. *The Guardian*, p. 3 (Sport).

Rees, P. (2011f, October 11). Wales eager to seize their best chance to be the best in the world. *The Guardian*, p. 4 (Sport).

Rees, P. (2012a, March 10). Forcing errors from Priestland offers the only prayer for Italy. *The Guardian*, p. 10 (Sport).

Rees, P. (2012b, May 19). South African steel turns Ulster's world around. *The Guardian*, p. 13 (Sport).

Reid, A. (2011, June 22). Edinburgh bring in Billy McGinty as defence coach. *The Daily Telegraph*. Retrieved June 23, 2011, from http://www.telegraph.co.uk/sport.

Reid, J. (2010, December 6). Defense must improve mental toughness: London Fletcher. *The Washington Post*. Retrieved June 1, 2011, from http://www.washingtonpost.com.

Reilly, T., Bangsbo, J., & Franks, A. (2000). Anthropometric and physiological predispositions for elite soccer. *Journal of Sports Sciences*, *18*, 669–683.

Reiss, M. (2006, September 27). One step at a time: Fellow kickers advise patience with rookie Gostkowski. *The Boston Globe*. Retrieved September 27, 2006, from http://www.bostonglobe.com.

Rej, A. (2011, April 10). Queens Park Rangers suffer shock to the system as 'reliable players' found wanting at Scunthorpe. *The Daily Telegraph*. Retrieved April 11, 2011, from http://www.telegraph.co.uk/sport.

Rezae, A., Ghaffari, M., & Zolfalifam, J. (2009). A survey and comparison of team cohesion, role ambiguity, athletic performance and hardiness in elite and non elite football players. *Research Journal of Biological Sciences*, *4*, 1010–1015.

Rich, T. (2008, September 30). Arsenal desperate to clear their heads. *The Daily Telegraph*, p. S2 (Sport).

Rich, T. (2010, March 27). Ferguson reveals pre-game nerves as title race closes. *The Guardian*, p. 5 (Sport).

Rich, T. (2011, April 24). Ferguson: We can win title in two weeks. *The Observer*, p. 1 (Sport).

Rich, T. (2012, April 16). Young's sideshow helps United romp home. *The Independent*, pp. 6–7 (Sport).

Richards, G. (2012, May 6). Age no barrier for pioneer Tweddle. *The Observer*, p. 16 (Sport).

Ridley, I. (2009, October 4). Harry's men show their steely side. *The Mail on Sunday*, p. 6 (Football).

Ridley, M. (2003). *Nature via nurture: Genes, experience and what makes us human*. London: Harper Perennial.

Robinson, L. (1999). Following the quality strategy – the rationale for the use of quality programmes. *Managing Leisure: An International Journal*, *4*, 201–217.

Robinson, L. (2003). The business of sport. In B. Houlihan (Ed.), *Sport & society: A student introduction* (pp. 165–183). London: Sage.

Roebuck, P. (2006, December 6). Old masters discover a new lease of life. *The Independent*, p. 57 (Sport).

Roebuck, P. (2009a, July 10). Old guard may not be in vogue but they can still turn on the style. *The Independent*, p. 59 (Sport).

Roebuck, P. (2009b, July 13). Ponting knows McGrath would have got it done. *The Independent*, p. 6 (Sport).

Roebuck, P. (2009c, July 17). Plumber's mate runs hot and cold. *The Independent*, p. 56 (Sport).

Rogers, T. J., Alderman, B. L., & Landers, D. M. (2003). Effects of life-event stress and hardiness on peripheral vision in a real-life stress situation. *Behavioral Medicine*, *29*, 21–26.

Roper, M. (2007, December 3). Saracens show rivals their winning mentality even in defeat. *The Daily Telegraph*, p. S23 (Sport).

Rosenberg, M. (1965). *Society and adolescent self-image*. Princeton, NJ: Princeton University Press.

Ross, R. (2007, October 7). Lewis Hamilton could be bigger than Beckham. *The Daily Telegraph*. Retrieved April 9, 2009, from http://www.telegraph.co.uk/sport.

Rotter, J. B. (1954). *Social learning and clinical psychology*. Englewood Cliff, NJ: Prentice Hall.

Rowan, P. (2009, April 12). Niko Kranjcar's late strike eases Portsmouth's woes. *The Sunday Times*. Retrieved April 12, 2009, from http://www.timesonline.co.uk/tol/sport.

Rowan, P. (2012, April 15). Blue blood: Roberto di Matteo can prove his mettle today with Chelsea at Wembley. *The Sunday Times*, p. 5 (Sport).

Rozin, P., & Royzman, E. B. (2001). Negativity bias, negativity dominance, and contagion. *Personality and Social Psychology Review*, 5, 296–320.

Rudd, A. (2010, September 29). Taarabt probes in vain as QPR's progress slows. *The Times*, p. 79 (Sport).

Rudd, A. (2011, June 30). Lisicki's powers of recovery gain fresh admirers home and away. *The Times*, p. 78 (Sport).

Rudd, A. (2012, May 14). West Brom 2 Arsenal 3: Arsenal do it the hard way right till finish. *The Times*. Retrieved May 22, 2012, from http://www.timesonline. co.uk/tol/sport.

Rushton, J. P., Bons, T. A., & Hur Y.-M. (2008). The genetics and evolution of a general factor of personality. *Journal of Research in Personality*, 42, 1173–1185.

Rushton, J. P., & Irwing, P. (2009). A general factor of personality in the Comrey Personality Scales, the Minnesota Multiphasic Personality Inventory-2, and the Multicultural Personality Questionnaire. *Personality and Individual Differences*, 46, 437–442.

Rutherford, S. (2012, April 30). Rodgers feels cheated of proper credit. *The Times*, p. 8 (The Game).

Rutter, M. (1987). Psychosocial resilience and protective mechanisms. *American Journal of Orthopsychiatry*, 57, 316–331.

Rutter, M. (1999). Resilience concepts and findings: Implications for family therapy. *Journal of Family Therapy*, 21, 119–144.

Ryan, C. (2009, September 24). NFL injury report: Week 3. *Sports Illustrated*. Retrieved November 10, 2009, from http://www.sportsillustrated.cnn.com.

Ryan, M. (2005, December 9). From Ashes to dust [Letter to the editor]. *The Daily Telegraph*, p. S10 (Sport).

Ryba, T. V., Stambulova, N. B., & Wrisberg, C. A. (2009). Forward to the past: Puni's model of volitional preparation in sport. *International Journal of Sport and Exercise Psychology*, 7, 275–291.

Saferstein, D. (2005). *Win or lose: A guide to sports parenting*. Ann Arbor, MI: Trusted Guide Press.

Saferstein, D. (2006). *Strength in you: A student-athlete's guide to competition and life*. Ann Arbor, MI: Trusted Guide Press.

Sagar, S. S. (2009, February). Fear of failure in youth sport: Building on the momentum of the new research. *Sport & Exercise Psychology Review*, 5, 5–15.

Sagar, S. S., & Stoeber, J. (2009). Perfectionism, fear of failure, and affective responses to success and failure: The central role of fear of experiencing shame and embarrassment. *Journal of Sport and Exercise Psychology*, 31, 602–627.

Salama-Younes, M. (2011). Towards a positive sport psychology: A prospective investigation in physical practice. *World Journal of Sports Sciences*, 4, 104–115.

Saleeby, D. (Ed.). (1997). *The strength perspective in social work practice* (2nd edn). New York: Longman.

Sanders, D. (2011, September 20). Tony Romo isn't over the hump yet. *The Dallas Morning News*. Retrieved October 4, 2011, from http://www.dallasnews.com/ sports.

Scanlan, T. K., Russell, D. G., Beals, K. P., & Scanlan, L. A. (2003). Project on Elite Athlete Commitment (PEAK): II. A direct test and expansion of the Sport Commitment Model with elite amateur sportsmen. *Journal of Sport and Exercise Psychology, 25*, 377–401.

Scarnati, J. T. (2000). Beyond technical competence: Developing mental toughness. *Career Development International, 5*, 171–176.

Schaubhut, N. A., Donnay, D. A. C., & Thompson, R. C. (2006, May). Personality profiles of North American professional football players. Poster session presented at the meeting of the Annual Convention of the Society for Industrial and Organizational Psychology, Dallas, TX.

Scheier, M. F., Carver, C. S., & Bridges, M. W. (1994). Distinguishing optimism from neuroticism (and trait anxiety, self-mastery, and self-esteem): A reevaluation of the Life Orientation Test. *Journal of Personality and Social Psychology, 67*, 1063–1078.

Schmid, J., & Leiman, J. M. (1957). The development of hierarchical factor solutions. *Psychometrika, 22*, 53–61.

Schoel, J., Prouty, D., & Radcliffe, P. (1988). *Islands of healing: A guide to adventure based counselling.* Hamilton, MA: Project Adventure, Inc.

Schoon, I., & Bartley, M. (2008, January). The role of human capacity and resilience. *The Psychologist, 24–27.*

Schwartz, S. H. (1994). Beyond individualism/collectivism: New cultural dimensions of values. In U. Kim, H. C. Triandis, Ç. Kâgitçibasi, S. Choi, & G. Yoon (Eds.), *Individualism and collectivism: Theory, method, and applications* (pp. 85–119). Thousand Oaks, CA: Sage.

Schwarzer, R., & Jerusalem, M. (1993). *Measurement of perceived self efficacy: Psychometric scales for cross-cultural research.* Berlin: Freie Universität.

Scott, M., & Hunter, A. (2011, April 11). Kroenke takes full control of Arsenal. *The Guardian*, p. 1 (Sport).

Scott-Elliot, R. (2011, December 31). Falling stars and strikes: America's year of shame. *The Independent*, p. 19 (Sport).

Sedor, D. L. (2008). *Model coach: A common sense guide for coaches of youth sports.* Bloomington, IN: iUniverse.

Segall, M. H., Dasen, P. R., Berry, J. W., & Poortinga, Y. H. (1999). *Human behaviour in global perspective: An introduction to cross-cultural psychology* (2nd edn). Boston, MA: Allyn and Bacon.

Seligman, M., & Csikszentmihalyi, M. (2000). Positive psychology: An introduction. *American Psychologist, 55*, 5–14.

Selvey, M. (2011a, March 23). Survival instincts put World Cup peak in reach for Strauss and co. *The Guardian*, p. 7 (Sport).

Selvey, M. (2011b, March 24). Chanderpaul's defiance swept aside by Pakistan. *The Guardian*, pp. 6–7 (Sport).

Selvey, M. (2011c, March 30). Samaraweera adds the final spark to see Sri Lanka home. *The Guardian*, p. 5 (Sport).

Selvey, M. (2011d, July 18). Sandwich 2011 was a good place to be old, unheralded or American. *The Guardian*, p. 5 (Sport).

Seward, H., Orchard, J., Hazard, H., & Collinson, D. (1993). Football injuries in Australia at the elite level. *Medical Journal of Australia, 159*, 298–301.

Shafer, A. B. (1999). Factor analyses of Big Five Markers with the Comrey Personality Scales and the Howarth Personality Tests. *Personality and Individual Differences*, *26*, 857–872.

Shakespeare, W. (1998). *The Tempest*. In S. Wells & G. Taylor (Eds.). *The Oxford Shakespeare: The complete works* (pp. 1167–1189). Oxford, England: Oxford University Press. (Original work published 1623)

Sheard, M. (2003, June 27). How not to win at Wimbledon [Letter to the editor]. *The Times*, p. 25 (Comment).

Sheard, M. (2006, December 6). Testing times [Letter to the editor]. *The Times*, p. 18 (Comment).

Sheard, M. (2008a, July). Personality hardiness distinguishes elite-level sport performers. Poster session presented at the meeting of the 29th International Congress of Psychology, Berlin, Germany.

Sheard, M. (2008b, July). Construct validation of the alternative Psychological Performance Inventory (PPI-A) and the Sports Mental Toughness Questionnaire (SMTQ). Poster session presented at the meeting of the 14th European Conference on Personality, Tartu, Estonia.

Sheard, M. (2009a). Hardiness commitment, gender, and age differentiate university academic performance. *British Journal of Educational Psychology*, *79*, 189–204.

Sheard, M. (2009b). A cross-national analysis of mental toughness and hardiness in elite university rugby league teams. *Perceptual and Motor Skills*, *109*, 213–223.

Sheard, M. (2009c, November 4). Strong men, strong minds [Letter to the Editor]. *The Guardian*, p. 10 (Sport).

Sheard, M. (2009d). *Mental toughness: The mindset behind sporting achievement* (1st edn). London: Routledge.

Sheard, M., & Golby, J. (2003). Mental toughness and hardiness: A cross-sport investigation. In J. Henry (Ed.), *European positive psychology proceedings 2002* (pp. 48–59). Leicester, England: British Psychological Society.

Sheard, M., & Golby, J. (2006a). Effect of a psychological skills training program on swimming performance and positive psychological development. *International Journal of Sport and Exercise Psychology*, *4*, 149–169.

Sheard, M., & Golby, J. (2006b). The efficacy of an outdoor adventure education curriculum on selected aspects of positive psychological development. *Journal of Experiential Education*, *29*, 187–209.

Sheard, M., & Golby, J. (2007a, March). Psychological characteristics that identify elite level sport performers: The moderating role of hardiness. Poster session presented at the annual meeting of the British Psychological Society, York, England.

Sheard, M., & Golby, J. (2007b). Hardiness and undergraduate academic study: The moderating role of commitment. *Personality and Individual Differences*, *43*, 579–588.

Sheard, M., & Golby, J. (2008, September). Resisting stress in sports officiating: The moderating role of positive psychology. Poster session presented at the meeting of the 14th World Congress of Psychiatry, Prague, Czech Republic.

Sheard, M., & Golby, J. (2009). Investigating the 'rigid persistence paradox' in professional rugby union football. *International Journal of Sport and Exercise Psychology*, *6*, 101–114.

Sheard, M., & Golby, J. (2010). Personality hardiness differentiates elite-level sport performers. *International Journal of Sport and Exercise Psychology, 8*, 160–169.

Sheard, M., Golby, J., & van Wersch, A. (2009). Progress toward construct validation of the Sports Mental Toughness Questionnaire (SMTQ). *European Journal of Psychological Assessment, 25*, 184–191.

Sheldon, K. M., Kasser, T., Smith, K., & Share, T. (2002). Personal goals and psychological growth: Testing an intervention to enhance goal attainment and personality integration. *Journal of Personality, 70*, 5–31.

Shepherd, R. (2007, June 6). Giants referee 'got it right'. *Yorkshire Post.* Retrieved June 6, 2007, from http://www.yorkshirepost.co.uk.

Shpigel, B. (2008, September 11). For the Mets' Stokes, renewal springs from his arm and mind. *The New York Times.* Retrieved May 1, 2011, from http://www.nytimes.com.

Shpigel, B. (2011, October 1). Jets' Mason, taught to endure pain, now shows others the way. *The New York Times.* Retrieved October 1, 2011, from http://www.nytimes.com.

Simpson, P. (2011, October 1). Jankovic falls at first hurdle in Beijing. *Chicago Tribune.* Retrieved October 4, 2011, from http://www.chicagotribune.com/sports.

Simpson, R. J., Gray, S. C., & Florida-James, G. D. (2006). Physiological variables and performance markers of serving soldiers from two 'elite' units of the British Army. *Journal of Sports Sciences, 24*, 597–604.

Slack, T., & Hinnings, B. (1992). Understanding change in national sports organisations: An integration of theoretical perspectives. *Journal of Sport Management, 6*, 114–132.

Slot, O. (2005, June 2). Injury report highlights danger zones for elite English players. *The Times*, p. 87 (Sport).

Slot, O. (2007a, October 13). England told to search for hero inside themselves. *The Times*, p. 120 (Sport).

Slot, O. (2007b, October 15). Ashton's film buffs barely able to believe their own box-office hit. *The Times*, p. 80 (Sport).

Slot, O. (2009, April 30). Analysing errors and not ability the key as Cech bounces back. *The Times*, pp. 88–89 (Sport).

Slot, O. (2011a, March 28). Britain look to hit back in 2012 as rivals create new world order. *The Times*, p. 64 (Sport).

Slot, O. (2011b, October 3). Sex taunts row shames England stars. *The Times*, p. 3.

Slot, O. (2011c, October 11). Williams ready for 'biggest game in Welsh history'. *The Times*, p. 72 (Sport).

Slot, O. (2012, February 2). Battle joined against head-turning agents. *The Times*, p. 65 (Sport).

Smith, A. (2010, September 12). Talent still not fully fledged since Brown flew the Hibs nest. *The Scotsman*, p. 13 (Sport).

Smith, A. L., Gustafsson, H., & Hassmén, P. (2010). Peer motivational climate and burnout perceptions of adolescent athletes. *Psychology of Sport and Exercise, 11*, 453–460.

Smith, A. L., Lemyre, P.-N., & Raedeke, T. D. (2007). Advances in athlete burnout research. *International Journal of Sport Psychology, 38*, 337–341.

Smith, E. (2009, February 21). Strauss becomes a leader by example. *The Daily Telegraph*, p. S15 (Sport).

Smith, E. (2010, June 25). These two have left a deeper imprint than many greats and won a prize bigger than victory. *The Times*. Retrieved June 29, 2010, from http://www.thetimes.co.uk/tto/opinion.

Smith, E. (2011a, March 25). The demons that destroy us also drive us on. *The Times*, p. 30 (Opinion).

Smith, E. (2011b, November 28). Top two in rankings will feel threatened by second coming of Roger the Great. *The Times*, p. 67 (Sport).

Smith, P. (1996, November 14). Scrum down. *London Review of Books*, pp. 26–27.

Smith, R. (2012a, April 17). Great escape a step closer after Roberto Martínez's men humble Arsenal. *The Times*. Retrieved April 17, 2012, from http://www.times online.co.uk/tol/sport.

Smith, R. (2012b, April 25). Terry's shame, Chelsea's game. *The Times*, p. 72 (Sport).

Smith, R. E. (2006). Understanding sport behaviour: A cognitive-affective processing systems approach. *Journal of Applied Sport Psychology*, *18*, 1–27.

Smith, R. E., & Smoll, F. L. (1989). The psychology of 'mental toughness': Theoretical models and training approaches to anxiety reduction in athletes. In C. C. Teitz (Ed.), *Scientific foundations of sport medicine* (pp. 391–402). Philadelphia, PA: B. C. Decker.

Smith, R. E., & Smoll, F. L. (2002). *Way to go, coach! A scientifically-proven approach to coaching effectiveness* (2nd edn). Portola Valley, CA: Warde.

Smithies, T. (2007, January 23). Jets work on mind games. *The Daily Telegraph (Australia)*. Retrieved January 23, 2007, from http://www.news.com.au/ dailytelegraph.html.

Smoll, F. L., & Smith, R. E. (2005). *Sports and your child: Developing champions in sports and in life* (2nd edn). Palo Alto, CA: Warde.

Smyth, R. (2009, July 12). Ashes: England v Australia – as it happened. *The Guardian*. Retrieved July 27, 2009, from http://www.guardian.co.uk/sport.

Snow, M. (2008, August 17). The taking part? Pah! *The Sunday Times*, p. 32 (Life & Style).

Snyder, A. W. (1999, June–July). Mind, body, performance. *Olympic Review*, 71–74.

Snyder, C. R., Lopez, S. J., & Pedrotti, J. T. (2011). *Positive psychology: The scientific and practical explorations of human strengths* (2nd edn). Thousand Oaks, CA: Sage.

Soderstrom, M., Dolbier, C., Leiferman, J., & Steinhardt, M. (2000). The relationship of hardiness, coping strategies, and perceived stress to symptoms of illness. *Journal of Behavioral Medicine*, *23*, 311–328.

Souster, M. (2003, November 24). Jones generous in defeat after pre-match attrition. *The Times*, p. 35 (Sport).

Souster, M. (2007, October 15). Backbone of England with spirit of a bulldog. *The Times*, p. 72 (Sport).

Souster, M. (2009a, March 13). Wounded hero finally set to take his leave in pursuit of fresh challenge. *The Times*, p. 84 (Sport).

Souster, M. (2009b, March 30). Rampant Bristol delay the inevitable. *The Times*, p. 62 (Sport).

Souster, M. (2009c, June 15). Johnson looks on the bright side as England fall short in comeback bid. *The Times*, p. 65 (Sport).

Souster, M. (2009d, August 20). Revealed: The Bloodgate bunglers and Harlequins' secret cheat file. *The Times*, p. 64 (Sport).

Souster, M. (2009e, November 28). Courage shown by Robinson in rebuilding his reputation rubs off on Scotland. *The Times*, p. 18 (Sport).

Souster, M. (2011a, May 16). Owen Farrell finds aim to hand Saracens a second tilt at final glory. *The Times*, pp. 62–63 (Sport).

Souster, M. (2011b, October 3). Johnson back on the defensive as off-field problems escalate. *The Times*, pp. 70–71 (Sport).

Souster, M. (2011c, October 6). Time arrives for Johnson's men to fulfil their promises. *The Times*, pp. 90–91 (Sport).

Souster, M. (2011d, November 23). Rifts in squad left campaign doomed from the beginning. *The Times*, p. 74 (Sport).

Souster, M. (2012a, February 10). Unchanged England keep focus on discipline for Rome mission. *The Times*, p. 84 (Sport).

Souster, M. (2012b, April 23). Chiefs' battle cry falls silent as they pay price for not trusting instincts. *The Times*, p. 60 (Sport).

Spiers, G. (2008a, January 31). Ferguson on target to put Rangers into final. *The Times*, p. 96 (Sport).

Spiers, G. (2008b, March 29). McCoist: 'We now have a toughness, an ability to win games.' *The Times*, p. 108 (Sport).

Spiers, G. (2009, July 18). Age no barrier for veteran if the spirit remains on his side. *The Times*, p. 11 (Sport).

Stanimirovic, R., & Hanrahan, S. (2010). Psychological predictors of job performance and career success in professional sport. *Sport Science Review*, *19*, 211–239.

Starkes, J. L., Weir, P. L., Singh, P., Hodges, N. J., & Kerr, T. (1999). Aging and the retention of sport expertise. *International Journal of Sport Psychology*, *30*, 283–301.

Stead, D. (2003). Sport and the media. In B. Houlihan (Ed.), *Sport and society: A student introduction* (pp. 184–200). London: Sage.

Stern, J. (2009, July 12). Hauritz gets his turn. *The Sunday Times*, p. 4 (Sport).

Stewart, R. (2010, April 1). Gopperth boots life into Newcastle. *The Daily Telegraph*, p. S20 (Sport).

Stoeber, J., & Stoeber, F. S. (2009). Domains of perfectionism: Prevalence and relationships with perfectionism, gender, age, and satisfaction with life. *Personality and Individual Differences*, *46*, 530–535.

Stone, S. (2009, May 6). Devils reach Rome in stunning style. *The Northern Echo*, p. 42 (Sport).

Stone, S. (2010, May 19). England call too strong for Carragher. *The Independent*. Retrieved June 29, 2010, from http://www.independent.co.uk/sport.

Strelan, P., & Boeckmann, R. J. (2006). Why drug testing in elite sport does not work: Perceptual deterrence theory and the role of personal moral beliefs. *Journal of Applied Social Psychology*, *36*, 2909–2934.

Stuart, L. (2008, February 29). Macfadyen puts his injury woes behind him to focus on return. *The Times*, p. 85 (Sport).

Stuart, L. (2009a, March 14). Three reasons for Scotland to have hope. *The Times*. Retrieved March 14, 2009, from http://www.timesonline.co.uk/tol/sport.

Stuart, L. (2009b, April 20). Edinburgh and Glasgow reveal lack of mental strength. *The Times*. Retrieved April 21, 2009, from http://www.timesonline.co.uk/tol/sport.

Stuart, L. (2011, October 3). Robinson will aim to instil winning habit after inquest. *The Times*, p. 67 (Sport).

Stuart, M. J. (2005). Gridiron football injuries. *Medicine and Sport Science, 49*, 62–85.

Sweeney, M. (2009, June 22). In final round, mental toughness can be decisive. *The New York Times*. Retrieved June 6, 2011, from http://www.nytimes.com.

Syed, M. (2007, October 15). Heroes? No, just men doing their job. *The Times*, p. 71 (Sport).

Syed, M. (2009a, February 4). Nadal's priceless gift to Federer – defeat. *The Times*, p. 59 (Sport).

Syed, M. (2009b, February, 11). Giggs knows path to greatness has no end. *The Times*, p. 71 (Sport).

Syed, M. (2009c, July 1). Chasing a ranking alongside heroes of '66. *The Times*, p. 69 (Sport).

Syed, M. (2009d, July 21). One putt almost put the Grim reaper in his place. *The Times*, p. 20 (Opinion).

Syed, M. (2009e, September 16). Tennis world axis tilts towards Argentina. *The Times*, p. 75 (Sport).

Syed, M. (2009f, November 25). Beckham's bravery puts critics in a spin. *The Times*, p. 87 (Sport).

Syed, M. (2009g, December 22). Phelps going to great lengths still in search of the impossible. *The Times*, p. 58–59 (Sport).

Syed, M. (2010). *Bounce: How champions are made*. London: Fourth Estate.

Syed, M. (2012a, March 14). Curse of the sledge nothing to shout about. *The Times*, p. 62 (Sport).

Syed, M. (2012b, April 11). Culture of cheating makes fall guys of us all. *The Times*, p. 57 (Sport).

Syed, M. (2012c, April 25). Hard to forget as cheats seek forgiveness. *The Times*, p. 57 (Sport).

Syed, M. (2012d, April 26). Loving Chelsea is a bridge too far, but miracle makes us reluctant admirers. *The Times*, p. 72 (Sport).

Szczepanik, N. (2009, October 26). Ancelotti enjoys warm glow of a Cole-fired performance. *The Times*, p. 8 (The Game).

Tabachnick, B. G., & Fidell, L. S. (2007). *Using multivariate statistics* (5th edn). Boston, MA: Allyn & Bacon.

Taniguchi, S., & Freeman, P. A. (2004). Outdoor education and meaningful learning: Finding the attributes to meaningful learning experiences in an outdoor education program. *Journal of Experiential Education, 26*, 210–211.

Taylor, D. (2009a, August 8). United get to grips with life after Ronaldo. *The Guardian*, pp. 8–9 (Sport).

Taylor, D. (2009b, November 21). 'It was a terrible feeling, such a sense of fear.' *The Guardian*, p. 7 (Sport).

Taylor, D. (2010a, March 6). After 18 months, two operations and a crushing diagnosis, Hargreaves is back. *The Guardian*, p. 3 (Sport).

Taylor, D. (2010b, April 26). Berbatov bubbles as United show grace in adversity. *The Guardian*, p. 7 (Sport).

Taylor, D. (2011a, March 12). Blip must not become slump, says Ferguson. *The Guardian*, p. 3 (Sport).

Taylor, D. (2011b, March 16). Smalling makes better case in United's defence. *The Guardian*, p. 3 (Sport).

Taylor, D. (2012, April 25). Chelsea in wonderland. *The Guardian*, p. 54 (Sport).

Taylor, J. (1989). Mental toughness (Part 2): A simple reminder may be all you need. *Sport Talk*, *18*, 2–3.

Taylor, J., & Taylor, S. (1997). *Psychological approaches to sport injury rehabilitation*. Gaithersburg, MD: Aspen Publication.

Taylor, J.-J. (2011, June 14). Dirk has shown Tony Romo that the ring is the thing. *The Dallas Morning News*. Retrieved October 4, 2011, from http://www.dallasnews.com/sports.

Taylor, L. (2009, October 2). No offence to Beckham or Scholes but Giggs was the certainty to be a superstar. *The Guardian*, p. 5 (Sport).

Taylor, L. (2010, March 2). Has roughing up Arsenal become part of the plan? *The Guardian*, p. 5 (Sport).

Tenenbaum, G., Fogarty, G., Stewart, E., Calcagnini, N., Kirker, B., Thorne, G., et al. (1999). Perceived discomfort in running: Scale development and theoretical considerations. *Journal of Sports Sciences*, *17*, 183–196.

Terracciano, A., Abdel-Khalek, A. M., Ádám, N., Adamovová, L., Ahn, C.-k., Ahn, H.-N., et al. (2005). National character does not reflect mean personality trait levels in 49 cultures. *Science*, *310*, 96–100.

The England Cricket Team. (2005). *Ashes victory*. London: Orion.

Thelwell, R. C., Such, B. A., Weston, N. J. V., Such, J. D., & Greenlees, I. A. (2010). Developing mental toughness: Perceptions of elite female gymnasts. *International Journal of Sport and Exercise Psychology*, *8*, 170–188.

Thelwell, R., Weston, N., & Greenlees, I. (2005). Defining and understanding mental toughness within soccer. *Journal of Applied Sport Psychology*, *17*, 326–332.

Thelwell, R. C., Weston, N. J. V., & Greenlees, I. A. (2007). Batting on a sticky wicket: Identifying sources of stress and associated coping strategies. *Psychology of Sport and Exercise*, *8*, 219–232.

Thelwell, R. C., Weston, N. J. V., Greenlees, I. A., & Hutchings, N. V. (2008). Stressors in elite sport: A coach perspective. *Journal of Sports Sciences*, *26*, 905–918.

The Secret Footballer. (2012, April 28). Mind games: The truth behind the clichés. *The Guardian*, pp. 1, 4 (Sport).

Thomas, P. R., Murphy, S. M., & Hardy, L. (1999). Test of performance strategies: Development and preliminary validation of a comprehensive measure of athletes' psychological skills. *Journal of Sports Sciences*, *17*, 697–711.

Thomas, P. R., & Over, R. (1994). Psychological and psychomotor skills associated with performance in golf. *The Sport Psychologist*, *8*, 73–86.

Thomas, P. R., Schlinker, P. J., & Over, R. (1996). Psychological and psychomotor skills associated with prowess at ten-pin bowling. *Journal of Sports Sciences, 14*, 255–268.

Thompson, B. (2004). *Exploratory and confirmatory factor analysis: Understanding concepts and applications*. Washington, DC: American Psychological Association.

Thompson, J. (2003). *The double-goal coach: Positive coaching tools for honouring the game and developing winners in sports and life*. New York: Harper Information.

Thomson, C., & Morris, T. (2009). Improving the hardiness of elite rugby players. *Journal of Science and Medicine in Sport, 12S*, S80.

Thomson, W. C., & Wendt, J. C. (2010). Contribution of hardiness and school climate to alienation experienced by student teachers. *Journal of Educational Research, 88*, 269–274.

Thurstone, L. L. (1947). *Multiple factor analysis*. Chicago, IL: Chicago University Press.

Tibbert, S., Morris, T., & Andersen, M. (2009). Mental toughness and recovery in athletes. *Journal of Science and Medicine in Sport, 12S*, S33.

Tillich, P. (1952). *The courage to be*. New Haven, CT: Yale University Press.

Tomase, J. (2007). Beating Chargers left players feeling Super. *The Boston Herald*, p. 74 (Sport).

Tomlinson, A., & Young, C. (Eds.). (2006). *German football: History, culture, society*. London: Routledge.

Tongue, S. (2008, June 27). Fabregas: 'Our mental strength has been the key.' *The Independent*, p. 70 (Sport).

Trainis, N. (2009, December 29). Peterborough roar back from the dead. *The Daily Telegraph*, p. S10 (Sport).

Tremayne, P., & Tremayne, B. (2004). Children and sport psychology. In T. Morris & J. Summers (Eds.), *Sport psychology: Theory, applications and issues* (2nd edn, pp. 529–546). Milton, Australia: Wiley.

Trott, J. (2010, November 15). Aussie crowds silenced and our squad is buzzing. *The Daily Telegraph*, p. S23 (Sport).

Tugade, M. M., & Fredrickson, B. L. (2004). Resilient individuals use positive emotions to bounce back from negative emotional experiences. *Journal of Personality and Social Psychology, 86*, 320–333.

Tunney, J. (1987). Thoughts on the line. Mental toughness: Biceps for the mind. *Soccer Journal, 32*, 49–50.

Turner, B. (2007, July 31). Happiness is . . . being Danish and enjoying life. *The Times*, p. 8 (Times2).

Tutko, T. A., Lyon, L. P., & Ogilvie, B. C. (1969). *Athletic Motivation Inventory*. San Jose, CA: Institute for the Study of Athletic Motivation.

Tutko, T. A., & Richards, J. W. (1972). *Coach's practical guide to athletic motivation*. Boston, MA: Allyn & Bacon.

Tutko, T. A., & Richards, J. W. (1976). *Psychology of coaching*. Boston, MA: Allyn & Bacon.

US Open 2010. (2010, June 21). Ryder Cup captain Colin Montgomerie hails Graeme McDowell's mental strength. *The Daily Mail*. Retrieved June 22, 2011, from http://www.dailymail.co.uk/sport.

Vadocz, E. A., Hall, C., & Moritz, S. E. (1997). The relationship between competitive anxiety and imagery use. *Journal of Applied Sport Psychology*, *9*, 241–252.

Vallée, C. N., & Bloom, G. A. (2005). Building a successful university program: Key and common elements of expert coaches. *Journal of Applied Sport Psychology*, *17*, 179–196.

Vallerand, R. J., Blanchard, C. M., Mageau, G. A., Koestner, R., Ratelle, C., Léonard, M., *et al.* (2003). Les passions de l'âme: On obsessive and harmonious passion. *Journal of Personality and Social Psychology*, *85*, 756–767.

Vallerand, R. J., Deshaies, P., Cuerrier, J.-P., Brière, N. M., & Pelletier, L. G. (1996). Toward a multidimensional definition of sportsmanship. *Journal of Applied Sport Psychology*, *8*, 89–101.

Vallerand, R. J., & Miquelon, P. (2007). Passion for sport in athletes. In D. Lavallee & S. Jowett (Eds.), *Social psychology in sport* (pp. 249–262). Champaign, IL: Human Kinetics.

Van den Heever, Z., Grobbelaar, H. W., & Potgieter, J. C. (2007). A survey of psychological skills training in South African netball. *African Journal for Physical, Health Education, Recreation, and Dance*, *13*, 254–266.

Vaughan, M. (2009, July 1). I made one last effort but now it's time to go. *The Daily Telegraph*, p. S10 (Sport).

Vaughan, M. (2010a, January 8). Newland spirit can take Team Strauss to No. 1. *The Daily Telegraph*, pp. S2–S3 (Sport).

Vaughan, M. (2010b, September 17). I am what I am due to Freddie's one-off talent. *The Daily Telegraph*, pp. S2–S3 (Sport).

Vaughan, M. (2010c, December 9). England can become world's best. *The Daily Telegraph*, p. S9 (Sport).

Vealey, R. S. (1994). Current status and prominent issues in sport psychology interventions. *Medicine and Science in Sports and Exercise*, *26*, 495–502.

Vickers, A. (2010, October 18). Get ready for Radio Gaga! *Evening Gazette*, pp. 4–5 (Sport).

Vickers, A. (2011a, April 11). Boro's men of steel. *Evening Gazette*, pp. 4–5 (Sport).

Vickers, A. (2011b, April 12). Turning back the tide. *Evening Gazette*, p. 38 (Sport).

Viner, B. (2009, June 26). Humble master. *The Independent*, pp. 54–55 (Sport).

Volz, M. (2009, March 16). Painful truth is that we're not always faking it. *The Times*, p. 19 (The Game).

Walker, G. (2011, April 23). Farrell late show breaks brave St Helens' hearts. *The Guardian*, p. 13 (Sport).

Walker, N., Thatcher, J., Lavallee, D., & Golby, J. (2004). The emotional response to athletic injury: Re-injury anxiety. In D. Lavallee, J. Thatcher, & M. V. Jones (Eds.), *Coping and emotion in sport* (pp. 91–103). Hauppauge, NY: Nova Science Publishers.

Walker, T. B., Lennemann, L. M., McGregor, J. N., Mauzy, C., & Zupan, M. (2011). Physiological and psychological characteristics of successful combat controller trainees. *Journal of Special Operations Medicine*, *11*, 39–47.

Wallace, H. M., Baumeister, R. F., & Vohs, K. D. (2005). Audience support and choking under pressure: A home disadvantage? *Journal of Sports Sciences, 23,* 429–438.

Wallace, S. (2011, January 17). United defend title credentials. *i,* p. 53 (Sport).

Wallston, K. A. (1989). Assessment of control in health-care settings. In A. Steptoe & A. Apple (Eds.), *Stress, personal control, and health* (pp. 85–101). Chichester, England: Wiley.

Walrond, N. (2012, April 16). Resilient Exeter head to Europe on a high. *The Daily Telegraph,* pp. S22–S23 (Sport).

Walsh, D. (2007, October 21). Accidental heroes. *The Sunday Times,* p. 6 (Sport).

Walsh, D. (2008a, February 24). Ashton's battling bruisers punch above their weight. *The Sunday Times,* p. 2 (Sport).

Walsh, D. (2008b, November 16). Arsenal title challenge fades after 2–0 defeat by Villa. *The Sunday Times,* p. 1 (Sport).

Walsh, D. (2009a, March 29). Paul O'Connell: Warren Gatland and me. *The Sunday Times.* Retrieved March 29, 2009, from http://www.timesonline.co.uk/tol/sport.

Walsh, D. (2009b, December 27). Stiliyan Petrov is all heart. *The Sunday Times.* Retrieved January 4, 2010, from http://www.timesonline.co.uk/tol/sport.

Walsh, D. (2012, April 15). Cup cheer for Dalglish. *The Sunday Times,* p. 3 (Sport).

Wankel, L. M., & Mummery, W. K. (1990). The psychological and social benefits of sport and physical activity. *Journal of Leisure Research, 22,* 167–182.

Warburton, S. (2012, February 10). Tip tackles not necessarily malicious. *The Daily Telegraph,* p. S12 (Sport).

Wark, P. (2003, February 26). You need emotion to be a winner. *The Times.* Retrieved July 30, 2009, from http://www.timesonline.co.uk/tol/sport.

Warne, S. (2007). *My complete illustrated career.* London: Cassell Illustrated.

Warne, S. (2008, September 29). Pietersen can become the best batsman in the world. *The Times,* pp. 66–67 (Sport).

Warne, S. (2009). *Shane Warne's century: My top 100 Test cricketers.* Edinburgh, Scotland: Mainstream.

Warne, S. (2010, May 18). A brilliant win, now for the toughest test Down Under. *The Daily Telegraph,* pp. S2–S3 (Sport).

Watson, D., Clark, L. A., & Tellegen, A. (1988). Development and validation of brief measures of positive and negative affect: The PANAS scales. *Journal of Personality and Social Psychology, 54,* 1063–1070.

Watson, D., Wiese, D., Vaidya, J., & Tellegen, A. (1999). The two general activation systems of affect: Structure findings, evolutionary considerations and psychobiological evidence. *Journal of Personality and Social Psychology, 76,* 820–838.

Watts, F. N., Webster, S. M., Morley, C. J., & Cohen, J. (1992). Expedition stress and personality change. *British Journal of Psychology, 83,* 337–341.

Waugh, S. (2006). *Out of my comfort zone.* Camberwell, Australia: Penguin.

Weaver, P. (2009, May 9). Back on track: England charge to three-day success. *The Guardian,* p. 1 (Sport).

Weaver, P. (2011, May 28). Magic of Monaco still casts a spell on Button. *The Guardian,* p. 11 (Sport).

Weaver, P. (2012, March 11). Refocused Hamilton has sights on Vettel. *The Observer*, p. 17 (Sport).

Weeks, J. (2010, February 15). Mattock keeps his focus to earn West Brom a second crack. *The Guardian*, p. 4 (Sport).

Weiss, A., Bates, T. C., & Luciano, M. (2009). Happiness is a personal(ity) thing: The genetics of personality and well-being in a representative sample. *Psychological Science, 19*, 205–210.

Weissensteiner, J., Abernethy, B., & Farrow, D. (2009). Towards the development of a conceptual model of expertise in cricket batting: A grounded theory approach. *Journal of Applied Sport Psychology, 21*, 276–292.

Werner, A. C., & Gottheil, E. (1966). Personality development and participation in collegiate athletics. *Research Quarterly, 37*, 126–131.

Westerby, J. (2008, December 9). Aaron Mauger relishes Dan Carter reunion. *The Times*. Retrieved December 9, 2008, from http://www.timesonline.co.uk/tol/sport.

Westerby, J. (2009a, July 23). Have Australia become too nice for own good? *The Times*, p. 71 (Sport).

Westerby, J. (2009b, August 12). Kevin Pietersen injury exposes England's Achilles' heel. *The Times*. Retrieved August 12, 2009, from http://www.timesonline.co.uk/tol/sport.

Westerby, J. (2011, June 27). Baby Blacks are run close by battling England. *The Times*, p. 53 (Sport).

Westman, M. (1990). The relationship between stress and performance: The moderating effect of hardiness. *Human Performance, 3*, 141–155.

Wheatley, J. (2009, June 27). Cricket teaches you vital lessons. *The Times*, pp. 4–5 (Weekend).

White, J. (2009a, June 27). Lillee still firing out rockets. *The Daily Telegraph*, pp. S18–S19 (Sport).

White, J. (2009b, July 4). Oddly, this defeat might make Murray easier to love. *The Daily Telegraph*, p. 3.

White, J. (2009c, July 4). Pietersen craves place on big stage. *The Daily Telegraph*, pp. S12–S13 (Sport).

White, J. (2010a, March 9). Walcott: I've never won a thing. Nothing. *The Daily Telegraph*, pp. S4–S5 (Sport).

White, J. (2010b, May 15). Twenty20? Just a good old beer match. *The Daily Telegraph*, p. 26.

White, J. (2010c, May 18). Planner supreme setting British wheels in motion. *The Daily Telegraph*, pp. S10–S11 (Sport).

White, J. (2011a, June 8). Katich sacrificed on the altar of youth. *The Daily Telegraph*, p. S16 (Sport).

White, J. (2011b, October 4). A little voice whispers: I hope they lose. *The Daily Telegraph*, p. 23 (Comment & Features).

White, J. (2012, April 26). Neville's scoregasm the perfect climax for Sky. *The Daily Telegraph*, p. S7 (Sport).

Whitmarsh, B. G., & Alderman, R. B. (1993). Role of psychological skills training in increasing athletic pain tolerance. *The Sport Psychologist, 7*, 388–399.

Whittell, G. (2010, February 6). Times man signs on with the NFL's school of hard knocks. *The Times*, p. 43.

Whittell, G. (2012, March). Perfecting the human machine. *The Times*, pp. 34–35 (Eureka).

Wiebe, D. J. (1991). Hardiness and stress moderation: A test of proposed mechanisms. *Journal of Personality and Social Psychology*, *60*, 89–99.

Wilde, S. (2009a, May 10). Andy Flower saw 'wow factor' in young Ravi Bopara. *The Times*. Retrieved June 9, 2009, from http://www.timesonline.co.uk/tol/sport.

Wilde, S. (2009b, July 12). Aussies send Strauss back to drawing board. *The Sunday Times*, pp. 2–3 (Sport).

Wilde, S. (2009c, July 12). Ponting wants first-round KO. *The Sunday Times*, p. 4 (Sport).

Wilde, S. (2010a, April 18). Peak performers. *The Sunday Times*, p. 13 (Sport).

Wilde, S. (2010b, April 18). Sorry Surrey slip to brink of defeat. *The Sunday Times*, p. 13 (Sport).

Wilhelm, K., Mitchell, P. B., Niven, H., Finch, A., Wedgwood, L., Scimone, A. R., *et al.* (2006). Life events, first depression onset and the serotonin transporter gene. *British Journal of Psychiatry*, *188*, 210–215.

Wilkinson, J. (2008). *Tackling life*. London: Headline.

Wilkinson, M., & Ashford, B. (1997). Psychological profiling and predictive validity. *Journal of Sports Sciences*, *15*, 111.

Williams, A. M., & Davids, K. (1995). Declarative knowledge in sport: A byproduct of experience or a characteristic of expertise? *Journal of Sport and Exercise Psychology*, *17*, 259–275.

Williams, J. M., & Krane, V. (2001). Psychological characteristics of peak performance. In J. M. Williams (Ed.), *Applied sport psychology: Personal growth to peak performance* (4th edn, pp. 162–178). Mountain View, CA: Mayfield.

Williams, R. (2003, November 24). A new set of heroes – and even Australia agrees. *The Guardian*, p. 2.

Williams, R. (2009a, August 17). City find elusive team spirit with ominous intent. *The Guardian*, pp. 6–7 (Sport).

Williams, R. (2009b, November 17). Big hits but little joy: A game trapped in the dark ages. *The Guardian*, p. 10 (Sport).

Williams, R. (2010, November 9). Button catches England's once-is-enough syndrome. *The Guardian*, p. 10 (Sport).

Williams, R. (2011a, February 28). Victors over Barcelona left feeling like beaten Bayern. *The Guardian*, pp. 2–3 (Sport).

Williams, R. (2011b, March 15). Unlike Ferguson, Wenger's real blind sport is captaincy. *The Guardian*, p. 12 (Sport).

Williams, R. (2011c, March 20). Johnson's red roses left wilting in the antiseptic greenery of Dublin 4. *The Observer*, p. 3 (Sport).

Williams, R. (2011d, April 19). Arsenal currently flap where Vieira once fought. *The Guardian*, p. 10 (Sport).

Williams, R. (2012, March 18). Team of captains lacked melody but were focused in bid for immortality. *The Observer*, p. 2 (Sport).

Williams, R. M. (1988). The US Open character test: Good strokes help. But the most individualistic of sports is ultimately a mental game. *Psychology Today, 22*, 60–62.

Willstrop, J. (2010, September 28). New Delhi will be intriguing. *The Daily Telegraph*, p. S15 (Sport).

Wilson, A. (2008, October 6). Smith and Leeds rewarded for persistence with sweetest of prizes. *The Guardian*, pp. 10–11 (Sport).

Wilson, A. (2009a, February 23). Long helps make short work of Giants. *The Guardian*, p. 14 (Sport).

Wilson, A. (2009b, April 9). Pryce takes Saints back to the top but Wigan close the gap. *The Guardian*. Retrieved April 9, 2009, from http://www.guardian.co.uk/sport.

Wilson, A. (2009c, October 8). Wigan appoint Maguire to give Australia nine Super League coaches. *The Guardian*, p. 8 (Sport).

Wilson, A. (2010, March 6). Bradford back from the dead as Wigan lose their perfect record. *The Guardian*, p. 10 (Sport).

Wilson, A. (2011a, February 28). Wigan make brave attempt but the Dragons are still worlds apart. *The Guardian*, p. 13 (Sport).

Wilson, A. (2011b, March 19). Charnley puts determined Wigan back on top. *The Guardian*, p. 15 (Sport).

Wilson, A. (2011c, March 25). 'He's a nice bloke and a hard bloke – if it gets you, you've got to let it out.' *The Guardian*, p. 3 (Sport).

Wilson, A. (2012a, March 10). Hood pounces at the death as Leeds end Warrington's unbeaten run. *The Guardian*, p. 11 (Sport).

Wilson, A. (2012b, April 29). Shaun Lunt's try secures hard-earned victory for Leeds at Salford. *The Guardian*. Retrieved April 29, 2012, from http://www. guardian.co.uk/sport.

Wilson, C., Edwards, D., & Collins, T. (2005). Long-term rider development. Retrieved September 20, 2008, from http://www.sportscoachuk.org.

Wilson, G. V., & Kerr, J. H. (1999). Affective responses to success and failure: A study of winning and losing in competitive rugby. *Personality and Individual Differences, 27*, 85–89.

Wilson, J. (2007, November 26). England role could be tempting, says Klinsmann. *The Daily Telegraph*, pp. S2–S3 (Sport).

Wilson, J. (2009a, February 23). Lampard reveals his debt to Ranieri ahead of reunion. *The Daily Telegraph*, p. S5 (Sport).

Wilson, J. (2009b, May 20). Frenchman keeps focus on 'project'. *The Daily Telegraph*, p. S3 (Sport).

Wilson, J. (2010a, March 27). Eduardo takes the final step on long road to recovery. *The Daily Telegraph*, pp. S6–S7 (Sport).

Wilson, J. (2010b, June 20). Starless Slovenia have mental toughness to send England home. *The Sunday Times*. Retrieved June 29, 2010, from http://www. thesundaytimes.co.uk/sto/sport.

Wilson, J. (2010c, November 15). Character of Noble and Parker a beacon in West Ham gloom. *The Daily Telegraph*, p. S11 (Sport).

Wilson, J. (2011, February 27). Revealed: The 117 questions that decide the fate of aspiring Gunners. *The Sunday Telegraph*, p. S8 (Sport).

Wilson, P. (2009, June 27). Stosur ready to lift game against focused Ivanovic. *The Australian*. Retrieved July 13, 2009, from http://www.theaustralian.com.au/sport.

Wilson, P. (2011a, April 10). No sweat for Berbatov as United stroll on. *The Observer*, pp. 2–3 (Sport).

Wilson, P. (2011b, April 10). Ferguson's better half knew better about Rooney. *The Observer*, p. 4 (Sport).

Wilson, P. (2011c, April 24). Unsung Park looms large in Euro vision. *The Observer*, p. 11 (Sport).

Wilson, P. (2012, April 15). Me and my coach: 'We are both perfectionists'. *The Sunday Telegraph*, p. 11 (Sports Life).

Winner, D. (2001). *Brilliant orange: The neurotic genius of Dutch football*. London: Bloomsbury.

Winter, H. (2005, May 27). How Liverpool defied belief. *The Daily Telegraph*, p. S2 (Sport).

Winter, H. (2006, September 5). England have mindset to survive Balkan cauldron. *The Daily Telegraph*, p. 3 (Sport).

Winter, H. (2007, November 26). Peril awaits on Eastern Front. *The Daily Telegraph*, p. S2 (Sport).

Winter, H. (2009a, March 31). 'Today's kids have it too easy': Lampard says pampered young players should go back to cleaning the senior professionals' boots. *The Daily Telegraph*, p. S1 (Sport).

Winter, H. (2009b, May 11). Ruthless Chelsea expose frail Arsenal. *The Daily Telegraph*, pp. S6–S7 (Sport).

Winter, H. (2009c, May 18). Ferguson the alchemist. *The Daily Telegraph*, pp. S6–S7 (Sport).

Winter, H. (2009d, May 23). Rooney maturing into perfect blend. *The Daily Telegraph*, p. S5 (Sport).

Winter, H. (2009e, May 25). Newcastle fall from grace without a fight. *The Daily Telegraph*, pp. S2–S3 (Sport).

Winter, H. (2009f, June 1). Money talks, but character counts for just as much. *The Daily Telegraph*, pp. S4–S5 (Sport).

Winter, H. (2009g, June 27). Gentleman on land, warrior on water. *The Daily Telegraph*, pp. S22–S23 (Sport).

Winter, H. (2009h, August 8). Ferguson backing Rooney to lead from front. *The Daily Telegraph*, pp. S10–S11 (Sport).

Winter, H. (2009i, August 18). Wenger's vision of united Europe. *The Daily Telegraph*, p. S2 (Sport).

Winter, H. (2009j, August 18). Warnock should turn his fire on City players. *The Daily Telegraph*, p. S5 (Sport).

Winter, H. (2010a, January 20). Tévez makes his point as City slickers down United. *The Daily Telegraph*, pp. S2–S3 (Sport).

Winter, H. (2010b, February 9). Leading light Parker can halt West Ham's descent into darkness. *The Daily Telegraph*, p. S9 (Sport).

Winter, H. (2010c, April 1). Fabregas delivers hope as Barça pay penalty. *The Daily Telegraph*, pp. S2–S3 (Sport).
Winter, H. (2010d, April 1). Injury hysteria shows up English game's twisted logic. *The Daily Telegraph*, p. S7 (Sport).
Winter, H. (2010e, April 12). Glorious tale of unexpected. *The Daily Telegraph*, pp. S6–S7 (Sport).
Winter, H. (2010f, April 14). Anelka timing is spot on for jittery Chelsea. *The Daily Telegraph*, p. S2 (Sport).
Winter, H. (2010g, April 15). Capello's candid views on the English game. *The Daily Telegraph*, pp. S4–S5 (Sport).
Winter, H. (2010h, May 15). Final act of a passion play. *The Daily Telegraph*, pp. S4–S5 (Sport).
Winter, H. (2010i, May 19). England make penalty plans. *The Daily Telegraph*, p. S4 (Sport).
Winter, H. (2010j, August 10). Cole and company would do well to follow Ainslie's winning example. *The Daily Telegraph*, p. S8 (Sport).
Winter, H. (2010k, August 26). Webb laments violent end to World Cup. *The Daily Telegraph*, pp. S6–S7 (Sport).
Winter, H. (2010l, September 20). Majestic Berbatov rises to the rescue. *The Daily Telegraph*, pp. S2–S3 (Sport).
Winter, H. (2010m, October 7). Robert Green has mental fortitude to revive his England career, says Ray Clemence. *The Daily Telegraph*. Retrieved October 13, 2010, from http://www.telegraph.co.uk/sport.
Winter, H. (2010n, November 6). Ancelotti: Gerrard is the world's complete midfielder. *The Daily Telegraph*, pp. S14–S15 (Sport).
Winter, H. (2010o, November 15). Core of steel makes Arsenal contender of real substance. *The Daily Telegraph*, p. S5 (Sport).
Winter, H. (2011a, January 2). Ancelotti victim of a perfect storm. *The Sunday Telegraph*, p. S7 (Sport).
Winter, H. (2011b, February 28). Martins pounces to expose Arsenal's defensive flaws. *The Daily Telegraph*, pp. S2–S3 (Sport).
Winter, H. (2012a, April 19). Barcelona stunned as Didier Drogba gives Chelsea Champions League hope with 1–0 first-leg victory. *The Daily Telegraph*. Retrieved April 19, 2012, from http://www.telegraph.co.uk/sport.
Winter, H. (2012b, April 25). Chelsea heroes hold firm as Torres has the final word. *The Daily Telegraph*, pp. S2–S3 (Sport).
Winter, H. (2012c, April 26). Real pay penalty as Bayern win in shoot-out drama. *The Daily Telegraph*, pp. S2–S3 (Sport).
Winter, H. (2012d, April 26). The blue flag of unity was too much for Messi. *The Daily Telegraph*, p. S5 (Sport).
Winter, H. (2012e, April 30). Manchester City v Manchester United: Blue Moon rising as Roberto Mancini consigns slapstick image to history. *The Daily Telegraph*. Retrieved April 30, 2012, from http://www.telegraph.co.uk/sport.
Woodcock, J. (2009, October 9). Have we really reached stage where Spirit of the Games needs rewriting? *The Times*, p. 107 (Sport).

Woods, R., Hocton, M., & Desmond, R. (1995). *Coaching tennis successfully.* Champaign, IL: Human Kinetics.

Woodward, C. (2012, April 29). Competing on their own patch is a huge plus for our Olympians. *The Sunday Times*, p. 14 (Sport).

World Cup 2010. (2010, July 6). Spain legend Fernando Hierro hails 'mental toughness of champions' inspired by Vicente del Bosque. *The Daily Mail*. Retrieved June 3, 2011, from http://www.dailymail.co.uk/sport.

Xie, P., Kranzler, H. R., Poling, J., Stein, M. B., Anton, R. F., Brady, K., *et al.* (2009). Interactive effect of stressful life events and the serotonin transporter 5-HTTLPR genotype on posttraumatic stress disorder diagnosis in 2 independent populations. *Archives of General Psychiatry, 66*, 1201–1209.

Young, E. (2001, March 30). Mind game: Psychological superiority alone could explain why Australia has won every rugby league World Cup since 1975. Retrieved April 10, 2001, from http://www.newscientist.com.

Young, J., & Pearce, A. (2010). Teaching mental toughness in tennis. *Journal of Science and Medicine in Sport, 13S*, e44.

Zakin, G., Solomon, Z., & Neria, Y. (2003). Hardiness, attachment style, and long term psychological distress among Israeli POWs and combat veterans. *Personality and Individual Differences, 34*, 819–829.

Zhang, L. F. (2011). Hardiness and the Big Five personality traits among Chinese university students. *Learning and Individual Differences, 21*, 109–113.

Zheng, X., Smith, D., & Adegbola, O. (2004). A cross-cultural comparison of six mental qualities among Singaporean, North American, Chinese, and Nigerian professional athletes. *International Journal of Sport and Exercise Psychology, 2*, 103–118.

Zuckerman, M. (2005). *Psychobiology of personality* (2nd edn). New York: Cambridge University Press.

Index

Walker, T. B. 73
Wall, M. 134
Wallace, H. M. 136
Wallace, S. 159
Walley, M. 101
Wallston, K. A. 87
Walrond, N. 158
Walsh, D. 13, 157, 160
Walsh, J. A. 101
Wang, C. K. J. 134
Wankel, L. M. 23
wanting the ball at all times 37, 51
Warburton, S. 162
Wark, P. 75
Warne, Shane (cricket) xv, 6, 15, 20,
   119, 158
Warren, R. F. 162
Warrington (rugby league) 107
Washington Redskins (American
   football) 8
Wasps (rugby union) 13
Watson, D. 82, 140, 155
Watson, T. 134
Watts, F. N. 112
Waugh, Steve (cricket) xv, 7, 87,
   118–119, 127–128
Weatherby, N. L. 134
Weaver, P. 4, 24, 159
Weber, Dick (ten-pin bowling) 71
Webster, S. M. 112
Weeks, J. 159
Weigand, D. A. 101
Weihenmayer, Erik (blind/visually-
   impaired extreme sports) xv
Weinberg, R. S. 54, 99
Weir, P. L. 126
Weiss, A. 132
Weiss, M. R. 155
Weissensteiner, J. 85, 96, 119
Wellens, Paul (rugby league) 7
Wendt, J. C. 162
Wenger, Arsène (soccer) 12, 13, 14,
   112
Werner, A. C. 32
Wessels, Kepler (cricket) xv, 14
West Bromwich Albion FC (soccer) 17
West Indies (cricket) 86
Westerby, J. 108, 109, 157, 159, 160
Westman, M. 57
Weston, N. J. V. 34, 55, 92, 97

Wetherington, J. M. 54
what you do when it matters most
   17, 21
Wheatley, J. 128
Whelan, J. 157
White, A. 54
White, J. 4, 19, 93, 108, 117, 159, 160
Whitley, M. A. 134
Whitmarsh, B. G. 103
Whittell, G. 158, 162
Widmeyer, W. N. 136
Wiebe, D. J. 57
Wiese, D. 82
Wiese-Bjornstal, D. M. 99
Wilde, S. 109, 120, 158, 159, 160
Wilhelm, K. 131
Wilkinson, Jonny (rugby union) xv, 7,
   105–106
Wilkinson, M. 69
will 19
will and conviction 160
Williams, A. M. 134, 136
Williams, Jean M. 4, 87
Williams, L. R. T. 115
Williams, R. 12, 16, 121, 158, 159,
   160, 162
Williams, R. M. 60, 161
Williams, Serena (tennis) 14
Williams, Shane (rugby union) 8, 11,
   14, 18
Williams, T. J. 162
willingness to take responsibility 86
Willis, A. 160
willpower 95, 161
willpower to burn 13
Willstrop, J. 158
Wilson, A. 119, 127, 157, 158, 160
Wilson, Betty (cricket) xv
Wilson, C. 94
Wilson, G. V. 24
Wilson, J. 15, 69, 112, 157, 158, 160
Wilson, P. 7, 109, 158, 159, 160
Wimbledon tennis championships, The
   2009 19
Winfield, L. F. 57
Winner, David xiv
Winning and losing 22–27
winning at all costs 27, 117
winning mentality 24, 86, 117,
   123, 137